Transportation Economics

NATIONAL BUREAU OF ECONOMIC RESEARCH
Special Conference Series

Transportation Economics

A CONFERENCE OF THE

UNIVERSITIES-NATIONAL BUREAU COMMITTEE

FOR ECONOMIC RESEARCH

PUBLISHED BY

National Bureau of Economic Research

NEW YORK

DISTRIBUTED BY

Columbia University Press

NEW YORK AND LONDON

1965

UNIVERSITIES-NATIONAL BUREAU COMMITTEE FOR ECONOMIC RESEARCH

This Committee is a cooperative venture of universities and the National Bureau. Its guiding objective is the encouragement of economic research on problems susceptible of objective treatment and of sufficiently broad scope to merit attention by institutions serving a scientific and public interest.

RELATION OF NATIONAL BUREAU DIRECTORS TO PUBLICATIONS REPORTING CONFERENCE PROCEEDINGS

Contents

Introduction

JOHN R. MEYER

HARVARD UNIVERSITY

The occasion of publishing the proceedings of a Universities-National Bureau Commitee Conference on Transportation Economics seems an appropriate moment to evaluate the general state of transportation economics, as a profession, science, art, or however one may view it. Perhaps the first and most obvious observation is that some revival of professional interest has occurred in transportation economics. Though once a very large recipient of professional attention, transportation could hardly be construed a major interest of economists from approximately 1930 to the middle of the last decade. During that period other matters, quite rightly, were deemed more worthy of professional study, the business cycle being the most obvious new focus of attention. In a very broad sense, transportation and other microeconomic problems went into abeyance as professional attention turned to macroeconomic problems. Furthermore, as firms in other industries grew larger and government became more and more involved in many different aspects of national life, the historic confrontation of big transportation firms and government became, at least relatively, less important.

It would be bold, though, to suggest that any revival in transportation economics has proceeded very far or has been markedly new in character. The rise in interest that has occurred almost certainly represents, in large though not exclusive measure, an almost classical response to the challenges posed by very immediate, public policy issues. These issues in many respects reflect older and long-standing policy problems, though with some new departures. One of the more dramatic and newer issues is the nearly total deterioration in labor-management relations within the railroad industry; some have gone so far as to characterize this deterioration as the most serious challenge yet posed to the institution of collective bargaining in American economic life. Another important set of public policy issues has been created by the serious financial difficulties, in many cases near or actual bankruptcy, of several major transportation companies; it is perhaps all the more significant that these financial difficulties have occurred not only in the oldest of the regulated transportation industries, railroading, but also the newest, the airlines. Closely related to these financial problems is the revival of interest in still another old policy issue, the proper role of mergers in regulated industries. Finally, another problem of long standing, urban congestion, considered of little major concern for public policy in preceding decades, suddenly has elicited a substantial concern at virtually all levels of government. This interest has been stimulated by the accelerated rate of change of urban location patterns which, in turn, is related to the development of new intracity transportation technologies associated with the internal combustion engine.

Revived interest in transportation economics also may have been stimulated by the coming to power of a new generation of transportation managers. This, of course, has been evolutionary rather than revolutionary, but the rate of change has been quite marked in the l. st decade. The change takes different forms in different transportation industries. In the airlines it has meant the emergence of a "second generation" of management that has replaced the original, and often highly colorful, pioneers who established the industry in the nineteen thirties and forties. In railroading the change has been the rise to top management of a group that grew up with the industry in its period of greatest adversity, as contrasted with predecessors who often first came to the industry at a time when it still enjoyed a considerable monopoly position. In general, the new management would seem to be more strictly professional and, most importantly, somewhat more oriented toward profit, as contrasted with public service or regulation in its thinking. In keeping with these trends, which correspond to somewhat similar trends in industry in general, transportation managements have become increasingly more receptive to outside advice and, indeed, have increasingly sought such advice. One source, among many, of such advice has been professional economists with interests in costing, operations research, and marketing problems.

Without much question, this volume, for better or worse, reflects this state of transition in both the industry and the economics profession. There is a bit of the old and of the new throughout. Every effort has been made, moreover, to find good representation of all interests, new and old. Whether or not this effort is deemed successful by the individual reader, it does seem certain that, again for better or worse, this volume is fairly representative of the present state of the art or science of transportation economics.

The volume is divided into four major parts, roughly corresponding to four major themes. Two, the first and the last, are of long-abiding interest to transportation economists: costing and public policy. The other two are relatively new: the nature and implications of technological change for transportation and urban transportation problems.

As noted, old and new ideas are to be found in every topic. For example, even in Part I, concerned with the old, classic concern of costing and the uses of cost data, some significant new departures are reported. The papers by J. R. Nelson, R. J. Gordon, and G. Kraft, are particularly relevant in this regard, all three almost certainly being controversial in some of their innovative tendencies.

Nelson, for instance, traces the dynamic interactions between transportation costs, prices, and the private prosperity or difficulties of individual transportation companies. His analysis begins with the late nineteenth century and proceeds to the present day. He hypothesizes that it is the dynamic interactions between transport prices and costs that best explain certain long-standing paradoxes in transportation history, such as the widespread prevalence of a profitless prosperity in railroad securities in the late nineteenth century.

Gordon, by contrast, is much more concerned with the contemporary problem of the depression in airline earnings that occurred in the early 1960's. He argues, quite persuasively, that much of the recent adverse earnings experience of the U.S. domestic trunk airlines is due to a failure of their managements to properly control costs. In particular, he feels that some of the larger domestic trunk lines have been slow to adjust expenses to match variations in travel demands. An implicit corollary is that the financial difficulties of the airlines in the early 1960's should, in most cases, be short lived, being correctable by either bringing costs more in line with requirements or by holding costs relatively constant in the face of future improvements in traffic—or by some of both.

Kraft is concerned with a very thorny issue, empirically, theoretically, and for public policy. This is the determination of the extent, if any, of the relationship between advertising outlays and growth of business volume for an industry or a firm. His particular focus is the case of airline advertising expenditures. Because of difficult identification problems, no conclusive answer seems possible to the question he poses. Kraft is always confronted with the problem of specifying whether increased advertising outlays are caused by improved business or vice versa, the actual answer almost certainly being some of both. He does, though, produce an estimate of advertising effects which might be most accurately portrayed as a maximum or upper limit estimate of the potential impact of advertising expenditures on business volumes. He also develops some tentative policy implications based upon this estimate.

More conventional in approach are the other three papers in the initial section on cost data and uses. M. J. Roberts presents a definitive statement of the point of view that transportation rates, specifically railroad rates, should be considerably less regulated in the interests of economic efficiency. His arguments are based primarily on static considerations and therefore are, not surprisingly, challenged mainly (though not exclusively) on dynamic grounds. Specifically, a clear difference of opinion obviously exists on the relative importance to attach to these different considerations, static and dynamic, and the locational-investment implications of transport rate policies, when arriving at public policy decisions.

More empirical in character is the W. J. Stenason and R. Bandeen paper which reports on what is probably the most elaborate and complete statistical cost study yet made. This study, done jointly by the Canadian Pacific and Canadian National Railroads and jointly designed by Stenason and Bandeen as representatives of their respective railroads, was a major submission made by the Canadian railroads to the recent Canadian Royal Commission on Transportation. Besides its thoroughness, the hallmark of this study was its imaginative use of data on system subcomponents to estimate maintenance of way-cost relationships.

In the last of the cost studies, Harbeson revives, with a careful study of recent urban-rural division of highway funds, the very old argument of whether "over-all system" or specific sector needs as measured by use should be dominant in determining allocations of state and federal highway funds. Obviously, the actual or practical divisibility of highway construction technology is most important in the final evaluation of this point, as the two discussants of the Harbeson paper point out either explicitly or implicitly. Clear-cut differences may also exist on less tangible but strongly held beliefs about what constitutes a desirable incidence of highway benefits between urban and rural users.

The second major part of the volume, concerned with problems of investment, innovation, and technological change, incorporates two papers dealing with very different aspects of these subjects, though in both cases heavy emphasis is placed on the implications of an accelerated rate of technological change for certain basic policy problems in transportation economics. Mansfield is concerned with answering for the railroad industry such questions as: at what rate has productivity been increasing, what has been the rate of diffusion of innovations, who has made these innovations, what prospective and recent changes in technology seem most promising, and what the probable impact of future innovations will be upon railroad employment. His projections of future developments, particularly for employment, will surprise at least some readers and, at a minimum, will be somewhat controversial.

The second paper in this section, that by M. J. Peck and J. R. Meyer, attempts to adapt a modern capital budgeting approach to assessing the old problem of determining a "fair return" for regulated industries. The paper also incorporates some comparative empirical data on the performance of different transportation companies and industries in recent years; these comparisons are based upon estimates using both capital budgeting measures and conventional administrative or regulatory concepts for measuring the returns on capital in regulated industries.

Part three contains four different yet complementary papers on urban transportation. The first of these, by J. F. Kain, represents an effort to empirically test a simple theory of economic behavior as it relates to the commuting and residential decisions of central business district workers. Kain, in his model, hypothesizes several different cost trade-offs being available to an urban commuter when making his joint decisions on residential location and commuter modal choice. The most important decision is considered to be the trade-off between housing and transportation costs. Kain also incorporates a number of socioeconomic variables, such as family status, number of employed persons in the family, and racial characteristics, into his model. Some of his conclusions, particularly those concerning the implications of race and the regressive fiscal character of urban transport subsidies, are bound to be contested by many.

Controversiality also characterizes the second paper in the urban transportation section, Vickrey's on "Pricing as a Tool in Coordination of Local Transportation." Vickrey suggests that departures from marginal cost pricing principles in urban transportation have much to do with explaining the existence of certain urban transportation problems. He also presents empirical estimates, strongly contested by some, of the extent of these discrepancies. In a similar vein, that of applying more rigorous economic analyses to urban problems, Kuhn discusses the potential applicability and also limitations of employing more formal capital budgeting procedures in transport planning for urban areas. Finally, Healy discusses certain problems of formulating a sensible urban transportation policy under today's circumstances. He argues for a greater sense of perspective about urban transportation policy; in particular, he challenges assumptions of the continued importance or even existence of high-density urban cores.

The fourth and final section of the volume deals with the *pièce de sustenance* of all transport economists, issues of public policy. These range widely from the question of labor "featherbedding" to common carrier regulation. The first paper, by R. A. Nelson and W. Greiner, discusses the relevance of the common carrier under modern economic conditions. Specifically, they argue that much of modern regulation of common carriers is not at all concerned with achieving economic rationality, but, instead, is often quite consciously undermining the achievement of economic efficiency in order to serve other objectives of public or social policy.

The second paper in the public policy section, by J. C. Nelson, deals with "The Effects of Entry Control on Surface Transport." Nelson presents considerable documentation for the view that the economic costs of certain common carrier regulatory practices are quite high. In fact, he leaves a clear impression that he considers these costs of sufficient magnitude to call into question the entire propriety of continued regulation as now practiced, at least of entry controls to common carriage.

The paper by J. Dunlop deals with the difficult labor and work rule problems which have been at issue for some time between railroad managements and the rail operating brotherhoods. He outlines the historical genesis of the problems and summarizes some of the more important recent findings by a Presidential Railroad Commission (of which he was a member) established to study railroad operating employment practices. Dunlop relates the manpower problems of the railroad industry to a broader context of similar problems encountered elsewhere in the economy. He presents a six-point program or set of suggestions on how the needed manpower adjustments in the railroad industry might be expeditiously effectuated.

The final paper in Part IV touches upon virtually all major issues of public policy but within the specific context of the Canadian experience. The author is F. W. Anderson, staff director for the recent Canadian Royal Commission on Transportation. It would appear that Canada's transport problems are not too dissimilar, at least conceptually, to those encountered in this country, although some quite significant special circumstances are to be found. Particularly interesting divergences are encountered in Canada's problems of regional development and the movement of grain from the Canadian Prairies to lake ports for export.

In sum, considerable diversity is to be found in this volume—diversity both in topics covered and points of view expressed. This is perhaps not surprising when dealing with a technology and set of institutions changing as rapidly as those in transportation do. Somewhat surprising, though, may be the strength and vigor with which the many participants defend their particular viewpoints. This too may be symptomatic of change if the following quotation from an earlier economist is an indication of earlier professional practice:

The expense of maintaining good roads and communications is, no doubt, beneficial to the whole society, and may, therefore, without any injustice, be defrayed by the general contribution of the whole society. This expense, however, is most immediately and directly beneficial to those who travel or carry goods from one place to another, and to those who consume such goods, The turnpike tolls in England, and the duties called peages in other countries, lay it altogether upon those two different sets of people, and thereby discharge the general revenue of the society from a very considerable burden.[1]

Obviously, if a positive, distinct point of view assiduously advanced is a sign of self-confidence and consensus, transportation economics may be progressing. On the other hand, allowance perhaps should be made for the possibility that in the absence of full unanimity earlier circumspection had a certain justification.

Special thanks are due to Leon Moses and his staff at the Transportation Center, Northwestern University, for their help in handling the many conference arrangements. In addition, Dr. Moses, who served as conference secretary, handled the bulk of correspondence with authors and discussants during my stay in Europe in early 1963. Other members of the planning committee were G. H. Borts, M. Hoffenberg, J. C. Nelson, J. Stenason, and E. W. Williams.

Some of the conference papers are not included in this volume for various reasons. Most of them have been published elsewhere in one form or another. The authors and original titles are: "An Analysis of the Costs of and Demand for Private Carriage" by Meyer Burstein, "An Economic Evaluation of Different Modes of Military Airlift" by William Niskannen, "The Spatial Structure of the American Economy" by Benjamin Chinitz, "Transportation and Economic Development"

---

[1] Adam Smith, *An Inquiry into the Nature and Causes of the Wealth of Nations*, Random House, Inc., 1937, p. 767.

by Louis Lefeber, "Cost Estimation, Capital Budgeting and Transportation Planning in Underdeveloped Countries" by Robert Brown, and "A Survey of the Current State of Public Policy and Research in the Transportation Industry" by Ernest Williams.

The papers presented here were prepared for press by Margaret T. Edgar and Joan Tron. H. Irving Forman drew the charts.

PART I

The Uses and Measurement of
Costs for Transport Policy

Transport Costs, Pricing, and Regulation

MERRILL J. ROBERTS

UNIVERSITY OF PITTSBURGH

In approaching the interrelationships among costs, pricing, and regulation, it is assumed that our interest is in allocative efficiency. Regulation may be construed as a measure designed to bridge any gaps between private and public interests that might be occasioned by inappropriate price-cost relations stemming from managerial pricing policies. Such gaps may arise at either end of the pricing scale, or from rates that are inimicable to the public interest because they are too low as well as from those that are too high.

Relevant questions with respect to rate floors include the cost concepts that appropriately govern private and regulatory pricing policy in competitive situations and the way costs are employed in this crucial aspect of regulation. Since the primary downward pressures on rates are generally conceded to be attributable to the railroads, a special look at their pricing policies is in order. While specific patterns and applications may be changing as a result of new competitive pressures, discrimination remains the hallmark of rate systems. Although frequently inferred, it has certainly not been established through present regulatory tests that inappropriately high price-cost ratios are out of the question. Accordingly, our discussion will be concerned with the appropriate employment of costs by regulators in setting both the upper and lower pricing boundaries within which managerial discretion should be free to operate.

Costs and Pricing: Governing Cost Concepts

It may seem surprising that a matter so thoroughly explored in the literature of economics as the costs which are relevant for pricing should require further attention. But it is apparent from a review of recent literature on transportation economics that the matter is not so straightforward as might be expected. There is no reason to be concerned about the wild and heated controversy over principles among affected partisan transportation interests. But there is evidence of intellectual disagreement among disinterested students of the transport pricing problem which extends to either or both the governing economic principles and their applicability to transport as a special case. Accordingly, it will be useful to review some recent views on the subject, both to illustrate the areas of disagreement and, hopefully, to rationalize the main points of contention.

The basic issue to which most other questions are subsidiary is whether competitive rates should be "predicated on" or "related to" some measure of incremental or marginal costs as a floor, or whether they should be formally tied to "full costs" through regulatory dicta. The latter contemplates a formal "accounting" assignment to specific services or classes of output of those cost elements which escape measurement under the marginal principle.

The most recent statement supporting the unique relevance of incremental costs as a pricing reference is that advanced by a panel of ten economists in the October 1962 issue of the *Journal of Business*.[1] Being a member of that group and, along with the others, a subscriber to the principles it advanced, I consider this article a useful starting point for the present discussion. It is essentially a restatement of orthodox principles generally accepted, at least in the abstract, by most economists, and can be summarized very briefly.

1. Railroads manifest a greater proportion of unallocable costs than is found in most industries. These unallocable components arise from both the high level of fixed costs and the significant elements of joint and common costs that characterize the industry.

2. Of vital importance for the argument and for further discussion is that, while fixity lapses into variability as the time dimension extends and sights are changed from short- to long-run considerations, a substantial proportion of rail costs remain fixed even over time spans far longer than are really relevant for any managerial or regulatory decisions. Since the cost fixities persist and the joint and common components are unaffected by the time dimension, the unallocability of costs is far more than a short-run phenomenon and untraceable

---

[1] William J. Baumol *et al.*, "The Role of Cost in the Minimum Pricing of Railroad Services," *The Journal of Business*, October 1962, pp. 1–10. The complete panel of authors includes William J. Baumol, Burton N. Behling, James C. Bonbright, Yale Brozen, Joel Dean, Ford K. Edwards, Calvin B. Hoover, Dudley F. Pegrum, Merrill J. Roberts, and Ernest W. Williams, Jr.

elements are extremely important even for relatively long-term considerations. This is far less true of truck and barge line costs.

3. The relevant cost reference for pricing decisions is marginal (or incremental) cost since this measure provides the test for the profitability of a pricing decision. In social terms, comparative marginal costs, which provide the economically valid measure of the value of resources used, offer the appropriate guide as to which agency is the most efficient alternative.

4. Coverage of the overheads created by the common and joint and the persistently fixed costs can only be achieved through "assignments" to specific services or classes of services that reflect market conditions and thus depend upon service demands. Rates higher than those thus dictated would restrict utilization of the fixed rail plant, artificially inflate shipper costs, and thus contribute to economic inefficiency.

5. Derivations of fully allocated costs through arbitrary assignment of the unallocable, as a means for recovering the overheads, is an economically invalid and pernicious device to measure comparative efficiency or to establish relative competitive prices for different modes.

But the lack of unanimity on these matters is manifest by some citations from other recent literature. One striking case is found in the so-called "Doyle Report" prepared for the Senate Committee on Interstate and Foreign Commerce.[2] This study concludes that, with some minor qualifications, rate changes which enhance departures from fully distributed costs are presumptively unreasonably related to costs.[3] Professor George Wilson in his recent volume of essays unequivocally prescribes that competitive rates should be based on the fully allocated costs of the low cost carrier, who would be identified by this measure.[4] Although clearly not accepted as a guide to their own policy recommendations, Professor Meyer and his associates indicate in their study that one of the historical purposes of minimum rate control was to prevent a carrier (or agency) with lower short-run marginal costs but higher average (or long-run marginal) cost from uneconomically usurping traffic from a competitor.[5] Although other

[2] *National Transportation Policy*, Preliminary Draft of a Report Prepared for the Committee on Interstate and Foreign Commerce, U.S. Senate, by the Special Study Group on Transportation Policies in the United States, Committee Print, 87th Congress, 1st Session, 1961.

[3] *Ibid.*, p. 444.

[4] George Wilson, *Essays on Some Unsettled Questions in the Economics of Transportation*, Bureau of Business Research, Indiana University, 1962, pp. 83–84.

[5] John R. Meyer, Merton J. Peck, John P. Stenason, and Charles Zwick, *The Economics of Competition in the Transportation Industries*, Harvard University Press, 1960, p. 249.

citations might be offered, these bring into focus the significant issues and are frequently cited by others to establish the intellectual respectability of the "full-cost doctrine" in transportation pricing policy. It will be noted that one of the main sources of difficulty is the persistent failure to deal realistically (in terms of relevance for public and private decision making) with the time horizons of cost variability.

The Doyle Report gives lip service to the economic attributes and virtues of long-run marginal costs:

> ... The recommendation that long-run marginal costs be defined as the appropriate floor to competitive ratemaking is sound long-range policy and will provide a basis for achieving rate structures which reflect the true cost advantages of the diverse modes. . .[6]

But the Doyle Report's definitions of long-run marginal and long-run out-of-pocket costs, which are regarded as virtually synonymous, embrace some puzzling references. At first glance these appear to be simply matters of loose terminology but they color the use of the concepts and cloud some vital relationships. For example, long-run out-of-pocket cost gives due consideration "to all *fixed* and *indirect* costs which are incurred because of the extra unit of production." [7] While confusing, this usage might be harmless if it did not influence further thought about cost relations.

The vitiation of the important conceptual distinction between fully-distributed costs and long-run marginal (or out-of-pocket) costs spawned by the defective definitions begins in earnest with the observation that the fixed costs of the past may or may not be appropriately considered in evaluating "the true fixed costs of additional production." And "if, in fact, they are appropriate guides to fixed costs which are incurred in additional production, it makes little difference in practice whether one refers to fully-distributed costs or long-run marginal or long-run out-of-pocket costs." [8] It is then an easy step to the proposition that "suitable" long-run marginal costs include a return sufficient "to defray all appropriate fixed and indirect costs, thus insuring continued production." [9]

This view suggests that over the long run, all costs are variable, and that if full account is taken of investment requirements and the associated costs imposed by added traffic, all costs will be traceable and

---

[6] *National Transportation Policy*, p. 441.
[7] *Ibid.*, emphasis mine.
[8] *Ibid.*
[9] *Ibid.*

no arbitrary allocations will be required. But the "theoretically pure" long run (contemplating complete variability) is, in the railroad case, an abstraction completely devoid of practical significance. As is well known, large elements of rail plant are not reproduced over very long time periods, and other investment as well lags far behind output. Substantial elements of rail cost remain fixed over any period relevant for either management or regulatory decisions. The variability that would be required to identify empirically fully-distributed costs with long-run marginal costs would have to be based on calculations stretching out into such an indefinite future as to be meaningless, because of the unpredictability of technological change as well as other factors, such as demand shifts.

The "long-run" concept may be employed in another way which is far more meaningful for railroads—that is, as a time period adequate to permit full accommodation of the plant to any output changes which may be realized. In this meaning, investment levels may change and short-run fixed costs will vary, but it is not necessary to contemplate that *all* investment costs must have thus varied before a meaningful "long-run" calculation can be made. This is, of course, the conception of the "long-run" that is implicit in the cross-section analyses that undertake to measure cost variability. These analyses cover the wide range of outputs and traffic densities that characterize the nation's railroads and provide empirical support for the reality of "long-term" fixities. Precisely because they do cover such a wide range of densities these analyses tend, if anything, to understate the fixed components and to overstate the long-run marginal costs that are really relevant for economic decisions; accordingly, they represent a highly conservative technique. In their measurements of long-run marginal costs, Meyer and his associates identify costs totalling a "reasonably substantial sum" which "represent unallocable overhead costs in the best empirical meaning of that term." [10] Accordingly, any realistic measure of "long-run" marginal costs will not exhaust all costs to insure against bankruptcy, and uncovered overheads will have to be assigned either arbitrarily or on a demand basis. Furthermore, the untraceability attributable to common and joint costs will not be washed out regardless of the time horizon of cost measurements.

Failure to recognize this empirical distinction between fully distributed and long-run marginal costs is reflected in the final recommendations on cost and pricing of the Doyle Report. One prescription

[10] Meyer *et al.*, *Economics of Competition*, p. 49.

is that "rate changes which result in rates that depart further from fully distributed costs than at present, may be presumed to produce rates unreasonably related to costs, unless specific evidence can be presented to demonstrate that such rates are reasonably related to long-run marginal costs." [11] Except for changes in the prices of factor inputs, long-run marginal cost (as realistically defined) will be less than fully distributed costs. Unless a rate is already below marginal costs, any reduction will inevitably bring it more closely into line with that measure.

Wilson does not merely flirt with fully distributed cost as does the Doyle Report, but embraces it affectionately. He finds that "the most sensible policy would be to have the rates based upon the fully allocated costs of the low-cost carrier (that is, the carrier whose *fully* allocated cost is lowest) . . . ." [12] He is explicitly led to this espousal of fully distributed costs through the traditional rule that "in the long run all costs are variable and the fixed-cost category disappears." [13] But, unlike the Doyle Report, he does not argue from this to the practical identity of fully allocated and long-run marginal costs. Rather, he realistically recognizes the distinction between train-journeys as the basic output unit and tons or ton-miles as the sales unit; this creates indivisibilities for pricing purposes that persist over the long run. It is these indivisibilities that are arbitrarily prorated in his concept of fully distributed cost. He explicitly rejects what he defines as the usual meaning of fully distributed cost, which involves the allocation of short-run fixed costs, and presumes away any problem of allocating fixities in something greater than the short run.

The earlier comments regarding appropriate and realistic time horizons for the railroad case are applicable here and need not be repeated. However, the *pro rata* allocation of the indivisible variables requires a closer look. Wilson observes with respect to these indivisible costs that *pro rata* allocation is both simple and based on precedent[14]— attributes that are respectively questionable and irrelevant. These costs appear to be nothing more than members of the common and joint cost family which, as Wilson himself recognizes in another section of his volume, can only be recovered on a noncost (or demand) basis.[15]

He is, nevertheless, dubious about the cost allocating function of

[11] *National Transportation Policy*, p. 442.
[12] Wilson, *Some Unsettled Questions*, pp. 83–84.
[13] *Ibid.*, p. 81.
[14] *Ibid.*, p. 82.
[15] *Ibid.*, p. 77.

demand in competitive markets (although the endorsement mentioned is not apparently reserved for noncompetitive situations), arguing that there is "a 'critical' point in the operation of an enterprise with large elements of indirect or indivisible costs beyond which further applications of the marginal cost principle can only lead to economic loss; along with this is a corresponding withdrawal of capital or elimination of operations for which rates not much above directly traceable costs have been quoted." [16] It is not particularly helpful, however, to suggest that profit maximizing through demand pricing is acceptable for some portion of output, but that the bulk of sales must be made at prices above the best the market will permit.

This suggestion that competition in transportation is inherently ruinous is of doubtful validity.[17] But even if it is true, there is no particular reason for seizing on fully distributed cost as a pricing reference point, plagued as it is with such serious defects as arbitrariness and circular relationships with volume.[18] If Commission intervention is needed to prevent the ruinous gravitation of rates, other less objectionable standards are available, including, for example, some minimum markup above long-run out-of-pocket costs.

Despite his formal adherence to fully distributed cost as a competitive pricing guideline, Wilson fortunately does not allow it to intrude too seriously into his substantive policy recommendations. Indeed, he expresses great admiration for "value of service pricing," where the cost and quality of a rival's offerings are the key value measures. Much of this retreat is dictated by wholesome respect for the power of actual or potential private carriage as a market conditioner. It would appear that the fully distributed cost concept, however defined, is as flabby in practice as it is in principle.

Although cited only as an historical argument for minimum rate control and clearly not a reflection of the policy conclusions of the study, a passage in the work of the Meyer group has been loosely used as theoretical support for full-cost pricing. Accordingly, it offers a useful focus for a further consideration of some significant issues of

---

[16] *Ibid.*, p. 83.

[17] For one contrary set of arguments on this subject see Merrill J. Roberts, "The Regulation of Transport Price Competition," *Law and Contemporary Problems*, Autumn 1959, pp. 557–585.

[18] Wilson seems to get into somewhat the same box that the Doyle Report did with respect to the ambiguity in the measurement of fully distributed cost: "What the full cost criterion basically means is that rates in intercarrier competition should be based upon the average cost of *normal, anticipated* traffic volumes." Wilson, *Some Unsettled Questions*, p. 85 (emphasis mine).

competitive price regulation. This passage refers to regulatory policy which is designed to prevent the movement of traffic by a carrier with lower marginal but higher average costs than a rival.[19] Apparently this policy is concerned with the inefficiency of penalties if a highly transitory cost advantage is converted to higher resource costs.

The railroads characteristically introduce the anomaly of lower marginal but higher average costs than a competitor. But further consideration of comparative cost structures reveals that the marginal cost advantage of rails, predicated on the realistic "long-run" concept that full plant adjustment is made to output increases, is apt to be quite persistent. Marginal cost, it will be recalled, is not a component of total cost at a given output level, but the *addition to* total costs associated with increasing volume.[20] Social efficiency is, for example, concerned with a comparison of the added rail or truck costs that will result if a given block of output is carried by one mode or the other. Precise determinations of the added costs that might be expected in specific situations undoubtedly require close consideration of the layering and cycling of railroad investment. But appropriately designed cross-section analyses, extrapolating from the cost experience of other companies with higher output levels, provide a valid indicator of the investment requirements and the associated costs that can generally be expected from output increments. Such "long-run" marginal costs provide at least the basic foundation of rail cost measurements from which efficiency may be realistically determined. Cost measures exceeding this level reflect an artificial or contrived degree of variability and thus offer a poor test of comparative efficiency.

As the foregoing suggests, a number of efficiency penalties may be incurred by hewing too closely to the comparative average cost line. Since reproduction of much of the rail investment that is reflected in average costs is long deferred, while truck investment turnover is relatively rapid, it might be worthwhile to take advantage of the free capacity availability reflected in the lower marginal costs of rails. If one or two generations of truck investment (over, say, five to ten years) can be avoided, a clear social saving is realized regardless of longer term outcomes. In addition, increases in output levels may by themselves change the average cost relationships and put the railroad in the low-cost position by that standard as well. Furthermore, technological improvements may intervene to produce the same result. These

[19] Meyer *et al.*, *Economics of Competition*, p. 249.
[20] This is a reminder which Professor Samuelson felt compelled to offer in his *Foundations of Economic Analysis*, Cambridge, 1947, pp. 241–242.

considerations suggest the folly of excluding railroads from markets where they demonstrate lower long-run marginal costs, regardless of comparative average costs.

Although not so clear cut, the foregoing considerations are applicable in some degree to relatively short-run pricing situations, as well as to the "long-run" in which there is full plant adjustment to expanded output. The relevant pricing horizon for management is clearly determined by the duration of the expected revenue change. According to the panel statement:

The decision is governed by such revenue dimensions as the nature and amount of the comtemplated change in volume, the length of the commitment to carry the traffic, the duration and geographic scope of the changed rate, the alterations of the service that might require added investments, and the time period in which changes may legally or practically take place.[21]

Accordingly, profit considerations may dictate a strictly short-run view of costs. This is clearly true if the pricing decision involves a temporary rate (such as one covering the movement of material to a construction project), but extends also to the general case where fuller plant utilization requires a consideration of short-run demand characteristics. There are good reasons to presume that pricing based on short-run marginal costs is not only profitable but is also consistent with efficient resource allocation, particularly since the railroad short run corresponds closely with the long run of a truck competitor. If rail prices predicated on a short-run cost reference are all the market will allow, replacement of the assets required to produce the service involved will be neither socially economic nor privately profitable, dictating substitute investment in an alternative mode. In the meantime, the economy will have enjoyed the use of the available capacity. However, economies realized from fuller utilization of available facilities must be weighed against the costs associated with such possible short-run dislocations as the elimination of firms with greater long-run efficiency. Accordingly, some "compromise" restrictions on strictly short-run pricing by railroads in competitive situations may be a required function of regulation.

As these considerations imply, maximizing returns with rates above marginal costs and below full costs does not occasion a reduction of investment below some socially desirable level. Full cost pricing, which necessarily reflects past investment costs which are unrelated to facility use, does not supply valid investment guidance. Enforcing

[21] Baumol *et al.*, in *The Journal of Business*, October 1962, p. 3.

this pricing policy where such costs are higher than "maximizing" prices (the relevant and interesting regulatory case) will in itself impose artificial restrictions on future investment levels. Sensible management and public policy requires prices that will permit the assets employed to earn as much as the market will allow. Whether the replacement ultimately occurs depends upon the fruitfulness of the maximizing goal, with the decision necessarily made at replacement time. Such a process can be socially objectionable only if the earnings are excessive. The stifling of marginal costs—particularly those associated with reasonably long-term horizons that reflect the investment requirements of traffic increments—cannot serve the public interest.

Market-Oriented Rates and Distribution Efficiency

Despite the established relevance of marginal costs as a measure of comparative efficiency and as a price floor, a system of market-oriented rates predicated on profit maximizing may still be open to question. There may be concern, for example, about unduly high charges in inelastic markets, or excessive discrimination (which is discussed in a later section). But the pricing system contemplated must also pass muster in other important respects, particularly on the validity of the resulting intermodal traffic allocation. The question is whether intermodal price relations may be expected to square with relevant cost relations when prices are designed to maximize contributions above incremental costs. This discussion is independent of the contention that this goal will produce a disorderly gravitation of rates to "ruinous" levels. It may be assumed either that such ruinous pricing is not to be expected or that regulation will prevent it.

Where the services of the various agencies in a given market are homogeneous, carrier demand functions are identical and in the maximizing process the carrier with the lower marginal cost presumably can (and will) generate the lower price. As a result, shippers will generally select the low-cost mode to achieve both private and social efficiency. Such service-quality homogeneity is certainly not unknown in some market situations. In others, shippers' requirements may make them indifferent to qualitative differences. In either case, traffic allocations are sensitive only to lower rates predicated on lower costs.

But it is more probable that such homogeneity or shipper indifference is a special case. Where qualitative differences enter into shippers' calculations, it is important to recognize the rather obvious (but occasionally overlooked) proposition that efficient traffic allocations are not determined exclusively by comparative transport (movement) costs, but must also take account of the different level of nontransport distribution costs associated with the employment of alternative agencies. As a result of these quality disparities, the simple proposition that low movement costs are determinative is inapplicable.

According to this reckoning, the most efficient carrier is the one offering the lowest sum of transport costs (measured by MC) and nontransport distribution costs associated with its employment (NTC). Employing the rail-truck illustration, distribution efficiency is determined by a comparison of $MC_r + NTC_r$ and $MC_t + NTC_t$. Shippers, however, are swayed by the comparative prices (P) and not carrier costs, requiring a consideration of $P - MC$ margins, or "markup" (MU). Accordingly, distribution efficiency requires that where (for example) $MC_r + NTC_r$ exceeds $MC_t + NTC_t$, then $P_r + NTC_r$ must exceed $P_t + NTC_t$. In other words, the concern is whether rates which would be established under a market-oriented pricing system would divert traffic from the alternative agency offering the lower total distribution cost ($MC + NTC$). Serious consideration of this question offers scope for a major inquiry, but it is useful to give some attention to it even in a preliminary and tentative way.

It is simplest to proceed by assuming at the outset an "all or nothing" situation, where all available traffic in the market will be allocated to one or the other of the rivals depending on comparative distribution costs. This condition would be realized if there were only one shipper in the market or if all shippers had identical distribution requirements and thus qualitative evaluations. The governing relationships are illustrated in Figure 1.

In case I, one agency has both lower MC and lower NTC, and in II, one has lower MC but higher NTC. The shipper in case I will employ trucks so long as the "markup" does not produce a rate which makes the cost of rail distribution less. In a system of market-oriented prices, there is no reason to expect a rate to be established at that level. In this case, the traffic moves by the carrier affording both the lower marginal cost and the lower distribution costs. The indicated truck rate appropriately attracts the traffic to the more efficient system.

In case II A, rail enjoys lower marginal cost but truck affords lower distribution cost. The indicated rate limits are the same as above. In this case, however, in the interest of over-all efficiency, traffic moves by the carrier with the higher MC. Case II B illustrates another important point: if the relative prices were governed by a rule requiring each competitor to observe the same P/MC ratio, the traffic would be

Figure 1

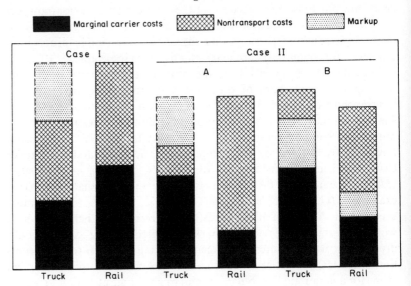

forced to the agency occasioning the higher distribution cost at a sacrifice of over-all efficiency.

Alternatively formulated, a carrier's maximum markup, and therefore price (e.g., the railroad's), is established by:

$$\text{Max. } MU_r = (MC_t - MC_r) + (NTC_t - NTC_r) + MU_t$$

Introducing illustrative values:

$$\text{Max. } MU_r = (.60 - .20) + (.40 - .60) + .20 = .40.$$

In this case, a markup of less than 40 cents (35 cents) will attract the traffic to the railroad. The following price-cost relations will prevail:

$$MC_r + NTC_r = \$0.80$$
$$MC_t + NTC_t = 1.00$$
$$P_r + NTC_r = 1.15$$
$$P_t + NTC_t = 1.20$$

In this circumstance, which appears to be a general case under the "all or nothing" assumption, the competitive price system operates to channel traffic to the agency affording the lowest real distribution costs.

The "all or nothing" limitation may be relaxed by assuming a number of shippers in the market with varying distribution system requirements and hence qualitative evaluations. This necessitates consideration of different shipper reactions to given rate relations. Thus, instead of a single *NTC* for each agency, there will be a variety of them, depending on the specific distribution requirements. At any given price, shippers will compare $P + NTC$ and select the mode which minimizes their distribution costs. If they are rank-ordered according to the *NTC* associated with (for example) rail movements, they will be successively attracted to rail service by progressively lower rates (assuming, as in the traditional demand function, that the price of the substitute truck service remains unchanged). They will come over to rail, in other words, when for them $P_r + NTC_r$ is less than $P_t + NTC_t$.

In establishing "maximizing" rates, the competitors will be confronted with comparative costs (*MC*) and *NTC* measurements. Prices will be set at a point where the $P + NTC$ values attract the traffic volume which will maximize net revenues. The carrier with the generally lower set of $MC + NTC$ values will, in a sense, "control" the market as in the previous case. Accordingly, the "all or nothing" situation previously postulated appears to be representative of discrete points along a demand function. It can be roughly equated with a "consensus" or a weighted average of the comparative *NTC* measures of shippers with varying distribution requirements. In this case, competitive considerations will sufficiently restrain the $P - MC$ ratio of the carrier with the lower range of $MC + NTC$ combinations in a specific market to prevent a higher $P + NTC$ combination. The result is thus the same as was indicated for the "all or nothing" market, and the price relations described there may be regarded as representative of a specific maximizing price.

The situation here is complicated by the variety of shipper reactions to specific price relationships. If prices are set as in the foregoing illustration ($P_r = 55$ and $P_t = 80$ cents) some traffic will be shipped by each alternative, depending on particular *NTC* measures. Although higher or lower *NTC* values will appear identically in both the measures of shipper distribution costs ($P + NTC$) and of real costs ($MC + NTC$), a simple illustration reveals that the variation in these values can occasion price-cost relations inimical to efficient distribution. With the former *NTC* values ($r = .60$, $t = .40$) rail transportation was most efficient and, under the resulting comparative rates, also represented the shipper's choice. But for a shipper with higher NTC_r (70 cents) and lower NTC_t (35 cents) measures, the efficiency results are quite different with the same set of prices. The following relationships emerge in this case:

$$P_r + NTC_r = \$1.25 \qquad MC_r + NTC_r = \$.90$$
$$P_t + NTC_t = 1.10 \qquad MC_t + NTC_t = .95$$

Here truck transport offers lower distribution costs to the shipper, but higher real costs. It appears that variations in shipper distribution requirements in the face of a single market price (and price relationship) may indeed defeat efficiency as measured by the criterion employed.

As the foregoing illustration suggests, this anomaly arises where the intercarrier *NTC* differences are large in terms of marginal transport cost differences. It can arise predominantly from one direction—that is, where the services of the carrier with the low marginal cost are "undervalued" by some shippers in terms of the concensus value upon which the rate was predicated. It might be inferred from this that efficiency departures are most apt to be associated with truck movements of traffic where rail offers the lowest real distribution costs. If, however, the maximizing prices represent a consensus or weighted average, the probability is good that most traffic allocations will pass the efficiency test. In this case, there is reason for hoping that market-oriented rates built on the foregoing model will do a reasonably adequate job of preserving and fostering distribution efficiency.

Full evaluation requires, however, some consideration of how closely the model represents the real world. Although it probably reflects what enlightened shippers and carriers do or should try to do, it clearly contemplates perfect and unattainable knowledge on the part of both, including (as a particular difficulty) carrier measurements of *NTC*. This is perhaps not really serious and is certainly no indictment of market-oriented transport prices, since perfection of knowledge and measurements is not achieved in the economy generally. But it is apparent that rational carrier pricing requires intimate understanding of shipper distribution systems. It is equally clear that distribution efficiency depends at least as much on rational shipper purchasing decisions as it does on carrier pricing policy.

Costs and Minimum Rate Regulation

The ICC's distrust of marginal costs (or the "long-run out-of-pocket costs" generated by its staff) as a comparative efficiency measure is well documented.[22] It is necessary only to emphasize that the Commission is wed to the proposition that the competitor with the lower full costs is the more efficient and that his costs should set the floor under competitive rate adjustments. The governing viewpoint has frequently been characterized by this quotation from Commissioner Freas:[23]

[22] See, for example, Roberts, in *Law and Contemporary Problems*, Autumn 1959, pp. 560–561.

[23] *Rate-Making Rule*, Hearings before the Senate Committee on Interstate and Foreign Commerce on S. 3778, 85th Congress, 2nd Session, 1958, p. 172.

In many instances, however, the full costs of the low-cost form of transportation exceed the out-of-pocket costs of another. If, then, we are required to accept the rates of the high-cost carrier merely because they exceed its out-of-pocket costs, we see no way of preserving the inherent advantages of the low-cost carrier.

According to the principles enunciated earlier, the general result of this policy is apt to be a misallocation of traffic and presumably of investment, where, as is usually the case, long-run, out-of-pocket cost measures are involved.

It might be noted additionally that these cost doctrines are apparently becoming more thoroughly solidified through the processes of judicial review. In a recent appeal from a Commission decision, a Federal District Court took occasion to elaborate on the cost considerations governing competitive rate determinations under regulation.[24] This Court uncritically accepted the assumed identity between "long-run" and "fully-distributed" costs, reflecting the common failure to gear cost generalizations to the cost situations of particular agencies. Accordingly, it found that "the inherent advantages of lower cost refers to the long-run or fully-distributed costs of carriage." [25] By the same token, out-of-pocket costs are regarded as being identified necessarily with the short run. The Court is, therefore, concerned that "rates set by reference to out-of-pocket cost may favor what in the long run is the less efficient, higher cost mode."[26]

These pronouncements reflect the failure to recognize some of the distinctions pointed out in this discussion, particularly that in the railroad case incremental costs can have a long-run meaning that clearly differentiates them conceptually and empirically from fully-distributed costs. As previously argued, preventing a carrier with a strictly transitory short-run cost advantage from taking traffic from a competitor with lower long-run costs may represent an economically valid exercise of regulatory authority. But because of its confused long- and short-run

[24] U.S. District Court, District of Connecticut, *The New York, New Haven and Hartford Railroad Company v. United States and Interstate Commerce Commission*, Civil Action No. 8679 (1961) (Mimeo).

[25] *Ibid.*, p. 10.

[26] *Ibid.* In a decision on review, rendered after the completion of this paper, the U.S. Supreme Court overturned some of the District Court's opinions, but not those pertaining to the role and interpretation of costs. It observed that: "It is not for us . . . to decide in advance precisely how either carrier's inherent advantage should be measured or protected." But the Court continued with a further observation of some possible future significance: "It may be, for example, that neither a comparison of 'out-of-pocket' nor a comparison of 'fully-distributed' costs, as those terms are defined by the Commission, is the appropriate method of deciding which of two competing modes has the cost advantage on a given movement." Cited in *Traffic World*, April 27, 1963, p. 134.

identifications, the Court fails to realize that achieving this objective does not require the adoption of "fully-distributed" costs as a railroad rate floor. It is clear that greater economic understanding must be introduced into the processes of regulation if viable rate relations are to be fostered and permitted.

In supporting its application for reductions in grain rates, the Southern Railway introduced an abundance of economic evidence designed to clarify the crucial cost concepts and relations that have been examined. While the reduced rates were authorized by Division 2 over barge line protests, there is no evidence that this is attributable to any change in the Commission's thinking regarding the governing role of fully-distributed costs in competititive situations.[27] Rather, it effectively dodged the question of relevant cost references for intermodal competition by introducing a novel notion for such proceedings. It found that the uncompensated costs for publicly provided waterway (and presumably highway) facilities should be included in cost comparisons designed to identify the most efficient carrier. Although Southern introduced some measurements, the Commission found them of questionable accuracy. Not having definitive measurements of these public costs, it concluded that it was unable to reach a decision regarding "inherent advantages" and, since the rates were "compensatory," permitted them to become effective.

This aspect of the case is consistent with past policy. The Commission is quite willing to accept out-of-pocket cost evidence in testing whether proposed rates are compensatory. Such a showing will often suffice unless the record of a case shows that, although compensatory as thus measured, the proposed rates are designed to attract traffic for a more "efficient" competitor—that is, one with lower full costs.

A recent classic illustration is found in the decision in *Coal—Southern Mines to Tampa and Sutton, Florida*, where the Commission authorized the reduced rates, finding that they were compensatory in terms of out-of-pocket cost coverage.[28] It is noteworthy that the traffic was moving by private water transportation and beyond the reach of the protesting barge lines, regardless of the rail rate. It seems clear that the rates would not otherwise have been approved.

Some additional insights regarding the role of costs in competitive rate regulation are provided by a survey of 350 Commission decisions

[27] Cited in *Traffic World*, January 26, 1963, pp. 11–14. Approval was subsequently denied by the full Commission in an opinion handed down after this paper was completed. This reversal, however, provides no significant new insights regarding the role of costs in such litigation.

[28] I. & S. Docket No. 7179, October 1, 1962 (Mimeo).

in rate reduction cases decided between March 14, 1960, and May 25, 1962.[29] Formal cost evidence was introduced in 252, or 80 per cent, of the cases surveyed. Costs were introduced exclusively by the proponents in 95 cases and by the protestants in 69, but both offered such showings in most situations.

In terms of competitive relations, the bulk of the cases (319) fall into three classes: truck intramodal (152); intermodal, with truck proponents and rail protestants (112); and intermodal, with the role of the parties reversed (38). The relatively small representation of cases involving rail reductions with motor carrier protests is noteworthy. Cost evidence is more prominent in intermodal than in intramodal cases, appearing in 90 per cent of the former (165 of 185 cases) but in only 71 per cent of the latter (117 of 165). These percentages varied significantly, however, with the participating agencies. Of the 152 truck intramodal cases, costs were introduced in only 72 per cent. But the ratio rose to 88 per cent in cases involving truck proponents and rail protestants and jumped further to 95 per cent when the roles of the parties were reversed. It is also noteworthy that motor carriers are less prone to rely on cost evidence than the railroads. In rail rate cases, motor carrier protestants supplied cost evidence in 55 per cent of the cases; but in truck rate cases, the railroads used cost evidence in 80 per cent.

Surprisingly, in only 8 of the 252 cases did the cost evidence pertain to fully-distributed costs. Out-of-pocket measures were involved in 219 cases, while in the others the report did not specify, possibly because of the vagaries of the presentations. This suggests that the limitations imposed by fully-distributed costs may not be as pervasive as one might be led to believe. While it plays a great part in some important cases, it does not seem to intrude routinely into competitive rate adjustments.

For the cases as a whole the denial rate was quite high (70 per cent), with little difference based on whether or not cost evidence was involved. The comparative figures were 68 and 72 per cent. But in the cases invoking this evidence, cost reasons were very important for the denials, either because the rates were found to be noncompensatory or because the cost evidence was inadequate to support the case. Such factors were instrumental in 144 of the 192 denials, or 80 per cent. It is not surprising that the denial rate is lower where only the proponent submits cost evidence. This obtained in 59 of 93 cases, for a 63 per cent rate. Similarly, where the protestants only supplied such evidence (69 cases), denials rose to 78 per cent. A correlation analysis confirmed the validity of the foregoing percentage relationships.

[29] Covering volumes 309–316.

These comparisons suggest some rather interesting and perhaps surprising propositions. The great majority of cases involved reductions in motor rather than rail rates. This balance, which prevails for intermodal as well as for intramodal relationships, undoubtedly reflects the greater competitiveness of the trucking industry. But it certainly indicates that, despite their restiveness, the railroads are not above invoking the protective cloak of regulation. Cost evidence figures prominently in these proceedings and denials are generally related to cost considerations. However, the evidence is predominately related to out-of-pocket and not full-cost measurements. Since the main denial basis is failure to establish the compensatory character of the proposed rates (as measured by out-of-pocket costs), it appears that the restrictions on pricing freedom imposed by full-cost tests do not characterize the litigation. These restrictions may, however, be relatively more important when measured in terms of associated traffic volumes, a criterion which could not be tested in this survey.

The Effectiveness of Railway Rate Policy

It has been alleged that railroad pricing in markets involving intermodal competition has been inept, bringing distress not only to competitors but to the railroads themselves. This point was emphasized in a paper delivered recently by a barge line official who based his contentions on personal experiences.[30] In more general terms, it is argued by their competitors that railroads keep reducing rates and get worse off financially year after year, with the clear implication that rate reductions are at fault. If true, such allegations suggest either irrational decision processes or a hopeless pricing situation. Whatever the cause, such contentions must be of interest to students of transportation pricing policy. The fruits of any consistent default of responsibility are apt to be uneconomic price relationships and transport investment levels, while the prospect of a continued drying-up of railroad revenues is also a cause for concern. As the acknowledged price leaders in the transport sector, railroads must pursue rational pricing goals and act with reasonably adequate information inputs if competitive stability

[30] Noble C. Parsonage, "Costs, Pricing and Discrimination," delivered at the annual meetings of the American Transportation Research Forum, Pittsburgh, Pa., December 27, 1962. In Mr. Parsonage's words: "I have actually participated in a case where the facts have shown that if the entire volume of the movement divided between water and rail were to move all rail at the proposed reduced rates, it would generate less gross revenue to the railroads than was being realized on the volume handled at the higher rail rates" (p. 1).

is to be achieved without the heavy hand of regulation.[31] For example, if railroad price makers are unduly fascinated by volume at the expense of profits, the results may indeed be unfavorable for themselves as well as for their competitors and even for the economy generally.

A detailed case-by-case evaluation of the results of railroad pricing policy is well beyond the scope of this undertaking. But the problem is of sufficient importance to warrant even generalized analysis in the hope that some tentative conclusions may be reached.

The rate indexes published annually by the I.C.C. indicate, for all commodities combined, an increase from 108 to 121 between 1954 and 1958 and a steady decline thereafter to 114 in 1961 (1950 = 100).[32] The indexes for the 60 major commodities and commodity classes which are computed individually conform generally to this same pattern, but with rather substantial variations in the rates of change. For example, between 1958 and 1961 the rate index for industrial sand declined from 128 to 127, while for automobiles it shot down 44 points from 122 to 78.

The following analysis attempts to evaluate the profitability of the pricing actions underlying these index movements, with particular reference to the reductions. It is based on interrelationships for the 1957–1960 period between the rate indexes and changes for each of the commodities in rail tonnage carried, total market size (production less local consumption), railroad market share, and railroad revenues.[33]

In over-all terms, the rate reductions have been modest and not particularly fruitful. The general results for all commodities combined are indicated for two periods in the following table.

Percentage Change in

Period	Rate Level	Tons Carried	Adjusted Production	Revenues	Ratio of Rail Tons to Adjusted Production
1958–59	−2.5	+3.7	+6.4	+3.3	−2.7
1959–60	−1.8	+1.0	+2.8	−3.1	−2.0

The rather small rate reduction of 2.5 per cent between 1958 and 1959 was accompanied by a 3.7 per cent increase in tonnage carried and a nearly comparable advance in revenues. However, adjusted production of all commodities (net of local consumption and thus

[31] For more detail on this rather obvious proposition, see Roberts, in *Law and Contemporary Problems*, Autumn 1959, pp. 570–78.

[32] I.C.C., Bureau of Transport Economics, *Indexes of Average Freight Rates on Railroad Carload Traffic*, 1953–1961 (Statement RI-1, 1963).

[33] From I.C.C., Bureau of Transport Economics and Statistics, *Fluctuations in Railroad Tonnage Compared with Production, Class I Line-Haul Railroads, 1958, 1959, and 1960*, Statement No. 6301 (1963).

representing the size of the aggregate market) jumped by 6.4 per cent, occasioning a decline in the railroads' market share. Thus, even with the reduction railroads were unable to get a proportionate share of the new volume. The 1959–60 story was about the same except that total revenue also declined.

More interesting than these gross figures, however, are some details for the sixty specific commodities or commodity classes for which rate indexes are separately computed. Table 1, which takes account of the 1957–58, 1958–59, and 1959–60 price changes, shows the results for each. Increases predominated in the 1957–58 period; rate indexes for forty-nine classes went up, compared with only six reductions and five cases of no change. At the same time, revenues increased for sixteen classes and declined for the other forty-four. In the other two periods, however, decreases predominated, representing forty-seven of the cases in 1958–59 and fifty-five in 1959–60. In these two periods revenues declined in twenty and forty-three of the cases, respectively.

Because of demand shifts induced by changed market size and other factors, the foregoing comparisons have little to say about railroad service demand elasticity. Where market size expands (for nonprice reasons), the total revenue figures overstate the true effect of the price change as such, while the reverse is true for shrunken markets. Deeper probing is thus provided by factoring the total revenue change into its components in order to isolate and subtract the portion attributable to the changed market size.[34]

Since most markets expanded, the revenue effect net of shifts in market size are generally less favorable than when total revenue change is measured. The direction of the adjusted revenue changes are shown by commodities for each period in Table 1, with the results summarized below.

	Three-Period Total	REVENUE INCREMENT							
PRICING MOVEMENT		1957–58		1958–59		1959–60		Total	
		Positive	Negative	Positive	Negative	Positive	Negative	Positive	Negative
Increases	58	13	36	4	2	1	2	18	40
No change	15	1	4	1	6	1	2	3	12
Decreases	107	0	6	7	40	7	47	14	93
Total	180	14	46	12	48	9	51	35	145

[34] Revenue changes attributable to the various influences were derived as follows:
1. Price change: price change (per cent) $\times$ R_1 (first period revenue).
2. Change in market size: per cent change in adjusted production $\times$ R_1.
3. Change in tons carried: per cent change in tons $\times$ R_1.
4. Price acting on tons carried: (3) − (2).
5. Interaction of market size and price change: price change (per cent) $\times$ (2).
6. Interaction of tons carried and price change: price change (per cent) $\times$ (4).
7. Combined effects: sum of (1) + (4) + (6) + (7).
8. Price change plus unmeasured influences: (8) − (2).

TABLE 1

RELATIONSHIP BETWEEN RATE CHANGES AND REVENUES FOR SIXTY COMMODITY CLASSES, 1957-60

	1957-58			1958-59			1959-60			
	A	B	C	A	B	C	A	B	C	D
Wheat	+4.1	+14.3	Neg.	+0.8	-4.4	Pos.	-2.4	+6.0	Neg.	196
Corn	0.0	-0.7	Neg.	-12.9	-19.5	Neg.	-4.5	-8.4	Neg.	142
Cotton in bales	+3.8	+0.8	Neg.	-0.9	+12.6	Neg.	-1.9	-10.8	Neg.	152
Potatoes, other than sweet	-1.7	-0.8	Neg.	-6.8	-3.4	Pos.	-0.9	-6.4	Neg.	84
Sugar beets	+5.8	+7.1	Pos.	0.0	+0.7	Neg.	-2.1	+1.3	Pos.	59
Prods of agric., NOS	+3.3	-11.5	Pos.	-3.2	+2.9	Neg.	-6.7	-0.5	Neg.	104
Cattle and calves, S.D.[a]	+4.7	-4.8	Neg.	-1.5	-8.0	Neg.	-2.3	-12.1	Neg.	79
Meats, fresh, NOS	-4.8	-11.4	Neg.	-0.8	+3.4	Neg.	-0.8	-3.2	Neg.	109
Anthracite coal, NOS	+1.8	-25.5	Neg.	-2.6	-11.3	Neg.	-0.9	-14.8	Neg.	120
Bituminous coal	+1.8	-17.2	Neg.	-1.8	-3.7	Neg.	-0.9	-2.3	Neg.	110
Coke	+4.4	-29.5	Neg.	0.0	+31.3	Pos	-0.8	+0.3	Neg.	103
Iron ore	+10.4	-31.2	Pos.	0.0	-7.1	Neg.	0.0	+32.5	Pos.	114
Clay and bentonite	+5.4	-3.8	Pos.	0.0	+11.4	Neg.	-2.2	-4.5	Neg.	151
Sand, industrial	+5.8	-11.8	Pos.	0.0	+23.2	Neg.	-0.8	-5.9	Pos.	124
Gravel and sand, NOS	+1.7	-3.5	Neg.	-1.7	+7.0	Neg.	-1.7	-13.0	Neg.	76
Stone and rock: broken, ground and crushed	+0.9	+3.1	Neg.	-1.7	-0.2	Neg.	-0.9	-8.6	Neg.	87
Fluxing stone and raw dolomite	+5.4	-24.1	Pos.	+2.2	+14.8	Pos.	+0.7	+2.4	Neg.	93
Asphalt	+4.3	-0.8	Neg.	0.0	-11.2	Neg.	-4.9	-9.4	Neg.	130
Salt	+5.4	-4.5	Neg.	-2.5	+1.2	Neg.	-0.9	+0.4	Neg.	134
Phosphate rock	-4.5	-2.0	Neg.	+5.7	+5.5	Neg.	-5.0	-3.2	Neg.	99
Products of mines, NOS	+4.0	-8.6	Neg.	0.0	+9.7	Neg.	-1.6	-5.9	Pos.	131
Logs, butts, and bolts	+10.4	-11.4	Neg.	+4.3	+13.7	Pos.	0.0	-6.9	Neg.	65
Posts, poles, and piling: wooden	+0.8	-10.6	Neg.	-7.9	+3.0	Neg.	-2.6	-6.3	Neg.	123
Pulpwood	+0.8	-4.7	Pos.	+0.8	+2.9	Neg.	+1.7	+5.0	Pos.	75
Lumber, shingles, and lath	+2.4	-1.8	Neg.	-2.4	+8.6	Neg.	-0.8	-12.5	Neg.	136
Products of forests, NOS	+6.0	-2.3	Neg.	-2.1	+12.1	Neg.	-2.2	-12.1	Neg.	109

(continued

TABLE 1 (continued)

	1957-58			1958-59			1959-60			
	A	B	C	A	B	C	A	B	C	D
Gasoline	0.0	-10.2	Neg.	-1.9	-2.9	Neg.	-6.7	-13.1	Neg.	93
Fuel: road and petroleum, residual oils, NOS	+3.6	-15.8	Neg.	-0.9	-4.6	Neg.	-1.8	-15.8	Neg.	104
Lubricating oils and greases	+3.2	-8.2	Pos.	-1.6	+4.3	Neg.	-3.9	-6.1	Neg.	123
Petroleum products, refined	+1.6	-3.6	Neg.	-7.9	-3.0	Neg.	-3.4	-3.1	Neg.	96
Chemicals, NOS	+3.2	-9.5	Neg.	-2.3	+10.1	Neg.	-2.4	-7.3	Neg.	179
Sodium (soda) products	+2.6	-4.2	Neg.	-5.0	+6.2	Neg.	0.0	-4.1	Neg.	173
Fertilizers, NOS	+1.7	+3.9	Neg.	-5.0	+3.8	Neg.	-3.5	-1.3	Neg.	145
Iron, pig	+8.8	-38.9	Neg.	-0.7	+36.0	Pos.	-1.5	-26.2	Neg.	187
Iron and steel: billet, bloom, and ingot	+1.6	-40.8	Neg.	-1.6	+72.4	Pos.	-2.4	-24.1	Neg.	155
Iron and steel: bar, rod, and slab	+8.5	-30.6	Neg.	+4.7	+21.3	Pos.	-6.7	+5.3	Neg.	184
Mfg. iron and steel	+1.8	-30.1	Neg.	-1.7	+12.8	Neg.	-3.5	+1.1	Neg.	193
Iron and steel pipe and fittings, NOS	+3.6	-45.1	Neg.	-3.5	+16.1	Neg.	-1.8	-10.1	Neg.	191
Machinery and machs., NOS	+3.9	-18.4	Neg.	-1.5	-7.1	Neg.	-2.8	-5.6	Neg.	246
Automobiles, passenger	+6.1	-21.3	Pos.	-2.5	+24.6	Neg.	-0.8	+62.5	Pos.	187
Vehicle parts, NOS	+6.2	-23.3	Neg.	-1.4	+25.4	Pos.	-0.7	+5.1	Pos.	195
Cement: natural and portland	-1.9	-1.8	Neg.	-7.8	-5.4	Neg.	-10.5	-27.0	Neg.	142
Lime, NOS	+4.8	-8.6	Pos.	-3.1	+6.7	Neg.	-2.4	-9.4	Neg.	142
Scrap paper and rags	-1.5	-5.1	Neg.	-10.0	+9.3	Neg.	-3.4	-9.7	Neg.	120
Printing paper, NOS	+0.8	-0.2	Pos.	-4.9	+3.5	Neg.	-3.4	+4.8	Neg.	159
Paperbd., fibrebd., pulpbd.	+0.9	-0.8	Neg.	-2.7	+14.0	Neg.	-1.9	+0.8	Neg.	168
Wallboard	+0.9	+11.0	Pos.	-5.1	+11.3	Neg.	-0.9	-13.6	Neg.	165
Glass bottles, jars, pkg. glass, NOS	+5.6	-11.7	Neg.	-0.8	+7.9	Pos.	-0.8	-14.7	Neg.	138
Refrig., freezing apparatus	+3.9	+0.3	Neg.	+0.7	+22.9	Neg.	-1.5	-9.3	Pos.	150
Furniture, NOS	+5.5	-3.4	Neg.	-6.7	+6.1	Neg.	-1.6	-8.1	Neg.	141

(continued)

TABLE 1 (concluded)

	1957-58			1958-59			1959-60			
	A	B	C	A	B	C	A	B	C	D
Liquors, malt	-0.9	+0.1	Neg.	-3.6	-2.8	Neg.	-2.8	-2.6	Neg.	118
Sugar	0.0	+5.0	Neg.	-6.7	-3.7	Neg.	-7.2	+7.0	Pos.	160
Food prod., NOS, in cans and pkgs.	0.0	+0.9	Neg.	-3.6	-1.2	Neg.	-1.9	+2.3	Neg.	127
Feed, animal and poultry, NOS	0.0	+3.4	Pos.	-2.3	-4.1	Neg.	-3.2	-6.4	Neg.	79
Containers, metal	+6.8	-5.3	Neg.	-0.7	+3.6	Neg.	-1.4	-13.8	Neg.	144
Containers, fibrebd. and paperbd., Knocked down	+2.3	-9.1	Neg.	-1.5	-1.4	Neg.	-2.3	-8.8	Neg.	141
Scrap iron and scrap steel	+8.2	-30.5	Neg.	-2.3	+28.9	Pos.	-1.6	-8.6	Neg.	161
Furnace slag	+2.6	-8.8	Pos.	-6.7	-5.2	Neg.	-0.9	-13.6	Neg.	76
Waste materials, NOS	+6.2	-12.4	Neg.	-5.1	+16.1	Neg.	-4.6	-8.8	Neg.	110
Manufacturers and misc. NOS.	+3.4	-5.1	Neg.	-7.4	+14.1	Pos.	-2.7	+3.5	Neg.	120

A = Per cent change in rate index.
B = Per cent change in revenue.
C = Direction of revenue change after adjustment for market size.
D = Revenue-cost ratio.

Source: A. *Indexes of Average Freight Rates*
B. *Fluctuations in Railroad Freight Traffic.*
C. Derived from data in sources indicated under (A), (B), and (D).
D. I.C.C. Bureau of Accounts, *Distribution of Rail Revenue Contribution by Commodity Group* . . .
1960 (Stmt. 2-62).

a
Single deck, i.e. shipments in single-deck rather than double-deck stock cars.

The strong inference from the table is that railroad pricing actions have indeed been singularly unfruitful. Only in scattered cases has a decline in the rate index been associated with an increase in the revenue attained from a particular class of traffic when change in market size is taken into account.

The direction of the revenue increment is a reflection of the effectiveness of railroad pricing policy in the face of the strategy or any "inherent" market advantages of their competitors. A closer look reveals the strength with which other market forces have actually counteracted increases in market size, as well as the potential traffic-stimulating effect of most rate reductions. In a number of extreme cases, in fact, large increases in market size were so completely counteracted that the volume after the price decrease was less than in the initial period.

In the 1959–60 period, thirty-five rate reductions were accompanied by a market expansion. Despite this favorable market trend, tonnage increases occurred in only fifteen cases, eight of which increased more slowly than the market enlargement. The rate reductions induced an output expansion beyond what would have been expected from increased market size in only seven (or one-fifth) of the cases. But in an even more extreme instance, twenty of the thirty-five price reductions were associated with an absolute decline in tonnage carried, perversely suggesting a positively sloping demand function and indicating the power of the forces eroding the railroad's market position.

The strength of these antirailroad forces can be roughly measured by relating the increased output expectable from the market expansion to the actual tonnage contractions. The sum of the potential revenue increment attributable to market growth, plus the decline actually realized, provides a rough absolute measure of the contributing influences in the twenty cases. Dividing this sum by the first amount reduces this measure to relative terms and produces a "revenue shrinkage ratio" based on the values derived from the factoring processes previously described (footnote 34). A ratio of one denotes a complete offset of the increased market potential, while a higher ratio indicates an even greater revenue depression. A ratio of two, for example, means that the counteracting forces depleted revenues by double the expansion dictated by the enlarged market, despite the reduced prices. The "shrinkage ratios" thus derived for 1959–60 generally range up to nearly seven, with a further jump to seventeen. Extremely powerful adverse market forces are clearly at work here.

The relationship of rate policy to prevailing revenue/out-of-pocket ratios is also of interest (see Table 1). Most surprising is the rather large number of cases where reductions occurred in the face of ratios below 100, which was true of ten of the fifty-five downward adjustments in the 1959–60 period. Although the revisions were generally nominal, they ranged on occasion up to 7 per cent. Unless rather sharply declining variable costs are anticipated, the rationale for these price changes is most obscure. On the other hand, a number of the reductions were associated with ratios well above the 129 all-commodity average, including twenty-nine of the fifty-five recorded in the 1959–60 period. This suggests that cost considerations frequently did not impose tight limits on the reported rate decreases.

While the data are too sparse and too generalized to permit any real diagnosis or prescriptions, several tentative conclusions are suggested by the foregoing discussion. It is evident that, in general, railroad price reductions have not thus far contributed to profitability in *absolute* terms. It is possible, of course, that market reactions are sticky and that any positive benefits from rate cuts will emerge only over a longer time period than was observed here. This effect, however, does not show up in the data studied. In any case, it is apparent from the demand shifts that railroad pricing policy faces extreme difficulties (including possibly an inexorable trend away from rail transportation), substantial price insensitivity of much traffic, or the rather consistent ability of competitors to outmaneuver the railroads in pricing actions. Price reductions of the kind reviewed clearly offer no panacea for dealing with the industry's financial ills.

While commonly unprofitable in a positive way, it is obviously possible that reduced rates may still yield larger revenues than higher ones. Although judgments about such relative profitability are extremely cloudy because of the lack of information about the course of nonrail rates and other vital factors, some of the cited evidence is relevant. The observed limitation on tonnage and revenue expansion, imposed by the contrary market forces, must stem from either inelastic demand, unfavorable demand shifts, or both. To the extent that inelastic demand is the cause, the reductions are certainly a mistake. Demand shifts are clearly an important factor unless the anomaly of positively sloping demand functions is accepted. Some additional clues to the relative profitability of reductions are thus afforded by a consideration of the character and basis of these shifts. If, in particular, they are due to changes in the prices of substitutes, a vital question is whether these price movements were induced by or occasioned the railroad rate reductions. Although it is impossible to generalize about the antecedents of the price changes examined here, the railroads are commonly regarded as the price leaders. Where they did start the action (and the changed price relationships are the cause of the demand shift), they would have been better off to maintain the *status quo*. In this situation the absolute unprofitability of a reduction also spells relative unprofitability. In other words, rate reductions are not generally profitable even in these relative terms where there is a reasonable chance of maintaining market shares with rate stability.

It is probable, however, that much of the unfavorable shift in demand is due to forces other than price relationships, or to a continued change in the transportation service requirements of the economy. In this case, no generalizations regarding the relative profitability of price reductions can be drawn from the available data. But it seems likely that decreases may be the appropriate response in such a situation. It is noteworthy, however, that in the cases observed price policy has not generally coped effectively with demand changes. It may be significant that these price changes have been rather modest. Many, furthermore, were associated with relatively high revenue-cost ratios, offering an opportunity to counter both such adverse market forces and competitive price responses. This suggests that in some cases at least reductions should possibly be far bolder than they appear to be from this sample. The potential expansivity of the traffic involved is indicated by the very low rail market shares that characterize these commodities, all running below, and most far below, 50 per cent.[35]

Regardless of other lessons that this discussion might offer, it seems clear that fully effective railroad pricing policy under present adverse conditions undoubtedly requires far greater insights into market behavior than are presently available. A great deal of attention has been devoted to the cost (or supply) side of transportation markets. Certainly the same intensive effort is required on the demand side.

Transport Costs and Discrimination Control

The pricing system obtained by maximizing net revenues in particular markets is, of course, highly discriminatory. When unallocable costs find their way into prices through differentiated demand functions, there will generally be an inequality of $P - MC$ relationships. However, the system does improve utilization of railway plant that is fixed

---

[35] Bureau of Transport Economics and Statistics, *Fluctuations in Railroad Freight Traffic Compared with Production, Class I Line-Haul Railroads, 1958, 1959, and 1960* (Statement No. 6301, 1963).

over relatively long time periods, and permits a reasonable degree of managerial discretion in responding to market forces. In this process some prices will be set below average costs at the prevailing output level, creating "downward discrimination." Others will rise above this measure where demand elasticities permit.

In theory, shippers paying below-average and above-average rates benefit along with the transportation companies from these price relationships. The gain to the shippers from the downward discrimination is apparent, while transport companies ostensibly benefit from the greater utilization and lower average costs induced by the relatively low charges. But completely happy results are not assured from the workings of this pricing system. To the extent that transport rates depart differentially from costs, uneconomic patterns of resource use are encouraged in the nontransport sectors of the economy. Furthermore, it is not necessarily true that the shippers paying rates reflecting upward discrimination are better off.[36] In other words, in the abstract at least, some form of discrimination control is indicated to limit the unfavorable effect on the nontransport sector of the economy and to insure that the rates assessed in the highly inelastic markets do not injure rather than benefit the affected shippers.

In this context, low rates are justified only if they contribute more than higher rates to the support of the system and thus diminish the financial burden on other traffic. The basic social justification for discrimination requires, therefore, that the high rates are less than they would be with nondiscriminatory charges. Accordingly, higher than average rates are unjustified if they exceed amounts dictated by the output and unit cost that would be associated with rates represented by uniform relations with marginal costs.[37] To illustrate, assume output (sales) of 50,000 units under discrimination but only 30,000 under uniform pricing, with unit costs of 2.0 and 2.3 cents respectively. In this case, shippers paying more than 2.3 cents would be better off without discrimination; such rates thus assess an unjustified burden of support which violates the basic social rationale of this pricing system. This test contrasts sharply with the present comparative

[36] Others have, of course, pointed this out. See, for example, Merton Miller, "Decreasing Average Cost and the Theory of Railway Rates," *Southern Economic Journal*, Vol. 21, p. 39.

[37] Since different services are not homogeneous but incur varying direct or out-of-pocket costs, discrimination is not eliminated by uniform rates per unit of output, but by a uniform ratio between rates and out-of-pocket costs. In the following discussion, this is the meaning attached to the removal of discrimination and to references to "uniform pricing."

system which, devoid of external or objective measurements, circularly permits one high rate to justify another.

It would be strictly an academic exericse to labor the question of rate ceilings if the present degree of transport competition insures that economic limits of rates are not exceeded. But it is apparent that substitution elasticity varies widely among transport markets, depending on such factors as haul distance and commodity characteristics. Furthermore, the substitutional impact of one major alternative, barge transportation, is rather restricted geographically. It is possible, therefore, that residual monopoly powers (or even regulatory rate floors) may permit degrees of discrimination that exceed socially acceptable standards. Meyer and his associates conclude from their analysis of the demand characteristics of transportation that they "do not set an effective ceiling on the rates of non-competing traffic at a level that precludes monopoly profits." [38]

Although not providing evidence regarding its economic legitimacy, the I.C.C.'s revenue contribution studies describe the sweep of discrimination in rail rates through revenue/out-of-pocket cost ratios for the different territorial movements of the various commodity classes. Table 2 shows the 1960 distribution of ton-miles by revenue-cost ratios which exceed that year's average of 129. The ratios rise to relatively high levels, ranging to over 500 per cent of out-of-pocket costs. Significant traffic volumes are involved, with nearly 17 per cent of 1960 traffic bearing rates representing revenue-cost ratios over 170. There may be some basis for suspecting that rates in these extreme reaches of discrimination are unduly high. If so, it is worthwhile to indulge in some speculations regarding the reasonableness of these rates in terms of the cost-oriented uniform pricing test that was previously advanced.

Cost studies of the Commission's staff indicate that, at generally prevailing traffic densities, costs are about 70 per cent variable and 30 per cent fixed in the "long run." The actual behavior of the out-of-pocket or variable portion of total costs is conjectural, but the cost studies indicate that these outlays are unchanged per unit as volume changes. This behavior will be adopted as a simplifying assumption in this analysis. Based on these cost functions, it is possible to measure the inflation in unit costs from a given percentage decline in traffic and the resulting percentage increase in the average rate level that would be required to meet all costs, including present overhead coverage. For example, if uniform pricing occasioned a 40 per cent traffic reduction,

[38] Meyer *et al.*, *Economics of Competition*, pp. 201–202.

fixed costs would increase by 100 per cent but total unit costs by only 20 per cent. To cover this increase and maintain the same total revenue contribution, rates would have to be set for all traffic at 155 per cent of out-of-pocket costs (where 1960 was 129).

The indicated traffic and revenue effect of uniform pricing at any given ratio of out-of-pocket costs depends upon the price elasticity of rail transport demand in particular markets, and upon the distribution of total traffic volume in terms of revenue-cost ratios. The latter factor is associated with the former since it determines the percentage changes in price (both increases and decreases) which would be involved in moving to uniformity at a given level. For example, output would be less seriously affected by the shift to uniformity if there are substantial blocks of traffic, moving at relatively high rates, which would be benefited by the contemplated reduction (representing the effect of traffic distribution). This would be particularly true if the reductions occasioned sharp increases in the movements of these commodities (representing the elasticity effect). On the other hand, large volumes at lower rate levels, with heavy price increases, would enhance the output reduction, particularly if the associated demands are highly elastic.

Traffic distribution is available from the Interstate Commerce Commission's 1 per cent waybill sample, and the rate-cost ratios from the revenue-contribution studies. But since the elasticities are subject to conjecture at this stage of transport market analysis, it is impossible to assess accurately the traffic effects of uniform pricing, or to determine the uniform level of rates which would permit full overhead coverage. Some general indications may be provided, however, by testing the possibility of achieving a traffic level 60 per cent of the present level, with rates uniformly set at 155 per cent of out-of-pocket cost. This is the level that would be required for full overhead coverage, if costs are 70 per cent variable.

On the surface, at least, it appears that the prospects of retaining the required portion of present output with such prices are not at all remote. According to the I.C.C. waybill data, nearly one billion ton-miles (or about one-quarter of the sample total), entail rates exceeding the indicated level.[39] This traffic nucleus by itself represents nearly half of the required output, and a reduction in these relatively high rates (ranging to over 500 per cent) to a level 155 per cent of out-of-pocket

[39] Computed from data in I.C.C., Bureau of Transport Economics and Statistics, *Territorial Traffic and Revenue by Commodity Classes*, Carload Waybill Statistics, 1960, Statement TD-1; and, *Distribution of Rail Revenue Contribution by Commodity Groups, 1960*, Statement 2-62.

TABLE 2

DISTRIBUTION OF TON MILES BY REVENUE COST RATIOS, 1960
(based on 1 per cent waybill sample)

Revenue–Cost Ratio Classes	Total Ton-Miles	Per Cent	Cumulative Per Cent
130–149	745,727,000	17.183	17.183
150–169	453,546,000	10.450	27.633
170–199	359,050,000	8.273	34.906
200–249	347,974,000	8.018	43.924
250–299	27,856,000	0.641	44.565
300–349	1,982,000	0.045	44.610
350–399	763,000	0.017	44.627
400–449	998,000	0.022	44.649
450–499	224,000	0.005	44.654
500 and over	1,686,000	0.038	44.692

Source: Revenue-cost ratios from I.C.C., Bureau of Accounts, *Distribution of the Rail Revenue Contribution by Commodity Groups ... 1960* (Statement No. 2-62, 1962). Ton miles from I.C.C., Bureau of Transport Economics and Statistics, *Territorial Distribution Traffic and Revenue by Commodity Classes,* Carload Waybill Statistics, 1960 (Statement TD-1, Supplement, 1961).

costs should occasion a significant expansion in this volume. The transport demands for many of these commodities were undoubtedly quite inelastic when the high-rate patterns were established in the days of extensive railroad monopoly. They are undoubtedly more elastic now in view of the heavy inroads that have been made by competitive transportation. Rate reductions of the order premised here, therefore, would probably stimulate much additional volume.

The potential expansibility of this sector is indicated by the fact that during 1960 the railroads handled an over-all average of only about one-quarter of the total tonnage movement of the commodities involved.[40] The hypothetical level of rates should be competitively attractive in tapping the huge balance in this traffic reservoir; rates at 155 per cent of out-of-pocket costs would, in 1960, have averaged only 2.5 cents per ton-mile—well below the regulated average cost for trucking. It seems reasonable to conclude that most of the output required to sustain present overhead coverage (60 per cent of existing volume) would be realized from traffic now moving at ratios exceeding the 155 ratio.

Furthermore, a substantial volume of traffic moving at ratios less than 155 could probably be retained. This would particularly be true in the sector involving ratios between 130 and 155 where rates are above

[40] Computed from data in *Fluctuations in Railroad Freight Traffic.*

average. In the waybill sample, this sector included 800 million ton-miles, another fifth of the total. Assuming this volume to be evenly distributed within the indicated ratio limits, the resulting average rate advance amounts to only 10 per cent. Many of the transportation demands associated with these above-average rates would probably be somewhat inelastic, indicating that rate increases would occasion a less than proportionate volume reduction from the rate advance premised. But even if unitary elasticity is assumed, most of this traffic could be retained, along with the expanded assured amount in the ratio sector over 155. Finally, although the demands are in many cases highly elastic, some of the vast volume moving at ratios less than 130 would continue to move at higher rates.

Although far from conclusive, the foregoing considerations at least suggest that a uniformly established rate ratio of 155 could sustain the level of traffic volume required to support present overhead coverage. But even if it should fall a little short, so that average cost (including overhead) would rise somewhat above the level associated with the 155 ratio, these considerations call into serious question the present rates which are at levels substantially exceeding this ratio. This would certainly appear to be true of rates exceeding double out-of-pocket costs.

The foregoing arguments should not be construed as advocating cost-based pricing with uniform overhead contributions. The possible effect of this system was considered only in order to visualize its implications for volume, average costs, and appropriate discrimination limits. Discrimination is still a valid railroad pricing device, but its range may quite possibly be excessive in terms of the cost structures associated with present-day traffic densities. Any rates that exceed a ceiling indicated by the test described here are questionable since the shippers involved are worse and not better off with discrimination. Assuming, however, that the lower rates make their best contribution to overhead, neither public or private purposes would be served by arbitrarily increasing them to some stipulated ratio. Discrimination below the ceiling facilitates overhead coverage and reduces average costs and over-all rate levels, thus truly benefitting those paying above-average rates. But to confine discrimination within the stipulated limits would minimize the distortions associated with uneconomic patterns of resource use. In short, discrimination thus restricted would be both more equitable and more economic.

The reduction of excessively high rates may imply a revenue gap and less complete overhead coverage, but this is by no means certain. It is more than possible that many of the offending rates are not only excessive by the standards advanced but are uneconomically high in terms of maximizing overhead coverage. Furthermore, any realistic system of discrimination control should insure that rates at the other end of the axis are not uneconomically low in terms of their revenue contribution potential. The large number of movements failing to cover the Commission's measure of out-of-pocket costs aggregated a deficit of $243 million in 1960.[41] The mere elimination of these deficits (e.g., by dropping the traffic) would enhance overhead coverage by nearly 15 per cent. It is likely that much of the traffic involved would, if appropriately priced, make a positive contribution. Furthermore, there must be an interesting volume which does not produce deficits but which is favored by rates which are still uneconomically low.

It is possible, however, that further restraints on upward discrimination might restrict over-all earnings and prevent overhead coverage. Such restrictions are certainly not inconsistent with present regulatory policy since the rate structure is honeycombed with maximum rate orders, at least some of which must be of more than token significance. But the desirability of tighter discrimination limits represents a transport policy problem of some magnitude.

From one viewpoint, there is no apparent reason for "monopoly" traffic *as a class* to contribute significantly more to the financial support of the system than does competitive traffic under a system of regulation which is designed to restrict rates to "reasonable" levels. It is precisely in the competitive sector of the economy that, by definition, a "normal" return is earned. In other words, where competition is at work, the market determines financial rewards and investment returns. Fair competition does not generally provide undue restraints on earnings and there is no reason to expect it to do so in transportation, particularly with the usual regulatory limits on the pressures of price competition. If a normal return is appropriately construed as that accorded under competition, there is no reason to have to "make up" anything on that portion of a company's business that is not subject to competitive pressures. If realizable returns are not adequate, in the face of competition, to induce and support additional investment, it should not be made; certainly it should not require the support of monopoly returns in noncompetitive markets.

On the other hand, hewing too closely to the line of more rigorous discrimination control and thus curtailing profit opportunities in the

---

[41] *Distribution of Rail Revenue Contribution by Commodity Groups—1960*, p. 22.

railroad industry may have an adverse effect on innovation and other socially desirable elements of progress. If investment beyond that dictated by competitive market forces (either actual or as simulated by regulation) are regarded as desirable, the available alternatives are, apparently, to subsidize the railroads or permit them to tap markets for all they can get. There are strong arguments for subsidy since the cost of social objectives can thus be born by the economy as a whole rather than by a limited number of consumers and producers or ecomonic sectors.

If the subsidy approach is neither feasible nor palatable, and earnings in excess of competitive allowances are indeed required, recourse to highly discriminatory rates is indicated. In this case, the elimination of present maximum rate controls may be called for. If, on the other hand, it is regarded as desirable to limit discrimination in order to strike a more judicious balance between its advantages and its costs, a close look at governing standards and other criteria is required. Although such control has been one of the important functions of regulation, it is questionable whether the historic concepts and methods are adequate to maximize the gains and minimize the costs of discrimination. The comparative method of testing rates was perhaps adequate in earlier years when the forms and procedures of regulation were developed. In the era of lower traffic densities, the legitimate sweep of discrimi- nation was much broader than at present, and the opportunity for developing refined tests was limited by the relative crudity of the available analytical techniques and machines. Although perhaps formerly necessary and adequate, the comparative method under which one high rate justifies another is plagued with circularity and provides no standards of any real vitality and validity.

As the need has changed, analytical methods and opportunities have improved immeasurably. But rational data exploitation is impossible without a comparable improvement in the concepts of rate control. If maximum rate control is to be continued, the feasibility of employing the "uniform pricing" test suggested here should be explored.

Conclusions: Concepts and Their Operationality

In this paper I have argued for the conceptual validity of transport rates related to incremental rather than to "full" costs; rates geared to demand conditions rather than to cost allocation formulas. According to this argument, "market-oriented" rates pass muster reasonably well in terms of significant economic criteria. Specifically, they are not inimicable to viable investment levels or to interagency traffic allocations consistent with efficient distribution patterns. Stated more positively, rates not fettered by regulatory ties to full-cost criteria can produce economic results as satisfactory as those realized from the operation of the price system in the economy generally. Commission regulation, however, is prone to distrust these results and to stifle market forces in key cases by inappropriately gearing competitive rates to fully distributed costs.

But the virtues of the market-oriented prices depend on the quality of the performance of both regulation and private management. Regulation must guard against any excessive discrimination that might arise from the pursuit of maximum profits in separate markets. Effective performance of this function requires far more refined and sophisticated tests—including both concepts and measurements—than have been applied in the past. Costly inefficiencies can also creep into "market-oriented" prices from the private (management) side. Clearly some modification of the historic monopoly-based "value-of-service" rates are in order. But gratuitous rate reductions that do not improve net revenues (and that are not required to realign rates exceeding the acceptable limits of discrimination) undermine the financial integrity of the transport system, impair investment adequacy, and create inefficient long-run traffic allocations. On the other hand, undue pricing conservatism, particularly on the part of the railroads, may produce the same results.

Unfortunately, the right path is not clearly marked. The zeal for "cost-finding," important as it is, digs up only part of the answer; cost measures tell only the scope of rate reductions that is tolerable, not what is socially efficient or privately desirable. All of the ordinary complexities of oligopolistic (and, with the rate bureaus, duopolistic) price behavior are compounded by the intricate interrelationships of transport costs, rates and total distribution systems. As shippers perceive and measure these interrelationships with greater refinement, distribution requirements become the key to transport demand. It seems to be a safe assertion that despite all of the complexities, far more is known about the measurement of transport costs than of demand. It is questionable, indeed, whether the problem of demand measurement has even been fully conceptualized in the specialized context of transportation since commodity value lost its meaning.

The need for greater understanding of demand, and of transport markets generally, is urgent for both pricing and its regulation. This can be accomplished only by broad-scale research efforts in this sector of the economy. Only through the improved insights thus afforded will there be a reasonable expectation that transport prices—with or without regulation—will produce tolerably efficient allocations.

COMMENT

James W. McKie, Vanderbilt University

This paper confirms again what has often been remarked about the comparative-statics approach to the theory of cost: the inadequacy of the long-run cost curve of the firm as a tool of economic analysis. Its inadequacies are not in logic but in application. In public utility economics, much more than in analysis of competitive firms, the long-run cost curve repeatedly fails to tell us what we want to know about long-run costs. It almost always turns out that some functional relationship other than the classic one is the one that counts. The classic relationship is that between simple volume, moving in an unchanging grid of time and space, and average cost with all factors fully variable. In railroad economics, the volume measure for such a concept, as Nelson points out elsewhere in this volume, is density of use per mile of railroad. Yet the dimensions of a real problem for decision may include this one only secondarily, if at all, and usually turns on some other—on geographical extensions or cross-connections, secondary systems, bottlenecks, different bases of service, central-station balance in different distributive configurations, or load-factor problems of one kind and another. These produce cost relationships that are hybrids of long- and short-run elements, reflecting several output dimensions and often containing some effects of technological change. These essentially nonreversible cost functions, rather than the classic envelope cost curve, are the ones that are relevant to the problems that have actually arisen.

What confronts us now is a problem of transition—from monopoly toward competition, and from value-of-service pricing toward cost-of-service pricing in transportation. But, because the railroads still have prodigious economies of scale, indivisibilities, and inflexibilities, they cannot simply be fitted into the new pattern like a small piece into a mosaic. Though their size and scope will be reduced compared with what they were in the days of monopoly, they cannot simply be squeezed down to the appropriate size along the same path they followed when they were expanding. The railroads can be squeezed right out of existence while we are still trying to find what their ultimate role will be in that transportation equilibrium that we have had so much difficulty in visualizing. If the railroads do survive, some indivisibilities must remain, and no doubt some value-of-service prices will remain along with them.

Professor Roberts asks the right questions: what will be the size of the railroad system in equilibrium, when all agencies of transport have finally been fitted into the optimum pattern? And will the costs, the rate structure, and volume of traffic appropriate to that equilibrium permit the railroads to survive and prosper? One might suggest additional considerations for the answers. Some kinds of service, and some of the costs associated with them, can be eliminated without affecting the cost-density relationship on trunk lines. Roberts himself notes that dropping the traffic which fails to cover out-of-pocket costs would itself enhance overhead coverage. Some of this traffic would still move at higher rates. Such measures as dropping passenger traffic, or at least handing over commuter services to some welfare agency, would greatly reduce losses without appreciably affecting unit costs on the remaining traffic. The abandonment of spur lines, backwater traffic, and lightly used branches might do likewise without necessarily affecting the density of traffic on main lines, since much traffic is shifting its locus with the increasing geographic polarization of population and economic activity. Where spur lines or weak branch systems are thickly grafted onto a trunk line which would otherwise be strong, some means must be found for lessening the load of debt and capital claims left behind when such unecomonic facilities are abandoned. It seems to me that this would be a most fruitful way to use government financial help, since the only other way to reduce the burden of claims in line with a reduced plant is through bankruptcy and reorganization.

Turning now to the question of rate structure, a consensus seems to be emerging among economists who have recently been studying the problem of interagency competition. It is roughly as follows: (1) Short-run fully allocated (average) costs are not an appropriate basis of pricing for railroads. (2) The appropriate minimum standard of price for railroads is long-run marginal cost. (3) This is also an appropriate minimum standard for other transport agencies, but because of their particular cost relationships, long-run marginal cost will be very close to short-run average cost (for all except pipelines—a special case with a decisive advantage in one commodity). (4) Hence, a rational allocation of freight traffic (excepting pipelines) among competing agencies will be achieved if prices are equal to minimum short-run average costs including a competitive profit for motor trucking and water transport. Railroad rates would depend on the cost-plus-service-advantage of competing agencies for the traffic in question, but the railroad's long-run marginal cost would be a minimum. This much of value-of-service pricing would remain in the equilibrium of transport rates. Of course, the railroads might well be priced out of the market for short hauls, or where speed of delivery is either very important or so unimportant that the waterways' advantages in bulk transport will tell.

But what is this long-run marginal cost that is to be the minimum for railroad rates? Not the same marginal cost that the railroads could look forward to if they were building their entire plant *de novo*. It is, instead, one of those hybrid concepts. If we take the present plant and shake out the uneconomic parts of it mentioned earlier, the long-run marginal cost is the incremental cost of equipment and long-run maintenance, plus the variable-factor cost, associated with increases in the volume of traffic in the neighborhood of the volume that will move when priced competitively as suggested. Rates equaling or exceeding this "LMC" are economic. It should not be hard to find a reasonably correct measure of this minimum. It is clearly lower than fully allocated short-run average costs for the railroads.

The concept of nontransport distribution cost (NTC) suggested by Roberts is a useful measure of "service advantage." The rule contemplated is that the railroad should be permitted to capture any traffic from other carriers if its LMC, as defined above, plus its NTC is less than their minimum SAC plus their NTC for the traffic. The rail rate may be brought as low as necessary to accomplish this result, provided it exceeds LMC. Since most types of traffic are diverted from competing carriers only by degrees, this rule for the railroad would amount virtually to value-of-service pricing above LMC, adjusted to the new competitive circumstances which have greatly increased demand elasticity for most railroad transportation services.

If this interpretation of the consensus is correct, it also means that the regulatory authority should not use short-run average cost as a minimum standard for rail rates, but it would be justified in preventing cuts below rail LMC down to short-run out-of-pocket cost or below it. Many critics believe, however, that the antitrust laws, rather than rigid rate regulation, are the best weapon against "predatory" pricing by railroads, and that the regulatory authority often insists on a "fair" division of traffic and preservation of competing vested interests when wholly unjustified by the underlying economic relationships.

What would the suggested principles of rate-making do to the present allocation of traffic? What would the equilibrium allocation be, under projected cost conditions? We do not know nearly as much about this as we should, considering that we need to predict whether the railroads could survive under those circumstances and whether massive reallocations and shrinkages in capacity of other agencies of transport might be necessary during the transition. The indivisibilities and economies of scale of the railroad are good reasons for our special solicitude for its traffic volume, to say nothing of its remaining position as the sole available carrier for some types of freight movement. It is much easier to effect a shrinkage in truck or waterway capacity without strong effects on unit costs. If such shrinkage were indicated, ways could be found to ease the transition for those carriers. (It is probably too much to hope in addition for imposition of full user charges and a cessation of uneconomic waterway development.)

Many of the estimates of minimum railroad freight volume under flexible pricing that I have seen seem to be on the low side. Some of these estimates are based on inferences from simple commodity characteristics rather than on calculations of cost and transportation demand. Roberts' own calculations are not designed to answer this question, but to show what might happen under strict cost-of-service pricing. We can take this as a minimum estimate or most pessimistic limit of the railroads' share in the total transport volume, assuming uniform rates. If the rules indicated above were followed instead, traffic for the railroads would very likely increase markedly instead of diminishing. Recent experience suggests that more rational pricing may recapture large volumes of remunerative traffic. One can refer to the multiple-car rates for coal, or the reduced grain rates which have elicited cries of unfair competition from the waterway carriers in the South. Minimum-volume rates and all-commodity rates are also promising, and the lower rates for automobiles combined with technological innovations in automobile carriage have apparently been successful. Rail-truck piggyback service may decisively reduce the railroad handicap of high terminal costs and slow service on package freight and manufactured goods, for all except very short hauls. In spite of Roberts' unfavorable findings on past experience with railroad rate reductions, the general picture of prices and demand elasticities at present leads me to believe that a massive and comprehensive reform of transport price policy would not only increase the rails' share of traffic but also have a strongly favorable effect on their revenues. But I agree with Nelson that these reorganizations, abandonments, rejuvenations and pricing reforms must be put into effect without delay; else the momentum of decline for the railroads may become too strong to reverse, short of government receivership.

HOWARD W. NICHOLSON, Clark University

Roberts' paper deals with controversial issues of minimum and maximum rate regulation. He stresses the desirability of permitting railroads to lower rates to incremental costs, by which he means costs incurred in producing additional units of service. Roberts states that he is interested in allocative efficiency and he argues that, in view of the existence of large fixed costs, maximum use of the rail system can be encouraged by discriminatory rate policies, that is, by stressing demand factors in the determination of rates. Despite evidence which he has collected which suggests that rate cuts may prove to be disappointing in increasing profits, Roberts appears to be relatively hopeful that the elasticity of demand for rail service will be high when cuts of sufficient size are undertaken. He also seems optimistic about the success of aggressive discriminatory pricing policies in contributing to the revenue needs of the railroads. The contrast between the views of Nelson and Roberts in this regard is striking, and it is a matter of considerable importance as to which position is correct. This subject deserves more careful examination.

Important as it is, the question of the effectiveness of rail-rate reductions in attracting additional revenue to the railroads is but part of the current problem of transportation pricing policy, and concern with railroad rate-making has tended to obscure more fundamental pricing questions. Complete analysis of transport pricing policy should involve consideration of the implications of pricing arrangements for: 1. investment in transport facilities, 2. use of existing facilities, and 3. the cost and quality of transportation service.

Although Roberts flirts with cost considerations and occasionally alludes to the relevance of price-cost considerations for investment decisions and industrial location, his paper creates the impression that he is primarily interested in rate-making practices that will encourage fuller utilization of existing railroad plant. He does not seem to be vitally concerned with the implications of pricing from the standpoint of the long-run problem of encouraging efficient investment in transport facilities, nor does he seem to attach much significance to development of transport rate structures which will encourage a more rational pattern of industrial location. The essential difference between Roberts and those—like myself—who advocate the development of rate policies in which rates are encouraged to bear a reasonable relationship to long-run marginal costs is that the disputants are concerned with different aspects of the total problem of transport pricing policy.

Roberts deserves credit for emphasizing, as he has done, the danger that emphasis on costs in transportation rates may in practice produce policies that tend to keep rates too high. I agree that policy does better to err somewhat on the side of encouraging flexibility in rate-making. But I regard as either wrongheaded or shortsighted economists who push transport investment problems under the rug and assume that by disregarding the problems of fixed costs in rate-making and letting nature take its course, somehow problems of resource allocation in transportation investment and problems of industrial location will be smoothly resolved. Is it not paradoxical that the competition that has developed in transportation and upon which we economists have come to depend for rationalization of domestic transportation affairs, is in fact a competition for railroads from transportation agencies which derive very large amounts of fixed capital from government sources. A crucial issue for modern transport pricing policy and one to which Roberts' analysis does not give sufficient weight is that of investment policy and the relationship which transport pricing bears to investment flows into the transportation system as a whole.

The Dynamic Interdependence of

Transportation Pricing,

Transportation Costs, and the

Rates of Growth or

Decline of the Various Modes

of Transportation

JAMES R. NELSON

AMHERST COLLEGE

This paper is concerned with the *interactions* of prices, costs, and rates of growth; it is especially concerned with the *cumulative effects* of such interactions. In view of the much-publicized recent difficulties of the American railroads—with emphasis on those serving official territory—it is still more particularly concerned with the possible dangers inherent in *cumulative decline*.

Statistical Background

Freight transportation as a whole has not kept pace with the economy. The decline of passenger travel by rail is too well known to require any documentation. Moreover, passenger travel may often be noncommercial in motivation as it is overwhelmingly noncommercial in performance. So this presentation will confine itself to the most favorable example in terms of both rail service and commerical transportation generally.

The following table indicates that even intercity freight movements have lagged behind the growth of the economy:

	Index for 1962	
	1947 = 100	1957 = 100
Gross national product (1962 prices)	168.8	115.7
Industrial production	179.9	117.4
Intercity freight, ton-miles[a]	136.9	104.5

[a] Excludes coastal and intercoastal shipping. Includes estimated private carriage.
SOURCES: Gross national product and industrial production, from *Economic Report of the President*, January 1963, pp. 172, 210; freight ton-miles, from Testimony of A. E. Baylis, I.C.C. Docket No. 21989, Exhibit H- 23 in *New York Times*, September 1, 1963, Section 4, p. 10.

Inclusion of coastwise ton-miles would not appreciably change the freight indexes given above. If petroleum were excluded, coastwise ton-miles would even show a strong downward trend. It is tempting to blame the ton-mile record on the continuing decline of coal, but this explanation would not justify an assumption of a reversal of trend in the future. For traditional methods of transport are threatened from all sides in the critical electric power market for coal: not only by natural gas and coal pipelines, but also by higher and higher transmission voltages for electricity, and more and more efficient nuclear power plants. Therefore, it seems reasonable to predict that ton-miles by traditional methods of transport will, at the very least, have trouble holding their own against a changing economy and changing patterns of fuel use within this economy.

This conclusion should require no proof. The further trend which *does* require emphasis, for the purposes of this discussion, is the tendency for an *absolute decline* in railroad ton-miles. These ton-miles have never recovered their 1947 level; nor their 1956 level. Meanwhile, truck ton-miles are about three times as great as they were in 1947, and 20–25 per cent above 1956. The relative shift from rail to truck has not continued, during the last decade, at the pace set during the years immediately after World War II. But recent statistics do not indicate that the decline in the railroads' relative share will be halted, or even slowed enough to halt the absolute rail decline.

So much, then, for recent trends. But what was the economic position of railroads during the era of greatest railroad expansion? Does an examination of that period provide any clues to diagnosing their

present problems? It will be specifically argued here that every condition of differentiated oligopoly, of which railroading is surely an
example, is likely to be *sui generis*. The annalist, therefore, must
precede the analyst.

Dynamic Interdependence on a Rising Market

That useful compendium, *Historical Statistics of the United States*, is
full of surprises. Where else, for example, would one find depicted on
the cover a town which can only be Lexington, Massachusetts mis-
labeled Hannibal, Missouri? Where else would one learn that—in
apparent defiance of near-money, liquidity preference, and the pre-
cautionary and speculative motives—long-term interest rates in much
of the nineteenth century were actually below short-term interest rates?
And where else—to state the theme of this paper—would one discover
that, during the golden era of railroad expansion in the generation after
the Civil War, rates of return on the book value of railroad investment
were below rates of return on the most nearly risk-free securities?

The stated value of outstanding railroad securities more than doubled
between 1867 and 1870; more than doubled once again between 1870
and 1880; and almost doubled between 1880 and 1890. A doubling
in ten years requires growth at a rate of 7 per cent, compounded; yet
"net earnings" (a concept with a close affinity to "net operating
income") rose above 5 per cent only in the first two years for which such
earnings are reported: 1871 and 1872. As a percentage of stated value
of railroad securities, these earnings never recovered from the panic of
1873. They averaged just above 3 per cent per annum during the late
1880's.[1] Interest on funded debt, which averaged just over 4 per cent
throughout the 1876–90 period, was more than double "dividends paid"
from 1885 on.[2] In general, the impression conveyed by the statistics is
one of profitless prosperity carried to an extreme in both directions:
extreme prosperity, extremely profitless.

The basic point is not much changed if the argument is related to
"investment in railroad and equipment." This was not quite 10 per cent
less than the stated value of securities in 1876, and had declined slightly
in relative size to just under 14 per cent less by 1890.[3] But neither the
small difference in percentage nor the even smaller difference in trend
would affect the comparison to any meaningful degree.

[1] *Historical Abstract*, Series Q 33–42, p. 428.
[2] *Ibid.*
[3] *Ibid.*

It is tempting at this point to contradict the evidence of a rapid rate of growth combined with a low rate of return by denying the accuracy of the basic data. The financial antics of Jay Gould have thrown a lurid light across this whole period. Before the days of stocks with no par value, even the best-intentioned promoters must often have accepted physical assets in exchange for stock at inflated nominal prices. A full picture of this problem would require an endless sojourn among the Valuation Dockets. Meanwhile, Professor Melville Ulmer estimates that 21 per cent of the change in book value of railroad plant and equipment between 1880 and 1890 was a product of write-ups of assets.[4] Adjustment for these would raise the reported return on investment, but it might not lower the nominal rate of growth. It could even raise this nominal rate if the average write-ups in 1880 exceeded 21 per cent of recorded 1880 values.

Moreover, much railroad investment was not primarily intended to yield profits from the operation of the railroad itself. The economic history of the United States from independence to World War I could be written, with a surprising approach to completeness, as a series of variations on the theme of land speculation; and railroads were a source of higher property values that even the most unenlightened community fathers could appreciate.

Finally, railroads in the nineteenth century had an active, if not creative, role to play in relation to corporate accounting. In various ways, the railroad did more to create the accounting profession than the accounting profession managed to achieve in restraining the imagination of railroad entrepreneurs. But, if retirement accounting offered wide scope for the movement of earnings backward and forward through time, this same accounting tended to *increase* reported rates of return in a growing industry over anything that could be achieved by depreciation accounting. Holding asset values intact on the books until assets were discarded tended to inflate net property accounts by equating them with gross property accounts; but failure to depreciate meant that annual charge-offs were a function of some much smaller level of past assets rather than of the entire spectrum of assets in service.

All in all, if we indulge in qualitative guessing as a complement to quantitative but dubious "facts," the net result would still not be a high rate of return on assets used and useful in the public service: hardly 8 per cent; possibly 6 per cent; not impossibly even less than that.

---

[4] *Capital in Transportation, Communications, and Public Utilities: Its Formation and Financing*, Princeton University Press for National Bureau of Economic Research, 1960, Appendix J, Sources and Uses of Funds, p. 501.

This ability of a really major industry to raise very important sums of money from all kinds of sources in the face of extreme uncertainties can scarcely be explained in terms of persistent bullishness on the part of investors. Twenty-five years is too long to be bullish, even during the Gilded Age. Besides, a combination of world price trends and the continued movement of the United States toward resumption of specie payments produced a rapid and almost continuous decline of wholesale prices from 1865 through 1879, and on down right through 1890. This may help to explain a willingness to accept low immediate nominal rates on long-term securities; but it does not help to explain why liquid funds should rush to lock themselves up in a physical embodiment with an unusually long life-cycle and in an industry subject to a rapid rate of technical improvement.

So much for the various aspects of the problem. How may all of these be combined to throw useful light on the period of fastest railroad development in this country? This step requires a return to a familiar static concept—that of differentiated oligopoly. This concept keeps overflowing its economic box: sales expenses involve costs which in turn affect the demand curve; a firm's market position at time (t) will affect its policies and performance at time ($t + 1$), and so on. But these problems are normally overlooked in order to put differentiated oligopoly on the same logical plane as other forms of market organization. The familiar oligopolistic pecularity—that of mutual interdependence—is assumed to involve special uncertainties; but these are often supposed to be most significant for pure oligopoly, and to be amenable, in any case, to logical extensions of static analysis.

When differentiated oligopoly appears in industries with such heavily-decreasing costs, and subject to so many internal and external influences for dynamic change, as nineteenth-century railroading, the result is not likely to be "mutual interdependence recognized" or an attempt to flee the rigors of competition by carving a small private market out of the larger general one. Instead, the result is likely to be a tendency toward out-and-out monopoly. If entry is difficult—for such obvious reasons as the gradual disappearance of public subsidies as local areas either achieved their transportation ambitions or lost out in the economic race because they had failed—then there must be some advantage in buying up competitors. But the stick may be employed along with, or prior to, the carrot: even if the competitor could not be driven out, he could be demoted from trunk-line to local status, deprived of other forms of economic importance and power, and bought out or leased at a lower price commensurate with his weakened position.

This monopoly goal was never achieved over any really wide area—with the possible exception of parts of the West Coast—during the late nineteenth century, although E. H. Harriman frankly described this as his objective early in the twentieth. But its interrelationship with the dynamic factors already mentioned may go far to explain the puzzling contrast of profits and expansion which has already been described.

For the outright loser in the corporate race for position, the profit record needs no explanation. This loser earned a low rate of return on a specialized investment which could not easily be withdrawn from the industry. Presumably the loser could not obtain capital for expansion. His fate was seldom abandonment, and often not even absorption by more prosperous and powerful rivals. Whether technically independent or no, the loser was relegated to branch-line status: low traffic density, low outlays for maintenance and capital purposes generally; slow technical progress; a continued existence more or less at the will of better-situated enterprises. This loser may not even have been the proverbial "weak" road, so dear to commentators on the Transportation Act of 1920, or to expounders of the justification for long- and short-haul discrimination. For "weak" roads were generally assumed to be competitive with, or in some sense comparable to, their stronger brethren. The losers we are discussing were more nearly complementary than competitive.

For the outright winners, the profit record sometimes also needs no explanation because it was high. The Pennsylvania and the New York Central were the classic money-earners of the late nineteenth century, and would have been even more outstanding if monopoly gains to predecessor interests had not become imbedded in the structure of asset valuations and leases of the successor concerns. But the New York Central also illustrates the vulnerability to existing competition of even a well-situated railroad. It also shows the particular vulnerability of such a railroad to new entries before the railroad map became frozen, due to the unwillingness of public interests to support new ventures. First, Gould engaged the Central in savage rate wars, even with a manifestly higher-cost property; Gould did not sell the Erie to Commodore Vanderbilt only because Vanderbilt thought he had bought it. Gould cheerfully met Vanderbilt's common stock purchases by conversion of debentures held in the Erie treasury, and thus kept voting control of that unhappy enterprise. Second, the Nickel Plate could not have been more of a threat to the Central if it had been designed solely with that purpose in view—which was obviously the opinion of the Vanderbilts, who bought it on behalf of the New York Central immediately upon its completion. Third, the West Shore-South Pennsylvania stand-off, although not explicable in terms of sheer blackmail, contained elements of

> Mirror, mirror on the wall—
> Who is the fairest of them all?

Silvering the mirrors cost both the Central and the Pennsylvania a great deal of money.

The great bulk of railroad mileage, and of railroad capital, fell in between the "hopeless" low return and the high return, with more or less dilution. Ask the question—what do the following railroads have in common, aside from conspicuous relative profitability since World War II: Chesapeake & Ohio and Norfolk & Western; Southern; Santa Fe and Union Pacific? One answer would be that all were in reorganization during the 1890's. As the subsequent record has proved, these difficulties were not due to poor original choice of location, or particularly bad luck in the development of the territory served. Most were not due to bad management, or to speculative financing in the sense that more conservative alternatives could have been chosen. A very complex series of episodes in American transportation history may perhaps be summarized as follows: with the possible exception of the Union Pacific, all of the railroads listed above had seen that they would drift back into the short-line group in Category 1 unless they built, and bought, on a gigantic scale. A railroad which really started at Atchison and ended at Santa Fe would have done very little. Instead, roads like the Santa Fe, with particularly strong leadership, aimed at the rank of the New York Central and Pennsylvania—which was a long way from their unpretentious origins. These roads were able to raise the funds required to *aim* at this rank because of the rapidly expanding demand for the services of the industry. They were all driven aground by a sharp downturn of the business cycle, but were rapidly refloated on the incoming business tide at the turn of the century.

The preceding comments offer a highly schematic version of a most "dynamic" stretch of transportation history. What analytical possibilities emerge from this record?

1. Present profits may be *subnormal* in a rapidly expanding industry, and not necessarily abnormal (in order to provide a flow of internal funds and attract finance from outside).

2. The first step toward explaining the apparent paradox of subnormal returns in an abnormally expanding industry is to make the

paradox even sharper by noting that an abnormal rate of physical expansion does not, in itself, furnish any promise of an abnormal rate of growth, or an eventual abnormal level, of profits.

3. The missing link in the argument must be a condition of decreasing costs on such a scale, for each firm, that aggressive tactics may be expected both to drive present lower-density firms to the wall and to act as a strong deterrent to entry—once the existing firms become able to develop volume and density by growth of the market and both parallel and end-to-end consolidation.

4. Such aggressive tactics were encouraged, in rail transportation, by the fact that one element in differentiation consisted of building private sidings to the premises of large shippers. Once these shippers became established, and committed fixed investment to the services of one railroad, this railroad could begin to earn abnormal returns without any possibility of entry—*as long as the shippers were not stimulated to encourage entry by their own efforts* (as Andrew Carnegie was stimulated to support the South Pennsylvania project).

5. As the scale of the market expanded longitudinally (rail shipment feasible for greater distances) as well as laterally (heavier density of rail shipments to and from given areas), the range of possible competition increased. The larger number of different routes for larger volumes over longer distances also increased the actual and possible degree of differentiation. This increase in the size of the available worlds to conquer also enhanced the risk of being conquered: but here, as in horse-racing, lengthening the odds possibly operated to *reduce*, or in some cases perhaps to reverse, the risk premium.

6. A view of market prospects from both sides—prospects of gain, and dangers of loss—indicates that new investment may have been rational even with low average and marginal returns on existing investment. The marginal productivity of new investment need not be positive in a *net* sense (after allowance for depreciation, or retirement and replacement, as the case may be) as long as it is positive in a *gross* sense (increment to gross flow of cash discounted by a *low* current rate possibly increasing with time, in excess of current cost of asset). In a static model, this would seem to amount to a recommendation to throw good money after bad. But the present case is not the profits treadmill of a purely competitive industry, with stationary profits possible only after unremitting effort. The profits prize might go not only to the greatest *amount* of capital investment per unit of length or area, but to the *fastest rate* of capital investment. Kalecki's "principle of increasing risk" may, in fact, have been reversed in this case.

7. This capital investment could take three very distinctive forms, yielding *three dimensions* of differentiation; intensive (higher capacity per unit of length), extensive (including more units of length *in a given area* already served), and qualitative (more efficient embodiments of capital). The first yields familiar "decreasing cost" conditions. The second involves every possibility, from an outward push on the collective demand curve to sheer cancellation because of duplicate effort. The third provides the most obvious relationship of differentiation to "progress."

Both the first and third of these dimensions would make rate decreases possible directly; the second might make decreases possible indirectly, by feeding increased volumes of traffic onto the "main line." In turn, rates could be—and were—differentiated, customer-by-customer, just as service was differentiated in typically larger units. Price differentiation may permit larger sales for a given rate of profit; which, in turn, may permit price *reduction*, further growth in volume, and so on.

8. Even without competition from the internal combustion engine after World War I, capital supply, "normal" rate of profit, and other railroad problems might have been affected by a combination of factors: more rigorous regulation; fewer additional gains to be made at the expense of railroad competitors; and possibly a slower rate of growth in "inherent" transportation demand, as the marginal physical product of extensive development slowed down and further extensions were not undertaken.

But these considerations are now leading us into the problems of maturity. Is there a critical rate of growth—year-by-year, or cumulative—below which internal repercussions begin to develop which slow growth even further?

The Point of No Return

This title is necessarily metaphorical, since the "life cycle" of an industry is not a precise concept. But, unless the industry should be rejuvenated by a cluster of innovations or by other external influences, it will reach a point in its aging process when the cumulative, interacting forces making for growth will be overborne by retarding influences.

The simplest illustration of this concept is provided by the contrast between the learning curve and the featherbed.

With age, every industry develops a staff of skilled laborers, sources for the collection and dissemination of technical information, facilities for systematic education of its labor force, experienced suppliers of equipment and raw materials, and all the other desirable by-products of continued existence. Many of these by-products will retain their importance even if the individual firms in the industry come and go.

The other side to this maturing process is the development of habit patterns: how much can be done, how it should be done, who should do it, under what working conditions, in the context of what kind of hierarchy for enforcement of discipline and distribution of incomes, at what rates of pay or rates of pay increase. These habit patterns involve a mixture of the technical and the financial. In the extreme case, there may never be any technical loss from freezing the job structure, enforcing seniority rules, or prohibiting the introduction of new methods. But the "habit" aspect of maturing will still have caught up with the growth aspect, from the standpoint of this industry's competitive position in the entire economy, if even a normal rate of technical improvement is accompanied by a tendency for factor costs to rise at a faster rate than the average for industries in general. Leads in factor prices will have the same effect as lags in factor efficiencies on demand, and on the mutual interrelationships of demand, cost, and price.

The aeronautical analogy of "stalling speed" could be used, i.e., a rate of growth which, as it declines, adds power to the forces operating to slow the industry rate of growth, and thereby helps prevent a return to the previous rate of growth. But this concept is not truly independent. The relevant rate of growth of demand would vary with the age of the industry and hence the behavior of its costs.

The important questions, from the standpoint of this paper, are those relating to trends and not turning-points. Therefore, this intermediate stage will not be examined in detail, but it may be noted that the point of no return may come sooner, rather than later, under the following conditions.

1. It will come sooner if market dominance comes earlier. The high demand elasticity of differentiated oligopoly combines with a profusion of opportunities to shift the entire demand curve of the firm and capture previously unexploited segments of the market. Additional differentiation becomes pointless by definition once monopoly is reached, and probably more or less pointless in fact at some intermediate stage. Hence, there will be possibly less waste from duplicated facilities, but probably also less need on the part of the dominant firm for technical progress. Moreover, hope for a big new prize cannot attract new capital at low current rates of return. The prize, big or small, has already been won.

2. If regulation inhibits competition it can produce a facsimile of market dominance, but without the security for investors that market dominance provides.

3. It will come sooner if differentiation takes the form of near duplication of facilities instead of innovation.

Beyond this point, generalizations tend to become a guessing game. The next section will carry on the argument in more concrete terms.

Dynamic Interdependence on the Way Down

The essential problem here is the savage reprisals of the capital market once an industry has disappointed its hopes. This may seem to introduce a paper dragon, since the main problem of a declining industry is to release embodied capital as rapidly and painlessly as possible. But the realities are:

1. A downward shift in the demand for an industry's services may *increase* the need for capital betterment to provide a cheaper or more efficient service, at the same time as it decreases the flow of funds available to meet the need;

2. Any going concern is caught in a web of contractual obligations and "legitimate expectations." Interest payments, and even dividends, tend to hold up longer than net operating income. Moreover, the acquisition of new capital from private sources bumps up against the historical fact of the existing capital structure. In the railroad industry, various devices for financing rolling stock have built a temporary detour around the balance sheet of each debtor railroad; but what is to happen if the whole industry faces a declining demand and a heavy outstanding debt in the form of equipment trusts and conditional sales contracts?

3. The discontinuity between returns expected on internal and external "new money" may actually increase. A hardy perennial of corporation finance is the proposition that new securities must sell at a discount. But, as we have seen, this discount when applied to an expanding industry may simply raise effective yields toward "normal profit." In a declining industry, with equities already selling well below book value, issuance of new stock at a discount from even this level would not be easy to explain to stockholders. Meanwhile, internally generated funds are dropping with the decline in sales, or much faster, since the short-run inflexibility of costs tends to become even more stubborn in an industry with long-run costs containing ingredients which are also inflexible. As a result, the rate of discount applicable to

yields from *better* investment begins soaring; an industry whose troubles may stem from low-quality investment thereupon says goodbye to improvement.

4. Theoretically, "better" investment and "more" investment are two entirely different things. In practice—and especially in transportation practice—it may be almost impossible to segregate the qualitative from the quantitative. In so far as improvements are more capital-intensive, they are likely to add to capacity, *somewhere* and in *some* respect. A firm which must anticipate either a decline in physical use of its facilities, or a decline in receipts per unit of use as the price of continued utilization, may find itself facing two ways at once: toward increased capacity, as a by-product of "improvement"; and toward a decreased flow of internally generated earnings available to pay for this capacity.

5. With technical progress slowed down just when it is most needed, can or should the decline be arrested *economically*, or *financially*?

Before examining this dilemma, we must go further in establishing that it really exists. Specifically, by any customary measure, the technical progress of American railroads has been very considerable over the last twenty or thirty years. Is there any evidence of a vicious circle here—especially for an industry with a century of technical progress already behind it a generation ago?

It would be most ungracious to deride railroad technical achievements, especially when they are viewed against the background of the industry's difficulties with finances, operating rules, regulatory bodies, etc. This paragraph will merely suggest that the recent historical record of technical progress in railroading may be used to prove too much about the future. The diesel locomotive provided a very important source of productivity gains before, and especially after, World War II. This locomotive owed much of its success to the application of certain of the principles of automobile manufacture: standardization of production methods; standardization of product; and an approach to mass production. Elsewhere in railroading, the product was already more standardized—or more resistant to standardization. The peak of the shift to diesels occurred at about the time of peak optimism about prospects for rail tonnage and revenues: ergo, of peak marketability for rail equipment obligations. Even today, improvements in equipment are much more easily financed than improvements in way and structure; and standard equipment is more easily financed than highly specialized equipment which can be used in only one area or for a limited range of services.

So the record of technical change in railroading should not lull us into complacency about the future, especially since truck competition has been most sharp on the small-volume, light-loading, short-haul movements which were bound to depress railroad productivity indexes as long as they were an important element in railroad service.

To return, then, to the economic and financial prospects, *economically*, two possibilities exist: *marginal cost pricing* and *intensified price discrimination*.

MARGINAL COST PRICING

Rigorously applied, this would have the advantage of eliminating accumulated areas of internal subsidy. It would have the further advantage of cushioning the downward shift of demand curves by intersecting each one at a level of lower price and higher volume.

The disadvantages would all stem from financial difficulties. Bankruptcy may not frighten an economist, but both the threat and the actuality may sometimes galvanize corporate managements. The long descent into bankruptcy is as demoralizing to employees as to stockholders. Bankruptcy is a temporary legal expedient appropriate to an economy in which one firm, more or less, is assumed to make practically no difference. The issue may lie between the former management and the current creditors; or it may turn on the continuation or liquidation of the firm itself. In a world of competitive firms, there is no economic difference. But in a world of decreasing costs, differentiated oligopolists, and long-run shifts in demand curves, marginal cost pricing under private ownership might eventually produce a tag-end service provided by the physical assets which cling to life most stubbornly. Assets with high opportunity costs could be shifted elsewhere or into other uses; assets with short life spans would have to be retired. Meanwhile, on the way down, shifts in demand curves would be accelerated by service deterioration affecting the form of transport whose popularity was tending to wane even with previous service standards. And the discontinuous character of the disinvestment process might plunge shippers directly down from quite good service by each of the competing forms of transport to no service at all by one or more of them.

INTENSIFIED PRICE DISCRIMINATION

One of the obvious drawbacks of the aging process in an industry is the tendency to freeze yesterday's price structure in the face of today's costs. If both marginal cost pricing and public subsidy are ruled out, a decreasing cost firm is likely to increase its interest in price discrimination; and, if the demand curve for its services is shifting downward, it must comb through its existing rate structure in search of opportunities to maintain volume, or net earnings, or both.

In a stationary world, this is well and good. A declining business should examine its demand structure as carefully as its cost structure—and act promptly on any discoveries it makes.

But in a dynamic world, "too late" cancels out everything. The high elasticity of demand which justifies a price cut may have been the end product of a minor share of the market; this, in turn, may have been the end-product of earlier price and service inflexibilities. All of which may simply prove that the best way to regain business is not to lose it in the first place.

Intensified price discrimination in the railroad industry faces two real problems: (1) For a wide range of commodities, the controlling rates are now truck rates; (2) trucking is a rapidly expanding industry in which the relevant costs, for purposes of examining rates, are *long-run costs*—of operation, of vehicles, of the highways themselves.

There is nothing wrong with intensified price discrimination in principle; but, in practice, it may simply offer an excuse for locking the barn door after the horse is stolen.

FINANCIAL SOLUTIONS

Financially, the problem is to find out whether an industry which has always believed in charging what the traffic will bear can benefit from yet another turn of the screw while external competition is steadily growing. Even with constant volume, the firm may still be able to check the downward spiral by massive rate readjustments which align the pricing structure to current cost of service. But this possibility of realignment assumes both that the market is strong enough to yield additional revenues and the regulatory authorities will permit a readjustment which must be rapid and drastic to be effective.

This same financial result may be approximated, within limits, by a realignment of service to gain more net revenue out of a frozen pattern of rates. The service spectrum may, of course, be too narrow to yield all the freedom available through rates themselves. The only feasible way to vary service may be to abandon large portions of it—passenger service, all service on certain lines—even at a cost of considerable decrease in volume of business, and possibly in volume remaining per mile of residual system.

The preceding paragraphs have only sketched in possibilities. This is partly due to the time dimension implicit in this section, which extends from the clear past into the overcast future. It is partly due to the fact that regulatory policy is a much more important influence now than it was in the era of greatest railroad growth (one purpose of this paper is to abstract from regulation, per se, to the utmost degree compatible with some resemblance to reality). But it is mainly due to a belief that the road downhill may end at a precipice. The possible existence of this cut-off point, below which a downfall becomes a disaster, is precisely the cause of deepest anxiety about public policy for the industry. It is bad enough if decisions turn an orderly industry retreat into a rout; it is surely much worse if these decisions drive, or push, the industry to its own annihilation.

This kind of statement can be intensely irritating, because it intimates that radical policy changes may be essential and yet offers no clue as to the form these changes might take. But one thing, at least, can be said without departing from the present context: decisions based on static assumptions as to "most efficient," or "least cost," or "best service" are likely to produce only puzzlement, as the industry continually develops new symptoms which are not covered by the original diagnosis. Specifically, "what is wrong with the railroads" from the standpoint of public policy—either in themselves, or as they compete with other media of transportation—may be due in part to the fact that both regulation and promotion look too closely at past conditions and not closely enough at the nature, meaning, future course, and destination, of current trends. This backward-looking view may be inseparable from regulation. If so, it is an argument against regulation as such.

Conclusion

Finally, this paper has not begun to live up to its title. The "transportation" so broadly promised turns out to be railroads, and usually just railroads hauling freight. At least something must be done to restore the balance.

The technical origin of interdependence in the early days of railroading was the existence of permanent way under the control of the firm operating the facilities and offering final transportation services to the consuming public. The permanent way was the outstanding single source of decreasing costs. The vertical integration was the outstanding source of the ability to carry elaborate forms of price differentiation right through to final consumers. These technical sources are not duplicated in any other major form of transportation. Airlines and shipping obviously do not require permanent way. Trucks and buses do not provide their own. As a matter of sheer technique, it would be possible to have oligopolistic warfare between turnpike authorities, but this possibility has been foreclosed, supposedly for all time, by the institutional development of the highway "industry."

Conversely, modern methods of transport must adhere to schedules, or operate within maximum time limits. Nothing could have been farther from the freight practices of American railroads in the nineteenth century. Express lines sprang up, sometimes with railroad sponsorship, but the shipper who did not want to pay a substantial premium had to wait indefinitely to hear that the goods had arrived.

The necessity for scheduling also brings in the possibility of decreasing costs with additional capital investment, as more units of service per route or per firm may help to fill all units (better load factor) or to permit each unit to serve for longer hours on the average (utilization factor). In the infancy of the airlines, these could be very important considerations; on routes with low traffic densities, they still are. But this scheduling problem, at its worst, is not really identical with the decreasing cost situation of the early railroads. Scheduling involves load factors; and load factors bring in the possible relevance of joint costs and of peak and off-peak use. These present thorny problems of analysis and policy, but they are likely to have cumulative or dynamic attributes only in the early stages of growth—or the last stages of decline.

The future of the railroads may be foreshadowed with startling clarity by the history of coastal shipping. As a general carrier of coastal cargo, shipping is approaching a watery grave. This is true in spite of the fact that practically all of the arguments for the superiority of railroad efficiency to truck are also arguments for the superiority of sea to land efficiency. The trouble obviously is a combination of high terminal costs and slow and relatively unattractive service. Once the decline is well under way, the hiatus between calls tends to lengthen; the job of profitably operating any liner service tends to become more difficult; and the stage is set for a further decline of the industry. In view of present railroad problems, there may be at least some poetic justice in the fact that the past decline of coastwise "liner service" was hastened by aggressive pricing and service tactics on the part of the railroads.

What does this discussion have to contribute to public policy?

1. An emphasis on the necessity for continuous exploration of future solutions, on the basis of reasonable alternative hypotheses, and with the aid of models which incorporate the *interrelationships* of demand, cost, price, and service.

2. Possibly, also, an argument for de-emphasis of regulation under just those conditions of industrial age and converging industrial problems which seem to make regulation most secure and most necessary. For age tends toward inflexibility, even in the absence of regulation. New competition, from new quarters, may require greater flexibility if the original service is to maintain itself. And regulation may therefore weight the scales against flexibility just when this flexibility is most required.

COMMENT

HOWARD W. NICHOLSON, Clark University

Nelson attempts to explain the large flows of private capital into the American railroad system during the late 19th century, despite seemingly subnormal returns. His paper is also concerned with the current capital needs of railroads. Nelson stresses that, in the absence of suitable demand conditions, railroads may experience difficulties in obtaining adequate revenue for current capital requirements with either marginal cost or discriminatory pricing policies. He seems skeptical as to whether elasticity of demand is sufficiently high to effectively contribute to capital needs through rate cutting. In the absence of policies which will have the effect of shifting the demand curve for rail transportation upward, Nelson expresses doubt that even the most aggressive system of discriminatory pricing will enable the railroads to obtain a supply of capital adequate to make full use of modern technological possibilities.

Nelson's paper is specifically addressed to the relationship between price and investment in transport facilities. But I regret that he conceived of his problem so narrowly and that the ingenuity he demonstrates in analyzing investment motives influencing private capital flows into the rail system was not directed to analysis of basic determinants of flows of capital into other significant areas of the transportation plant.

In short, I am criticizing his failure to provide the breadth of analysis, the analytical framework against which to adequately judge the pressing pricing policy issues of today. What are these issues? What is this unmet challenge to price analysis?

In the 1870's, the Windom Committee reported that the transportation problem of that day was unsatisfactory rail service and unsatisfactory railroad rates. The Committee's report proposed that the problem be dealt with by construction of government railroads and waterways which would bring competitive pressures on the railroads to reduce their rates and improve their service. This policy was not immediately adopted. Instead, in 1887, Congress passed legislation providing for regulation of railroad rates. Shortly after this, however, the federal government began to promote competitors for the railroads, beginning with waterways, then highways, and finally air transportation. Today, national transportation policy is a mixture of the policies recommended by the Windom and Cullom Committees in the 1870's and 1880's. The Doyle Report provides evidence that present policies are producing instabilities in the transport system. Existing policies tend to produce large government investment in transport facilities, creating a chronic tendency toward a total supply of transport facilities in excess of the demand which exists for transport service. More serious may be the tendency of present policies to produce an imbalance in the mix of transport facilities. This, in essence, is the railroad problem. Moreover, there is evidence that pricing and other aspects of present policy discourage efficient utilization of existing transport facilities and do not tend to promote the best quality of service.

The fundamental question for pricing policy is whether, by suitable changes, a pricing system can be developed which will help to correct imbalances in transportation investment while encouraging a more rational utilization of existing facilities, lower cost and better quality service. The emphasis which the Doyle Report places on cost-related pricing is designed to emphasize the need for development of transportation policies which will produce rates that contribute to development of a more efficient and better coordinated transportation system. This involves a consideration of the effect of rate policies on investment, on use of existing facilities, and on the cost and quality of service produced by the existing system.

The challenge for transportation economists is to clarify understanding of how alternative price policies will affect all of these vital areas. We need to know much more than we do about what these effects are, and we need to be able to evaluate specifically the implications of different pricing policies both for use patterns of existing facilities and for transportation investment.

Airline Costs and
Managerial Efficiency

ROBERT J. GORDON

MASSACHUSETTS INSTITUTE OF TECHNOLOGY

The drastic decline in profits of domestic trunk airlines after the
introduction of jet service in 1959 brought many complaints from
the airlines and financial columnists. In the winter of 1961–62, when the
clamor was loudest, one analyst said that the airlines "as a whole are
seriously sick, perhaps almost as much as their rivals, the railroads." [1]
Most explanations of low profits centered on "CAB-induced over-
competition" [2] and "an abrupt slowdown in the growth of passenger
traffic." [3] In other words, it was assumed that lower profits were
caused by a decline in revenues relative to costs, and not much attention
was given to the possibility that costs were higher than necessary. But
some of the airlines were making substantial profits, and at the same
time there was considerable intercarrier variation in the level of average
cost. A curious observer would notice, for example, that in 1960 the
average cost of the operations of Continental Airlines was 74 per cent
of that at United Air Lines. Was this inevitable? Were all intercarrier
cost differences dependent on route structure, fleet structure, and
other economic variables over which management had no control, or
could more skillful managerial cost control have substantially lowered
costs and raised profits? [4] The economist wonders: do the inefficient
firms, protected by the CAB from price competition with their more
efficient rivals, penalize the public by choosing to petition for fare
increases instead of putting more effort into cost control?

NOTE: This paper was originally submitted in April 1962 as part of a senior honors
thesis at Harvard College.
[1] *Forbes*, January 1, 1962, p. 34.
[2] *The New York Times*, January 8, 1962, p. 81.
[3] *Ibid.*, December 13, 1961, p. 13.
[4] These questions should interest the Civil Aeronautics Board, which has been
requested to grant important mergers on the ground that a more highly concentrated industry will be better able to make a profit.

"Managerial efficiency" is not often discussed in empirical micro-economic work. It is usually necessary in *theoretical* writings to treat managerial talent as a constant. "Economic Theory often simply assumes that the individual businessman will find and use the lowest cost method of production." [5] "We must assume that it is not the case that a few firms, managed by men of superior gifts, can and will continue to attract the small number of superior managers, and thus will be enabled to outperform all rivals in all fields." [6] But perhaps this assumption has been too rigidly retained in empirical work; even when managerial efficiency is mentioned, the difficulties involved in quantifying it scare most authors away. Caves, in his recent industry study, thinks that although some inefficiency may be lurking about, "the extent of the inadequacy of the airlines' performance due to inefficiency is impossible to measure." [7]

What statistical techniques are appropriate to quantify the elusive concept of managerial efficiency? In the first place, there is no general airline industry cost function to work with. As Caves shows, every writer who has tried to compute such a function by multiple regression analysis has failed, primarily because the sample is small and the relevant variables are many. [8] However, while computation of a *general* cost function has failed, it is possible to disaggregate reported costs into separate accounting cost categories. The working hypothesis of this paper is that after elimination of intercarrier cost differences due to identifiable economic variables over which management has no control, there remains a substantial residual in each cost category which can be statistically related to differences in managerial efficiency. We should expect effective cost control to be consistently applied by some managements in each cost category, and some managements, likewise, to be consistently inefficient—hence we shall be looking for evidence that the ranking of the carriers' "adjusted" costs (i.e., after elimination of differences dependent on identifiable economic variables) in each category should be similar.

This study is static. Since 1960 was the first full year of jet operations, no earlier period is suitable for analysis; nothing later than the third quarter of 1961 was available when the statistical work was done in early 1962. Furthermore, important strikes made an analysis of the

---

[5] H. Thomas Koplin, "Public Utilities and Transportation," *American Economic Review*, May 1961, p. 335.

[6] C. Kaysen and D. Turner, *Anti-Trust Policy*, Cambridge, 1959, p. 9.

[7] R. E. Caves, *Air Transport and Its Regulators*, Cambridge, 1962, p. 420.

[8] *Ibid.*, pp. 63–64.

TABLE 1

AVERAGE TOTAL COST BY CARRIER, 1960-61
(cents per available ton-mile)

	1960 Quarters				1961 Quarters		
	1st	2nd	3rd	4th	1st	2nd	3rd
American	31.2	30.0	29.1	29.3	32.0[a]	29.1	28.8
Braniff[b]	29.0	28.8	29.1	28.9	30.4	30.0	28.3
Capital[b]	35.0	33.0	34.4	34.2	33.9	--	--
Continental	24.5	23.1	22.8	23.7	25.0	22.7	22.5
Delta	29.4	28.8	29.3	31.0	30.0	30.0	30.3
Eastern	24.8	28.0[a]	25.6	25.2	27.8[a]	26.5	25.4
National	27.5	27.6	27.6	27.1	28.7[a]	22.6	22.8
Northeast	30.9	31.1	32.6	40.0	32.5	29.5	29.6
Northwest	26.6	24.8	25.8	29.6[a]	49.6[a]	27.7[a]	24.9
TWA	32.3	29.4	27.5	27.4	30.1[a]	26.1	26.3
United[b]	34.4	30.2	28.8	29.7	30.0	29.3	28.3
Western	29.2	29.5	29.6	32.5[a]	35.3[a]	28.3[a]	26.5

Source: CAB, *Air Carrier Traffic Statistics,* and *Air Carrier Financial Statistics,* various issues, 1960-61.

[a] Carrier was affected by a strike during this period.

[b] Capital figures from April 1 to May 31, 1961, included with United.

TABLE 2

AVERAGE CARRIER COST BY CATEGORY, THIRD QUARTER, 1961
(cents per available ton-mile)

	Flying Operations[a]	Maintenance	Passenger Service	Aircraft and Traffic Service	Promotion and Sales	General and Administrative	Depreciation[a]
American	7.2	6.0	2.4	4.9	3.5	1.3	3.5
Braniff	8.2	5.8	2.4	5.3	2.9	1.1	2.6
Continental	6.7	4.1	1.9	2.8	2.4	1.3	3.2
Delta	8.0	5.9	2.3	4.9	3.4	.9	3.4
Eastern	7.8	4.4	2.0	3.8	3.0	1.0	3.5
National	6.8	4.2	1.4	3.4	3.0	.6	3.4
Northeast	8.4	6.0	2.4	4.8	2.8	.8	4.4
Northwest	7.5	4.1	2.0	2.9	2.9	1.3	4.2
TWA	7.4	5.2	2.3	3.9	3.2	1.3	4.0
United	8.1	5.0	2.1	5.1	3.5	1.0	3.5
Western	7.0	4.0	2.1	3.5	3.6	1.3	5.1

Source: CAB, *Financial Statistics* and *Traffic Statistics,* September 1961 CAB, Form 41, September 30, 1961, Schedule P-9.2.

[a] Costs within the flying operations and depreciation categories have been rearranged from the officially reported figures. Carriers which lease flight equipment report this expense as "flying operations" even though, as a substitute for buying equipment, it should be considered equivalent to depreciation.

full 1960–61 period impossible. Table 1 shows that there were only three quarters during which strikes had no dislocating influence on cost levels. Fortunately, an analysis limited to the last of these periods, the third quarter of 1961, will not discriminate against any carrier or carrier group, since during this three-month period all carriers achieved their lowest cost levels of 1960–61 (with a few exceptions of only one- or two-tenths of a cent). Also, by concentrating just on the summer quarter, there will be no need to wonder to what extent unexplained intercarrier cost differences are due to differing winter weather conditions.

Table 2 shows average cost by categories for the third quarter of 1961. Flying operations consist of fuel costs and pilots' salaries; maintenance represents the costs of plane overhaul; passenger service includes stewardess salaries and food; aircraft and traffic servicing is mostly payroll for airport personnel who check in passengers, fuel planes, and load baggage; promotion and sales represents reservations agents, salesmen, and advertising; general and administrative covers the central office; and depreciation includes rental of planes as well as amortization of planes and ground equipment. Four of these categories cannot be considered in this analysis because a carrier's cost perform- ance therein may be related to its marketing success, and thus economies might reduce revenues instead of increasing profits. These are: passenger service, promotion and sales, general and administrative, and depreciation (which, of course, reflects the structure and size of the fleet each carrier has chosen for competition on its routes). But the remaining three categories, flying operations, maintenance, and aircraft and traffic servicing, are relatively unrelated to attracting passengers, and so any savings from increased efficiency would increase profits.

Flying Operations

Pilot salaries and fuel are the major cost items in the flying operations category. The average cost of these items should vary inversely with the average length of flight hop. With costs measured per ton-mile, the longer the flight, the greater the proportion of salary and fuel expended in cruising, and the less spent in taxiing, landing, and taking off. Surprisingly enough, however, almost no statistical relationship can be established between average length of hop and average cost of flying operations: the correlation coefficient is only −.09.

Two possible causes for intercarrier differences in average costs of flying operations are: the varying presence of relatively economical

Figure 1

Average Cost of Flying Operations Related to
Average Length of Hop, Boeing 707

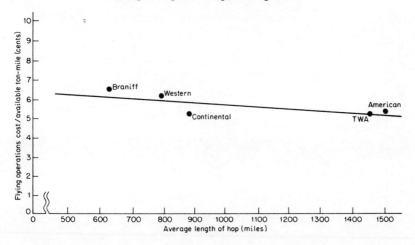

SOURCE: CAB Form 41, September 30, 1961. Regression line calculated to be
$Y = 6.6 + -.0009X$.

Figure 2

Average Cost of Flying Operations Related to
Average Length of Hop, Douglas DC-8

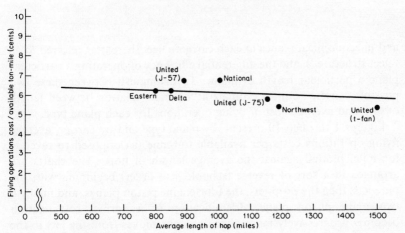

SOURCE: CAB Form 41, September 30, 1961. Regression line calculated to be
$Y = 6.55 + -.0004X$.

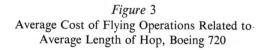

Figure 3
Average Cost of Flying Operations Related to·
Average Length of Hop, Boeing 720

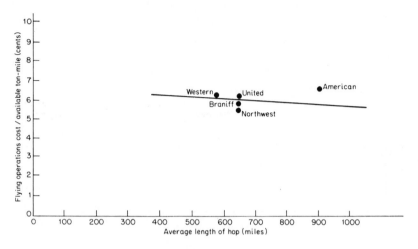

SOURCE: CAB Form 41, September 30, 1961. The calculated regression line has an upward slope, which conflicts with *a priori* expectations. The relatively high cost reported by American gives the curve an upward bias, but this may be due to some sort of inefficiency rather than to a fixed operational characteristic of the plane itself. Since the plane should have roughly the same cost characteristics at the relevant hop lengths of 500–900 miles as its big brother, the Boeing 707, the curve calculated for the latter has been used here.

and uneconomical planes in each carrier's fleet (hereafter referred to as "fleet structure"), and the differential efficiency of operating a particular plane a particular length of flight. To distinguish between these two possible causes, we must estimate a "normal" relation between length of hop and average cost of flying operations for each plane type.

Figures 1 through 10 present, by plane type and by carrier, average flying operations costs per available ton-mile (as opposed to revenue ton-mile) plotted against the average length of hop. The charts are arranged in a sort of reverse technological order, beginning with the pure jets, then the prop-jets, the four-engine piston planes, and finally a two-engine piston plane. Identification of a normal cost relation becomes progressively more difficult as one moves from the jets to the older planes. In fact, conventional regression analysis yields meaningful results only for the Boeing 707 and DC-8. After that, intuition must

Figure 4

Average Cost of Flying Operations Related to
Average Length of Hop, Convair 880

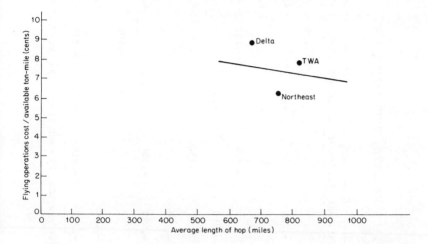

SOURCE: CAB Form 41, September 30, 1961. The calculated line has an extreme downward slope, which is illogical at the 600–800 mile length of hop relevant here. The curve was plotted, instead, with a slope similar to, but slightly steeper than, that of the 707, and raised upward to conform with the relatively high-cost performance reported for the 880.

take over the job; for instance, the calculated regression for Figure 3, the Boeing 720, would show costs *rising* with increasing length of hop! Intercarrier deviations become extreme for Figures 5 through 10; for instance, the three carriers using the Viscount have an almost identical average length of hop, but widely differing costs. A mathematically calculated curve for the Viscount would be vertical.

Most of the "normal" curves shown, then, are freehand, visual, and inductive representations rather than precise calculations.[9] Since any estimate of individual carrier deviations from the normal will be no more precise than the normal itself, the succeeding investigation must be taken as a description of general tendencies only.

Table 3 shows the calculation of each carrier's deviation from the "normal cost" of operating its fleet. This estimate is derived by

[9] Caves' study (*ibid.*, p. 68) presents some general information helpful in determining the relative expense of flying different plane types at different stage lengths.

TABLE 3

WEIGHTED CARRIER DEVIATIONS FROM THE "NORMAL" COST OF FLYING OPERATIONS, THIRD QUARTER, 1961
(cents per available ton-mile)

	American	Braniff	Continental	Delta	Eastern	National	Northeast	Northwest	TWA	United	Western
Boeing 707	+.036	+.080	-.350						-.150		+.080
Douglas DC-8				+.027	-.019	+.288		-.114		+.039	
Boeing 720	+.320	-.016						-.072		+.036	+.022
Convair 880				+.238			-.624		+.132		
Lockheed Electra		+.119			-.084	-.210		+.505			-.380
Viscount			0				-.750			+.343	
Douglas DC-7	+.072	+.099		-.125	-.540	-.170		0		+.040	
Douglas DC-6	+.176	+.140		-.195		-.090	+.960	0		+.234	-.190
Constellation					-.150				+.405		
Convair Piston	+.125	+.184		0	0	-.140				+.026	
Total	+.983	+.606	-.350	-.055	-.755	-.322	-.414	+.319	+.387	+.718	-.468

Source: Figures 1 through 10 for normal costs; percentage of service provided by each plane type from CAB Form 41,
9-30-61, Schedule T-3. For method of estimation, see text.

Figure 5

Average Cost of Flying Operations Related to
Average Length of Hop, Lockheed Electra

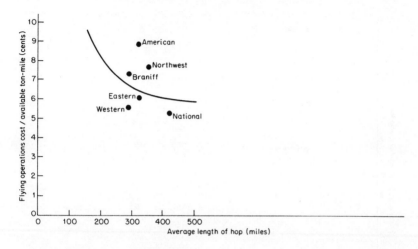

SOURCE: CAB Form 41, September 30, 1961. This curve and those for the DC-6 and DC-7 were difficult to draw; almost anything could be justified. It was assumed that at some hop length in the vicinity of 100 miles the curves would become vertical, and that constant costs would eventually be reached between 500 and 1000 miles. Caves reports some general figures for these planes. With these in mind, the figures for this plane, the DC-7, and DC-6 were superimposed on each other, and the curves were drawn approximately parallel, with the DC-7 highest, the DC-6 next, and the Electra lowest.

multiplying the cost deviation for each plane type by the percentage of service provided by that plane type. For instance, Northwest reported 7.6 cents per available ton-mile for its Lockheed Electras (Figure 5) which flew an average hop of 356 miles; the "normal cost" at 356 miles was approximately 6.2 cents. Since the Electra contributed 36 per cent of Northwest's available ton-miles, the deviation of 1.4 cents is multiplied by .36, to obtain the .505 cent figure shown in Table 3. When these deviations are summed for all plane types, it can be seen that Northwest's average cost of flying operations would have been lower by .319 cents per available ton-mile if it had flown each of its planes at "normal cost." If we adjust each carrier's cost figures for their deviation from "normal," we provide some clues to the explanation of the absence of correlation between *reported* average cost of flying operations and length of hop. Length of hop related to *adjusted* costs

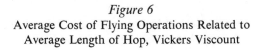

Figure 6
Average Cost of Flying Operations Related to
Average Length of Hop, Vickers Viscount

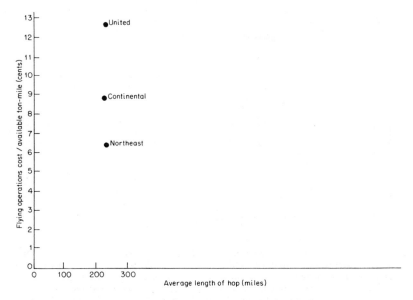

SOURCE: CAB Form 41, September 30, 1961. No curve was attempted here, since all carriers report the same length of hop. Continental is taken as "normal."

yields a —.77 correlation coefficient, as opposed to —.09 before adjustment. Most of the remaining unexplained difference is probably due to the structure of each carrier's fleet: the normal curves indicate, for example, that in general the Boeing 720 is cheaper to operate than the Convair 880.

Thus we conclude that intercarrier differences in flying operation costs are attributable to length of hop, fleet structure, and deviations from normal cost, as shown in Table 3. But what accounts for these deviations—why do some carriers operate more efficiently than others? It is difficult to believe that carriers differ greatly in the gas mileage they obtain from a particular plane type. Pilot salaries, on the other hand, may be susceptible to cost control. Pilots are paid a flat rate per month, with supplementary pay based on aircraft type, night flying, over-water flying, and so on; the maximum permissible flying time is eighty-five hours per month. Given this pay set-up, an efficient carrier would be

Figure 7
Average Cost of Flying Operations Related to
Average Length of Hop, Douglas DC-7

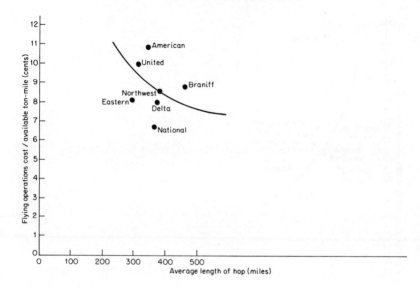

SOURCE: See note to Figure 5.

TABLE 4

A "PILOT STAFFING INDEX," THIRD QUARTER, 1961

	Man-Hours Required (1)	Flight Crew on Payroll as of 9/30/61 (2)	Column 1 Divided by Column 2 (3)
American	280,700	2,018	139.2
Braniff	80,800	510	158.0
Continental	61,900	287	215.0
Delta	121,900	785	155.0
Eastern	306,900	2,334	131.6
National	73,800	447	165.0
Northeast	62,800	363	172.9
Northwest	71,400	660	108.2
TWA	239,600	2,010	119.0
United	448,400	3,044	146.8
Western	57,900	353	163.8

Source: CAB Form 41, September 30, 1961, Schedules P-10 and T-3.

Figure 8

Average Cost of Flying Operations Related to
Average Length of Hop, Douglas DC-6

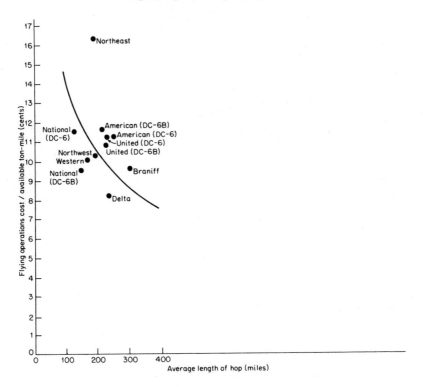

SOURCE: See note to Figure 5.

sure to schedule its pilots as close to 85 hours per month as possible,
to spread the fixed base pay over maximum pilot output. An excess of
pilots on a carrier's payroll might mean that some of the men were
receiving full base pay for substantially less than 85 hours of work.
(For instance, a former Northeast pilot cites instances of working three
hours a month while receiving full base pay.[10]) Second, the presence
of relatively few pilots on the payroll indicates that savings are being
made in training expense.

Table 4 presents computations designed to indicate relative pilot
understaffing or overstaffing. The total number of man-hours required

[10] Related to the author in a conversation with the former pilot, February 1962.

Figure 9
Average Cost of Flying Operations Related to
Average Length of Hop, Constellation (All Models)

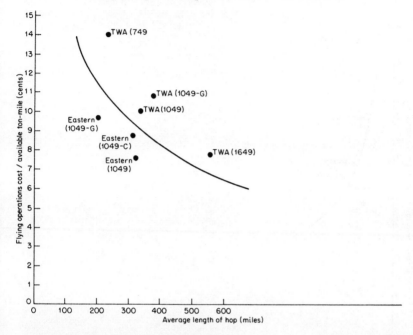

SOURCE: CAB Form 41, September 30, 1961. Since only two airlines report substantial use of this plane, it was impossible to achieve any idea of the "normal" when the many different models were viewed separately. Here they are combined. The curve, drawn parallel to, and between, the DC-6 and DC-7 curves, appears a good fit.

during the third quarter is divided by the total number of pilots, co-pilots, and flight engineers on the payroll as of September 30, 1961. (Total man-hour requirements take account of differing labor contracts and the fact that different plane types require different numbers of men in the cockpit.) Inspection of a scatter diagram indicates that this "staffing index" is negatively related to the deviations from normal cost calculated in Table 3. The fitted regression is clearly significant

$$y = 186.8 - 1.12x.[11]$$
$$(.52)$$

[11] Eastern was eliminated in this calculation. Its achievement of a substantial deviation below "normal cost" for its fleet, despite relative pilot overstaffing, may be due to its practice of cramming a large number of seats into its propeller planes.

Figure 10

Average Cost of Flying Operations Related to
Average Length of Hop, Convair Piston (Two-Engine)

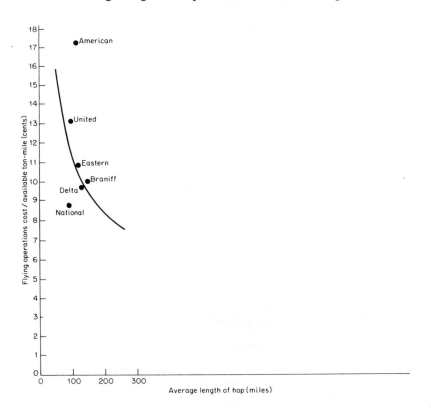

Average length of hop (miles)

SOURCE: CAB Form 41, September 30, 1961. The lower portions of this curve are parallel to the DC-6 and DC-7 curves; the upper portions are drawn almost vertical to represent the high average cost of stages under 100 miles. At all relevant stage lengths shown here, the curve represents lower cost than the DC-6, because the Convair was designed for relatively economical performance on short hops.

Although the use of freehand curves necessarily means that this analysis is imprecise, it is tempting to calculate total cost savings attainable through improved managerial efficiency. This will at least show the general orders of magnitude involved. In the preceding analysis, intercarrier cost differences were first adjusted for differing lengths of hop and fleet composition. Then the residual cost differences proved to be significantly related to a fleet staffing index. Let us postulate a "normal" carrier as one which has a zero deviation in Table 3. The regression line calculated above indicates that the five carriers which had deviations above "normal" in Table 3 would have saved money if they had achieved the same staffing index as the hypothetical "normal" carrier. Cost savings for the five high-cost carriers are calculated in Table 5.

TABLE 5

POTENTIAL COST SAVINGS FOR FLYING OPERATIONS,
THIRD QUARTER, 1961

	"y" Indicated by Regression (dollars per ton-mile)	Actual Output (ton-miles)	Cost Savings (dollars)
American	.00309	356,186,000	1,100,000
Braniff	.00099	65,459,000	64,000
Northwest	.00657	83,174,000	546,000
TWA	.00536	291,521,000	1,563,000
United	.00224	470,896,000	1,054,000

Source: Tables 3 and 4.

The first column shows the "y" indicated by the regression equation for each carrier's reported staffing index; i.e., the average cost deviation above normal which is related to each carrier's subnormal staffing. This is multiplied in Table 5 by output to obtain an actual dollar figure of potential savings for the third quarter of 1961.

Maintenance

The economic variables affecting the level of average maintenance cost should be identical with those affecting average flying operations costs, with the addition of expected economies of scale. Length of hop is again revelant, since the government fixes overhaul intervals in hours for all plane types. High average speed (achieved by relatively long flight length) implies that a relatively large percentage of the time between overhauls is productive. Cost levels would be affected also by the structure of a carrier's fleet—airlines have different proportions of planes that are relatively expensive or inexpensive to maintain. A priori, economies of scale should be present, since a large carrier with large numbers of a specific plane type would presumably be better able fully to utilize its maintenance base, and would also make savings on spare parts. If our hypothesis regarding differential managerial efficiency is correct, we should expect the assembly-line techniques of airplane overhaul to show substantial potential for cost control.

TABLE 6

AVERAGE MAINTENANCE COST AND LENGTH OF HOP BY CARRIER
AND PLANE TYPE, THIRD QUARTER, 1961

Plane Type	Carrier	Length of Hop (miles)	Maintenance Cost (cents per available ton-mile)
Boeing 707	American	1,500	4.7
	Braniff	630	3.9
	Continental	880	3.1
	TWA	1,445	3.3
	Western	795	3.0
Douglas DC-8	Delta	855	6.3
	Eastern	800	2.7
	National	1,010	2.5
	Northwest	1,190	3.0
	United (J-57)	897	3.7
	United (J-75)	1,162	3.3
	United (T-fan)	1,500	3.1
Boeing 720	American	900	4.7
	Braniff	650	2.6
	Northwest	650	2.2
	United	650	3.9
	Western	575	3.7
Convair 880	Delta	663	6.4
	Northeast	755	4.8
	TWA	815	6.0
Lockheed Electra	American	313	8.9
	Braniff	280	8.2
	Eastern	324	3.7
	National	415	4.0
	Northwest	356	3.8
	Western	298	4.1
Vickers Viscount	Continental	231	7.7
	Northeast	236	4.5
	United	230	8.6
Douglas DC-7	American	342	10.1
	Braniff	467	6.0
	Delta	381	6.2
	Eastern	307	4.9
	National	370	6.3
	Northwest	388	7.4
	United	315	7.2
Douglas DC-6	American (DC-6)	244	9.3
	American (DC-6B)	222	9.3
	Braniff	299	7.2
	Delta	239	6.8
	National (DC-6)	135	9.0
	National (DC-6B)	152	8.0
	Northeast	190	11.8
	Northwest	204	6.0
	United (DC-6)	234	7.0
	United (DC-6B)	233	6.4
	Western	179	5.5

(continued)

TABLE 6 (concluded)

Plane Type	Carrier	Length of Hop (miles)	Maintenance Cost (cents per available ton-mile)
Lockheed	Eastern (1049)	322	7.8
Constellation	Eastern (1049-C)	317	3.9
	Eastern (1049-G)	198	5.1
	TWA (749)	215	12.8
	TWA (1049)	348	4.9
	TWA (1049-G)	347	10.7
	TWA (1649)	557	4.4
Convair Piston	American	134	14.9
	Braniff	155	5.9
	Delta	144	4.2
	Eastern	126	10.8
	National	97	7.2
	United	112	9.2

Source: CAB Form 41, September 30, 1961.

The correlation between average maintenance costs and length of hop has a coefficient of .16, implying a very weak connection between high maintenance costs and *increasing* length of hop. Again we must look further and examine carrier fleets by plane type. These statistics are presented in Table 6.

To distinguish between the structure of a carrier's fleet and its efficiency in maintaining a given plane, we must consider "normal" maintenance costs for each plane type. This is a considerably easier task than the preceding analysis of flying operations. Table 6 shows no relation at all between length of hop and average maintenance cost for any type of plane. In some cases a carrier reports relatively high costs for a relatively short flight, but always there is a carrier reporting lower costs for about the same hop. For instance, Delta reports average maintenance cost for the DC-8 of 6.3 cents per ton-mile for an 855-mile trip, while Eastern achieves a 2.7 cost figure at an 800-mile trip. The lowest-cost carriers etch a constant average cost curve over relevant trip lengths for most plane types.[12]

Eliminating length of hop, then, as an explanation of differences, we need not develop normal curves. Instead, the lowest-cost carrier is considered "the efficiency norm" for each plane type; Table 7 presents deviations of costs of individual carriers from those of the lowest-cost carrier, weighted by the percentage of output contributed by each plane type in the carrier's fleet (thus, Table 7 is the equivalent of Table 3).

[12] To save space, these statistics are shown in tabular form instead of graphically as in Figures 1 through 10.

TABLE 7

INDIVIDUAL CARRIER DEVIATIONS FROM THE "EFFICIENT" COST OF MAINTENANCE,
WEIGHTED FOR FLEET STRUCTURE, THIRD QUARTER, 1961
(cents per available ton-mile)

	American	Braniff	Continental	Delta	Eastern	National	Northeast	Northwest	TWA	United	Western
Boeing 707	.61	.14	.07						.15		0
Douglas DC-8				.76	.07	0		.10		.39	
Boeing 720	.80	.06						0		.31	.31
Convair 880				.30			0		.26		
Lockheed Electra	.57	.77			0	.11		.04			.15
Viscount			.67				0			.28	
Douglas DC-7	.21	.12		.32	0	.14		.25		.23	
Douglas DC-6	.42	.24		.17		.25	1.09	.09		.20	0
Constellation					.08	0			.84		
Convair Piston	.21	.44		0	.12	.12				.10	
Total deviation	2.82	1.77	.74	1.55	.27	.62	1.09	.48	1.25	1.51	.46
Adjusted cost[a]	3.20	4.00	3.40	4.40	4.10	3.60	4.90	3.60	3.90	3.50	3.50

Source: Tables 2 and 6.

[a] Adjusted cost is each carrier's actually reported maintenance cost minus the total deviation calculated in this table.

For example, if American had been able to overhaul each of its plane types as inexpensively as the lowest-cost carrier for each plane, it would have saved about 2.8 cents per ton-mile, lowering its reported average maintenance cost from 6.0 cents to 3.2 cents.

Adjusted costs after elimination of the "efficiency deviation" are shown in Table 7. Relating these costs to length of hop again, the correlation coefficient is −.45, as compared to .16 before adjustment for differences in efficiency. The structure of each carrier's fleet probably accounts for much of the remaining intercarrier difference. Northeast, Delta, and TWA could have improved their standing, for instance, by having ordered the Boeing 720 instead of the Convair 880 as their medium-range jet. Braniff flies the same selection of planes as American, but its shorter average trip length (dictated by its route structure) forces it to fly a much greater percentage of its output at unproductive low speeds.

Is this analysis reasonable? The individual carrier deviations for each plane type bear a marked resemblance to deviations from the "normal" curves calculated for flying operations. The .86 correlation coefficient between deviations in flying operations and maintenance is strikingly high, indicating that cost control is a talent which certain carriers apply with equal success to both flying operations and maintenance costs. Table 8 shows that maintenance deviations are strongly related to the productivity of maintenance labor, just as flying operations deviations are related to a "pilot staffing index." The data in Table 8 yield a linear regression given by the equation:

$$y = 2.49 - .0000145x.\text{[13]}$$

$$(.0000063)$$

Potential cost savings are calculated in Table 9. Let us postulate an "efficient" carrier which repairs each of its planes as efficiently as the lowest-cost actually reported performance (i.e., this hypothetical carrier has a zero deviation in Table 7). The regression line calculated above indicates that carriers would have saved money if they had achieved the maintenance employee productivity of the postulated zero-deviation carrier. In Table 9 the first column shows the "y" calculated from the regression equation for each carrier's reported level of maintenance productivity. This is multiplied by output to obtain an actual dollar figure of potential savings for the third quarter of 1961.

[13] See footnote 11.

TABLE 8

RELATION OF MAINTENANCE DEVIATIONS TO PRODUCTIVITY
OF MAINTENANCE LABOR

	Available Ton-Miles Divided by Maintenance Labor on Payroll (1)	Deviations from "Efficient" Cost of Maintenance (cents per available ton-mile) (2)
American	72,500	2.82
Braniff	61,000	1.77
Continental	113,000	.74
Delta	75,000	1.55
Eastern	76,000	.27
National	124,000	.62
Northeast	81,000	1.09
Northwest	85,000	.48
TWA	86,000	1.25
United	67,000	1.51
Western	169,000	.46

Source: Col. 1 from CAB Form 41, September 30, 1961,
Schedule P-10. Col. 2 from Table 7.

TABLE 9

POTENTIAL COST SAVINGS FOR MAINTENANCE, THIRD QUARTER, 1961

	"y" Indicated by Maintenance Cost Regression (dollars per ton-mile)	Actual Output (thousands of ton-miles)	Cost Savings (thousand dollars)
American	.0144	356,186	5,129
Braniff	.0161	65,459	1,053
Continental	.0074	66,878	494
Delta	.0140	122,169	1,710
National	.0062	88,210	547
Northeast	.0132	48,860	645
Northwest	.0109	83,174	906
TWA	.0124	291,521	3,614
United	.0152	470,896	7,157
Western	.0046	62,544	300

Source: Tables 7 and 8.

Aircraft and Traffic Servicing

The aircraft and traffic servicing payroll includes most of the airline personnel at the airport. A relatively long hop should be related to low average cost in this category, since a long flight requires more or less the same airport operations as a short one. Different airports may have differing pay scales; some very large airports may require extra personnel because the check-in area is a long distance from the plane boarding area—thus an airline's costs may be affected by the varying requirements of its particular set of airports. Since the costs of cleaning, fueling, and checking a plane are greater at the end of a flight than at intermediate stops, an airline with a relatively large number of dead-end route segments should have a cost disadvantage. Differing managerial efficiency in cost control may also explain some intercarrier variation in the average cost of aircraft and traffic servicing.

Relating length of hop to average cost in this category yields a +.30 correlation coefficient, although there is an a priori presumption of a negative relation. But Table 10 looks strangely familiar. American, Braniff, TWA, and United, identified earlier as relatively inefficient in the flying operations and maintenance categories, again show higher costs and *longer* hops than Continental, Eastern, National, and

TABLE 10

RELATION OF AVERAGE LENGTH OF HOP TO AVERAGE
COST OF AIRCRAFT AND TRAFFIC SERVICING,
THIRD QUARTER, 1961

	Average Length of Hop (miles)	Average Cost of Aircraft and Traffic Servicing (cents per available ton-mile)
American	430	4.9
Braniff	344	5.3
Continental	298	2.8
Delta	278	4.9
Eastern	239	3.8
National	310	3.4
Northeast	232	4.8
Northwest	354	2.9
TWA	525	3.9
United	340	5.1
Western	294	3.4

Source: CAB Form 41, September 30, 1961, Schedule T-3; CAB, *Traffic Statistics*, and *Financial Statistics*, various issues.

TABLE 11

AVERAGE COST OF AIRCRAFT AND TRAFFIC SERVICING BY CARRIER,
THIRD QUARTER, 1961

	Aircraft and Traffic Servicing Cost (thousands of dollars)	Seats Departing (thousands)	Cost Per Seat Departing (dollars)
American	16,442	4,497	3.34
Braniff	2,871	1,832	1.57
Continental	2,119	1,282	1.65
Delta	5,037	3,003	1.67
Eastern	10,959	7,222	1.52
National	2,863	1,681	1.70
Northeast	2,059	1,362	1.51
Northwest	2,621	1,651	1.59
TWA	9,643	3,386	2.85
United	19,935	8,864	2.25
Western	1,855	1,418	1.31

Source: CAB Form 41, September 30, 1961, Schedules
P-9.2 and T-4; *Official Airline Guide Quick Reference
Edition,* July 1, 1961; and Appendix A.

Western, which were efficient performers in the previous analysis. Is it possible that managerial cost control will again explain the illogical relation between average cost and length of hop? It is possible to isolate the effect of cost control from intercarrier differences in route structure?

We can extract trip length from average cost by changing our output denominator. Until now, output has been measured in available ton-miles. Airport operations, however, are better measured by "seats departing"—the product of departures and available sets per plane. This measure accounts simultaneously for frequency of operations and the size of planes used at each particular airport. We can account for the high cost of servicing turnaround flights by classifying each airline station as "turnaround," "through," or "mixed," and treating each type separately. Table 11 shows the wide variation among the carriers in average cost per "departing seat"—note that American's cost is more than twice Eastern's!

The analysis of flying operations and maintenance costs developed "normal" or "efficient" costs for each plane type in an attempt to separate the effects of managerial cost control and fleet structure. The same technique can be applied to aircraft and traffic servicing, to separate the effects of route structure and managerial efficiency, although the computation is more complicated (there are 254 airports with 568 separate airline station operations producing 8,600 departures per day, or 475,000 departing seats). When two or more airlines serve an airport with the same type or operation (turnaround, mixed, or through), the carrier/type with the lowest average cost is considered "normal." Thus, in Table 12, United has the lowest average cost, of the mixed carriers at Cleveland. Therefore $2.08 per "departing seat" is considered the efficient cost for the other mixed carriers, American and TWA. Similarly, Northwest's performance is the better of the two through operations, so its cost is considered efficient for Eastern (the other through operation). When a carrier is the only one of its type serving a particular airport, its costs can be compared to a regional model—the airline station of the same size and type achieving the lowest cost in a three- or four-state region.

When we follow the procedure of Table 12 for all 254 airports (the detailed results are too bulky to be shown in detail), we obtain the totals shown in Table 13. At one extreme, American (quite consistently the "inefficiency champion") spent $8,763,000 more than the "efficient cost" of operating its set of airport stations. This means that its actual costs were more than twice as much as the "efficient cost." Western, on the other hand, exceeded efficient cost by only 7 per cent.

Route structure explains much of the variation in average "adjusted cost" (col. 3 in Table 13). An examination of the raw statistics showed that costs are relatively higher at large airports, and also at terminal stations. A crude "route structure index," the percentage of output provided in large airports (more than 300,000 seats departing in the third quarter of 1961) multiplied by the percentage of output produced in terminal stations, has a .66 rank correlation with adjusted cost. This is shown in Table 14.

To further check our original assumptions, we again tested the relation of average cost to length of hop. "Raw" cost showed an illogical .30 correlation coefficient; adjusted cost yields a −.76 coefficient. As another support for the consistency of the analysis, the computed average *deviations* show a strong negative relation to airport output per airport employee, as shown in Table 15. The regression line relating aircraft and traffic servicing deviations to airport employee productivity is $y = 2.214 - .00126x$. As noted in the

$$(.00029)$$

analyses of flying operations and maintenance, inefficiency seems to be a matter of overstaffing. The data strongly support the claim that a particular management is consistently efficient or inefficient across several cost categories. The carrier standing in aircraft and traffic

TABLE 12

CALCULATION OF "EFFICIENT" COST OF AIRCRAFT AND TRAFFIC
SERVICING AT CLEVELAND, THIRD QUARTER, 1961

	American	Eastern	Northwest	TWA	United
A. Type of operation	Mixed	Through	Through	Mixed	Mixed
B. Seats departing (thousands)	102.2	141.5	54.4	23.6	434.2
C. Cost (thousand dollars)	253.0	169.5	50.6	73.0	903.0
D. Average cost (line C divided by line B)	2.48	1.20	.93	3.09	2.08
E. "Efficient cost"	2.08	.93	.93	2.08	2.08
F. Average cost deviation (line D minus line E)	.40	.27	.00	1.01	.00
G. Total deviation (line B times line F, thousand dollars)	41.0	38.2		23.8	

Source: See Table 11 and Appendix A.

TABLE 13

DEVIATION FROM "EFFICIENT COST" OF AIRCRAFT AND TRAFFIC
SERVICING, THIRD QUARTER, 1961

	Total Deviation (thousand dollars) (1)	Deviation Divided by Seats Departing (dollars) (2)	Adjusted Cost Divided by Seats Departing (dollars) (3)
American	8,763	1.78	1.56
Braniff	759	.41	1.16
Continental	456	.36	1.29
Delta	1,018	.34	1.33
Eastern	2,291	.32	1.20
National	798	.47	1.23
Northeast	231	.17	1.34
Northwest	353	.21	1.38
TWA	3,440	1.02	1.83
United	6,969	.78	1.47
Western	131	.09	1.22

Source: See Table 12 and Appendix A.

TABLE 14

CALCULATION OF A "ROUTE STRUCTURE" INDEX

	Percentage of Output[a] Provided in Large Airports (1)	Percentage of Output[a] in Turn-around Stations (2)	Column 1 Times Column 2 (3)	Adjusted Cost (dollars) (4)
American	69	22	1,520	1.56
Braniff	50	14	700	1.16
Continental	40	28	1,120	1.29
Delta	60	18	1,080	1.33
Eastern	60	19	1,140	1.20
National	62	27	1,670	1.23
Northeast	65	37	2,400	1.34
Northwest	68	20	1,360	1.38
TWA	80	31	2,420	1.83
United	68	21	1,430	1.47
Western	48	25	1,200	1.22

Source: The first two columns were computed from the basic data referred to in Table 13 and Appendix A. Col. 4 repeats col. 3 of Table 13.

[a]Here output is in terms of seats departing, not available ton-miles.

TABLE 15

A COMPARISON OF AIRPORT EMPLOYEE PRODUCTIVITY WITH AIRCRAFT AND TRAFFIC SERVICING COST DEVIATIONS

	Seats Departing (1)	Airport Personnel (2)	Column 1 Divided by Column 2 (3)	Cost Deviation (4)
American	4,927,000	6,184	797	1.78
Braniff	1,832,000	1,406	1,302	.41
Continental	1,282,000	801	1,600	.36
Delta	3,003,000	2,765	1,085	.34
Eastern	7,222,000	4,255	1,690	.32
National	1,680,000	1,269	1,320	.47
Northeast	1,362,000	913	1,495	.17
Northwest	1,651,000	1,083	1,525	.21
TWA	3,385,000	4,416	765	1.02
United	8,864,000	6,559	1,310	.78
Western	1,418,000	801	1,720	.09

Source: Col. 1, see Table 11; col. 2, CAB Form 41, Schedule P-10, Lines 6126.1, 6226.1, 6326.1, 6126.2, 6226.3, 6226.4; col. 4, see col. 2 of Table 13.

TABLE 16

ESTIMATED COST SAVINGS POSSIBLE IN THE AIRCRAFT AND
TRAFFIC SERVICING CATEGORY, THIRD QUARTER, 1961

	Dollar Deviation Indicated by Regression ("y") (1)	Output (Seats Departing) (2)	Dollar Cost Savings (3)
American	1.21	4,497,000	5,441,000
Braniff	.57	1,832,000	1,044,000
Continental	.20	1,282,000	256,000
Delta	.85	3,003,000	2,552,000
Eastern	.09	7,222,000	649,000
National	.55	1,681,000	925,000
Northeast	.33	1,362,000	449,000
Northwest	.29	1,651,000	478,000
TWA	1.25	3,386,000	4,232,500
United	.56	8,864,000	4,963,000
Western	.05	1,418,000	71,000

Source: Tables 13 and 15.

servicing deviations shows a .80 rank correlation with the average carrier ranking in the flying operations and maintenance deviations.

We again postulate an "efficient" carrier which services each of its airports at the minimum achieved cost for an operation of its type. (Note that Western is not far from achieving a perfectly efficient performance.) The regression line calculated above indicates that carriers would have saved money if they had achieved the airport employee productivity of the postulated zero-deviation carrier. Col. 1 of Table 16 shows the "y" calculated from the regression equation for each carrier's reported level of airport employee productivity. This is multiplied by airport output to obtain, as before, an actual dollar figure of potential savings for the third quarter of 1961.[14]

Conclusion

Clearly this investigation has revealed some rather extraordinary figures. On the assumption that inefficiency shows no seasonal variation, the

[14] Some of the high-cost performances in Table 16 may, to some extent, reflect sound long-run marketing strategy. For instance, extra people on the airport staff may be able to speed up check-in procedures or aircraft servicing during periods of peak traffic. Or, simply, having a large number of employees at the airport may improve an airline's marketing "image." But it is curious indeed that Continental, which maintains fewer airport personnel per departure-seat than its "high-cost" competitors, is able to service and turn around its planes in a shorter time.

quarterly savings calculated above for each cost category can be translated into an annual total of $176 million, as shown in the first column of Table 17. Table 17 also shows the potential improvement of profit margins and rates of return, on the assumption that potential economies in the three cost categories discussed above would not affect revenues and thus could be directly applied to operating profit. The industry's rate of return, on these assumptions, could have been more than tripled by more effective application of cost control.

Let us recall that the preceding analysis involved arbitrary assumptions and freehand curves, and to that extent the figures in Table 17 should be viewed with caution. It would be fair to conclude, however,

TABLE 17

NET PROFITS AND RATES OF RETURN BEFORE AND AFTER ADJUSTMENT
FOR COST SAVINGS, YEAR ENDING SEPTEMBER 30, 1961
(dollar figures in millions)

		Net Profit		Rate of Return (per cent)	
	Cost Savings for the Year (1)	Before Adjustment (2)	After Adjustment (3)	Before (4)	After (5)
American	44.9	8.7	30.2	5.02	10.49
Braniff	8.7	0.7	4.9	3.71	10.09
Continental	2.9	1.1	2.5	6.38	8.43
Delta	16.4	4.1	12.0	7.81	16.50
Eastern	2.6	−6.2	−5.0	.04	.53
National	5.3	−5.0	−2.5	−3.96	.00
Northeast	4.2	−11.8	−7.6	−51.70	−29.03
Northwest	6.4	0.7	3.8	3.90	7.47
TWA	33.2	−0.4	6.5	.70	6.85
United[a]	50.7	−2.7	21.6	3.84	8.52
Western	1.2	0.5	1.1	3.35	4.44
Total	176.4	−19.2	67.5	2.16	7.05

Source

Col. 1: Savings for each airline were added from Tables 5, 9, and 16, and then were divided by the percentage of annual costs incurred in the third quarter, from CAB, *Quarterly Report of Air Carrier Financial Statistics, September, 1961.*
Col. 2: *Ibid.*
Col. 3: Because operating savings would be taxed at the 52 per cent corporate tax rate, 48 per cent of col. 1 has been added to col. 2. In the case of Northeast, taxes are not deducted because of that carrier's large outstanding tax credit.
Cols. 4 and 5: Rate of return is the sum of net profit after taxes plus interest charges, divided by investment. The figures for each carrier's interest charges and investment are taken from *ibid.*

[a]United's figures include those of Capital for the period prior to merger on June 1, 1961.

that there are differences between the cost levels of the various carriers which, after adjustment for identifiable economic variables, show a reasonably strong statistical relation to overstaffing. Every statistician knows, of course, that merely stating a statistical correlation does not prove a relation of cause and effect. Nevertheless, some field work has convinced this author that managerial laxity is an important cause of the various poor performances shown in Table 17.

Managerial inefficiency could be due to simple lack of concern with costs; possibly costs are considered "determined" by fleet and route structures so that management makes no effort to keep costs down. Or, again, it is possible that management realizes the importance of cost control but exercises it ineffectively. This author has found each of these attitudes in his contacts with airline management.

At "Everywhere Airlines" (for obvious reasons, names of airlines criticized have been changed), one of the worst performers in the preceding analysis, management officials interviewed seemed relatively unconcerned about costs; the main emphasis was on the need for fare increases. Instead of comparing the poor cost performance of their company to the competition, "Everywhere" men seemed to look at their problems either in isolation or as "general industry problems." When asked bluntly why Continental, for example, achieved a much lower average cost level, an "Everywhere" management man answered lamely: "It (Continental) is just a small airline which hasn't grown up yet." This comment, with its implications of diseconomies of scale, is not only meaningless in terms of the statistics presented above, but almost amusing considering the repeated comments at "Everywhere" that low profits were some sort of inevitable and uncontrollable plague wrought by disappointing demand, bad weather, and the CAB.[15]

"Columbia Airlines" is also a poor performer in our statistical analysis. In this light it is interesting to examine the "Columbia" treasurer's explanation of Continental's low costs:

"What are the factors limiting [Columbia] and other lines from lowering their costs to the 22–23¢ per ton-mile achieved by Continental?
1. A common sense balance between equipment utilization and load factor.
2. Differences in equipment types, average trip length, station locations.
3. Extent of obsolete piston fleet.
4. Maintenance policy differences—progressive versus deferred major overhaul.

---

[15] Based on an interview, December 18, 1961.

Continental has achieved a ton-mile cost lower than the industry principally through higher utilization . . . . I question Continental's method of achieving lower costs as an industry panacea. It may eventually be Continental's undoing." [16]

This statement supports our statistical suspicions; every factor mentioned except "maintenance policy differences" has been accounted for in our analysis of deviations from efficient performance. Utilization has been eliminated as a matter of concern by limiting our attention to two variable cost categories—flying operations and maintenance—and one category, aircraft and traffic servicing, which is unrelated to actual airplane costs. Differences in equipment types were accounted for by analyzing each plane type separately. Average trip length (length of hop) was adjusted for in flying operations, irrelevant in maintenance, or eliminated in aircraft and traffic servicing. Station locations were accounted for by taking individual stations or regional models as efficiency norms in the analysis of aircraft and traffic servicing. "Extent of obsolete piston fleet" is the same thing as differences in equipment types. Attributing cost differences to Columbia's deferred major overhaul as opposed to Continental's progressive maintenance proves nothing, as most of the efficient carriers in the maintenance category use deferred major overhaul. Certainly all these factors have something to do with Columbia's high cost level, but they do not disprove the implication of our analysis that Columbia could have saved a great deal of money by improving its cost control.

Another possible reason for managerial inefficiency is that, despite recognition of the need for improved cost control, the wrong techniques are used. The author witnessed this in detail during the past several years. "Economy" often seemed to be a matter of skimping on pencils, ticket stock, and paper clips, instead of that most important component of costs—people. Another factor is management's misuse of the quota system: in many cases the personnel quota develops from year to year by adding one year's expected traffic growth to the actual number of employees from the previous year. In this way an initial distortion, or a bad forecast, leads to overstaffing. Thus, in one case, even though ticket and reservations agents were sitting around with no work to do, the office manager was congratulating himself on being "two under quota" (the reservations manager was less blind; he admitted that he had hired fifty too many reservations agents). Another wasteful factor is the excess of supervisory personnel. Above an

[16] From a letter to the author, dated January 2, 1962.

ordinary ticket counter salesman at this same office was: one senior agent, three supervisors, one "chief," one "assistant to the manager of city ticket offices," and the "manager of city ticket offices," not to mention the "ticket agent trainer."

In contrast to all this was a visit to Continental Airlines. The management seemed to pride itself on its low costs and require of itself that it lead the industry in low-cost performance.[17] On the desk of each executive was a company booklet (prepared monthly) comparing Continental's costs to those of other airlines. Continental keeps station costs down in small cities by, for example, sending employees home between flights, and in large stations by handling work for international carriers between peaks in its own operations. The budgeting director, in contrast to the officials from "Everywhere" and "Columbia" quoted above, was well aware that the principal way to keep costs low is to hire as few employees as possible.

This field work, then, provides a reasonable explanation of the statistical analysis. The inefficient carriers explain their unsatisfactory profits in terms of low revenues and CAB-induced over-competition, and do not concentrate enough on cost control. When these carriers do examine their costs, they explain their relative inefficiency in terms of fixed economic variables like route structure, over which management has no short-run control. Finally, on the basis of one close observation, it may be suggested that when the management of an inefficient airline does sporadically try to control costs, it concentrates too much on equipment and not enough on people.

Even if the industry had been able to save a *third* of the estimated potential cost savings calculated in Table 17, its rate of return would have been almost doubled. This raises an important question for the Civil Aeronatuics Board the next time it is asked by certain carriers to approve a merger or a fare increase because of low reported profits. Perhaps, in requesting fare increases, the inefficient carriers are penalizing the public. Perhaps more diligent cost control could eventually lead to a lower fare level. It is interesting in this connection that United, which recently has been a price leader upward, performed poorly in the statistical analysis of managerial efficiency, while Continental, a price leader downward, performed well. If efficient lines had more freedom to engage in free price competition, the inefficient lines would of necessity have to put a greater effort into cost contol or risk going out of business. This paper is in agreement with Caves' recent

<hr>

[17] Based on an interview, December 19, 1961.

recommendation that CAB price regulation of the domestic trunk airlines should be abandoned.[18]

An additional insight into the reasons for relatively effective or ineffective cost control comes from a close examination of each carrier's route structure. For instance, Continental is at a disadvantage in competing with American, TWA, and United, because Continental's routes stop at Chicago, while the larger carriers fly farther east. Thus Continental, on its routes west of Chicago, must subsist on local traffic and connections, while the larger carriers can feed traffic through from their eastern cities. To run the same flight frequencies as the larger carriers, Continental's load factors are thereby lower, and it is compelled to cut costs. In a similar case, Western, one of the smallest trunklines, must compete along the west coast with United, which is the largest private air carrier in the world and can shuttle its many planes up and down the coast between trips to the east. Thus Western, in order to maintain a fleet large enough to compete with United, feels compelled to cut its costs. By the same analysis, United, American, and TWA, inefficient performers in this analysis, with their large fleets and profitable long-haul high-density routes, can more easily than the smaller lines maintain a high load factor and thus feel less pressure to control costs. This semipsychological factor is probably more important than any possible diseconomies of scale as an explanation of the apparent relative efficiency of small carriers. Delta and Braniff, two other inefficient carriers, are relatively small lines, but have a relatively high proportion of monopoly traffic. Thus, they can easily maintain a high load factor and feel little pressure to control costs. If the CAB is interested in promoting a low fare level for the domestic trunk airlines, this analysis would suggest that it should maintain, or even perhaps increase, the present level of competition between the carriers on important routes.

The president of a major airline recently confirmed some of the conclusions of this paper. In our statistical analysis it was estimated that for the year ending September 30, 1961, American Airlines could have raised its net profit from about $9 million to about $30 million by more effective cost control. In a recent speech, C. R. Smith, president of American Airlines, said, "American should earn about $35 million after interest. American is trailing some of its competitors in doing a good job at cost control . . . we must find a way to do our work more economically." [19]

---

[18] Caves, *Air Transport*, Chapter 18.
[19] *American Airlines Flagship News*, January 21, 1963, p. 1.

APPENDIX A: *Notes on the Calculation of Seats Departing and the Cost of Aircraft and Traffic Servicing*

The calculation of seats departing involved adding daily seats for each station from the *Official Airline Guide Quick Reference Edition* (number of seats per plane was obtained from various airlines in Boston), and dividing by daily departures reported in the same source to obtain a daily average number of seats per plane for each station. The resultant figure was then multiplied by the total departures from each station during the third quarter as reported on Schedule T-4. A possible element of error was that several airline seating configurations were estimated.

Costs were obtained from CAB Form 41, Schedule P-9.2; costs listed in cols. 3, 4, 5, 8, 9, 10, and 12 of this schedule were added together. Some carriers listed large expenses in their home office, maintenance, or flight training cities which represented the costs of system, rather than station, expense. Thus cols. 9, 10, and 12 were excluded in each carrier's home office, maintenance, and flight training city. This had a small effect on intercarrier average cost ranking. The rank correlation between actual aircraft and traffic servicing expense and the adjusted figures is .86.

American's extraordinary cost at Fort Worth is discounted—some stewardess training or other system expense must have been reported.

Eastern's New Orleans cost figures were missed when these statistics were copied at the CAB.

COMMENT

CHARLES J. ZWICK, The RAND Corporation

I found this to be a very interesting and persuasive paper. Although much of the empirical analysis is shaky, due to inadequate data and the "first attempt" nature of the work, it does, I believe, represent an important contribution. My comments will be focused on the limitations of this first analysis and will include suggestions for improvement. I suspect that Gordon would in fact agree with most, if not all, of them.

The first point I would like to make concerns Gordon's equating of managerial efficiency with cost control. Certainly this is one aspect, and an important aspect, of managerial efficiency, but it is not the only one. He eliminates, for example, the whole general area of sales promotion, the material of direct interest to Kraft. Efficient firms should be both cost-conscious and effective marketers of their product.

Secondly, it would be highly desirable to reproduce the analysis using additional quarters of data. Gordon's analysis is based on one quarter's data. He extrapolates these results to an annual basis, assuming no differences with regard to seasonality. I would expect significant seasonal impact on cost performance since there are, as Kraft recognizes in his paper, important seasonal differences in demand.

I thought Gordon handled his data, given its limitations, with prudence. One way to increase our confidence in his conclusions is to reproduce the analysis with new data. I am sure unexpected analysis innovations would develop so that reproducing this analysis over a number of periods should increase significantly our confidence in the results. I would, however, like also to propose an alternative approach. Gordon infers standard or normal costs for an airline from historical data; an alternative procedure would be to model a carrier's operations, and cost these operations, using standard cost factors. This approach has, of course, been used in a number of situations,[1] and we do have fairly good data on costs of specific air carrier operations. I believe that in the long run this would be a more fruitful way of developing normal costs for an airline than inferring these from historical data. The alternative approach, of course, would be more expensive than the one employed by Gordon, and we therefore have the troublesome question of which approach is preferred on a cost-effectiveness basis. I suspect, however, that Gordon has done such a good job of pointing out that significant amounts of money are involved that we could make a case that a more refined costing approach would be worth the extra expense, especially if we could get a public agency, such as the CAB, to conduct these analyses in a continuing and competent manner.

Lastly, I want to suggest that being completely preoccupied with labor efficiency could lead a carrier into trouble. Gordon correctly points out that effective cost control is practically identical with efficient use of labor. It is clear, however, that one can push labor efficiency too far, as there is a stochastic element to producing air carrier services. Viewing the process from a queuing model point of view, there is an optimal waiting situation. Clearly, we do not want expensive equipment always queued up waiting for personnel—nor do we want to lose passengers because personnel unavailability affects schedule reliability. There is, in short, a balance in waiting times that must be struck in such

[1] See, for example, R. G. Bressler, Jr., *City Milk Distribution*, Cambridge, 1952.

a situation. There are real world examples where excessive concern with personnel utilization has lead to undesirable performance consequences.

Management efficiency has been considered, as Gordon points out, that part of firm behavior that is beyond the scope of economics. He has made an important contribution by indicating that it can be attacked in a systematic and useful way. I quite agree with his policy conclusion that it would be useful to generate these data on a continuing basis and to have them available in rate-making cases. We all can end our discussion, as Gordon did, with the hope that some day we may be so bold as to allow price competition as one form in which management efficiency could be reflected.

Over-all, I believe that it is important to stimulate additional empirical cost efforts in the transport industries. Important policy decisions will be facing us with regard to transportation over the next decade. It would be comforting to know that we have a significant body of cost analysis behind us when making these decisions. Outside of agriculture, detailed analysis of cost functions has been largely neglected.

The Role of Advertising Costs in the Airline Industry

GERALD KRAFT

CHARLES RIVER ASSOCIATES

Introduction

Economists have long recognized that there are different types of costs having different economic significance. This paper discusses the particular type of cost referred to as selling cost. While one finds some discussions of this type of cost in the literature, these are almost invariably oriented toward questions of a theoretical nature, such as optimum firm behavior, or the effects of selling costs on the allocation of resources. The latter generally associate expenditures on one important type of selling cost, advertising, with waste or inefficiency, although some value is often recognized for its informative aspects. Beyond these broad considerations economists have given little or no attention to the role of selling costs in specific situations. In particular, questions of public policy with regard to selling expenditures have been largely ignored. Establishment of standards for selling cost levels by the regulatory agencies have left much to be desired from both a theoretical viewpoint and a quantitative understanding. The basic objective of these costs, to shift the demand curve, is not explicitly considered. The lack of quantitative understanding of their behavior is an especially critical problem in the realm of economic regulation of industry, particularly in industries provided with publicly financed subsidy, such as the airline industry.

NOTE: This paper was prepared while the author was associated with Systems Analysis and Research Corporation. The author is particularly indebted to Lester B. Lave, Carnegie Institute of Technology, who worked closely with the author in preliminary research analyzing airline advertising costs; to Robert R. Glauber, Harvard, who very generously contributed his skills in data processing; and to John R. Meyer, Harvard, and Alan R. Willens, Charles River Associates, who provided helpful criticism and editorial suggestions. Computer time was made available at the Harvard Computing Center under a National Science Foundation Grant, NSF-GP-683.

In airline regulatory proceedings, great weight is often placed on evidence regarding cost-output relationships. Little consideration, however, is devoted to the relationships between output or revenue and selling costs.

This paper focuses on some of the considerations that should be given to advertising, an important component of selling costs, in the airline industry, and presents the results of a general study of airline advertising expenses. The paper begins with a discussion of the uses and effects of advertising and presents an historical review of Civil Aeronautics Board policies with respect to airline selling costs.

The Uses and Effects of Advertising

The primary purpose in advertising is not simply to alter the demand curve, but to shift it upward and to the right. For the industry as a whole, this requires that it either bring consumers into the market who who would not otherwise use the service, or encourage people who use the service to use it more frequently, or more intensively on longer hauls. For an airline in a competitive market, an increase in its demand may also accrue from a shift of passengers away from its competitors. This result of competitive advertising may lead to a requirement that all firms in the market advertise merely to retain their share, and such advertising, not creating new demand in appropriate amounts, leads to economic waste.

The bulk of airline advertising is directed toward, or at least results in, providing the potential traveler with specific information of a scheduling or price nature. Some is institutional, stressing the reliability, dependability, comfort, and convenience of air travel; some is almost purely competitive, stressing a sometimes nonexistent advantage, such as an alleged superiority of one aircraft or service over that of competitors. In a recent speech before the Airline Finance and Accounting Conference, CAB Chairman Alan S. Boyd said "Any day of the week we can open the morning newspaper and be assured that carriers A, B, and C will carry you to designated destinations in less time than their competitors. I fail to see how such an approach sells air transportation."

The intraindustry effects of advertising are perhaps most wasteful. Airlines competing for traffic on the same routes are compelled to advertise simply to maintain their share of the market. The question arises as to the possible effect on joint airline revenues of an over-all reduction of such advertising by all competing carriers. Could the potential savings be translated into reduced fares that might be a genuine stimulus to demand, perhaps leading to increased revenues, accompanying lower advertising expenditures? It will not be easy to arrive at a definitive answer to this question, but its answer has important implications for regulatory policy.

Another intraindustry use of advertising may occur when airlines serve different places through a common city. Here it is used to stimulate travelers to go to a place on one carrier's routes, rather than to one on the routes of a competing carrier. Although it is doubtful that such advertising has any effect on the business traveler, it may influence the pleasure traveler. The wastes of this type of advertising are not so clear-cut. Through it, new vacation spots are stimulated, which in the long run may be generally beneficial to the industry and to society; the short-run effects may appear uneconomic.

In addition to competing with other airlines for a share of the consumer's dollar, airlines advertise in competition with other transportation industries, and with other industries generally. If the market for air transportation is carefully considered, this interindustry effect shows great long-term promise for the airlines. Recent studies show that only 25 per cent of the population has ever flown, while only 8 or 9 per cent take an annual air trip.[1] At the same time, it is estimated that during the year 1961 over 50 per cent of the population took an automobile, bus, or train trip of at least 400 miles round trip, and thus could be considered logical members of the market for air transportation.[2]

To the extent that airline advertising diverts consumer expenditures from other industries, it is difficult to evaluate the economic implications. The study by Opinion Research indicates that a large proportion of the people interviewed were uninformed or poorly informed about the relative costs of travel by air and by auto. Often the respondents believe air transportation to be substantially more expensive than it actually is, and particularly they believe it to be more expensive than travel by auto, when the total costs may, in fact, be comparable. Unfortunately, it is very difficult for the airlines to change these beliefs. The price of an airline ticket is well established. The cost of traveling by auto, on the other hand, is not so easily determinable by the traveler. Some aspects of automobile operating expenses, for example, are not

[1] Opinion Research Corporation, *The Domestic Travel Market with Emphasis on Prospects for Diversion from Auto to Air*, Princeton, N.J., 1962; E. Mueller, J. Lansing, and T. Lorimer, *The Travel Market 1959–1960* and J. Lansing, *The Travel Market 1957*, Survey Research Center, Institute for Social Research, University of Michigan, Ann Arbor.

[2] Opinion Research Corporation, *Domestic Travel Market*.

directly associated by the traveler with the trip. In the Opinion Research survey, only 17 per cent of the auto traveler respondents indicated that they account for tire wear; 11 per cent accounted for servicing; and, somewhat surprisingly, only 69 per cent accounted for oil. Prices for train or bus transportation are also well established, but certain extra costs may be incurred such as enroute eating expenses. These different modes of travel may have economic and noneconomic compensating attractions to the traveler, such as enroute sightseeing, joy of driving, and having a car at the destination.

Since the price comparisons between forms of transportation are difficult to convey to the general public, the airlines often use other means to create psychological impact. They use advertising to stimulate the potential traveler by depicting glamorous vacations and exciting adventures in distant places, and they emphasize that these places are only a few hours away by air. There is also reason to believe that an image has been created that air travel is a measure of social status. Some indication of this lies in the results of most personal interview surveys of air travel. There seems to be a strong tendency for interviewees to exaggerate their air travel. Expansion of sample survey results to population estimates reveals more travel by air than reliable airline statistics indicate.[3] Although these results could be due to poor sampling techniques or to sampling variations, the reputability of the surveying organizations and the extraordinarily consistent overestimation makes respondent exaggeration more likely.

To the extent that people consider air travel a measure of social status and a luxury, they may tend to correlate it with high prices. In the past fifteen years there has been an attempt on the part of the airlines to transform flight as a mode of transportation for a select few to one available to the masses. This has been done largely through the introduction and development of coach services, family fare plans, and recently by special emphasis on no-reservation and air bus experiments.

The effects of advertising manifest themselves in both the short and the long run. In terms of intraindustry competition, an airline can at best only hope to use advertising as a means of increasing market share in the short run. Once its competitors become aware of their loss or potential loss of demand, they will retaliate, with the general

---

[3] In an unpublished memorandum of Systems Analysis and Research Corporation, reconciling actual air travel with the Survey Research Center's *Travel Market Surveys*, the following is indicated: The 1955 Survey overstates air travel by 84 per cent, the 1956 Survey by 115 per cent, the 1957 Survey by 110 per cent, and the 1959–1960 Survey by 135 per cent.

result that the total level of advertising in the market will be raised. The tendency for airlines to incur heavy advertising expenditures during their peak seasons may indicate some desire to capture the market, but it may also be appropriate for stimulating the use of air transport at a time when a particular type of trip is being considered. For example, airlines serving North-South markets spend considerable amounts on advertising in the winter months to attract travelers to the South.

Probably the most important effects of advertising to the airlines are its long-run influence on interindustry market shares. Continued advertising has a cumulative response. It produces an increased awareness of air transportation through constant exposure, and may create an identification of a particular carrier or carriers with a route, market, or region.

Appropriate policy and good decision making by both the regulatory agencies and by the firms in the industry require knowledge of the relative significance of advertising in both the short and the long run.

Regulatory Policy Concerning Advertising

In order to appraise regulatory policies concerning advertising expenditures, consideration must be given not only to the effect of the policy on the industry and its member firms, but also to the effect on the entire economy through the allocation of resources. The best case that could be made for airline advertising would be to show that it results in increased output while price is held constant or is reduced (without disturbing rates of return); and that the best allocation of resources for the movement of people is to provide air transportation. The determination of this last factor is not simple. There are formidable difficulties in determining the full cost of each service. Some services pay for the entire right-of-way directly; for other services, the right-of-way is provided by the public, and user charges are assessed. The evaluation of the appropriate level of user charges and of the proper allocation of charges to the individual users is a question too complex to be undertaken in this paper.

We must focus on the problem of the airline industry alone, in determining the importance that must be given to advertising expenditure in appraising rate levels. The Civil Aeronautics Board considers cost, among other factors, in evaluating rate proposals. The Board is required by law to take into consideration "the need of each air carrier for revenue sufficient to enable such air carrier, under honest, economical, and efficient management, to provide adequate and efficient air carrier service." [4] What items should be considered in establishing the carrier's need? In particular, what items of selling cost or advertising should be considered?

Appraisal of Board policies regarding selling costs and the establishment of standards requires a review of proceedings that took place during the era of subsidy and mail pay determined by need. Although subsidy is now restricted to the local service carriers, and revenue from the carriage of mail has declined in importance, historical review of Board policy can help to demonstrate the regulatory issues, the precedence established for their resolution, and the problems inherent in the type of standards developed.

In general, the Board has recognized selling expenditures as an important cost area for the airlines and has established and applied standards for them. Advertising expenses are almost always considered within the broader scope of selling expenses; consequently, the Board's views on advertising itself can be inferred only from its views of the broader cost category. It is important to recognize in these inferences, though, that the aggregate of selling expenses is three or four times the size of the advertising component.

The Board has recognized that higher-than-normal selling expenses are important in developing new markets, but that such levels of expenditure should not persist for very long. However, the Board has had a varying standard to apply. In an early mail rate case it stated ". . . expenditures in the past for advertising, publicity, solicitations, and the like were proper as a development program, but a continuance of the expenditures should be made only in the light of what past experience has indicated may provide a profitable return." [5] In establishing mail rates for American Overseas Airlines, which claimed costs for extension and development that included expenditures on advertising and public relations, prior to the inauguration of their new service, the Board stated "While we recognize the need for expenditures of this type in order to bring the name of a new member of the industry before the public, we also are of the opinion that such expenditures are not warranted until a reasonable period of time before the date on which service to the public is expected to begin." [6]

[4] Civil Aeronautics Act of 1938, Title X—Procedure, Rule of Rate Making.

[5] Mid-Continent Airlines, Inc., Mail Rates, I CAA 45 (52) Docket No. 1 3-406-(A)-1, 1939.

[6] American Overseas Airlines, Inc., Mail Rates, 9 CAB 695 (704) Docket No. 1666, 1948.

The CAB has used several standards in its appraisal of selling expenditures. These are most often of a comparative nature and generally measure the volume of these expenditures in terms of their ratio to revenue. In the Transatlantic Final Mail-Rate Case, the Board took the position "Since the selling-expense ratio is fixed in relation to revenues, and selling expenses are largely incurred in station activities affected by traffic volume, the significance of this factor of comparability is obvious." [7] The Board thus indicates a belief that the ratio is related to load factor and capacity. "At a given capacity, realization of a high load factor permits reduction of 'selling' expense." [8] It is undoubtedly true that the major portion of selling expenses does relate to traffic volumes as the Board indicates; however, advertising, if it is effective, has a different causal nature, i.e., it creates the volumes. Other discretionary cost portions of selling expense behave in the same way as advertising, affecting traffic volumes rather than being affected by them. The standards have been applied with caution, however. Comparisons have been made only between carriers with relatively homogeneous circumstances, or for a single airline over different time periods.

In a case deciding the mail rate for Colonial Airlines, the Board disallowed a portion of expense in the traffic and sales account in an amount ". . . based on excess of ratio of combined traffic and sales and advertising and publicity expenses to nonmail revenues over 17 per cent, which we consider reasonable for a carrier the size of Colonial." [9] In addition to the 17 per cent standard, consideration was given to the change that had taken place in Colonial's ratio of selling expense to revenue, from 14.9 per cent in an earlier period to 19.5 per cent in the then current period. In a subsequent case involving mail rates for Colonial, the Board applied the standard used for the other trunklines. [10]

At other times, the CAB has made comparisons within smaller groups for purposes of establishing a standard. For example, a ratio of selling expense to commercial revenue of 18.25 per cent, based on intra-Alaska carrier experience, was used as a standard for disallowing expenses of Wien Alaska. [11] The policy of group comparisons has not always been followed, however. In a case involving a local service

[7] Transatlantic Final Mail-Rate Case, 21 CAB 484(489), Docket No. 1706, 1955.
[8] Transatlantic Final Mail-Rate Case, 19 CAB 464 (545), Docket No. 1706, 1954.
[9] Colonial Airlines, Inc., Mail Rates, 15 CAB 279 (305), Docket No. 2724, 1951.
[10] Colonial Airlines, Inc., Mail Rates, Domestic Operations, 16 CAB 578, Docket No. 5497, 1952.
[11] Wien Alaska Airlines, Inc., Mail Rates, 18 CAB 130 (134), Docket No. 5800, 1953.

carrier, decided one year after the Wien Alaska case, the Board adjusted the carrier's forecast of advertising and publicity expense to the level it had experienced during the previous year.[12]

The prevailing opinion has been to apply a standard, but in addition, to consider other factors that may be significant in a particular situation. Special care has been taken in cases involving subsidized carriers. In the establishment of mail rates for the Latin American Division (LAD) of Pan American, the Board explicitly recognized that selling costs are an area "which is most susceptible to the control of management and which subsidy carriers must keep within reasonable bounds." [13] The Board went on to adopt the standard: "For this reason, the standard of 19 per cent of appropriate nonmail revenues is adopted as the benchmark from which to test the reasonableness of selling expenses for LAD and for the larger American-flag carriers in general. Any upward departures from the 19 per cent level will have to be specifically justified." [14] In applying the standard to Braniff operations in the same area of the world, the Board decided that the carrier's smaller size warranted a higher ratio.[15] For a local service carrier, the Board allowed a 55 per cent ratio on the grounds that there is a "fixed cost element inherent in selling expenses," and the carrier's experienced low passenger revenue.[16]

The Board clearly recognized the use of selling expenses, and particularly advertising, to affect a change in relative market shares. It has gone so far as to suggest the possibility, for example, of an airline with vast resources competing in this manner with less endowed carriers. In the All American Certificate Renewal Case, it stated ". . . the extent to which Eastern will suffer depends almost entirely upon the carrier itself for Eastern has not only greater advertising facilities, prestige, and resources than All American but also has unlimited authority schedule-wise." [17] Replying to arguments by Colonial for a larger allowance for advertising and publicity to support its competition with Trans Canada's then recent introduction of Montreal-New York service, the Board decided that the amount allowed was ample "for

[12] Southwest Airways Company, Mail Rates, 19 CAB 328 (337), Docket No. 6230, 1954.
[13] Pan American World Airways, Inc., Latin American Division, 17 CAB 775 (812), Docket No. 3308, 1953.
[14] *Ibid.*
[15] Braniff Airways, Inc., Latin American Operations, Mail Rates, 18 CAB 752 (758), Docket No. 2886, 1954.
[16] Lake Central Airlines, Inc., Mail Rates, 18 CAB 426 (434), Docket No. 4156, 1954.
[17] 17 CAB 400 (456), Docket No. 5053, 1953.

any measure Colonial's management reasonably had to take to meet the new competition." [18]

When TWA decided to use greater sales promotion effort, rather than a more attractive service, to combat the competition from Pan American's better equipment, the Board considered this "a sound action of economic management which resulted in a lower mail-pay claim." [19] It consequently allowed TWA a special increment over the standard of 19.5 per cent established in the case. In this situation the Board did take an important precaution by not allowing the increment for future periods, clearly indicating its fear of wasteful competitive advertising. It stated "Increased expenditures by one carrier in a competitive market start a vicious cycle of increased outlay by all to maintain prior shares of the traffic. Such uneconomic practices would unduly impede the industry's progress toward self-sufficiency." [20]

While the standards developed were crude and undoubtedly arose out of pragmatic considerations, the Board either implicitly or explicitly recognized many of the uses and effects of advertising. Nevertheless, its failure to recognize the explicit relationship between advertising and revenue or demand raises some question as to the validity or possibility of implementing standard ratios of selling expenditures to revenue in all cases. Situations might arise where application of the standard and its acceptance by the carriers could result in severe hardship for the carriers. The Board has applied a standard that implicitly assumes that the average carrier in the group is fully aware of the revenue-advertising relationships and behaves optimally. The application of the standard through disallowance of costs for the determination of mail rates is one thing; the implementation by the airline, another. Consider an airline whose selling expenditure ratio is "too high" according to the standard. It may be that a reduction in this expenditure category will so impair revenues that the cut will actually produce an even higher ratio. Application of the standard does not indicate the direction which airline management should vary their selling expenditures. If selling expenditures were very effective in stimulating revenue, they would have to be increased to reduce their ratio to revenue.

The policies discussed are largely of historical interest. In the early period of the airlines, when they were supported through subsidy or mail pay determined by need, the Board took a great deal of care in establishing the extent of need. During that period, subsidy and mail

[18] Colonial Airlines, Inc., Mail Rates, 15 CAB 279 (345), Docket No. 2724, 1951.
[19] Transatlantic Final Mail-Rate Case, 19 CAB 464 (486), Docket No. 1706, 1954.
[20] Ibid., p. 487.

pay were determined largely on a carrier-by-carrier basis. So long as the carrier had a "closed" rate fixed by the Board, it could operate any way it pleased. Any level of selling costs was permitted, the only use of the standard being the setting of subsidy, and there was no direct provision for the government to recapture earnings considered in excess of normal, or for the carrier to recover losses incurred. When a rate is open, however, the carrier's earnings are subject to Board policy; the Board sets a final rate that will apply to the entire period in which the rate is open, and thus has the power to create profits or losses for the carrier. During these periods, Board policy had a powerful influence on airline management decisions, and these periods were both frequent and long.[21]

Since the early 1950's, the trunklines have not been subsidized, mail pay has been considered separately, and, recently, subsidy for the local service carriers has been based on a class rate which considers needs in terms of factors that apply to the entire group of carriers. In addition, mail revenues are now of little significance to the airlines. Nevertheless, the Board must still consider costs in many of its regulatory decisions, and its power to define "honest, economical, and efficient management," provides it with an important tool that could be used to influence management policies.

In order to demonstrate the possible potential for advertising that should be considered in regulatory policy, let us consider a hypothetical situation. Figure 1 shows a curve describing the relationship between output and total cost, including return on capital, but excluding advertising costs.[22] Curve *ON* shows a total revenue curve assuming no expenditures for advertising.[23] If such expenditures are incurred, the total revenue relationship can be expected to shift upward, indicating that purchasers of air travel are willing to purchase larger quantities at each price, or pay higher prices for the same quantity. This upward shift of the total revenue curve corresponds to a shift of the demand curve upward and to the right. In the illustration, it is assumed that an amount *EO* is expended on advertising, and that the resulting total revenue curve is shifted downward by distance *EO* to construct a total

[21] R. E. Caves, *Air Transport and Its Regulators*, Cambridge, 1962, Chapter 11.

[22] Figure 1 is taken from Systems Analysis and Research Corporation, *The Cost of Air Cargo Service*, Boston, 1962. The total cost curve is assumed to include a normal rate of return as considered by the regulatory agency.

[23] This assumption is unnecessary, but simplifies the illustration. Some standard or average level of advertising expenditure could be assumed and added to the total cost function, in which case the analysis is directed to the effect of adding increments to the standard assumed, rather than to the effect of total advertising expenditures.

Figure 1
Illustration of the Effect of
Rates and Advertising on Profit

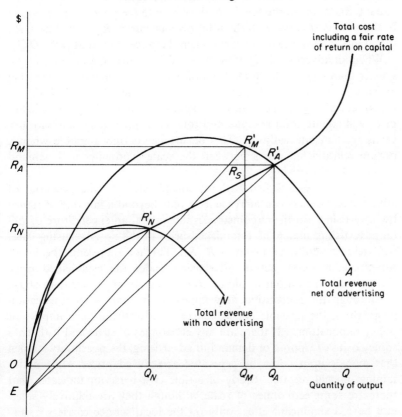

revenue net of advertising, curve *EA*. Consequently, at zero output, the total revenue with advertising is negative by an amount *EO*. Accepting the general policy that the Board "is unlikely to allow fares that will yield profits much above a normal level," [24] it is assumed in the example that Board rate decisions equate total cost, including a

[24] Caves, *Air Transport*, p. 360; and E. Troxel, *Economics of Transport*, New York, 1955, Chapter 19. In industries where entry is severely restricted by regulatory agencies, profit maximization is rarely permitted. The Civil Aeronautics Board restricts the entry of firms into the commercial airline industry, and, even for firms in the industry, controls the number operating any route and the conditions of service.

normal rate of return, and total revenue. In the absence of advertising, total cost and total revenue are equated for an output of OQ_N. This output will be produced if the price is set equal to OR_N/OQ_N, i.e., equal to the slope of the line from the origin to the point of intersection of the total cost curve with the total revenue curve, R'_N. The line OR'_N represents the total revenue curve when the price is fixed at OR_N/OQ_N.

When an advertising expenditure of EO is incurred, an output OQ_A, greater than OQ_N, will equate total revenue with total cost (advertising expense having been deducted from total revenue). The line ER'_A has a smaller value of slope than the original line, indicating that a lower price will equate total revenue and total cost under a system with advertising than one without. This occurrence is only possible when a certain relationship exists between the scale economies and demand response to advertising.

If a price is established without consideration of the potential of advertising, the firm can increase its profits beyond a fair rate of return by advertising. In the circumstances illustrated, an expenditure of EO on advertising, under the established price in the no advertising case, will yield an additional profit of $R'_M R_S$. The line represents the firm's total revenue curve net of advertising under the established price OR_N/OQ_N. The output would be OQ_M, an amount greater than OQ_N.

Although the illustration may appear to be only a demonstration in graphics, the possible consequences of advertising have important policy implications. If there are any economies of scale and if there is some positive response of demand to advertising, the possibility is open that more output could be generated at reduced prices while maintaining normal returns. Study of airline cost behavior indicates that there are some economies of scale, although they are relatively small and have a significant effect only on the local service carriers.[25] Establishment of the usefulness of advertising thus depends upon a determination of the effect of advertising on revenue.

Empirical Analysis

In an attempt to establish quantitative measures for the various effects of advertising on revenue, a limited empirical analysis was performed. Unfortunately, data in sufficient detail are not available for analysis of some of the more important aspects of airline advertising, particularly its effects on market shares. In addition, there has been no recent

[25] See the discussion in Caves, *Air Transport*, pp. 56–63; and Systems Analysis and Research Corporation, *Cost of Air Cargo*.

period in which the industry has remained relatively stable for long. Throughout the post-World War II years, there have been vast improvements in equipment, speed, capacity, and passenger comfort. Prices and services have been continually varied and promotional programs have been initiated. In addition, the period has seen a reduction in the number of carriers through merger, or through the Board's cancellation of operating authority, such as occurred with certain local service carriers. Important changes in airline route structures have been made also as a result of Board action. Finally, the trunk carriers have gone off subsidy, and the local service carriers now have their subsidies determined by a class rate. In addition to these internal industry changes, the economic environment has, of course, changed also. Undoubtedly all these factors have played a role in the growth of the airline industry and its revenues.

Since, without a substantial increase in scope, it is not possible to isolate the effect of economic factors other than advertising on revenue, our models assume that revenue is explained entirely on the basis of advertising expenditures and on a seasonal pattern. Many problems exist in obtaining reliable estimates under this single variable assumption. In particular, while advertising expenditures were increasing during the period analyzed, 1948–61, significant increases also took place in population, national income, and personal income (both total and per capita). The problems inherent in analyzing time series data are well known; and it is also well known that to the extent that independent variables excluded from the model are correlated with the included variables, statistical relationships between the dependent and the excluded variables will be reflected through the included variables.

It might be argued that all increases in airline revenue during the period 1948–61 are due to increases in national or personal income. On the other hand one might argue that advertising is directed toward creating, preserving, or changing the relationships between income and expenditure, and that in the absence of advertising the growth in income would not have resulted in the growth of airline revenue. Consideration of such arguments presents very complex identification problems. Because, of its correlation with income, the statistical measure of the effect of the single variable on revenue will include that of income (to the extent that there is an independent effect). Consequently, such measures might be overestimates, or perhaps upper bounds on the effectiveness of advertising.

While it is likely that the effect of a given level of advertising on airline revenues is dependent on the income level, it is also likely that revenues would be responsive to changes in advertising expenditures. Revenue would probably suffer severe deterioration if an airline ceased all advertising, but would not be expected to disappear entirely, in the short run, for several reasons: previous air travelers would continue to fly, word-of-mouth advertising would not cease, and the long-term effects of previous advertising would probably help sustain some level of revenue. Nevertheless, much airline advertising provides the prospective traveler with essential information on schedules and prices, leading one to believe that revenue could fall nearly to zero after some time.

Prices and service are other important factors influencing revenues. Although service characteristics improved considerably during the period under analysis, the behavior of passenger revenue per revenue passenger mile for the domestic trunks has been mixed, ranging from 5.73 and 5.75 cents in 1948 and 1949, respectively; declining to 5.25 cents in 1957; and then rising sharply to 6.19 cents in 1961.[26]

Although precise measurement of the effect of advertising on revenue requires a complex analysis of demand behavior and of the influence of the excluded variables (discussed earlier, and considered beyond the scope of this analysis), it was felt that gross measurements indicating the magnitude of these effects would be useful.

It is assumed that advertising has both short- and long-run effects on revenue and that the latter are cumulative over time. Hence, a distributed lag model was used. The general model takes the form

$$R(t) = K + b_0 A(t) + b_1 A(t-1) + b_2 A(t-2) + \cdots; \qquad (1)$$

where $R(t) =$ Passenger revenue, in quarter t, in dollars,

$\quad A(t) =$ total advertising and publicity expense, in quarter t, in dollars,

$\quad K =$ a constant, and

$\quad b_i =$ the effect of advertising in period $t - i$ on revenue in period t

$\quad (i = 0, 1, 2, \ldots)$.

Estimating the model in the form of Equation 1 presents two serious difficulties: First, if advertising has any very long-term effect, a large number of parameters have to be estimated; second, the intercorrelations between the independent variables are very high, presenting a severe multicollinearity problem. To overcome the first problem, the model is simplified by assuming a pattern to the b_i. It is specifically assumed that the effect of advertising on revenues in successive periods declines at a geometric rate, i.e.,

$$b_i = b\rho^i, \qquad 0 < \rho < 1, \qquad (2)$$

---

[26] *Handbook of Airline Statistics*, Civil Aeronautics Board, 1962, p. 103.

where ρ is the geometric ratio. This results in a simpler form of Equation 1 which can be written as

$$R(t) = K + bA(t) + b\rho A(t - 1) + b\rho^2 A(t - 2) + \cdots, \tag{3}$$

which is our Model I.

The method used in the analysis for eliminating much of the multicollinearity is attributable to L. M. Koyck.[27] Consider Equation 3 for $R(t - 1)$ and multiply the equation by ρ giving

$$\rho R(t - 1) = \rho K + b\rho A(t - 1) + b\rho^2 A(t - 2) + \cdots. \tag{4}$$

If Equation 4 is subtracted from Equation 3 and terms rearranged we obtain

$$R(t) = K(1 - \rho) + \rho R(t - 1) + bA(t). \tag{5}$$

Equation 5 is used to estimate the parameters of Equation 3. In the empirical analysis, seasonal dummy variables were appended to Equation 5 to eliminate the effect of seasonal variation. Equations 3 and 5 assume that the geometric series begins with the first period and do not allow for any separate short-term effects of advertising. Therefore, an alternative model was used to measure special short-term effects. Model I was slightly modified to begin the geometric series at the first lag, by introducing a separate long-run coefficient, c. The mathematical development is similar; the equation resulting is Model II:

$$R(t) = K + bA(t) + cA(t - 1) + c\rho A(t - 2) + c\rho^2 A(t - 3) + \cdots, \tag{6}$$

and the equation used for estimating the parameters is

$$R(t) = K(1 - \rho) + \rho R(t - 1) + bA(t) + (c - b\rho)A(t - 1), \tag{7}$$

again with appended seasonal dummy variables. This model has an even greater problem of multicollinearity than Model I.

The analysis was carried out for the domestic operations of U.S. trunk airlines on quarterly data for the years 1948 through 1961. Since the airlines, as well as the Board, seem to gear advertising expenditures to revenue in their budgeting, the problem arises as to which is the independent variable. To the extent that advertising expenditure is budgeted on prior-period revenues and is modified to reflect experience, annual data will tend to smooth, reflecting the modifications to a greater extent than would be expected in quarterly data. In the quarterly data, the period of time available for recognition of the need for and implementation of an adjustment is very limited. This is particularly true in advertising, where expenditures are often contracted for

[27] The methods have been described recently in H. Theil, *Economic Forecasts and Policy*, second revised edition, Amsterdam, 1961, pp. 217–219; and in J. Johnston, *Econometric Methods*, New York, 1963, pp. 216–217.

TABLE 1

SUMMARY OF REGRESSION RESULTS FOR MODEL I[a]

Airline	p^b	b^b	Degrees of Freedom	R^2
American	.8563	5.2253	49	.97
	(14.26)	(2.37)		
Braniff	.8867	4.4260	50	.99
	(21.82)	(3.26)		
Capital	.8954	6.0637	46	.96
	(18.53)	(2.92)		
Continental	.6130	8.6380	50	.99
	(8.36)	(5.71)		
Delta	.9021	3.8895	50	.99
	(13.17)	(1.95)		
Eastern	.7287	10.3927	49	.96
	(7.82)	(2.95)		
National	.6346	7.9139	45	.91
	(5.90)	(3.38)		
Northeast	.9052	2.3185	50	.95
	(18.90)	(2.92)		
Northwest	.6758	12.1481	49	.95
	(12.79)	(7.08)		
Trans World	.8936	4.8452	49	.97
	(20.43)	(2.87)		
United	.9212	5.4080	50	.97
	(16.35)	(2.19)		
Western	.4012	14.2590	45	.97
	(7.22)	(11.40)		
Total[c]	.8115	7.2592	50	.99
	(11.18)	(2.79)		

[a]The actual equations fitted also have a constant term and coefficients for the seasonal dummy variables.

[b]Figures in parenthesis below coefficients are t ratios and *not* standard errors of the regression coefficients.

[c]The total represents a regression based on total trunkline revenue and total trunkline advertising.

in advance. As a consequence, for quarterly data the budgeted relationship can be described as

$$A(t) = qR(t - 1), \tag{8}$$

where $q =$ the proportion of previous quarter revenue expended on advertising. In this relationship, $R(t - 1)$ can be regarded as a predetermined variable; but in a similar expression using annual data the following relationship would be more appropriate:

$$A(t) = qR(t), \tag{9}$$

and $R(t)$ is certainly not predetermined. If quarterly data are used, the models are then recursive and ordinary least-squares estimates,

TABLE 2

SUMMARY OF REGRESSION RESULTS FOR MODEL II[a]

Airline	ρ[b]	b[b]	$(c-b\rho)$[b]	c	Degrees of Freedom	R^2
American	.8034	2.8753	4.4600	6.7700	48	.97
	(12.02)	(1.12)	(1.69)			
Braniff	.8818	4.3881	.2188	4.0882	49	.99
	(16.42)	(3.14)	(.14)			
Capital	.8320	5.2028	3.8994	8.2281	45	.96
	(13.72)	(2.48)	(1.68)			
Continental	.4897	8.7639	2.6187	6.9104	49	.99
	(3.63)	(5.78)	(1.09)			
Delta	.8030	1.7851	5.3383	6.7717	49	.99
	(10.52)	(.86)	(2.49)			
Eastern	.6668	9.5791	3.3400	9.7273	48	.96
	(5.83)	(2.64)	(.94)			
National	.6700	8.0783	−1.0175	4.3950	44	.91
	(4.83)	(3.37)	(.41)			
Northeast	.8284	.3570	3.8768	4.1725	49	.96
	(18.23)	(.43)	(4.18)			
Northwest	.6028	10.8599	3.8871	10.4334	48	.95
	(9.00)	(5.90)	(1.72)			
Trans World	.9229	5.8457	−2.3085	3.0865	48	.97
	(18.28)	(3.08)	(1.15)			
United	.9908	6.7693	−4.6689	2.0381	49	.97
	(14.31)	(2.65)	(1.67)			
Western	.4125	14.3960	− .4192	5.5192	44	.97
	(4.65)	(9.51)	(.16)			
Total[c]	.8769	8.6234	−3.7820	3.7799	49	.99
	(9.93)	(3.08)	(1.28)			

For notes a, b, and c, see Table 1 notes.

although not necessarily maximum likelihood, are consistent.[28] The sample size when quarterly data are used is significantly larger than would result from the use of annual data, and consequently the estimates have the asymptotic properties desired even though the predetermined variables are not completely exogenous.

The best single source of consistent and accurate data is the airlines' financial and operating reports to the CAB and the various CAB publications of these data. Detailed financial data regarding advertising expenses and revenue by market are not available from these sources.[29] As a consequence, the empirical results presented are based on data for entire airlines rather than for individual markets.

Ordinary least-squares regression estimates of the parameters for the two models are presented in Tables 1 and 2. In both models,

[28] If the covariance matrix of the system of equations made up of the budget relationship and the revenue relationship can be assumed to be diagonal, the estimates will be maximum likelihood. See L. Klein, *A Textbook of Econometrics*, Elmsford, N.Y., 1953, pp. 110–113.

[29] Revenue estimates for individual markets could perhaps be derived from available traffic data, but would be very crude.

estimates of ρ are highly significant, as might be expected in view of the high serial correlation of the revenue series. In addition, the estimates of b in Model I are all significant at the 95 per cent level, and nearly all the variance in revenue is explained. Estimates of the parameters b and c in Model II are not as good with respect to statistical significance, although comparison of the results for different airlines indicates that at least one of b and c is statistically significant for all airlines, except American, and for the total.

The limitations of the statistical estimation procedures indicate that significance tests may not be reliable. Other general tests of the results, relying on reasonableness, can be applied. If the results are compared among airlines, both models show that estimates of all the parameters appear to be reasonably similar for all airlines. Model I implies that a dollar of advertising will provide b dollars of revenue in the period of expenditure; $b\rho$ dollars of revenue in the first future period; $b\rho^2$ dollars of revenue in the second future period; $b\rho^i$ dollars of revenue in the ith future period. If all the returns are discounted and summed, the present value of a dollar of advertising implied by the model can be determined. If we let P_I be the present value under Model I and r be the appropriate discount rate we obtain

$$P_I = b + \frac{b\rho}{1+r} + \frac{b\rho^2}{(1+r)^2} + \cdots. \tag{10}$$

The value of this geometric series with ratio $\rho/(1+r)$ is

$$P_I = b \frac{1+r}{1+r-\rho}. \tag{11}$$

For Model II the derivation is similar, resulting in

$$P_{II} = b + c \frac{1}{1+r-\rho}. \tag{12}$$

Results of these calculations for Model I and Model II are given in Table 3, under the assumption that $r = 0.12$ annually ($r = 0.03$ quarterly). Both models give similar results for the value of a dollar of advertising. It is not clear that this similarity is entirely due to multicollinearity, since the method for obtaining the values is not strictly a linear transformation. With the exceptions of American, Delta, and Northeast, the estimates of the short-run parameter b are approximately the same in both models; similarly ρ does not change greatly between models. If multicollinearity were much more serious in Model II than

TABLE 3

PRESENT VALUE OF GROSS REVENUE GENERATED BY
ONE DOLLAR OF ADVERTISING
($r = 0.03$ quarterly)

Airline	P_I (dollars)	P_{II} (dollars)
American	30.99	32.75
Braniff	31.81	31.97
Capital	46.40	46.76
Continental	21.34	21.55
Delta	31.32	31.62
Eastern	35.53	36.36
National	20.62	20.29
Northeast	19.14	21.05
Northwest	35.33	35.28
Trans World	36.59	34.66
United	51.20	58.76
Western	23.36	23.33
Total	34.22	33.31

in Model I, wide discrepancies would be expected between the parameter estimates of the two models, since the estimates would be extremely sensitive to small random variations.[30]

In view of the apparent stability of the relationship, Model II may be preferred to Model I for two reasons. First, it provides for an estimate of the short-run effect of advertising on revenue that is distinct from the assumed geometric decline in the long-run influence. Second, some airlines seem to have a slightly different lead time between advertising expenditure and the short-run response of revenue, and Model II permits such a distinction. Moreover, to the extent that the long-run relationships are of interest, the two models result in approximately the same values.

The results of the analysis were examined to determine whether any significant differences in the value of advertising to the carriers appeared to be correlated with carrier size, growth, or level of expenditure. Other than the fact that four of the smallest carriers in the sample, Northeast, Continental, Western, and National, have very low estimated values for advertising, no size-value relationships could be found. The four smallest airlines have values for advertising ranging between $19 and $24; the remaining carriers have values for advertising in the range between $31 and $37, except for Capital and United which have substantially higher values. The narrow range of variation precludes any statement regarding returns to scale of advertising.

[30] H. Wold and L. Jureen, *Demand Analysis*, New York, 1953, pp. 46–47.

One possible reason for the lack of any clear evidence on the correlation of advertising with carrier size may be the fact that larger carriers are generally larger in the sense that they serve more markets. The average advertising expenditure per market may be very similar for both large and small carriers. Furthermore, while the larger carriers have an advantage in that they can offer a wider variety of points served to potential travelers, this advantage is counteracted by the fact that they compete with each other in the most important markets. Analysis of advertising behavior in individual markets might provide better evidence regarding returns to scale.

A crude attempt was made to determine the effect of competitive advertising by using as a variable the proportion of total industry advertising provided by the carrier. The variable showed no significance. A better measure might have been the proportion of directly competitive advertising, but such data are not available.

One final important problem is the advertising budget relationship. The models imply that for a firm starting with zero revenue and introducing a constant quarterly expenditure on advertising, quarterly revenue will grow asymptotically to some determinable level. For Model I, a constant advertising expenditure of one dollar per quarter will provide revenues of $b/(1 - \rho)$ per quarter in the long run. On this basis, the long-run ratio of advertising expense to revenue can be calculated. The results, as shown in Table 4, are compared with the ratio of average advertising expense to average revenue for the period. The assumption of constant expenditures on advertising implies that,

TABLE 4

LONG–RUN AND AVERAGE RATIOS OF ADVERTISING
EXPENSE TO GROSS REVENUE

Airline	Long–Run Ratio Implied by Model I	Average Ratio of Advertising Expense to Average Revenue
American	.027	.027
Braniff	.025	.029
Capital	.017	.032
Continental	.045	.043
Delta	.025	.035
Eastern	.026	.028
National	.046	.046
Northeast	.041	.053
Northwest	.026	.029
Trans World	.021	.027
United	.015	.024
Western	.042	.038
Total	.026	.030

in the short run, ratios of actual advertising expenditure to revenue will be higher than the limiting ratio. In all but two cases, Continental and Western, the observed ratio is greater than or equal to the asymptotic ratio.

Of course, advertising expenditures are not constant. In fact, they are generally budgeted as a proportion of revenue. To determine the steady state ratios of advertising expenditure to revenue, consider the budget relationship. Suppose that advertising expenditure in a quarter is budgeted at a fixed proportion of previous quarter revenue as in Equation 8, i.e.,

$$A(t) = qR(t - 1). \tag{8}$$

If Equation 8 is substituted into Equation 5 for Model I we obtain

$$R(t) = K(1 - \rho) + (bq + \rho)R(t - 1). \tag{13}$$

The ratio of advertising to revenue that materializes from the expenditure is

$$\frac{A(t)}{R(t)} = \frac{qR(t - 1)}{K(1 - \rho) + (bq + \rho)R(t - 1)} \tag{14}$$

The ratio that emerges from the budgeting policy will be equal to the budgeted ratio only if the right hand side of Equation 13 is equal to q. Some algebraic manipulation provides the result:

$$q = \frac{1 - \rho}{b}\left[1 - \frac{K}{R(t - 1)}\right]. \tag{15}$$

The first factor in Equation 15 is simply the long-run ratio of advertising expense to revenue when advertising expense is constant over time. If revenue is growing over time, the second factor of Equation 15 approaches unity and the long-run limit for the ratio in the case of budgeted advertising is the same as that for constant advertising as given in Table 4. The model thus yields results that are consistent with the hypothesized budget relationship.

Alternative models to the budget relationship were tested. Models explaining advertising expenditure as a function of fund availability, as measured by lagged profit, lagged depreciation, and working capital, were estimated. None of the relationships tested demonstrated statistically significant behavior.

The results presented here are merely to indicate the general behavior of the advertising-revenue relationship. The data do not warrant very sophisticated analysis in view of their highly aggregated nature and the multitude of other factors, both within the industry and in the over-all economy, influencing revenue patterns. Consequently, the results must be used with caution.

As discussed earlier, there is reason to believe that the estimates of the value of advertising to the airlines may be regarded as upper bounds. They cannot be regarded in any way as conclusive proof that advertising is worthwhile. For example, during the period analyzed, both national and personal income grew at an average rate of between 5.5 per cent and 6.0 per cent annually. During the same period domestic trunk airline revenue from passenger service grew at an annual rate of 14.5 per cent annually. If the income elasticity of airline demand is between 2 and 3, the entire growth in revenue could be attributed to the change in income. It could be argued that, even if the income elasticity is in the required range, airline advertising creates and maintains the elasticity; nevertheless it could be as easily argued that had advertising expenditures remained at the 1948 level, the income changes would have produced the observed growth in revenue.

Furthermore, the model does not attempt to describe the profitability of advertising. Questions of the cost of services were not explicitly considered in the study. Subject to the cautions raised above, the results indicate that advertising does produce an upward shift in total revenue. This, coupled with the evidence of some economies of scale, leads to the conclusion that advertising can be used to generate more output at reduced prices while maintaining returns. Hence, it should be given explicit attention in regulatory rate proceedings.

Before adequate attention can be given to advertising, further research into its quantitative nature is needed. Analyses of its intra- and interindustry competitive effects, its scale effects in individual markets, and the types of traffic changes it stimulates are required.

More disaggregated data than were used here will be needed, in the absence of detailed knowledge of the demand function and its behavior over time. If data can be obtained for individual markets, it may be possible to use cross-section analysis for market groupings in which the nonmeasurable factors are homogeneous. The greatest hope for disentangling the complex interrelationships of demand and advertising lies in the use of carefully controlled experiments, where factors external to the model can be held constant or randomized so that the required measurements can be made. Results of such studies will be useful for airline management decision making as well as for regulatory policy.

COMMENT

CHARLES J. ZWICK, The RAND Corporation

I will comment on two aspects of the Kraft paper: first, on his general discussion of selling costs and their implications for research methodology; and second, on his empirical study which focuses on the productivity of advertising expenditures in the air carrier industry.

With regard to the first of these, I must admit that I found Kraft's discussion to be as unsatisfactory as other discussions I have read on the distinction between selling costs and costs of production. Apparently we face a dilemma. Either we can develop logically distinct classes of costs, such as Chamberlain[1] provides, and find that they are operationally useless; or we can come up with an operationally useful classification of costs but then find that we have logically overlapping classes.

I see little, if any, utility resulting from spending much time trying to distinguish selling costs from other production costs. Almost all firms that are of interest to economists will be producing a variety of products, rather than one homogeneous product and will use a number of inputs for this product mix. Certainly the statistical problem of separating out the various influences of different inputs on the variety of outputs is a very complicated and tedious process. When faced with this formidable task, we only do ourselves a disservice by creating distinctions which are either not operationally useful or logically fuzzy.

The last section of the Kraft paper reports an empirical investigation of the impact of advertising expenditures on airline revenues. As we are not provided with sufficient information to judge the quality of the work, I find this section difficult to comment on. I must say quite frankly, however, that from the evidence presented I am most skeptical. Kraft assumes a model that relates passenger revenue to advertising expenditures and seasonal variations in demand. He argues that by using quarterly data he solves his identification problem; that is, that advertising decisions lag behind revenue and therefore the fact that advertising expenditures are usually a function of revenue may be ignored. I wish I were as convinced as he is of this. The data employed were for domestic operations of the U.S. trunk airlines for the years

---

[1] E. H. Chamberlain, *The Theory of Monopolistic Competition*, Sixth Edition, Cambridge, 1950.

1948 through 1961. Certainly over the thirteen-year period all major airlines had substantial increases in revenue, and I would suspect that this long-term trend completely dominated any quarter-to-quarter variation in the analysis. It is surprising that Kraft did not use some of the more simple methods available for handling trend, e.g., fitting a least squares line to the data and taking deviations from it, or taking first differences.

I find the high productivity figures that he derives not surprising given the underlying relationships. Kraft relates revenue in period t to advertising expenditures in t and previous time periods. But advertising expenditures are, by CAB edict, approximately 19 per cent of revenues. If we therefore say that $R(t)$ is not a function of advertising in t but that $R(t)$ is a function of $.19\ R(t-1)$, we are not surprised that the coefficients that Kraft estimates are in the general range that he finds. In fact, if one looks at Tables 1 and 2, they seem to fit my view of the world very nicely. Postulate that there has been a continuous increase over the period in revenue and advertising expenditures. And note that another way of viewing the relationship Kraft has is to say that $R(t) = b\ .19R(t-1)$. Since revenue in t is greater on the average than revenue in $t-1$, you would expect the regression coefficient to be on the average greater than 5. Certainly the data fit this very nicely.

All of this, of course, is troublesome. I believe the most prudent thing that can be said is that the empirical work does little to advance our knowledge about the productivity of advertising expenditures in the air carrier industry.

WALTER Y. OI, University of Washington

In my opinion, Kraft's paper fails to be entirely convincing. That advertising is a potentially powerful competitive tool is surely reasonable. If his diagram of the potential profitability of advertising is accepted, and if one believes that there are economies of scale, then the larger airlines should have realized the greatest returns from advertising. Even if we accept Kraft's estimates, this result is not borne out. Furthermore, Gordon's work suggests that there are no significant economies of scale.

The distributed lag models of Koyck and Nerlove are extremely powerful analytic tools. Yet, as noted by Griliches (*Econometrica*, January 1961), they may sometimes lead to spurious conclusions. The high coefficients of determination reported in Tables 1 and 2 mean nothing. I am certain that equally high coefficients could have been obtained by regressing revenues on lagged revenues and any other secularly growing variable such as Soviet industrial production. To be more precise, consider a slight modification of Kraft's basic model. Suppose that revenues in year t, R_t, is a linear function of accumulated advertising expenditures, A_t^*, and some other variable, X_t^*. The true model can be written:

$$R_t = a_0 + a_1 A_t^* + a_2 X_t^* + e_t. \tag{1}$$

If we adopt Kraft's method of declining weights, we may define

$$A_t^* = A_t + p A_{t-1} + \cdots + p^i A_{t-i} + \cdots$$
$$X_t^* = X_t + p X_{t-i} + \cdots + p^i X_{t-i} + \cdots.$$

By appropriate algebraic manipulation the reduced equation becomes

$$R_t = (1 - p)a_0 + a_1 A_t + a_2 X_t + p R_{t-1} + e_t - p e_{t-1}, \tag{2}$$

or in regression notation we have

$$R_t = B_0 + B_1 A_t + B_2 X_t + B_3 R_{t-1} + u_t, \tag{3}$$

where $u_t = e_t - p e_{t-1}$.

Kraft, however, ignores the influence of any other pertinent explanatory variate such as X_t which might have affected the time series behavior of R_t. Hence, he estimates the regression by Equation 4, which deletes X_t.

$$R_t = b_0 + b_1 A_t + b_3 R_{t-1} + v_t. \tag{4}$$

The parameters of Equation 4 are, however, uniquely related to those of the larger model (Equation 3), even for fixed sample size, through the familiar analysis of specification errors of Theil (*Economic Forecast and Policy*) and Griliches (*Journal of Farm Economics*, 1956). The link is provided by the auxiliary regression of the excluded variable, X_t, on the included explanatory variables, A_t and R_{t-1}:

$$X_t = c_0 + c_1 A_t + c_3 R_{t-1} + f_t, \tag{5}$$

where f_t is a residual. We then have the three identities between the parameters of Equations 3 and 4:

$$B_0 = b_0 - c_0 B_2, \tag{6-a}$$

$$B_1 = b_1 - c_1 B_2, \tag{6-b}$$

$$B_3 = b_3 - c_3 B_2. \tag{6-c}$$

Suppose that X_t is real income and affects revenues, R_t, in a direct way, thus implying that B_2 is positive and large. The comovement of X_t with current advertising outlays, A_t, and lagged revenues, R_{t-1}, is described by the auxiliary regression Equation 4. Since all three variables have grown over time, it is likely that both c_1 and c_3 will be positive. To the extent that the estimated model, Equation 4, omits a pertinent variable such as X_t, the estimated parameters do not give unbiased estimates of the effects of changes in the explanatory variables. In the example I have cited b_1 will be an over-estimate of the corresponding parameter, B_1, in the correctly specified model (Equation 3). Similarly, b_3 will be larger than B_3. Indeed, his parameter estimates would be unbiased if and only if one of the following two conditions prevailed: (1) any pertinent excluded variables are statistically independent of both advertising expenditures and lagged revenues, or (2) excluded variables have no effect on current revenues. The possibility that either condition truly prevails contradicts intuition about the market for air transportation. Kraft's defense for omitting these "other variables" is that they produce too formidable a problem of collinearity. If collinearity is present the exclusion of the collinear variables will lead to false conclusions.

One method for handling the problem of collinearity has been suggested by Richard Stone. First differences or other statistical tricks have also been used. Until Kraft gives explicit consideration to other variables affecting an airline's revenues the empirical work will leave much to be desired.

Finally, the theoretical justification for the model strongly supports cross-sectional analysis. If relative advertising expenditures do not vary across firms then an empirical analysis cannot hope to succeed.

Transportation Costs and Their Implications: An Empirical Study of Railway Costs in Canada

W. J. STENASON AND R. A. BANDEEN

CANADIAN PACIFIC RAILWAY COMPANY
AND
CANADIAN NATIONAL RAILWAYS

In transportation economics, the efficient allocation of resources and the method of allocation whether by the market or by regulation require detailed knowledge of market, market structure, and costs. All too often the policy deliberations of economists are hampered by inadequate empirical study. This paper describes a study which resulted in producing costing systems currently used by the Canadian National Railways and the Canadian Pacific Railway Company. The purpose of the paper is to shed light on an important area of transportation economics—railway costs.

Brief History of Railway Costing

In the late 1890's, a number of engineers, notably Lorenz, attempted to approximate railway cost behavior through engineering formulas. The work of J. M. Clark[1] is, however, the starting point of modern cost analysis in railway transportation. Clark's procedure was to develop a cross-section statistical relationship based on a number of U.S. railroads to demonstrate that significant overhead or constant costs existed in railway transportation. Ford K. Edwards, a student of Clark's, applied his techniques, first, with the California Public Utility Commission and, second, with the Interstate Commerce Commission.

[1] J. M. Clark, *Economics of Overhead Cost.*

From this emerged cost-finding procedures still in use in railway pricing and regulation in the United States.

The ICC costing procedures have had a significant effect on the economics of railway transportation through extensive railway regulation, and the intermingling of regulation and management. Essentially, the ICC procedures are a compromise between the need of the accountant to record all the costs in a specific set of accounts, often on a somewhat arbitrary basis, and the desire of the economist to trace expenses to the output that occasions them, in order to determine the costs associated with specific changes in service or output.

Currently, all railway expenses are grouped on the basis of an accounting classification prescribed some eighty years ago by the Interstate Commerce Commission and still used with little modification in both the United States and Canada. The classification is designed to achieve a uniform reporting of railway expenses, but it does not facilitate cost analysis.

The first step in the ICC costing procedure is to distribute expenses in each account into five service areas: line-haul, switching, station and platform services, special or ancillary services, and overhead. Accounting methods are used in some phases of the allocation. For example, an analysis of the time spent in a sample of stations is used to distribute station labor expenses among the various services performed at stations. While the study itself may be arithmetically accurate, little can be inferred from it about the behavior of total station expenses as a result of changes in the volume of output or in its mix.

A method of analysis that would reflect the fact that not all railway expenses vary with traffic volume was needed. A simple, linear, cross-section regression analysis, based on total operating expenses, rents, and taxes, of a number of United States rail systems, as well as arithmetic comparisons of time variability of expenses with time variability of traffic volume, were developed and used by regulatory agencies. The dependent variable in the cross-section analysis was operating expenses per mile of road, and the independent variable, gross ton-miles per mile of road, or density. The procedure, in effect, was a simple regression on ratios. The value at the intercept on the dependent expense axis was then subtracted from the average value of expense among U.S. railways. The residual, expressed as a percentage of the average value of the dependent variable, was used to measure the per cent of variability among all railway operating expenses. A similar procedure was used to assess variability of road and equipment capital investment, to which was then applied a cost-of-money factor.

Certain basic steps in this procedure are unacceptable in any analysis designed to measure a marginal or variable cost function. The allocation of expenses among different service categories, not on the basis of behavior of the expense, but rather on the basis of arbitrary factors such as time allocation of employees, will not produce an estimate of the extent to which total expenses will change as a result of change in traffic volume, or in its mix. In addition, the procedure for development and application of an average per cent variable leads to serious distortions in the estimates of variable cost. The distortions arise for two reasons: linear regression, based on ratios, can lead to serious distortions if the error terms of both the numerator and denominator if the ratios do not follow a homogeneous distribution; and a constant per cent variable, regardless of length of haul, volume, density of traffic, or commodity carried, is inherently fallacious, even if the regression model used did accurately portray the cost relationship. The type of expense incurred can differ substantially for different types of commodities and different lengths of hauls. For example, yard expenses form a much greater proportion of the cost of commodities moving a short distance. Since yard expenses are almost entirely variable with traffic volume, application of an average per cent variability will underestimate variable costs of traffic volume having less than an average length of haul, and overestimate costs of traffic moving over much longer than average distances.

Another deficiency of the average per cent variable method is that it associates variation in all operating expenses with variation in one measure of output—gross ton-miles—and ignores the many different types of railway output produced, which have substantially different influences on cost. Size of plant, a factor known to influence railway expenses, is either ignored or improperly handled as the denominator of ratios.

For the reasons set forth above, a simple transplantation of ICC cost-finding procedures to the Canadian transportation scene was not desirable.

Railway Costing in Canada

Since 1959, the Canadian railways have carried out extensive research programs on costing methods in order to determine which will best produce accurate costs of railway operations. The detailed presentations by the two major Canadian railways to the recent Royal Commission on Transportation on the cost of moving grain and grain products at statutory rates were subjected to rigorous scrutiny by transportation experts and economists engaged by all interested parties, as well as those of the Royal Commission.[2] The weaknesses and strengths of the railways' methods were tested by that forum of expert witnesses and also in private meetings, sponsored by the Commission, of transportation, economic, and statistical experts from both Canada and the United States. The methods used by the railways were accepted with modification by the Royal Commission which also suggested fields for further study. Since then, the two railways have devoted much attention to refining and bringing up to date the costing methods presented to the Royal Commission. The research on costing methods and their application embraces the broad spectrum of applied transportation economics.

Costing methods must enable a railway to determine expenses variable with traffic volume, that is, those traceable to the traffic under study, given a period sufficient to allow management to make all necessary changes in operations and plant. The railways have not been concerned with a short-run cost function. Moreover, every effort has been made to avoid confusion between the short- and long-run cost functions. Basic sources are quantitative data on operations and expenses actually incurred as recorded in the accounts prescribed by the Board of Transport Commissioners, to which were added the results of special studies and operating, engineering, and technical knowledge.

MEASUREMENT OF PHYSICAL WORK, VARIABLE WITH TRAFFIC VOLUME

Essentially, there are two steps in developing the variable cost of moving a category of traffic. First, physical work requirements for movement of a particular category of traffic must be developed. Second, variable unit costs must be developed and attached to the traffic under study. The first step involves tracing individual movements in order to determine the associated car-days, car-miles, gross ton-miles, train-miles, and yard switching minutes used by the traffic under study.

To develop work requirements for moving the traffic, the first step is to establish, through a sample or by other means, the origin and destination points, as well as the route followed. This permits development of route-miles which, when combined with the loaded weight of the traffic and the tare weight of the equipment used, permits calculation of gross ton-miles, revenue ton-miles, car-miles, and car-days loaded.

[2] Report of Royal Commission on Transportation, Ottawa, 1962.

One of the most difficult aspects of developing basic output units is to determine the movement of empty cars traceable to the traffic under study. In theory, the empty movement traceable to a category of traffic is the difference between total empty movement with and without handling of the traffic. Such a calculation is impossible, however, with analytic procedures available at present. In addition, it has little meaning in the case of small categories of traffic where traffic patterns are subject to considerable variation. As a consequence, somewhat arbitrary methods are frequently used, including application of a general empty return ratio, or a more specific ratio, arrived at on a sample basis, through tracing the cars used in moving the traffic. Tests made indicate that such methods result in an accurate measure of avoidable car supply or empty movement, provided that unusual peaking characteristics are not present, and that the traffic under study is similar in its direction and distribution to that of freight traffic as a whole.

A good example of the complexity inherent in the determination of these measures is that of estimating the yard switching minutes required in handling a particular category of traffic. When the route and the trains used by a particular car have been determined, the yards through which the car moves are also known. Then it is necessary to determine the movement pattern of the car through those yards and to estimate the yard switching time required to perform that movement. Unfortunately for the cost analyst, each and every yard has a different physical layout as well as other varying operating characteristics. As a result, the amount of time required to perform similar switching moves may vary from yard to yard and, additionally, to put a car through a yard might well entail a different mix of moves.

To provide adequate data, it was necessary to conduct a study at all major yards as well as a good sample of the smaller yards. Each railway required a team of from eight to ten men with yard experience working for a six-month period to analyze only the yards in Western Canada. The men spent several days in each of the yards collecting detailed information on switching movements. An interesting aspect of applied economics in this case was the need for achieving cooperation of yard forces in assessing the productive time spent in various assignments and the total nonproductive time. When the minutes for each element of switching at each yard are known, it is possible to determine the total number of switching minutes assignable to a car for each yard through which the car passes.

Other principal measures of output to be made are: the gross ton-miles, that is, the total weight of shipment and car times the distance travelled; train-miles, usually calculated on the basis of actual train weight by train run; diesel unit miles, which reflect the number of diesel units used on a train for each train run; and car-days and car-miles.

VARIABLE COSTS INCURRED FOR
EACH UNIT OF WORK PERFORMED

The second major step is to estimate the expenses incurred for each one of the units such as car-days and car-miles, which are variable with a particular movement, and the expenses associated with possible changes in size of fixed plant. The operating expense accounts generally divide into three groups: those which vary directly with volume (about 37 per cent of the total operating expenses); those partially variable with volume (about 58 per cent of the total operating expenses); and those entirely unrelated to volume changes (about 5 per cent of the total operating expenses).

The unit costs for expense accounts entirely variable with volume can be calculated quite simply when the variability has been determined. The yard-crew wages and train-crew wages were tested by regression analysis to assess variability and were found over a long-term period to be completely variable with traffic volume. The same conclusion was reached with respect to the fuel expense for road and yard diesel locomotives.

As an additional test, the functional relationship between output and expense can be established through engineering analysis or an examination of operating procedures. Thus, in assessing variability of train costs with traffic volume, primary consideration was given to the dispatching decision rules, which determine how frequently trains are dispatched. For the lowest priority traffic, trains are dispatched when a sufficient volume of traffic has been accumulated to utilize the power available. However, schedules of other trains dispatched to provide service are fixed on a short-term basis but are adjusted extensively over a longer period, depending on the volume of traffic available. Local trains, operated primarily on branch lines, are adjusted to the volume of traffic available through changes in the frequency of train service.

In the case of yard expenses, once again, the rules for operating-yard engine shifts are based on traffic volume and subject to adjustment with relatively small variation. There are substantial differences between types of yards but, within each yard, statistical procedures were used to identify the variability between yard operations and traffic volume handled.

Car repair expense, by type of car, is available from accounting records. Engineering analysis made possible a division of car maintenance and capital costs between the portion variable with the passage of time, measured by car-days, and the portion variable with work performed by the car, measured by car-miles.

Train fuel expense is computed individually for each train run and is based, in part, on the grades over which the train travels, its speed, and its weight. Fuel consumption estimated on this basis has proved to be extremely accurate when matched against actual consumption on a train-run basis.

The group of accounts which are only partially variable with volume pose a more serious problem. For them, it is necessary to rely upon engineering knowledge, operating experience, and historical data pertaining to actual operations. These data reflect the cost variations associated with differing volumes of traffic, differing physical plant, and geographical influences. Engineering knowledge and operating experience suggest, in a general way, how these costs, traffic volumes, and other items are related, but do not provide detailed estimates.

Fortunately, regression analysis could be used to measure relationships between changes in volume of traffic and the changes in a particular category of expense. Both railways have historical data for their operating divisions, which numbered over thirty on each railway. The data showed the costs, by operating division, most measures of the volume of operations, by division, as well as measures of the physical plant, such as miles of track and number of bridges. Having the statistics recorded in this fashion made possible use of cross-sectional regression analysis. With the aid of electronic computers, it was possible to estimate the costs variable with a particular measure of traffic volume. In addition, the costs of performing special services were, in many cases, available in the accounts and could be directly traced to the services provided.

The accounts not entirely variable with volume were checked to find the relationship of volume and plant size to the various expenses. This involved estimating many hundreds of regression models and selecting those which best fitted the many tests made of them. The cost curve must, in each case, be tested to determine whether it is linear or curvelinear. The models were tested by arraying the data representing costs, size of plant, and output for all the operating divisions. The residuals from each regression model were plotted against the various measures of traffic volume to observe whether there was any indicated nonrandom pattern in these residuals. Such tests indicated that curvelinearity was not present in railway costs within the range of observations.

The problem of collinearity was, of course, the chief reason so many models were tested. The main test for collinearity was to determine the R^2 or coefficient of determination between the various pairs of independent variables. The coefficient of determination used to test the applicability of the model as a whole was in all cases statistically significant and—more than that—was such as to allow use of the model without misgivings. A "t" test was used to ensure the significance of the individual parameters in the model.

Aside from purely statistical tests, it was necessary to apply two others. One was the test of the models against the experience of a particular year's expenses, division by division, to find whether the models selected would have estimated the actual expenditures fairly accurately, given only the volume of traffic and the size of the division. The second nonstatistical test was the so-called common sense test. Did the models used make sense to the engineer and to the practical railroader? The models passed both tests.

In the third set of operating expense accounts, those not variable with volume of traffic, some accounts—notably maintenance of fences, snow sheds and signs, and snow, sand, and ice removal—were tested by regression analysis and found not to be variable with traffic volume.

The roadway property investment accounts present significant difficulties in railway cost analysis. As a result of regulatory requirements, property investment is accounted for on a subdivision and division basis, with full accounting breakdown, depending upon the type of property involved. Since there are not significant differences between divisions in the age of property invested in, it was possible to analyze variability of railway road property investment through multiple regression analysis. The cost of the capital must be applied to the variable railway property investment traceable to the particular segment of operations being costed. The cost of money was calculated as the amount which, after payment of corporate income taxes, was sufficient to make investors indifferent about the choice between retention of their investment in railway operations or placing it in other pursuits with similar risk and opportunity for gain.

There were left some expenses which could not be analyzed through direct and regression procedures. Such accounts were allocated to the traffic under study following survey or other procedures designed to assess general variability relationships.

Table 1 shows the methods used in analyzing the various accounts and groups of accounts by the Canadian Pacific Railway, the

TABLE 1

GROUPING OF EXPENSE ACCOUNTS IN THE COST STUDY AND METHODS
USED TO DETERMINE COST, CANADIAN PACIFIC RAILWAY

Account Number	Group of Accounts	Method
Road maintenance		
201,274,276,277	Road maintenance, superintendence and overhead	Regression analysis
202,208,212,214,216, 218,229,266 (Track) 269,271,273,281	Track maintenance and depreciation	Regression analysis
221-266	Fences, snowsheds, and signs, maintenance and depreciation	Regression analysis
227-266	Station and office buildings, maintenance and depreciation	Regression analysis
231-266	Water and fuel stations, maintenance and depreciation	Regression analysis and direct
235-266	Shops and enginehouses, maintenance and depreciation	Regression analysis
237-266	Grain elevators	Not applicable
241-266	Wharves	Not applicable
247	Rail communication systems	Allocated
249-266	Signals, maintenance and depreciation	Regression analysis
253-266	Power plant maintenance and depreciation	Regression analysis
265-266	Other structures	Not variable
270	Dismantling retired road property	Not variable
272	Removing snow, ice, and sand	Not variable
275,278-279	Insurance and joint facilities	Allocated
Equipment maintenance		
301,302,305,306,329, 332,333,334,335,336, 337	Equipment maintenance, superintendence and overhead	Regression analysis
308-311-331	Road locomotive repairs and depreciation	Direct
308-311-331	Yard locomotive repairs depreciation	Direct
314-331	Freight train car repairs and depreciation	Direct and allocated
317-331	Passenger train car repairs and depreciation	Not applicable
323-331	Vessels, repairs and depreciation	Not applicable

(continued)

TABLE 1 (continued)

Account Number	Group of Accounts	Method
Equipment maintenance (cont.)		
328–331	Other equipment, repairs and depreciation	Not applicable
Traffic		
351,352,353,354,356, 357,358,359	Agencies, advertising, associations, industrial and immigration bureaus, insurance, stationery, and other expenses, superintendence	Allocated and not applicable
Transportation		
371,374,410,411,415, 416,420	Transportation, superintendence and overhead	Regression analysis
372,373,376	Dispatching and station employees and expenses	Regression analysis
375	Coal and ore wharves	Not applicable
377	Yardmasters and clerks	Regression analysis
378,379,380,382,385, 389	Yard expenses	Regression analysis
386,388	Yard, other expenses	Regression analysis
390–391,412–413,414	Joint facilities and insurance	Allocated
392,394,401	Trains, enginemen, locomotives, fuel and power, trainmen	Direct
397	Train locomotive water	Direct
398,400	Trains, enginehouse expenses, and locomotives, other supplies	Regression analysis
402	Trains, other expenses	Direct and allocated
403	Operating, sleeping and parlor cars	Not applicable
404	Signals, operation	Regression analysis
405	Crossing protection	Not variable
406	Drawbridge operation	Not variable
407	Rail communications system, operation	Allocated
408	Operating vessels	Not applicable

(continued)

TABLE 1 (concluded)

Account Number	Group of Accounts	Method
Transportation (cont.)		
418	Loss and damage, freight	Direct
419	Loss and damage, baggage	Not applicable
Miscellaneous operations		
441	Dining and buffet service	Not applicable
442	News service and restaurants	Not applicable
443	Grain elevators	Not applicable
446	Other operations	Not applicable
447-448	Miscellaneous joint facilities	Not applicable
General		
451,452,453,454,455 457,458,460,461-462	General officers, clerks and attendants, office expenses, legal expenses, insurance, pensions, stationery, other expenses and joint facilities	Allocated
Equipment rents		
463-464	Equipment rents	Direct and allocated
Joint facility rents		
465-466	Joint facility rents	Allocated
Railway tax accruals		
468	Other railway taxes	Allocated
Investment		
	Road property	Regression analysis
	Locomotive, steam and diesel	Direct
	Freight train cars	Direct
	Passenger train cars	Not applicable
	Vessels	Not applicable
	Work equipment	Allocated
	Other equipment	Not applicable

TABLE 2

VARIABLE PORTION OF ROAD MAINTENANCE EXPENSES APPLICABLE TO THE
TRAFFIC UNDER STUDY, CANADIAN PACIFIC RAILWAY

Account Groups and Account Numbers	Independent Variable	Unadjusted Coefficient or Unit Cost (Canadian dollars as of Dec. 31, 1958)
Road maintenance: superintendence and overhead (201, 274, 276, 277)	Road maintenance expenses, excluding superintendence	0.03586
Track maintenance and depreciation (202, 208, 212, 214, 216, 218, 229, 266, 269, 271, 273, 281)	Freight gross ton-miles (000's)	0.16441
	Yard- and train-switching miles	0.41394
Station and office buildings: maintenance and depreciation (227, 266)	Carloads	1.33237
Water and fuel stations: maintenance and depreciation (231, 266)	Yard-locomotive miles	0.00626[a]
	Train miles	0.01677[a]
	Train-switching miles	0.02864[a]
Shops and enginehouses: maintenance and depreciation (235, 266)	Direct equipment maintenance ($)	0.03124
Signals: maintenance and depreciation (249, 266)	Train miles	0.04772
Power plants: maintenance and depreciation (253, 266)	Station employees ($)	0.01546
Insurance and joint facilities (275, 278, 279)	Road maintenance ($)	0.01060
Equipment maintenance: superintendence and overhead (301, 302, 305, 306, 329,332-337)	Direct equipment maintenance, excluding depreciation ($)	0.04990
Road locomotive: repairs (308-311)	Road-locomotive miles	0.38790
Road locomotive: depreciation (331)	Road-locomotive miles	0.17301
Yard locomotive: repairs (308-311)	Yard-locomotive miles	0.20848
Yard locomotive: depreciation (331)	Yard-locomotive miles	0.13106
Freight-train car: repairs (314)	Car miles	0.01529
	Car-days active	0.57354
Freight-train car: depreciation (331)	Car miles	0.00408
	Car-days active	0.47814
Work equipment: repairs (326)	Road maintenance ($)	0.01314
Work equipment: depreciation (331)	Road maintenance ($)	0.00498
Transportation: superintendence and overhead (371, 374, 410, 411, 415, 416, 420)	Transportation expens · ($)	0.02442
Dispatching and station: employees and expenses (372, 373, 376)	Carload	5.61490

(continued)

TABLE 2 (concluded)

Account Groups and Account Numbers	Independent Variable	Unadjusted Coefficient or Unit Cost (Canadian dollars as of Dec. 31, 1958)
Yardmasters and clerks (377)	Yard-switching mile	0.46992
Yard expenses (378–380, 382, 385, 389)	Yard-switching mile	2.37435
Other yard expenses (386, 388)	Yard-switching mile	0.14389
Train enginemen, train locomotive fuel and power, trainmen, train switching (392, 394, 401)	Direct	
Train enginehouse expenses and other train locomotive supplies (398, 400)	Locomotive miles	0.13997[b]
Train locomotive water (397)	Direct per locomotive mile	0.01298
Other train expenses (402)	Direct per car mile	0.00250
	Grain doors (direct), train miles	0.10819
Signals operation (404	Train miles	0.01146
Joint facilities and insurance (390, 391, 412–414)	Transportation ($)	0.01206
Freight loss and damage (418)	Direct	

procedures being explained in Appendix A. The unit variable cost coefficients which required adjustment for various overhead and other factors are set forth for the Canadian Pacific Railway in Tables 2 and 3. Data for the Canadian National Railways is not shown since it is very similar with a few differences in the models used and, of course, differences in the unit variable costs reflecting differences in the operations and management of the two railways.

COST VARIABLE WITH TRAFFIC VOLUME

Estimates of the cost variable with any particular point-to-point movement can be made by multiplication of the relevant variable traffic units by the appropriate variable costs. The procedure may be time consuming because it involves a large number of additions and multiplications which have to be carried out in a particular order, involving some hundreds of different factors. For this reason it was found advantageous to combine the various items into "unit" costs of the form, cents per 1,000 gross ton-miles, and cents per train-mile. Combining the various factors and formalizing the subsequent steps

TABLE 3

COST OF MONEY FOR INVESTMENT IN ROAD PROPERTY AND EQUIPMENT
APPLICABLE TO TRAFFIC UNDER STUDY, CANADIAN PACIFIC RAILWAY

Investment Category	Independent Variable or Output Unit	Unit Variable Cost (dollars)
Road property	Gross ton-miles	0.28926
	Yard- and train- switching miles	0.84033
Diesel yard locomotives	Yard-engine miles	0.25778
Diesel road locomotives	Train miles	0.30748
	Train-switching miles	0.23700
Steam locomotives	Train miles	0.04291
	Yard-switching miles	0.06055
	Train-switching miles	0.18979
Freight-train cars	Car miles	0.02470
Work equipment	Gross ton-miles	0.00786
Shop and power plant machinery	Train miles	0.02974

has made costing a readily available tool for management and regulatory purposes in Canada.

RESULTS OF COST ANALYSIS

When the cost method described here was presented to the Royal Commission, it heard, as well, submissions about costing by opposing parties and by employed staff analysts. While changes were made in certain of the treatments, and in others further analysis was recommended, the Commission accepted much of the analysis put forward by the railways, including the use of linear multiple regression analysis and many of the other procedures described. It used the amended costs as a basis for recommendations to the government for payment of a shortfall between revenues and variable cost, as well as a contribution to cover constant costs to the railways for movement of the traffic under study.

The cost procedures described here have been adopted by both railways in pricing and in many of the other management operations described. Since the studies were completed, the Canadian railways have continued their research into cost finding, and while some changes have been made in some areas, the basic methodological framework remains pretty well as described. We believe it has resulted in improved resource allocation in transportation in Canada.

Appendix A: Empirical Results

ROAD MAINTENANCE, SUPERINTENDENCE, AND OVERHEAD

Among models used in analyzing the expenses, a relationship with direct roadway expense provided the most satisfactory explanation of the expense. Divisions that had greater amounts of direct road maintenance expense had higher levels of supervision. Furthermore, on the Canadian Pacific, road maintenance superintendence was found to vary not only with direct road maintenance expense, but also with size of plant; that is, a division with extensive branch-line mileage requires more supervision than one with only main-line trackage, even though the maintenance expenses are the same. As might be expected, there is a high proportion of expense not variable with traffic volume in this category of costs.

TRACK MAINTENANCE AND DEPRECIATION

After testing with approximately three hundred models in each company, a model relating track maintenance costs to size of plant and freight, passenger, and yard output produced the best explanation of variation in this category of cost. Canadian National found also that the variable miles of tunneled track was related as a geographical variable to this category of cost. While recognizing that such influences were present, Canadian Pacific found that the influence of terrain was absorbed by the constant term in the regression analysis, and that introduction of a variable would not significantly affect the output coefficients used in estimating variable cost.

Road maintenance expenses are a good example of the blending of engineering and statistical analyses. The regression equation for the Canadian Pacific indicated a constant track maintenance cost of some $1,136 per mile of track. The estimate was confirmed through an examination of track maintenance expenses on many extremely light-density branch lines throughout the Canadian Pacific system. Similarly, because of collinearity between freight and passenger output measures, it was impossible to obtain separate statistically reliable coefficients for each of them. An engineering analysis, based on influence of speed and weight on track maintenance, was performed and used to obtain a weighting factor between freight and passenger traffic.

OTHER ROADWAY MAINTENANCE ACCOUNTS

As might be expected, maintenance of fences, snow sheds, and signals was found to be closely related to miles of roadway fences and not variable with traffic volume. Maintenance of station and office building expenses were found to be related to the number of less-than-carload cars originated, and to passenger car miles on the various divisions. This relationship indicates the primary use made of stations, and also reflects the fact that no strong relationship could be found with operations independent of the measures of output described. Water and fuel station maintenance and depreciation expenses were related to fuel and water expenses, which indicates that where there is a large charge-out of fuel and water for train service, there is a significant maintenance expense involved. Similarly, maintenance of shops and engine houses was found to be closely related to direct equipment expenses; signal maintenance and depreciation, to train miles; and power and protection, to station labor expenses. The last arises because power plants are used primarily to generate power for heating stations.

EQUIPMENT MAINTENANCE, SUPERINTENDENCE, AND OVERHEAD

These three accounts included all elements of supervisory expense involved in equipment maintenance and injuries, as well as shop machinery. The regression analysis indicated a relationship with direct cost of maintenance expense with a large constant term.

ROAD AND YARD LOCOMOTIVE REPAIRS AND DEPRECIATION

Regression analysis was not attempted on these accounts, since locomotives maintained on one part of a railway system usually run out their mileage over the system as a whole and, as a result, output on a division level may bear no relation to division expenses. A major portion of locomotive repair expenses on both Canadian railways is occasioned by inspection and preventive maintenance. Certain work is carried out on a diesel locomotive when it has completed a specified mileage, and such work, which may be approximated by an engineering function, accounted for a large portion of the expense. For major overhauls, analysis was made of the records which showed run-out mileage, locomotive number, and expense. It was possible to analyze the major overhaul work done in relation to mileage of the locomotive. As might be expected from the preventive maintenance policies, locomotive maintenance expenses were closely related to locomotive miles.

FREIGHT-TRAIN CAR REPAIRS AND DEPRECIATION

A special study was performed to segregate light and heavy repair expenses, as well as inspection, for various classes of freight cars. Following this, an ICC engineering study, which showed the relative effect of time and use as they influence freight-car expense, was brought up to date in the light of railway operating practices by mechanical officers. That study was used to divide freight-car repair expenses between those associated with the passage of time and those associated with mileage.

WORK-EQUIPMENT REPAIRS AND DEPRECIATION

Work equipment is used for road maintenance; hence a time-series analysis was used to relate work equipment repairs and depreciation to road maintenance expenses.

TRANSPORTATION SUPERINTENDENCE AND OVERHEAD ACCOUNTS

On the Canadian Pacific, these accounts were found to be closely related to dollars of direct transportation expenses on each division. On the Canadian National this expense was related directly to train miles and yard switching miles.

DISPATCHING AND STATION EMPLOYEE EXPENSES

These expenses were difficult to analyze on both railways. Somewhat different solutions were obtained for each railway, reflecting the different operating and station-organization patterns of the two. For Canadian Pacific, after a substantial amount of statistical analysis, the most satisfactory explanation was afforded by the number of cars of freight originated, less-than-carload cars originated, and passenger-car miles.

For Canadian National, the solution was somewhat different. After considerable investigation, two separate models were developed. The first covered a group of expenses called train control expenses, including the expense of maintaining and operating signal systems, as well as dispatching expense. The model expressed these expenses as a function of train miles and car loads originated. The second model embraced station employees' expenses and other station expenses. It expressed them as a function of car-load traffic originated and less-than-carload cars originated.

YARD EXPENSES

Yard expenses were found to be closely related to yard-switching miles—not surprising, since a majority of yard expenses vary with yard work performed. Little or no constant expense was found in this category of cost. Observation of the residuals against volume and size of yard indicated that there were no measurable economies in large yard operations.

TRAIN EXPENSES

Direct treatment of train expenses was possible because of special records kept on both Canadian railways. On Canadian Pacific, the records show labor and fuel expenses by direction, on each subdivision, divided between through and local trains, as well as the volume of traffic handled and the volume of train miles produced. On Canadian National, fuel required was computed for each individual move by use of an engineering formula which takes into account grade resistance, axle resistance, weight, speed, and wind resistance. Crew wages were also computed by train run, using current wage rates. The number of trains imputed to a particular traffic in the study was determined separately for each train run on the basis of gross tons per car plus axle resistance, as compared with actual average train handling achieved on each train run.

ROAD-PROPERTY INVESTMENT ACCOUNT

Reference was made earlier to the accounts which made possible estimates of the variability of road-property investment. These accounts were on a division basis, and regression analysis proved appropriate. The analysis showed, as one might expect, that investment was most closely related to size of plant, as measured by miles of track operated, and to gross ton-miles, as well as by yard and train switching miles.

EQUIPMENT INVESTMENT

Investment in the majority of the diesel locomotives was found to be completely variable with change in traffic volume. A few special-purpose diesel locomotives, used primarily in servicing branch lines, did not show that relationship.

Variability of freight-car investment with traffic volume proved to be an important area of analysis, and various methods were used to show the relation. A time-series analysis on the two Canadian railways proved difficult as a result of technological changes, both in size of equipment and speed of movement. Reliance, therefore, was placed upon internal management of the two railways in Canada both of which provide that freight-car inventory is adjusted to changes in traffic volume through car retirement and replacement policy. This is one more example of how an economist may, on occasion, have to rely on judgment rather than analysis.

Some Allocational Problems
in Highway Finance

ROBERT W. HARBESON

UNIVERSITY OF ILLINOIS

The manner in which highways are financed has long been of great interest to transportation economists because of its important bearing upon the broader problem of achieving an economical allocation of resources among competing agencies of transportation. There are, however, additional reasons for giving further consideration to this topic at the present time.

First, in recent years revenues and expenditures for highway purposes have grown at a rapid rate and have reached impressive totals. Receipts, excluding transfers and the proceeds of bond sales, totalled $11,899 million in 1963, which was nearly three times the figure for 1950 and not far from five times that for 1940.[1] Second, the growth of highway expenditures has been accompanied by a strong trend toward increased reliance upon user charges as sources of revenue. The ratio of user contributions to the total of user and nonuser contributions for highways, excluding bond issue proceeds, increased from 44 per cent in 1940 to 59.8 per cent in 1950 and 79.9 per cent in 1963.[2] Third, and most important, the increased reliance upon user charges has been accompanied by a trend toward extending user-charge support to an increased mileage of highways, and consequently toward devoting a disproportionate share of user revenue to roads and streets having very low traffic volumes. Hence, increased reliance upon highway user charges has been paralleled by a progressive departure from the matching of payments by, and benefits to, particular users or classes of users, which is the underlying rationale of these levies.

---

[1] Data for 1940 and 1950 from *Final Report of the Highway Cost Allocation Study*, House Doc. No. 54, 87th Congress, 1st Session, Washington, D.C., 1961, Table III-I. Data for 1963 from U.S. Dept. of Commerce, Bureau of Public Roads, Release, January 30, 1964, Table HF-1.

[2] *Ibid.*

Finally, the *Highway Cost Allocation Study* conducted by the U.S. Bureau of Public Roads in accordance with the terms of the Highway Revenue Act of 1956 has made available data which permit the determination, state by state, of the extent of the aforementioned departure from the benefit principle and which provide a basis for the adoption of corrective policies.[3]

The achievement of an economical allocation of highway resources is not a single problem but a complex of at least five interrelated problems. These involve the appropriate division of financial responsibility (1) between highway users as a group and nonusers; (2) among operators of different types of motor vehicles; (3) among users of different segments of the road systems of individual states; (4) among the users of highway systems of different states, a problem growing out of the collection and allocation of Federal highway user charges; and (5) between present and future highway users, a problem which arises when long-lived highway improvements are financed by means of current or accumulated user levies. This paper will be confined to the third and fourth of the foregoing problems, except to the extent that these also involve the question of the division of highway costs between users as a class and nonusers.

The problem of allocating resources among different segments of the road system of a state arises from a combination of circumstances. First, as shown in Table 1, roads and streets differ widely in construction and maintenance costs and in traffic volumes, with a resulting wide diversity in cost per vehicle mile. Moreover, with few exceptions, vehicle-mile cost varies inversely with traffic volume. The exceptions occur in connection with both very high cost and very low cost facilities. It should be noted that the figures in Table 1 are annual costs which reflect the spreading of capital costs over the estimated life of the facilities and not the annual expenditures incurred in a pay-as-you-go program.

Second, it would be administratively impracticable to take account of differences in vehicle-mile costs by maintaining separate schedules of user charges for different segments of a state's road system, although it is feasible to supplement state registration fees with special city motor vehicle licenses. The alternative—a universal toll road system with toll gates at every intersection—would not be seriously considered.[4]

---

[3] *Final Report of the Highway Cost Allocation Study*, Note 1.
[4] It may eventually be possible, as Professor Vickrey contends, that use of various electronic devices installed along the roadside and in vehicles will permit the direct pricing of highway services without the necessity of a universal system of toll gates.

Finally, to a large extent the users of different segments of the road system are different individuals.

The foregoing combination of circumstances constitutes a substantial limitation upon user charges as a method of highway finance. Because of differences in vehicle-mile costs, a level of user charges which would provide adequate intercity highways would not be adequate to finance local rural roads and many city streets. The latter would therefore necessarily have to be financed in large part from nonuser sources. It may be argued that this departure from user-charge financing would contribute to an over-all misallocation of resources as between highway and rail transportation, but two considerations reduce the force of this objection. First, most of the traffic carried by the roads in question is local in character and is not competitive with rail transportation. Second, if the share of the cost not covered by user charges is financed by special assessments on abutting property owners the effect of these levies is similar to that of a user charge, since the persons concerned will in almost all cases be road users. The assessments are analogous to the special contributions to defray the cost of line extensions which electric and telephone utilities sometimes require as a condition of serving isolated customers.

It is possible, of course, to finance light-traffic roads and streets to any desired extent by means of user charges, given a sufficiently high level of charges and an allocation of the proceeds which disregards the relative use made of different segments of the road and street system (as measured by vehicle miles or on some other basis). This is the situation which actually prevails in varying degrees at the present time. However, since this policy involves the allocation of user-charge revenue to the various segments of the road and street system without regard to the relative traffic volumes thereon, the connection between payments made and benefits received by particular users and groups of users is broken and the benefit principle is violated. When this occurs the light-traffic segments of the road and street system will be over-developed, and the heavy-traffic segments correspondingly under-developed, in relation to traffic requirements; there will be a significant

---

It would also be possible to convert much of the interstate system, by reason of its limited access feature, to toll roads, thereby extending the scope of direct pricing of highway services. Whether, on balance, such a step would be advantageous is a question which it is not feasible to consider here. It may be noted, however, that although a strong case can be made for the use of tolls to reduce congestion on, and secure efficient utilization of, certain urban facilities, their use under these circumstances is often impractical because of the need to maintain numerous access points to the facilities concerned.

TABLE 1

COMPARISON OF ANNUAL TOTAL COSTS PER MILE AND PER VEHICLE MILE
FOR ALL ROAD AND STREET SYSTEMS IN THE UNITED STATES[a]

Highway System and Surface Type	Rural			Urban		
	Cost Per Mile (dollars)	Cost Per Vehicle Mile (mills)	Vehicles Per Day Per Mile	Cost Per Mile (dollars)	Cost Per Vehicle Mile (mills)	Vehicles Per Day Per Mile
Interstate: high type	19,165	4.1493	12,655	73,798	3.7022	54,612
Other federal-aid primary:						
High type	10,012	7.0635	3,883	32,679	4.9714	18,010
Intermediate type	6,835	37.7804	496	6,667	22.2222	822
Low type	1,250	18.1818	188	--	--	--
Subtotal	9,634	7.5638	3,490	32,633	4.9727	17,979
Federal-aid secondary, state:						
High type	7,771	10.4862	2,030	17,445	4.6468	10,285
Intermediate type	2,288	18.5302	338	8,523	52.2059	447
Low type	2,664	77.2392	95	--	--	--
Unsurfaced type	461	24.1379	52	--	--	--
Subtotal	4,444	12.5376	971	16,147	4.9910	8,864
Federal-aid secondary, local:						
High type	3,861	8.1335	1,301	10,884	4.3337	6,880
Intermediate type	2,206	37.4289	162	5,910	63.1250	256
Low type	1,523	86.9296	48	2,151	25.0000	236
Unsurfaced type	--	--	40	--	--	--
Subtotal	2,401	16.2039	406	9,568	5.0473	5,193
All federal-aid systems	5,446	8.3239	1,792	30,140	4.5164	18,284
Other state highways:						
High type	9,601	16.6846	1,577	19,692	4.6262	11,662
Intermediate type	2,539	26.7629	260	5,702	22.1622	705
Low type	2,441	67.2222	100	--	--	--
Unsurfaced	--	--	--	--	--	--

(continued)

TABLE 1 (concluded)

Highway System and Surface Type	Rural			Urban		
	Cost Per Mile[b] (dollars)	Cost Per Vehicle Mile (mills)	Vehicles Per Day Per Mile	Cost Per Mile (dollars)	Cost Per Vehicle Mile (mills)	Vehicles Per Day Per Mile
Subtotal	5,464	18.7120	800	16,031	4.9856	8,810
Other local roads and streets:						
High type	4,941	13.8040	981	8,242	7.0109	3,221
Intermediate type	1,837	31.1759	161	3,853	55.2233	191
Low type	877	49.9616	48	2,434	121.1178	55
Unsurfaced type	203	21.9507	25	656	64.8649	28
Subtotal	1,134	25.6732	121	5,614	9.9717	1,543
All nonfederal-aid systems	1,275	24.4070	143	5,764	9.5876	1,647
Grand total	2,384	11.2296	582	7,746	7.0745	3,000

Source: *Final Report of the Highway Cost Allocation Study*, House Doc. No. 54, 87th Congress, 1st Session, Washington, D.C., 1961, adapted from Table III-G-1.

aDoes not include Alaska and Hawaii; includes District of Columbia. Does not include toll-facility mileage or the 2,012-mile expansion of the Interstate System.

bEstimated annual cost of investment in right-of-way and construction and estimated maintenance and construction costs. Costs at last half of 1956 price level and 0 per cent interest rate.

misallocation of resources both as between different parts of the highway transportation system and between highway and other forms of transportation.

A policy of allocating user revenues to the different segments of the highway system in accordance with the relative traffic volumes thereon would avoid the latter result and would also permit handling a larger volume of traffic with a given level of highway investment than is the case under present arrangements. This is a very important consideration in view of the magnitude of current highway expenditures and the rapid growth in demand for highway facilities.[5] Existing policies, by allocating a disproportionate share of user revenue to light-traffic roads and streets, contributed significantly to the deficiencies which have increasingly characterized main intercity highways and urban arteries since World War II. It has been pointed out that the modern toll road movement which was inaugurated largely to alleviate these deficiencies, has in turn helped to perpetuate existing revenue allocation policies.[6]

The justification of the proposed policy for the allocation of user-charge revenue in terms of its contribution to the achievement of an economical allocation of resources, and hence to the maximizing of economic welfare, is subject to two qualifications. First, the policy rests on the premise that user-charge financing should approximate as closely as possible the results which would be attained if highway services could be priced directly through the market mechanism, i.e., if the universal application of the toll principle were practicable. However, the attainment of an ideal allocation of resources within the framework of the market mechanism is ideal only to the extent that private and collective values coincide and this is not always the case. For example, national defense considerations might dictate an allocation of highway user revenue somewhat different from that based on individual user choices as reflected in relative traffic volume. It is the intent of this study neither to ignore such considerations nor to pass judgment on the extent to which they should be reflected in highway financing decisions, but merely to provide a basis for weighing the

[5] This statement does not imply that the objective should be *merely* to maximize ton-miles or vehicles miles per dollar of investment. It is equally important, for example, that highways handle only that volume and type of traffic which they can handle more advantageously than other means of transportation, and the policy regarding user-charge allocation recommended here would contribute to the attainment of this objective.

[6] See Wilfred Owen, *Toll Roads and the Problem of Highway Modernization*, Washington, D.C., 1951, Chapter 6; and D. Netzer, "Toll Roads and the Crisis in Highway Finance," *National Tax Journal*, June 1952, p. 110.

costs incurred in giving effect to such considerations against the resulting benefits.

Second, the proposal is subject to the limitations inherent in any partial application of the principles of welfare theory. In technical terms, the attainment of a Paretian optimum requires the simultaneous fulfillment of all the optimum conditions; if there exists some constraint which prevents the attainment of one of the Paretian conditions, a "second-best" optimum can be attained only by departing from all the other optimum conditions.[7] As applied in the case at hand, this means that policies designed to attain optimum allocation of a given total level of highway expenditure among different segments of the road and street system will contribute to maximizing welfare only if the total level of expenditures is also optimum. The analysis in this study therefore assumes that the total level of highway expenditures is, in some sense, optimum. Furthermore, it rests on the premise that, subject to the qualification noted in the preceding paragraph, adherence to the benefit principle of taxation will result in an optimum allocation of a given total expenditure among different parts of the road and street system. Subject to the stated qualifications, the preceding analysis suggests that there would be important advantages in adopting the policy of allocating user revenues among the various segments of the road and street system in accordance with the relative traffic volumes thereon.

The problem of allocating resources among the various segments of the highway system cannot be completely isolated from that of allocating highway costs between users as a whole and nonusers. This is true even under the so-called public utility approach to highway finance, which treats highway costs as almost entirely the responsibility of users. The reason is to be found in the fact that, as previously mentioned, it is necessary for administrative reasons to have a uniform schedule of user charges throughout a given jurisdiction, whereas there is a wide range in the vehicle-mile costs on different segments of the road system to which the user charges apply. The choice of the level of vehicle-mile costs to which user charges are to be equated will not only determine the proportion of the total highway system costs which will be borne by users as a whole, but also whether or not user-charge earnings on one segment of the highway system are to subsidize other parts of the system. The latter result can be avoided only if the

[7] For further discussion of this point see R. G. Lipsey and R. K. Lancaster, "The General Theory of the Second Best," *Review of Economic Studies*, 1956–57, No. 1, p. 11.

user charges are established at a level which will support the segment of the highway system which has the lowest vehicle-mile cost.

There are two closely related procedures for allocating total highway system costs between users as a whole and nonusers which avoid internal subsidization and the resulting violation of the benefit principle and misallocation of resources among different segments of the road system. One is the so-called standard road method, which is most often associated with Professor H. D. Simpson's Ohio highway study of 1951.[8] Under this method the allocation of user charges to each segment of the road and street system would be proportional to the number of ton-miles or vehicle-miles on it at a rate per ton-mile or per vehicle mile sufficient to support the state primary system. The additional revenue necessary to support the roads and streets below the primary level would be derived from nonuser sources. This method calls for a level of user charges which would provide 100 per cent support of that part of the road system having the heaviest traffic volume and lowest ton-mile or vehicle-mile cost.

The other procedure is known as the earnings-credit method and consists of threee steps.[9] The first step involves the same procedure as in the standard road method, i.e., the cost per vehicle mile on the primary system is taken as determining the user share and is applied to the entire road and street system. The nonuser share on roads and streets below the primary level is obtained by subtracting the amounts allocated on this basis from the total costs. The second step is to find the cost per mile of tertiary or access roads and streets having a minimum traffic volume. This is taken as determining the nonuser share and is applied to the entire road and street system. The user share is determined by subtracting the amount allocated on this basis to roads and streets above the tertiary level from the total cost thereof, and reducing the difference to a vehicle-mile basis. The third step is to take the mean of user cost per vehicle mile as determined in the first two steps and apply this vehicle-mile cost to the entire road and street system. The nonuser share is computed by subtracting the user share thus determined from the total cost of each road and street system. Whereas the first step results in assigning 100 per cent of the cost of the primary system to users and the second step 100 per cent of the cost of the tertiary system to nonusers, this last step results in dividing the cost responsibility of each road and street system between users and nonusers, though of course in widely differing proportions.

[8] H. D. Simpson, *Highway Finance, A Study Prepared for the Ohio Program Commission*, Columbus, Ohio, 1951.
[9] *Final Report of the Highway Cost Allocation Study*, Section III-G.

The earnings-credit method, like the standard road method, recognizes that the user-charge allocations to secondary and tertiary road systems should not exceed the rate per vehicle mile which can be used efficiently on the primary system. Unlike the latter method, however, it recognizes some degree of nonuser responsibility on the primary system as well as on the other systems. The fact that both the standard road and earnings-credit methods provide a reasonable basis for dividing highway costs between users as a whole and nonusers without interfering with an economical allocation of resources between different segments of the highway system is, in the writer's view, an important and somewhat neglected argument in their favor.[10]

If user-charge revenue is to be allocated to the various segments of the highway system in proportion to the relative traffic volumes thereon, it is necessary to have a measure of traffic volume which will accurately reflect the use made of highways by operators of various types of motor vehicles. Ton-miles would serve this purpose, since this measure reflects both the volume of traffic and its composition by vehicle type. However, ton-mileage figures broken down by class of road on a nationwide basis are not available, and it would be administratively very difficult and expensive to compile these data and to keep them up to date on a comprehensive basis. Fuel consumption appears to be the best available alternative, since it likewise reflects both the volume of traffic and its composition by vehicle type. However, it is not an accurate measure of ton-mileage, since fuel consumption for heavy trucks is more per vehicle mile but less per ton-mile than for automobiles; although a reasonably satisfactory measure of the benefit received by users as a whole from each segment of the road and street system, fuel consumption is not a satisfactory measure of the benefit received therefrom by operators of individual classes of vehicles.

Data showing aggregate fuel consumption by class of road are not available, but, this information can be derived from two other sets of data, namely, fuel consumption (both gasoline and diesel) by vehicle

[10] Mr. Zettel suggests another procedure, whereby the user share would be determined by applying the average cost per vehicle mile for the entire road and street system to each segment of the system. The nonuser share would be determined by subtracting the amount allocated on this basis to each segment of the road system from the total cost of each segment. Zettel holds that this procedure gives the minimum amount which is properly allocable to nonusers. He recognizes that it involves some internal subsidization in the case of roads having vehicle-mile costs above the average for the entire system but says that if this "subsidy" is not considered large, "it might be accepted on the ground that it helps provide an integrated plant and that feeder roads potentially contribute to traffic and earnings of the other roads." R. M. Zettel, "Some Problems of Highway Cost Assignment, With Special Reference to the Truckers' Share," *Proceedings of the National Tax Association*, 1953, p. 96.

type, and vehicle miles by type of vehicle for each class of road. These data have been compiled in connection with the *Highway Cost Allocation Study*, although some breakdowns of vehicle-mile data are not presently available in published form.[11] The vehicle-mile data are for 1957, with projections to 1964. They were derived by a scientific sampling procedure involving traffic volume counts at 365,000 stations plus nearly 29,000 classification counts for the purpose of differentiating traffic volume according to its vehicle-type components. Vehicle-mile data were collected for fifteen vehicle types on each of twelve classes of roads.[12]

On the basis of fuel-consumption data derived from the foregoing sources it is possible to compare the estimated percentage of total traffic carried by various segments of the road and street system with the percentage allocation of user-charge revenue. Such a comparison provides a rough measure of the degree to which existing policies have resulted in a departure from the benefit principle and in a misallocation of resources among different segments of the road and street system. Table 2 shows that for the United States as a whole in 1960 the allocation of state user-charge revenue to state highways was only slightly in excess of the amount justified by traffic volume, as measured by fuel consumption; whereas, on the same basis, the amount allocated to county and local roads was approximately 50 per cent greater than was justified, and the amount allocated to city streets less than half the amount justified. On the basis of relative traffic volume, approximately $135.6 million less should have been spent on state highways in 1960, $331.4 million less on country and local roads, and $467 million more on city streets. Table 3 indicates that for the East North Central Region there was a slight underallocation of user-charge revenue to state highways but, in comparison with the national situation, a heavier overallocation to county and local roads and a smaller underallocation to city streets. For the State of Illinois, as shown in Table 4, there was a substantial underallocation to state highways, a very heavy overallocation to county and local roads, and only a slight underallocation to city streets.[13]

[11] For making available unpublished data and generously assisting in other ways, the writer is indebted to Messrs. Robley Winfrey, C. A. Steele, Stanley Bielak, W. R. McCallum, and G. P. St. Clair of the U.S. Bureau of Public Roads.

[12] *Final Report of the Highway Cost Allocation Study*, p. 177.

[13] Fuel consumption data by road system for individual states can be computed only for 1957, since vehicle miles by states are available only for that year. Vehicle-miles data for 1957 were projected to 1964 only for census regions and the United States as a whole.

TABLE 2

ALLOCATION OF REVENUE FROM STATE MOTOR FUEL TAXES AND STATE MOTOR VEHICLE
REGISTRATION AND RELATED FEES TO ROAD AND STREET SYSTEMS IN THE
UNITED STATES, 1960, COMPARED WITH ESTIMATED FUEL
CONSUMPTION ON ROAD AND STREET SYSTEMS, 1964[a]
(dollars in thousands)

	Total	State Highways[b]	County and Local Roads	City Streets
Disposition of state motor fuel tax revenue[c]	3,176,013	2,226,546	654,441	295,026
Percentage distribution	100.0	70.1	20.6	9.3
Disposition of revenue from state motor vehicle registration and related fees[c]	1,315,381	922,789	296,790	95,802
Percentage distribution	100.0	70.1	22.6	7.3
Disposition of combined revenue from motor fuel taxes and motor vehicle registration and related fees	4,491,394	3,149,335	951,231	390,828
Percentage distribution	100.0	70.1	21.2	8.7
Estimated percentage distribution of fuel consumption, 1964	100.0	67.1	13.8	19.1

Source: U.S. Department of Commerce, Bureau of Public Roads, *Highway Statistics, 1960*, Tables G-3 and MV-3 and unpublished Bureau of Public Roads data.

[a] Forty-eight states and District of Columbia.

[b] Includes funds allotted for city streets forming urban extensions of state highway systems.

[c] Net funds available for distribution, less expenditures for state highway police and safety and nonhighway purposes.

As might be expected, a materially different picture emerges when fuel consumption is compared with the allocation of total highway revenue from all sources, including not only state user charges but also federal aid and other sources of revenue. This comparison is presented in Table 5. State primary rural roads show a substantial overallocation of revenue in relation to fuel consumption. State secondary rural roads and other state rural roads show a very large underallocation in relation to fuel consumption, whereas county and township roads show a slight overallocation. On the other hand, if state secondary rural roads and other state rural roads are classed with county and township roads, on the ground that the type of service rendered on much of the mileage of these systems is more nearly like that on local than on primary roads, there is a slight underallocation in relation to fuel consumption. The showing with respect to urban facilities is especially significant. Expenditures on municipal extensions of state highway systems conform closely to the amount indicated as desirable

TABLE 3

ALLOCATION OF REVENUE FROM STATE MOTOR FUEL TAXES AND STATE MOTOR VEHICLE
REGISTRATION AND RELATED FEES TO ROAD AND STREET SYSTEMS IN THE
EAST NORTH CENTRAL REGION, 1960, COMPARED WITH ESTIMATED
FUEL CONSUMPTION ON ROAD AND STREET SYSTEMS, 1964
(dollars in thousands)

	Total	State Highways[a]	County and Local Roads	City Streets
Disposition of state motor fuel tax revenue[b]	667,984	358,271	176,109	133,604
Percentage distribution	100.0	53.6	26.4	20.0
Disposition of revenue from state motor vehicle registration and related fees[b]	296,135	146,482	102,929	46,724
Percentage distribution	100.0	49.5	34.7	15.8
Disposition of combined revenue from motor fuel taxes and motor vehicle registration and related fees	964,119	504,753	279,038	180,328
Percentage distribution	100.0	52.4	28.9	18.7
Estimated percentage distribution of fuel consumption, 1964	100.0	57.4	14.3	28.3

Source: U.S. Department of Commerce, Bureau of Public Roads, *Highway Statistics,*
1960, Tables G-3 and MV-3 and unpublished Bureau of Public Roads data.

[a]Includes funds allotted for city streets forming urban extensions of state
highway systems.

[b]Net funds available for distribution less expenditures for state highway
police and safety, park and forest roads, and nonhighway purposes.

on the basis of fuel consumption, whereas other city streets show a
particularly serious underallocation on this basis.[14]

It must be emphasized that because of limitations of the available
data the foregoing analysis indicates only the general order of magnitude
of the discrepancy between the actual and an optimum allocation of
user-charge revenue among road and street systems. There is need for
a more detailed breakdown of data by road systems. For example, in
the analysis of state user charges in Tables 2, 3, and 4 it was necessary

---

[14] A recent study by Dr. Philip H. Burch, Jr., which appeared after the first draft
of the present paper had been completed, finds that, in contrast with the showing in
Table 5, there is a smaller overallocation of total highway revenue to state rural
roads, a larger underallocation to state and local urban arteries, and a heavy overallocation to local rural roads. It should be noted that, except for four states,
Burch defines local rural roads to include state secondary roads. He finds that the
allocation of total highway revenue for 1957–59 was 52.7 per cent to state rural
roads, 22.6 per cent to local rural roads, and 24.7 per cent to state and local urban
arteries; the proper allocations would have been 44.3 per cent, 11.0 per cent, and
44.7 per cent, respectively. Burch's allocations were derived, with various adjustments, from the relative rural and urban populations. He rejected the available

TABLE 4

ALLOCATION OF REVENUE FROM STATE MOTOR FUEL TAXES AND STATE MOTOR VEHICLE
REGISTRATION AND RELATED FEES TO ROAD AND STREET SYSTEMS IN ILLINOIS, 1960,
COMPARED WITH ESTIMATED FUEL CONSUMPTION ON ROAD AND STREET SYSTEMS, 1957
(dollars in thousands)

	Total	State Highways[a]	County and Local Roads	City Streets
Disposition of state motor fuel tax revenue[b]	143,632	38,012	45,606	60,014
Percentage distribution	100.0	26.4	31.8	41.8
Disposition of revenue from state motor vehicle registration and related fees[b]	75,925	55,088	11,867	8,970
Percentage distribution	100.0	72.5	15.7	11.8
Disposition of combined revenue from motor fuel taxes and motor vehicle registration and related fees	219,557	93,100	57,473	68,984
Percentage distribution	100.0	42.4	26.2	31.4
Estimated percentage distribution of fuel consumption, 1957	100.0	54.8	11.4	33.8

Source: U.S. Department of Commerce, Bureau of Public Roads, *Highway Statistics,
1960,* Tables G-3 and MV-3 and unpublished Bureau of Public Roads data.

[a]Includes funds allotted for city streets forming urban extensions of state
highway systems.

[b]Net funds available for distribution less expenditures for state highway
police and safety, park and forest roads, and nonhighway purposes.

to confine comparisons to three very broad divisions of the highway
system, thus neglecting a number of significant differences in vehicle-
mile costs within these divisions. Thus, it was not possible to take
account of the differences in vehicle-mile costs between the federal-aid
primary and secondary systems, to the extent that both are under state
control, or between the rural and urban portions of either of these
systems. Second, and of the greatest importance, the classification of
roads as primary, secondary and local does not correspond in any
close and consistent manner with a classification based upon the

---

vehicle-mile data as a basis for determining the proper allocations on the ground
that some of the state traffic surveys from which the vehicle-mile data were derived
were unreliable and produced inconsistent results. While this may be true in
individual instances the writer nevertheless is of the opinion that, on a national
basis at least, the vehicle-mile figures and the fuel-consumption figures derived
therefrom are likely to give a closer approximation to the actual relative traffic
volumes by road systems than the method used by Dr. Burch. See Philip H. Burch,
Jr., *Highway Revenue and Expenditure Policy in the United States*, New Brunswick,
N.J., 1962, pp. 174–175.

TABLE 5

ALLOCATION OF TOTAL HIGHWAY REVENUE TO ROAD AND STREET SYSTEMS IN THE UNITED STATES,
1960, COMPARED WITH ESTIMATED FUEL CONSUMPTION ON ROAD SYSTEMS, 1964[a]
(dollars in thousands)

Road System	U.S. Bureau of Public Roads Highway Classification Number[b]	Total Expenditure[c]	Percentage Distribution of Expenditure	Estimated Percentage Distribution of Fuel Consumption
State primary highways—rural	1, 3	3,534,344	51.9	35.9
State secondary roads—rural	5	418,083	6.1	9.3
Other state roads—rural	9	36,005	0.5	3.1[d]
County and township roads	7, 11	1,062,214	15.6	12.8[d]
Municipal extensions of state systems	2, 4, 6, 10	1,358,222	19.9	18.8[d]
Municipal streets	8, 12	407,307	6.0	20.1[d]
Total		6,816,175	100.0	100.0

Source: U.S. Department of Commerce, Bureau of Public Roads, *Highway Statistics, 1960*, Tables SF-2 and SF-4A and unpublished Bureau of Public Roads data.

[a] Forty-eight states, exclusive of toll facilities.

[b] The numerical code for road classification adopted by the Bureau of Public Roads in its *Highway Cost Allocation Study* is as follows:

1. Interstate—rural
2. Interstate—urban
3. Federal-aid primary—rural
4. Federal-aid primary—urban
5. Federal-aid secondary—rural, state
6. Federal-aid secondary—urban, state
7. Federal-aid secondary—rural, under local control
8. Federal-aid secondary—urban, under local control
9. Other state roads—rural

predominant function served by the respective road systems. Finally, the classification of roads as primary, secondary, and local does not correspond completely with the administrative classification of roads as state or county and local. Thus, roads on the federal-aid secondary system are partly under state and partly under local control in varying proportions in different states. The adoption of a road classification based upon functional principles, and a division of administrative responsibility between the states and their local governments which is consistent with such a classification, is essential to the improvement of highway financing policies.

The allocation of user-charge revenues to those segments of the road and street system which are not under state control involves the further problem of determining the share of these allocations to be received by the individual local governments concerned. Fuel consumption would not be a practicable measure for this purpose. The problem is therefore to find some alternative measure or combination of measures which would serve equally well in making apportionments to individual local governments in accordance with the requirements of the benefit principle.

A number of measures are currently used for this purpose, each of which is open to objection, and there is no general agreement as to which is most satisfactory. In the writer's view the choice is narrowed to vehicle miles, motor vehicle registration fee collections, and road mileage, singly or in some combination. Vehicle mileage is doubtless the best single available measure of relative use, but the surveys required for its determination involve considerable expense and need to be repeated at fairly frequent intervals. Instances have also been reported where vehicle mileage has been dishonestly manipulated by running a

---

NOTES TO TABLE 5 (concluded)

10. Other state roads—urban
11. Local rural roads
12. City streets, excluding municipal extensions of state
     highway systems

[c]Data for state highways and their municipal extensions cover capital outlays and maintenance expenditures; data for county and township roads and municipal streets cover total expenditures and fund transfers, excluding service of obligations for local roads.

[d]The percentages of total fuel consumption shown in this table for county and township roads and municipal streets, respectively, differ slightly from those shown in Table 2 because road system number 8 is included with county and township roads in Table 2 and with municipal streets in Table 5.

vehicle back and forth over the recording tapes. The dollar amount of motor vehicle registration fees is a better measure than the number of registrations, in that it reflects the composition of the registrations by vehicle types, but neither of these measures, unless supplemented by special local studies, indicates the use which the registered vehicles make of the roads in the jurisdiction concerned. Road mileage is not regarded as satisfactory unless adjusted to reflect differences in types of roads, and hence in traffic density and construction and maintenance costs, in different jurisdictions. One recent careful study recommends an apportionment formula weighted 50 per cent on the basis of vehicle miles and 50 per cent on the basis of road mileage adjusted in the manner just described; or, alternatively, if the collection of vehicle mileage data is regarded as impracticable, 50 per cent vehicle registrations and 50 per cent adjusted road mileage.[15]

The second major problem with which this paper is concerned is the appropriate division of financial responsibility for the highway system among users in different states. This problem arises from the fact that, with the passage of the Highway Revenue Act of 1956, the financing of federal highway appropriations was shifted from a general-fund basis to a user-charge basis, whereas the policy governing allocation of federal-aid funds among the states has not been altered to conform with the implications of the new method of financing.

Federal-aid funds, other than for the interstate system, are apportioned among the states on the basis of a formula which gives equal weight to population, area, and road mileage. Funds for the interstate system, originally apportioned according to the same formula, were modified beginning with the fiscal year 1956 to give a weight of two-thirds to population, one-sixth to area, and one-sixth to road mileage. Beginning with the fiscal year 1960, the interstate apportionment was changed to a cost-of-completion basis, i.e., the ratio that the estimated cost of completion of the system in each state bears to the estimated cost of completing the entire system. By contrast, the user-charge basis of financing adopted in 1956 would call for an allocation of funds proportionate to the contributions to the Federal Highway Trust Fund made by highway users in the respective states.

It should be noted that the recommended basis for the allocation of federal-aid funds among the states is the same as for the allocation

[15] Charles H. Bradford, "State Aid for Highways: Development of an Apportioning Formula," Unpublished doctoral dissertation, Harvard University Library, 1961. Quoted in Commonwealth of Massachusetts, *Report Submitted by the Legislative Research Council Relative to State Aid to Cities and Towns for Highway Purposes*, House Doc. 3580, Boston, 1962, p. 54.

of state user-charge revenue among the road and street systems within the individual states; namely relative volume and composition of traffic. But the measures of traffic volume used in the two cases differ somewhat. In the former case the measure used is the relative amount of federal user-charge revenue generated in the respective states; in the latter case it is the relative amount of fuel consumption, and hence fuel tax revenue generated, on the various road and street systems within the individual states. However, it is unlikely that the two measures of traffic volume would produce significantly different results, particularly in view of the dominant importance of the fuel tax among the federal user-charge revenues.

The discrepancy between the existing allocations and those which would be made on the proposed basis is shown in Table 6.[16] This discrepancy is a measure of the extent to which federal highway policies result in a misallocation of resources and in a departure from the benefit principle as among highway users in different states.[17] However, it will be observed from this table that, in general, the federal-aid apportionments for 1962 will probably reduce the magnitude of the discrepancies between the two bases of allocation, a trend which reflects the influence of the revised basis of apportionment adopted for the interstate system in 1960.

A special problem arises in the case of the interstate system. There is a conflict between the present basis of allocation, which is designed to accomplish completion of the entire system by the same date, and allocations which would be proportional to the contributions to the Highway Trust Fund made by users in the respective states. If the simultaneous achievement of both of the foregoing objectives be regarded as sufficiently important to justify some departure from the user-charge basis of financing, this could be accomplished by supplementary user-charge allocations based on the benefit principle with appropriations from general funds where necessary to insure a uniform completion date.

Even if the allocations of federal-aid highway funds were revised in the manner just suggested, thereby recognizing the benefit principle as

[16] It was necessary to compare payments to the Highway Trust Fund with federal-aid receipts rather than with federal-aid allocations because the latter are published on a fiscal year basis whereas payments to the Highway Trust Fund are reported on a calendar year basis.

[17] It should be noted that Table 6 does not imply that *total* road outlays are too high in states which receive more federal aid than is warranted on the basis of highway-users contributions to the Highway Trust Fund, or too low in states where the reverse situation prevails. The comparison merely shows the extent to which federal-aid allocations violate the benefit principle.

TABLE 6

FEDERAL-AID RECEIPTS AND USER PAYMENTS TO THE HIGHWAY TRUST FUND, CALENDAR
YEAR 1960, AND FEDERAL-AID ALLOCATIONS, FISCAL YEAR 1962
(dollars in thousands)

Rank by Federal-Aid Receipts	State	Federal-Aid Receipts	User Payments to Highway Trust Fund[a]	Ratio of Payments to Receipts	Federal-Aid Allocations, Fiscal Year 1962
1	Illinois	186,893	137,779	73.7	147,694
2	Texas	163,070	178,019	109.2	148,281
3	New York	160,437	178,961	111.5	157,248
4	California	146,640	264,294	180.2	273,564
5	Ohio	119,915	148,238	123.6	174,732
6	Michigan	94,736	119,224	125.8	116,262
7	Pennsylvania	78,813	151,291	192.0	125,175
8	Tennessee	77,889	52,304	67.2	80,749
9	Florida	74,140	80,712	108.9	74,852
10	Indiana	70,840	80,666	113.9	82,467
11	Louisiana	66,874	43,404	64.9	70,646
12	Minnesota	64,169	54,278	84.6	62,514
13	Alabama	56,412	47,493	84.2	58,732
14	Virginia	55,714	61,807	110.9	108,283
15	Georgia	55,009	62,254	113.2	72,721
16	Massachusetts	52,684	65,284	123.9	74,691
17	Missouri	47,623	73,470	154.3	83,822
18	Kentucky	46,374	40,644	87.6	51,862
19	North Carolina	44,156	68,471	155.1	31,846
20	Iowa	44,080	46,568	105.6	38,194
21	New Jersey	41,562	94,550	227.5	86,659
22	Wisconsin	41,085	57,438	139.8	41,791
23	Kansas	39,062	38,442	98.4	36,434
24	South Carolina	38,508	34,190	88.8	29,413
25	Mississippi	36,892	31,145	84.4	37,035
26	Oregon	33,945	32,567	95.9	49,745
27	West Virginia	33,312	23,279	69.9	35,259
28	Nebraska	33,294	26,088	78.4	26,706
29	Washington	32,751	43,888	134.0	52,995
30	Arkansas	31,931	29,807	93.3	32,623
31	Arizona	31,121	24,869	79.9	41,083
32	Colorado	28,918	31,207	79.2	29,830
33	Oklahoma	28,644	43,818	153.0	35,247
34	Maryland	27,862	41,703	149.7	58,652
35	Montana	27,537	13,249	48.1	37,263
36	South Dakota	26,008	12,068	46.4	19,100
37	Connecticut	25,947	35,844	138.1	33,861
38	North Dakota	24,585	10,467	42.6	18,482
39	Utah	24,080	15,114	62.8	28,951
40	Wyoming	24,049	8,867	36.9	30,156
41	New Mexico	23,248	20,454	88.0	37,376
42	District of Columbia	19,211	9,465	49.3	25,982
43	Vermont	19,030	6,272	33.0	23,922
44	Idaho	17,232	13,222	76.7	22,970
45	Maine	17,126	15,601	91.1	16,876
46	New Hampshire	16,660	9,381	56.3	15,957
47	Alaska	13,537	2,223	16.4	36,975
48	Rhode Island	11,847	11,488	97.0	14,596
49	Nevada	9,179	7,528	82.0	19,417
50	Delaware	7,415	8,248	111.2	11,325
51	Hawaii	5,312	6,370	119.9	16,384
	Totals	2,497,449	2,711,901	108.6	3,037,398

between highway users in different states, they would, unless co-ordinated with the allocations of state user-charge revenues, result in a misallocation of resources as among the different segments of the highway systems of the individual states. The problem arises from the concentration of federal-aid funds upon a limited portion of the highway systems of the states. Federal-aid funds, other than those for the interstate system, are apportioned 45 per cent to the federal-aid primary system, 30 per cent to the secondary system, and 25 per cent to the urban extensions of these systems. This concentration of federal-aid funds on the more heavily traveled segments of the state road and street systems counterbalances the tendency, previously noted, for the states to allocate a disproportionate share of their user-charge revenue to light-traffic roads. However, as Tables 7 and 8 indicate, the result may also be the allocation of a disproportionate share of total revenue to the federal-aid systems.[18] A comparison of Tables 2 and 5 leads to a similar conclusion for the United States as a whole.

In any event, the combination of federal-aid apportionments and allocations of state user-charge revenues is almost certain to result in total allocations to the various segments of the road and street systems of individual states which are materially different from allocations based on some measure of relative use, such as fuel consumption or vehicle miles. An obvious solution of this problem would be for the states to take account of federal aid in allocating their user-charge revenue, so that total allocations would reflect the relative use of each segment of their highway systems. However, in some instances this would call for state user-charge allocations smaller than the matching funds which states must currently appropriate in order to qualify for the full amount of federal aid. To the extent that this is the case, the elimination of the misallocation of highway revenue would appear to be virtually out of the question at the present time, since it would be

[18] It was necessary to make comparisons with vehicle miles in Table 7 because fuel-consumption data by road systems were not available for states other than Illinois. It will be noted that the vehicle-mile figures for Illinois in Table 7 are not greatly different from the fuel-consumption figures for Illinois in Table 8.

NOTES TO TABLE 6

Source: Computed from U.S. Department of Commerce, Bureau of Public Roads, *Highway Statistics, 1960,* Tables SF-1, E-7, E-8, and FA-4.

[a]Both the highway user portion of total taxes paid and the distribution by states were estimated by the Bureau of Public Roads, based on U.S. Internal Revenue Service collections. Amounts paid on U.S. government purchases, as estimated by the Bureau of Public Roads, have been excluded.

TABLE 7

ALLOCATION OF STATE USER-CHARGE AND FEDERAL-AID RECEIPTS
TO ROAD AND STREET SYSTEMS, 1960, COMPARED WITH
VEHICLE MILES, 1957, EAST NORTH CENTRAL STATES
(per cent)

States	State Highways[a]			County and Local Roads			City Streets		
	State User Charges[b]	State User Charges Plus Federal-Aid	Vehicle Miles	State User Charges[b]	State User Charges Plus Federal-Aid	Vehicle Miles	State User Charges[b]	State User Charges Plus Federal-Aid	Vehicle Miles
Illinois	42.4	66.3	52.5	26.2	16.7	11.6	31.4	17.0	35.9
Indiana	52.1	67.8	63.2	32.0	21.8	8.9	15.9	10.4	27.9
Ohio	61.0	71.1	54.4	26.1	19.7	13.6	12.9	9.2	32.0
Michigan	49.0	63.3	49.3	34.0	25.0	18.9	17.0	11.7	31.8
Wisconsin	55.6	63.4	47.6	28.8	25.5	25.8	15.6	11.1	26.6
Total	52.4	67.0	53.1	28.9	20.8	15.7	18.7	12.2	31.2

Source: U.S. Department of Commerce, Bureau of Public Roads, *Highway Statistics, 1960*, Tables G-3, MV-3, and SF-1 and unpublished Bureau of Public Roads data.

[a] Includes funds allotted for city streets forming urban extensions of state highway systems.

[b] Net funds available for distribution less expenditures for park and forest roads, state highway police and safety, and nonhighway purposes.

TABLE 8

ALLOCATION OF STATE USER CHARGES AND FEDERAL–AID
RECEIPTS TO ROAD AND STREET SYSTEMS, 1960, COMPARED
WITH FUEL CONSUMPTION, 1957, IN ILLINOIS
(per cent)

	Total	State Highways[a]	County and Local Roads	City Streets
Allocation of receipts from state user charges	100.0	42.4	26.2	31.4
Combined allocation of receipts from state user charges and Federal–aid	100.0	66.3	16.7	17.0
Estimated fuel consumption by road system	100.0	54.8	11.4	33.8

Source: U.S. Department of Commerce, Bureau of Public Roads, *Highway Statistics, 1960*, Tables G–3, MV–3, and SF–1 and unpublished Bureau of Public Roads data.

[a]Includes funds allotted for city streets forming urban extensions of state highway systems.

unrealistic to expect the states to adopt the suggested policy where it involved the sacrifice of a portion of the available federal-aid funds.

In conclusion, it seems probable that the allocational problems discussed in this paper have been relatively neglected partly because of preoccupation with other aspects of highway finance and partly because of the lack of data necessary for investigation. The latter deficiency has been at least partially remedied by the availability of data developed in connection with the *Highway Cost Allocation Study* of the Bureau of Public Roads. The financial consequences of the misallocation of resources revealed by these and other data are of sufficient magnitude to warrant both further investigation and remedial action along the lines suggested in this paper.

COMMENT

PETER O. STEINER, University of Wisconsin

Harbeson's paper is highly informative in its identification of the divergence between the pattern of incidence of highway user taxes and the allocation of expenditures on roads of different types. I have, however, some fundamental reservations about whether the discrepancies may be taken to be a demonstration of resource misallocation, and thus I have real reluctance in accepting his suggestions for remedial policies.

In order to focus on my doubts, I will put my understanding of his argument as baldly as possible:

1. Road services are predominantly a private commodity and ideally one would like to use the market mechanism (jointly) to: (a) allocate funds between road services and other goods; (b) allocate funds between types of roads and roads in different places; (c) assure optimal use of the roads constructed.

2. But direct pricing is impractical[1]—a toll booth at every intersection adversely affects the service—and this necessarily creates problems if we substitute indirect pricing in the form of user taxes.

(a) Since taxes must be based on vehicle use or upon residence, they will fail to reflect use of different types of roads (whose cost varies per vehicle mile) by different users.

(b) By virtue of being indirect, the allocative or rationing effect among roads is absent and thus optimal use may be lost.

---

[1] Although Professor Vickrey and others have suggested that some form of direct pricing may be practicable, I will accept this conclusion for the subsequent discussion.

(c) The appropriate total level of investment in road services is left undetermined. (This is implicit in the Harbeson paper. I add it now, because I deem it crucial to my subsequent comments.)

3. The best practical approach to the ideal is to raise the required total revenue through user taxes and to allocate it: (a) among types of roads within a state by a measure of relative traffic volume when no prices are charged; (b) among political subdivisions by size of user payments.

4. Using the best available measures, Harbeson finds allocation not optimal in either sense: too little goes to city streets and secondary state roads, too much to intercity highways; too little to New Jersey and Pennsylvania, too much to Vermont, Wyoming, South Dakota and Montana.

My reservations are several.

1. The "ideal," if it were feasible, would be ideal only if private and collective values coincided. These arguments are familiar and I will not rehearse them in detail. But there are collective benefits in a coherent road system, in at least minimum standards of access to all places, and (given lags) in anticipation of future demands. The major appeal of market determination would be that it would solve a major allocation problem and could, so far as it neglected collective needs, be supplemented by public roads. But let this pass: when near Rome, think as a Roman. I accept for the remainder of these comments the ideal as ideal.

2. Assuming the free market is not available, is the *benefit principle* as Harbeson uses it part of the second best? This is the very heart of the matter and its deserves discussion. This principle—to each according to his contribution—*is* a part of a market pricing scheme; economists have long called it consumer sovereignty. But, given the constraints that block use of the market system, the benefit principle is a proxy—and an imperfect one—for only *some* of the functions of the pricing mechanism. Unless those for which it *is* the proxy are of dominant importance, its use may be unwise or at least unimportant.

Indirect user payments, in the first place, do not provide a clue as to the level of the program of investment in road services. The benefit principle provides no help: it divides a pie according to the way it is collected. But how much should be collected, and in what way? These are important questions that are not independent of the allocational problems to which Harbeson addresses himself. To see this quickly, notice that any arbitrary amount and pattern of highway investment is "optimal" (according to the benefit principle) for some pattern of taxation; a change in the technique of taxation is as effective as a change in allocation in reducing discrepancies of the kind noted in the paper. "Optimal resource allocation," under the benefit principle, is no longer an independent goal toward which we strive, but is instead determined by the method of fund raising employed and the amount of taxes collected.

How *should* the level of investment be determined? Clearly, we do not choose to maximize something like ton-miles per dollar (which would mean building only the busiest road). Nor, at the other extreme, do we maximize the revenue we can extract from users by user related taxes. Instead, we plan a system whose size *and composition* is judged to be adequate (whether by the criterion of private or public needs is not critical in this discussion). One can visualize being very sophisticated within the private goods frame of mind: giving people what they would pay for in a free market, using an appropriate rate of discount that reflects private consumption and investment margins, and so on. Ranking of projects and selecting an optimal level of program is conceptually routine, although it is enormously complex and difficult in practice. But—and this is the point—once such an "optimal program" is selected, the allocational issues have all been decided. The question that remains is how and where to raise the funds. The benefit principle, if we use it, dictates the technique of taxation, not the expenditure of the receipts. Demonstrated discrepancies between users and taxpayers of the kind Harbeson develops suggest that we tax inequitably, not that we allocate resources among types of highways unwisely.

Put differently, Harbeson's use of the benefit principle substitutes taxpayer sovereignty for consumer sovereignty. Since the very essence of the allocative problems that Harbeson discusses is that taxpayers and users are imperfectly paired, the substitution is critical in evaluating the findings. The imperfect pairing of users and taxpayers may be partly a matter of conscious public policy, or it may be the result of some taxpayers being able to, and choosing to, avoid certain taxes (e.g., by operating a car with low fuel consumption). This however does not measure how much they value (and would pay for) roads of different types.

3. By neglecting the rationing function of prices, the use of the benefit principle fails to come to grips with the key element of peak load problems: the simultaneous solution of optimal investment and optimal use. This is the problem Vickrey discusses elsewhere in this volume. Relative traffic volumes of roads of different kinds (and of

different qualities and costs) when all are free, is both a poor and an uncertain guide to what use people would make of a different mix of roads with an optimal tariff on each.

To summarize my central criticism, the benefit principle does not seem to me to come to grips with the major allocative problems of highway finance. *If* the level of total expenditure and the forms of taxation precisely matched the pattern and amount of receipts of an "ideal" pricing scheme, the allocation of funds according to the benefit principle would assure perfect allocation. Without these conditions (and they are absent), a discrepancy between present allocation and present sources of funds is certainly ambiguous as to which is non-optimal (both may be, of course) and is very possibly of a second order of importance in the larger framework of determining the levels of need for highway construction and the optimal investment in roads of different kinds and in different places. The benefit principle may retain its significance as an element in the fabric of social justice, but this case must be made in very different terms.

Finally, a few questions about the more specific suggestions for policy. (1) Are relative traffic volume, as among roads within a state, and taxpayers' contributions as among states, equivalent principles of allocation? This may be true, but it is not apparent to me. (2) Why, for a given investment, is maximizing ton-miles per dollar a sensible objective? Not only would I weight people differently from freight, but I believe the comparative advantage in transportation by roads, rail, and water of different commodities is very different, and is systematically related to weight. (3) In what meaningful sense should road outlays in Vermont be judged three times too high; in Montana, Wyoming and South Dakota, more than twice as high as is proper? Conversely, why are New Jersey's roads receiving less than half of the proper amount? Having driven in all of these states the conclusions seem preposterous. Neither the access problems of the vast plains and mountain states nor the overpopulation and overcrowding of megalopolis will be solved by this sort of reallocation of funds. This is a pity, because it would be an easy solution to hard problems.

O. H. BROWNLEE, University of Minnesota

Harbeson is concerned with how to collect for highways and how to allocate the proceeds when it is not feasible to charge users of a given class different fees for different qualities of service. Although this typically is the kind of problem faced, I believe that we could decrease its relative importance by converting much of the so-called "interstate" system to toll roads with proceeds from gasoline tax revenues being credited to the various segments in accordance with the volumes of various kinds of vehicles which use each segment. Limited access highways usually are those that lend themselves to operation as toll roads without high collection costs. And toll roads permit charging different amounts per unit of distance traveled, on different roads at a given time or a given road at different times, which is what we want.

However, even if the "interstate" were to be converted into a toll road, there would still be much of the road and street system where tolls would not be feasible and for which Harbeson's problem would still exist. If the schedule of charges were optimal, then clearly the revenues returned to the various sectors of the road system should be proportional to the revenues earned. Whether, in absolute amounts, revenues returned should be less than, equal to, or greater than revenues earned depends upon whether there are increasing, constant, or decreasing returns technologically to highway production. However, it is unlikely that allocating revenues in the best manner for an optimal fee pattern also will be optimal when the fee pattern is not an optimal one.

Harbeson proposes two closely related procedures which he claims are such as to result in no transfer of earnings from any broad segment of the highway system to any other. In turn, he claims that there is thus no subsidization of some users from funds collected by taxing others, and thus no misallocation of resources among various broad sectors of the road system. (The over-all system may be too large or too small but Harbeson is not discussing this problem.) One of these procedures establishes the standard per mile fee at the average cost per mile of privilege fees (Harbeson calls then nonuser taxes) sufficient to cover average costs on the other sectors. The second procedure seems to do somewhat the same, although I cannot translate the verbal statement into an algebraic one so that I can check my conjecture.

Although I intuitively believe that Harbeson's proposed general procedure is superior to that currently used, I cannot prove this to be the case without specific cost and utility functions. Existing fee schedules largely ignore congestion costs—the principal item on much of the urban portion of the road system. Optimal fees cannot be based only on construction and maintenance costs, since the system produces joint products. And I believe that the measurement of benefits is operationally impossible.

Those who advocate a benefit approach to the allocation of highway costs typically argue that taxes paid by various classes of users and benefits per unit of use ought to be proportional. However, since a highway user can be expected to use a facility to the extent that any larger use would increase his costs (operating, *waiting*, etc.) by more than it would increase his benefits, the net benefit—at the margin—is zero. This will be the case (except for indivisibilities) on all kinds of highways.

The difficulties associated with an allocation scheme alloting revenues proportionate to traffic volume can be shown by the case in which there are two roads with equal volumes but much different levels of congestion. Both would (assuming identical construction and maintenance costs) receive the same revenue; but the more congested one should be charging more and also receiving more for expansion.

Although it is not a central idea in Harbeson's proposal, the suggestion is made that we should "use surplus revenue generated on urban arteries to assist in the financing of urban mass transit facilities." This could represent an improvement, insofar as highways are financed from nonuser sources and prices for highway service are below the optimal ones. However, removing the subsidy to highways would be still better.

PART II

Investment, Innovation, and Technological Change in Transport Industries

Innovation and Technical
Change in the Railroad Industry

EDWIN MANSFIELD

UNIVERSITY OF PENNSYLVANIA

I. Introduction

The importance of innovation and technical change to the railroad industry is widely recognized. In a recent paper, Healy has gone so far as to suggest that, under present conditions, they may be of paramount importance.

Because of the erosion of the other aspects of authority and responsibility, and the simultaneous appearance of major technological advances in other types of transportation, the responsibility for technological innovation among the various remaining responsibilities of management has become paramount. It is not an overstatement to say that both the place of railroads as a whole in the total transport picture and their individual economic success depend more than anything else upon the technological advances which managements develop and put into effect.[1]

Granting the significance of technical change, the following important questions arise concerning the extent of the technological advances that have occurred in recent years in the railroad industry and the process by which such advances have been introduced and have gained acceptance. How rapidly have labor and total factor productivity been increasing in the railroads? How rapidly has the production function shifted over time? How have important inventions in the railroad industry been distributed over time? Have the largest railroads tended

NOTE: The work on which this paper is based is part of a larger project on research, innovation, and economic growth, supported by a grant from the National Science Foundation. I am indebted to M. Hamburger, F. Levy, L. Rapping, and O. Williamson for comments on an earlier draft and to C. Phillips for assistance. My thanks also go to J. Schmookler for making unpublished data available and to the many people in the railroad and related industries who provided information.

[1] K. Healy, "Management and Technological Change," in *Technological Change and the Future of the Railways*, Evanston, 1961, p. 126.

Figure 1
Output Per Man-Hour: Railroads, All Transportation,
and National Economy, 1889–1953
(1929 = 100)

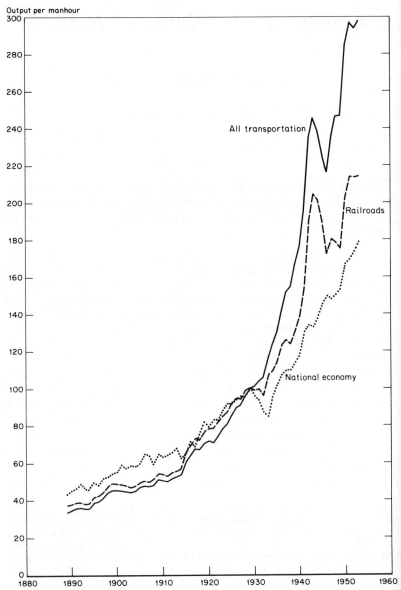

SOURCE: Kendrick, *Productivity Trends.*

to be the pioneers in introducing these new techniques? Once a new technique is introduced by one company, what determines how rapidly other companies take it up? What determines how rapidly its use spreads within a company? Specifically, what sorts of innovation have occurred in recent years in railroading? What prospective changes in technology seem most promising and what effects are they likely to have on railroad employment?

II. Increases in Productivity

There is an enormous literature concerned with the uses and misuses of average productivity measures—labor, capital, and total. If technical change is defined as a shift in the production function, it is generally agreed that increases in output per man-hour and in output per total factor input are incomplete measures of the rate of technical change.[2] Nonetheless, it is also agreed that, if properly used, they provide valuable, if only partial, information regarding changes over time in an industry's input requirements.

Figure 1 shows the pre-1954 movement in the railroad industry of output per man-hour, the most widely used average productivity measure. Between 1890 and 1925, output per man-hour went up about as rapidly in the railroad industry (2.5 per cent per year) as in all transportation (2.6 per cent per year),[3] but much more rapidly than in the economy as a whole (2.0 per cent per year). Between 1925 and 1953, although output per man-hour continued to rise more rapidly in railroads (3.0 per cent per year) than in the economy as a whole (2.4 per cent per year), it rose much more slowly than in all transportation (4.5 per cent per year).[4]

[2] It is obvious that changes in output per man-hour generally do not measure shifts in the production function. Moreover, only under quite restrictive conditions do changes in output per total factor input measure shifts in the production function (see E. Domar, "On Total Productivity and All That," *Journal of Political Economy*, December 1962).

[3] Of course, in view of the fact that the railroads were then such a large proportion of the transportation industry, this is what one would expect.

[4] These growth rates (and all others in this section) are only approximate, since they were computed by finding the rate of growth of output per man-hour between the initial and terminal years, ignoring the intermediate years. Nonetheless, they are reasonably adequate approximations and good enough for present purposes. Note too, when examining Figures 1 and 2, that the railroads have been operating at less than full capacity.

For discussions of various types of productivity measures, see *Output, Input, and Productivity Measurement*, Studies in Income and Wealth 25, Princeton University Press for National Bureau of Economic Research, 1961; and J. W. Kendrick, *Productivity Trends in the United States*, Princeton for NBER, 1961. For discussions

Over the entire period, 1890–1953, output per man-hour rose, on the average, about 2.8 per cent per year in the railroad industry. This increase was due partly to increases in the amount of capital utilized per man-hour. According to Kendrick's figures, the capital-labor ratio increased by about 50 per cent between 1890 and 1953. It was also due partly to changes in technology. Diesel locomotives replaced steam locomotives, automatic hump yards replaced flat yards, centralized traffic control and other signaling devices were introduced, mechanization of maintenance-of-way became important, and countless other improvements were made.[5]

Comparing years (1889, 1899, 1909, 1920, 1929, 1941, and 1950) when the railroad industry was operating at fairly high levels of capacity utilization, in an effort to exclude the effects of the business cycle, we find that apparently output per man-hour in the industry increased at a fairly steady rate through that long period. This is interesting, since one might suppose, with Fabricant and others,[6] that output per man-hour would tend to increase at a decreasing rate as an industry matured. These data, however, provide no indication of that.[7]

Figure 2 shows the long-term movement in the railroad industry of output per total factor input. Whereas data on output per man-hour take no account of changes over time in the amount of capital utilized per man-hour, the data in Figure 2 do take account of such changes, total factor input being a weighted combination of labor and capital inputs. The results indicate that output per total factor input rose more rapidly during 1890–1953 in the railroad industry (2.6 per cent per year) than in the economy as a whole (1.7 per cent per year), but less rapidly than in all transportation (3.1 per cent per year). Of

---

of railroad productivity indexes, see H. Barger, *The Transportation Industries, 1889–1946*, New York, NBER, 1951; D. Munby, "The Productivity of British Railways," D. W. Glassborow, "The Comparison of Partial Productivity Ratios for National Railway Systems," and M. E. Paul, "International Productivity Comparisons Over Time," all in *Bulletin of Oxford Institute of Statistics*, Feb. 1963; and E. Mansfield and H. Wein, "Notes on Railroad Productivity and Efficiency Measures," *Land Economics*, Feb. 1958.

[5] Kendrick, *Productivity Trends*, pp. 543–545, contains the data on which the figure in the text is based. For a detailed discussion of recent increases in railroad efficiency, see J. Nelson, *Railroad Transportation and Public Policy*, Washington, 1959, Chap. 8.

[6] S. Fabricant, *The Relations Between Factory Employment and Output since 1899*, Occasional Paper 4, New York, NBER, 1941.

[7] The rates of growth of output per man-hour (in per cent) were: 2.7 (1889–99), 1.1 (1899–1909), 3.3 (1909–20), 2.7 (1920–29), 3.6 (1929–41), 3.1 (1941–50), and 2.6 (1950–57). There is no indication of a decrease over time. This has also been pointed out by H. Barger, *The Transportation Industries*, p. 95.

Figure 2
Output Per Total Factor Input: Railroads,
All Transportation, and National Economy, 1889–1953
(1929 = 100)

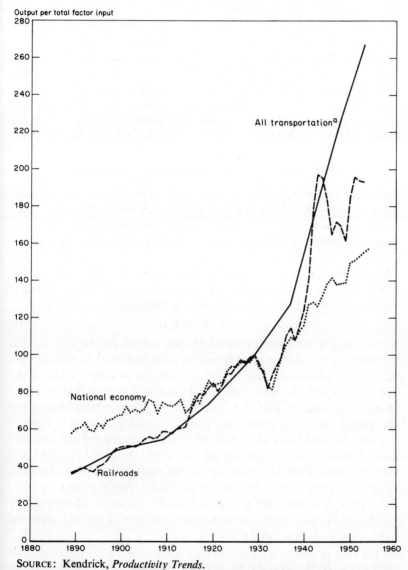

SOURCE: Kendrick, *Productivity Trends*.
ᵃ Figures are given at only about ten-year intervals. The graph simply connects
these points.

course, the more rapid increase in nonrailroad transportation may have been due partly to exclusion of government inputs like highways. Excluding years of deep depression and war, the rate of increase remained fairly steady in the railroad industry, the results being similar to those based on output per man-hour.[8]

Finally, a word should be added on the changes in railroad productivity since 1953. According to the Bureau of Labor Statistics, output per man-hour increased by about 5.8 per cent per year in the railroad industry during 1953–61. This was a much greater increase than had occurred previously in the railroads (3.0 per cent per year in 1925–53) or simultaneously in the private economy as a whole (2.7 per cent per year in 1953–61). The new techniques that helped to bring about the spurt in railroad productivity are described in Section VIII.

III. Shifts in the Production Function

Technical change is defined here as a shift in the production function. To measure such shifts in the railroad industry during 1917–59, I shall use the following highly simplified model, which was first employed by Solow[9] to analyze economy-wide data. First, I assume that all technical change in the railroad industry was capital embodied. To become effective, all innovations had to be embodied in new plant and equipment. Second, I assume that, for capital installed at time v which is still in existence at time t, the production function was

$$Q_v(t) = \beta e^{\lambda v} L_v(t)^\alpha K_v(t)^{1-\alpha}, \tag{1}$$

where $Q_v(t)$ is the output derived at time t from this capital, $L_v(t)$ is the amount of labor used at time t in combination with this capital, $K_v(t)$ is the amount of such capital in existence at time t, and λ is the rate of technical change. Note that Equation 1 implies that technical change was neutral, that it proceeded at a constant rate throughout the period, and that there were constant returns to scale. Third, I assume that all capital, regardless of vintage, depreciated at a constant annual rate of δ and that at any point in time the industry's total labor force is allocated efficiently among various vintages of capital. Featherbedding of many kinds is allowed by the model, since the working labor force may be larger than the firms consider optimal. Moreover, the results are not affected if a certain (fixed) per cent of the total time put in by labor is useless "make work."

---

[8] The rates of growth of output per total factor input (in per cent) were: 3.1 (1889–99), 1.8 (1899–1909), 3.3 (1909–20), 1.8 (1920–29), 2.9 (1929–41), 2.9 (1941–50). Again, there is no evidence of a decrease over time.

[9] R. Solow, "Investment and Technical Progress," in *Mathematical Methods in the Social Sciences*, Arrow, Karlin, and Suppes, Eds., Stanford, 1960.

Given these assumptions, one can easily show that

$$Q(t) = \beta e^{-\delta(1-\alpha)t} L(t)^{\alpha} S(t)^{1-\alpha}, \tag{2}$$

where $Q(t)$ is the total output of the industry at time t, $L(t)$ is the total amount of labor used by the industry at time t, and

$$S(t) = \int_{-\infty}^{t} e^{\sigma v} I(v)\, dv,$$

where $I(v)$ is the industry's gross investment at time v, and $\sigma = \delta + \lambda/(1 - \alpha)$. Letting $R(t) = Q(t)^{1/(1-\alpha)} \div L(t)^{\alpha/(1-\alpha)}$, it follows that

$$\ln \left[\frac{\dfrac{dR(t)}{dt} + \delta R(t)}{I(t)} \right] = \frac{\ln \beta}{1 - \alpha} + \frac{\lambda t}{1 - \alpha}. \tag{3}$$

Thus, one can estimate λ—the rate of technical change—in the following way. First, using data regarding $Q(t)$, $L(t)$, and α, it is an easy matter to compute $R(t)$. Second, substituting $\Delta R(t)$ for $dR(t)/dt$ and inserting data regarding $I(t)$ and δ, one can estimate the left-hand side of Equation 3. Third, if the left-hand side of Equation 3 is regressed against time, the product of the regression coefficient and $(1 - \alpha)$ is an estimate of λ.

This procedure was used to estimate the rate of technical change in the railroad industry during 1917–59. Following Bowden,[10] $Q(t)$ was set equal to the number of ton-miles plus 2.6 times the number of passenger-miles for Class I line-haul railroads during year t, the result being expressed as an index number (1929 = 100).[11] $L(t)$ was "total time paid for" by class I line-haul railroads in year t,[12] the result being expressed as an index number (1929 = 100). $I(t)$, expressed in millions of 1929 dollars, was measured by Ulmer's figures[13] on gross investment

[10] W. Bowden, "Productivity, Hours, and Compensation of Railroad Labor," *Monthly Labor Review*, Dec. 1933, pp. 1277–1278. For those years for which Barger (*Transportation Industries*) provided data, I used his figures on $Q(t)$. Of course, railroad output is multidimensional and this output index is very crude. For an analysis of technical change which takes account of the multidimensionality of an industry's output, see V. Smith, "Engineering Data and Statistical Techniques in the Analysis of Production and Technological Change: Fuel Requirements of the Trucking Industry," *Econometrica*, Apr. 1957.

[11] Of course, $Q(t)$ really should be measured by value added, but I assume that value added is proportional to output.

[12] For those years for which Barger (*Transportation Industries*) provided data, I used his figures on $L(t)$. Although they pertain to time worked, rather than time paid for, the index numbers are not affected much by the difference. Figures for later years come from *Statistics of Railways*.

[13] M. Ulmer, *Trends and Cycles in Capital Formation by United States Railroads, 1870–1950*, Occasional Paper 43, New York, NBER, 1954. Also, see his *Capital in Transportation, Communications, and Public Utilities: Its Formation and Financing*, Princeton for NBER, 1960.

by railroads (1917–50) and the corresponding figures issued by the Department of Commerce (1951–57). Finally, the average value of labor's share of the industry's value added during 1946–57 was used as an estimate of α[14] and, following Ulmer (p. 49), .02 was used as an estimate of δ. Needless to say, these estimates are very rough.

The resulting regression, omitting cases where $\Delta R(t) + \delta R(t) < 0$, is

$$\ln\left[\frac{\Delta R(t) + \delta R(t)}{I(t)}\right] = -413 + .213t. \qquad (r = .89) \qquad (4)$$
$$(.020)$$

The regression coefficient has the expected sign and is highly significant. Moreover, Figure 3 shows that this regression fits the data reasonably well. The regression coefficient multiplied by $(1 - \alpha)$, gives the estimate of λ, .030, its standard error being .003. This is higher than Solow's estimate of λ for the entire economy (.025), though the difference is probably statistically nonsignificant.

In Equation 4, I obviously had to omit cases where $\Delta R(t) + \delta R(t) < 0$. As Solow has pointed out, the omitted years tend to be those in which there was a serious drop in output; and this is a rough way of dealing with the fact that, although the model assumes the industry is always working up to capacity, obviously it has not been. As an experiment, I tried to handle this problem in another way. I obtained from various members of the industry rough estimates of the ratio of actual to capacity output and the ratio of actual to capacity labor requirements during each year.[15] Dividing $Q(t)$ by the former ratio and $L(t)$ by the latter, we obtain estimates of capacity output and capacity labor requirements. Using these figures rather than $Q(t)$ and and $L(t)$, we obtain the following regression:

$$\ln\left[\frac{\Delta R(t) + \delta R(t)}{I(t)}\right] = -23.8 + .007t. \qquad (r = .00) \qquad (5)$$
$$(.008)$$

The regression coefficient is not statistically significant, and the fit is extremely poor. Apparently, the estimates of the ratios were too inaccurate to be useful in this sort of analysis.

[14] In this model, as well as in the older ones where technical change was "disembodied," labor's share will equal α, if the value of labor's marginal product is set equal to the wage rate. Of course, in a regulated, highly unionized industry like railroads, this may not be a very suitable assumption. But the resulting estimate of α (.86) is very close to one made by L. Klein (.89) which rests on somewhat different assumptions (see L. Klein, *A Textbook of Econometrics*, Evanston, 1956, p. 234). These estimates are rough, but it is difficult to see what alternative procedures could have been used.

[15] These estimates were obtained in interviews with executives of several railroads and a railroad equipment company.

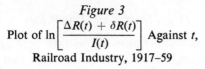

Figure 3

Plot of $\ln\left[\dfrac{\Delta R(t) + \delta R(t)}{I(t)}\right]$ Against t,

Railroad Industry, 1917–59

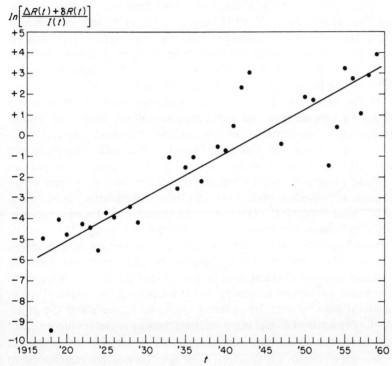

SOURCE: See Section III.

In conclusion, the rate of technical change in the railroad industry, as measured by λ, seemed to be about 3.0 per cent per year during 1917–59, which is higher—though perhaps not significantly so—than the corresponding estimate for the entire U.S. economy. Needless to say, the model underlying this estimate is oversimplified in some respects, and consequently the estimate, although reasonable, should be treated with caution.[16]

[16] Some of the difficulties are as follows: First, contrary to the model, technical change may not have been neutral, some of it may not have required new capital, there may have been economies or diseconomies of scale, labor inputs may not have been homogeneous over time and, once capital was installed, there may not have been the possibilities for capital-labor substitution envisaged in the model.

IV. Timing of Invention

The model in the previous section throws little light on the underlying processes of invention, innovation, and diffusion that are responsible for the estimated shifts in the production function. In this section, together with Sections V–VI, I turn to these processes. Specifically, the present section is concerned with the distribution over time of important railroad inventions, the object being to determine whether such inventions have been distributed in accord with various hypotheses put forth by Kuznets, Schmookler, and others.

At the outset, one should note that there are enormous problems in obtaining a meaningful and useful definition of an "invention" and in evaluating the contribution of a particular invention to an industry's technology. Results obtained are bound to be crude. The procedure adopted is to use Schmookler's chronology of patents and important railroad inventions and to analyze the distribution over time of all patents, all important inventions, and those considered by Schmookler to be "most important." Obviously, the findings can only be suggestive, since, as Schmookler points out, the data are very rough.[17]

Two hypotheses regarding the timing of invention have received considerable attention. First, there is the hypothesis, put forth by Kuznets, Burns, Fabricant, and others,[18] that the rate of occurrence of significant inventions decreases as an industry grows older. "Every technical improvement, by lowering costs and by perfecting the utilization of raw materials and of power, bars the way to further progress."[19]

Second, the railroads may have been operating off the production function during some of the period because of slack demand and inefficiencies. Third, the data used to estimate λ are rough. Fourth, technical change, as defined here, is a catchall that includes the effects of many factors other than the improvement of techniques (see E. Domar, "On the Measurement of Technological Change," *Economic Journal*, Dec. 1961, pp. 709–729).

Note too that the research and development underlying the technical change in the railroad industry have been carried out largely outside the railroad industry.

[17] J. Schmookler, "Changes in Industry and in the State of Knowledge as Determinants of Industrial Invention," in *The Rate and Direction of Inventive Activity: Economic and Social Factors*, Special Conference 13, Princeton for NBER, 1962. I am grateful to Schmookler for making his unpublished worksheets and the chronology of inventions used in his paper available to me.

[18] S. Kuznets, *Secular Movements in Production and Prices*, Boston, 1930; A. F. Burns, *Production Trends in the United States Since 1870*, New York, NBER, 1934; S. Fabricant, *Factory Employment and Output;* and J. Wolf, *Die Volkswirtschaft der Gegenwart u. Zukunft*, Leipzig, 1912.

[19] Quoted from *ibid.*, by Kuznets, *Secular Movements in Production and Prices*, p. 11.

Second, there is the hypothesis, put forth by Schmookler, that significant inventions tend to occur during periods when investment is high. "The trend and swings of invention are probably caused . . . by those in investment or by the same forces which dominate the latter." [20]

To test these hypotheses, we regress the number of inventions in year t on the amount of railroad capital formation (in millions of 1929 dollars) in year $(t - 3)$ and on t. A three-year lag is used for the investment variable, because this is the lag adopted by Griliches and Schmookler.[21] For all of Schmookler's "important" inventions, the results are:

$$n(t) = 39.0 + .0011I(t - 3) - .0200t, \quad (r = .46) \qquad (6)$$
$$(.0004) \qquad\qquad (.0048)$$

where $n(t)$ is the number of these inventions occurring in year t, and $I(t)$ is the railroad capital formation in year t. Figure 4 contains the time series of $n(t)$. Letting $n(t)$ be the "most important" inventions, the results are

$$n(t) = 14.1 - .00003I(t - 3) - .0071t. \quad (r = .17) \qquad (7)$$
$$(.00029) \qquad\qquad (.0034)$$

Letting $n(t)$ be the number of patents, the results are

$$n(t) = 4510 + .936I(t - 3) - 2.04t. \quad (r = .41) \qquad (8)$$
$$(.223) \qquad\qquad (2.63)$$

The results are usually in accord with the hypothesis of Kuznets, Burns and Fabricant, the regression coefficient of t being negative and statistically significant in two of the equations. The results are also in general accord with the Schmookler hypothesis, the regression coefficient of $I(t - 3)$ being positive and statistically significant in two of the equations. Of course, it may be objected that the number of inventions in each year should be weighted by some measure of importance. But

[20] Schmookler, "Changes in Industry," p. 215. Note that Schmookler's tests of this hypothesis are based on the same data used here, but the methods are entirely different.

[21] Z. Griliches and J. Schmookler, "Inventing and Maximizing," *American Economic Review* (September 1963). Their data do not pertain to the railroads and their techniques are different.

We use the period 1870–1950, because annual data on $I(t)$ do not seem to be available for earlier years and because of the particularly great difficulties in evaluating the importance of very recent inventions. Besides the regressions shown below, regressions including t^2 as an independent variable, as well as t and $I(t)$, were run. The effect of t^2 is not significant.

Figure 4
Number of Major Railroad Inventions,
Schmookler's Chronology, 1870–1950

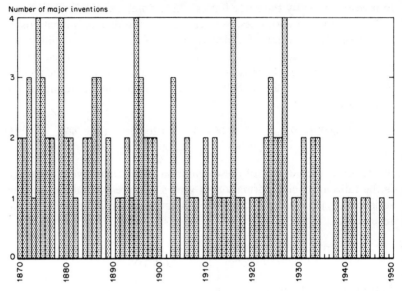

SOURCE: Schmookler, "Changes in Industry and in the State of Knowledge.'

if Schmookler's weights[22] (by technological and economic importance) are used in Equation 7, the results change very little. Unfortunately, such weights are not available for Equations 6 and 8.[23]

It is interesting that, although the probability of a major invention has decreased over time, the rate of productivity increase has not slowed down. Perhaps the rate of invention has decreased substantially only in fairly recent years and it has not yet had an effect on the rate of productivity increase. The data in Figure 3 seem to suggest that $n(t)$

[22] Schmookler, "Changes in Industry."

[23] In addition, I ran Cox's test of randomness against trend. The results indicate a downward trend. See D. Cox, "Some Statistical Methods Connected with Series of Events," *Journal of the Royal Statistical Society*, 1955; and E. Mansfield, "Power Functions for Cox's Test of Randomness Against Trend," *Technometrics*, Aug. 1962.

With regard to Schmookler's hypothesis, it should be noted that if $I(t)$, rather than $I(t - 3)$, is used, it is not statistically significant in Equations 6 or 7, but it is statistically significant in Equation 8. It is also interesting that Schmookler's hypothesis holds most strongly for relatively unimportant inventions. This seems reasonable to me and I suspect it is true in other industries as well.

was lower during 1930–50 than previously, and that the trend in $n(t)$ was relatively slight before 1930.[24]

V. Size of Innovators

The importance of the innovator—the firm that first introduces a new technique commercially—has been stressed by Schumpeter and others. Is it true, as Schumpeter claimed, that the innovators in recent years have tended to be very large firms? Have the largest firms been the first to introduce a disproportionately large share of important new techniques? This section is concerned with these questions, which are obviously important from the point of view of public policy, and which throw further light on the process of technical change in the railway industry.

First, consider the extent to which the largest railroads have been the innovators. Healy[25] includes the following in a list of ten major innovations introduced in the railroad industry since 1920: (1) four-wheel trailing trucks and large fire box for steam locomotives, (2) the diesel-electric switcher, (3) the diesel-electric passenger locomotive, (4) the diesel-electric freight locomotive, (5) the roller bearing, (6) the streamlined, lightweight passenger car, (7) the AB freight airbrake, (8) air conditioning, (9) car retarders, and (10) centralized traffic control. Taking this very small sample of innovations, I determined which firm was first to introduce each one and the size distribution of the innovators.[26]

The results, shown in Table 1, seem to support the Schumpeterean view. Almost all the innovators were among the ten largest firms, and

---

[24] Although there was some downward trend in $n(t)$ before 1930, it was relatively slight. Only after 1930 was there an appreciable drop. This would seem to be in accord with the hypothesis in the text, but another possible explanation is that it is very difficult to gauge the importance of recent inventions, and many important ones are omitted from the list. Moreover, the general decline in patenting may have been important too.

For some tentative results regarding the timing of innovations—not inventions—and their effect on investment, see E. Mansfield, "Timing of Innovation and the Investment Function," Carnegie Institute of Technology, 1963.

[25] K. Healy, "Regularization of Capital Investment in Railroads," in *Regularization of Business Investment*, Special Conference 4, Princeton for NBER, 1954.

[26] The innovator is defined as the first firm to introduce an innovation commercially. The identity of the innovator in each case was determined by a careful search of past issues of trade journals like *Railway Age*. Of course, there may be arguments over the definitions of "the innovation" and "commercially." Although it is possible that some of the information is incorrect, it is unlikely that there are any errors of real consequence.

TABLE 1

SIZE DISTRIBUTION OF INNOVATORS AND ALL CLASS I RAILROADS

Size of Firm (millions of ton-miles, 1920)	Number of:		
	Firms	Innovations[a]	Innovators
A. EACH SYSTEM REGARDED AS A UNIT			
Less than 4,000	77	0.0	0
4,001 – 8,000	6	0.0	0
8,001 – 12,000	7	0.0	0
12,001 – 16,000	8	3.0	3
16,001 – 20,000	3	0.5	1
20,000 and over	3	6.5	3
B. INDIVIDUAL CLASS I LINE-HAUL RAILROADS[b]			
Less than 4,000	159	1.0	1
4,001 – 8,000	9	0.0	0
8,001 – 12,000	12	2.0	2
12,001 – 16,000	4	1.0	1
16,001 – 20,000	1	0.5	1
20,000 and over	3	4.5	3

Source: See Section 5.

[a]When two firms began using an innovation at about the same time, the credit was split equally between them. Thus, fractions occur in this column.

[b]There is one less innovation in this part of the table than in the upper part, because one of the innovators, although part of a very large system, was not a Class I line-haul railroad.

about one-half were among the four largest. Moreover, although the largest four firms account for about 32 per cent of the industry's ton-miles, they account for 65 per cent of the innovations. Thus, if one assumes that these innovations are a representative sample, the largest four firms accounted for a significantly larger share than would be expected on the basis of their share of the freight traffic. By this criterion, their share of the innovations was disproportionately large.[27]

[27] The chances are less than .05 that the observed difference (between .65 and .32) is due to chance. Of course, no attempt is made to weight the small numbers of innovations included in Table 1 by their importance. Moreover, the smaller, less important innovations are excluded altogether. The results in Table 1 can only be regarded as a very rough, partial measure of the size distribution of the innovators. Note too that the criterion used to judge whether the largest firms' share is disproportionately large is not the only one that could have been used. But it seems to be a reasonable one.

In Table 1, two different definitions of a firm are used. In the upper panel, an entire system is regarded as a single unit. Thus, the firms are either entire systems or Class I line-haul railroads that do not belong to any system. In the lower panel, each Class I line-haul railroad is regarded as a single unit, whether or not it belongs to a system.

Next, consider a simple model designed to explain why the largest firms in some industries but not in others do a disproportionately large share of the innovating. Since this model, which I have described in more detail elsewhere,[28] seems to work reasonably well for other industries, it is of interest to determine how well it can explain our results for the railroads. Consider all innovations introduced during a given period in a particular industry which required, for their introduction, a minimum investment of I. Letting $\pi_j(I)$ be the proportion of these innovations introduced by the jth firm in this industry, the model assumes that

$$\pi_j(I) = \begin{cases} 0 & S_j \geq M \\ B_1(I) + B_2(I)S_j + E_j(I) & S_j \geq M \end{cases}, \tag{9}$$

where S_j is the size (measured in terms of assets) of the jth firm. Of course, $B_1(I)$, $B_2(I)$, and M vary among industries and time periods, $B_2(I)$ is non-negative, and $E_j(I)$ is a random error term.[29]

Firms below a certain size (M) introduce none of the innovations because they lack the volume of production required to use the innovation profitably.[30] For firms larger than M, we suppose that the proportion of these innovations introduced by a firm is a direct, linear function of its size. In addition, we assume that a firm's size has more effect on $\pi_j(I)$ if the innovations require relatively large investments than if they can be introduced cheaply. Consequently,

$$B_2(I) = a_1 + a_2 I / \bar{S}_M + z, \tag{10}$$

where $\bar{S}_M$ is the average assets of the firms with assets greater than or equal to M, a_2 is presumed to be positive, and z is a random error term.

It follows that the proportion of all the innovations carried out by the four largest firms equals

$$\pi = 4/N(M) + 4a_1(\bar{S}_4 - \bar{S}_M) + 4a_2\bar{I}(\bar{S}_4 - \bar{S}_M)/\bar{S}_M + z', \tag{11}$$

where $N(M)$ is the number of firms with assets greater than or equal to M, $\bar{S}_4$ is the average assets of the four largest firms, $\bar{I}$ is the average minimum investment required to introduce these innovations, and z'

[28] E. Mansfield, "Size of Firm, Market Structure, and Innovation," *Journal of Political Economy* (December 1963).

[29] It may turn out that $\pi_j(I)$ is a linear function of $S_j / \sum_{s_j > M} S_j$, rather than S_j. If so, the modifications required in the subsequent analysis are straightforward. See Mansfield, "Size of Firm."

[30] For simplicity, I assume that M is the same for all innovations. Although it complicates things, it is possible to allow for differences among innovations in M.

is a random error term.[31] Inserting estimates of a_1 and a_2 obtained from a study of the steel and petroleum industries,[32] we have

$$\pi = 4/N(M) + .0014(\bar{S}_4 - \bar{S}_M) + .0289I(\bar{S}_4 - \bar{S}_M)/\bar{S}_M + z'. \quad (12)$$

To what extent can this equation, based on experience in the steel and petroleum industries, predict the behavior of the largest four firms in the railroad industry? Since the value of π derived from Table 1 could, with reasonable probability, depart from the true value by as much as .25, simply because of sampling errors, it is clear that a test of this sort will not be very powerful. Nonetheless, it is worth carrying out. Ignoring z', the estimate of π obtained from Equation 12 is .54,[33] which is reasonably close to .65, the value of π derived from Table 1. Thus, taking account of the independent variables in Equation 12, it appears that, in comparison with other industries, the estimate of the largest four railroads' share of the innovations is higher than would be expected, but that the difference could easily be due to chance. Data of the sort presented in Table 1 will have to be gathered for more railroad innovations if we are to tell whether this difference is due merely to sampling variation or whether there is a real difference in this regard between the railroads and other industries.[34]

VI. Interfirm Rates of Diffusion

Once one firm introduced a new technique, how soon did others in the railroad industry come to use it? Apparently, twenty years or more elapsed before all major railroads began to use many of the important twentieth century innovations in locomotives, signaling, and yards. In particular, it took about fifteen years for the diesel locomotive,

[31] This also assumes that $\sum_j E_j(I) = 0$. Note that $\bar{S}_4$, $\bar{S}_M$, and I are expressed in millions of 1950 dollars.

[32] Mansfield, "Size of Firm, Market Structure, and Innovation." Of course there could be an identification problem in equation (11) (see my discussion in *ibid.*).

[33] To obtain this number, we needed rough estimates of M, $\bar{S}_M$, $\bar{S}_4$, and I. As a very rough estimate of M, 5 billion ton-miles in 1920 were used. (Although this is not measured in terms of assets, it makes no difference.) To estimate $\bar{S}_M$ and $\bar{S}_4$, the average ton-miles of (1) all firms with more than 5 billion ton-miles, and (2) the four largest firms were each multiplied by the average ratio of total assets to ton-miles for the ten largest firms. As a rough estimate of I, $1 million was taken. Although these estimates are crude they should not be too wide of the mark. To convert them from 1920 to 1950 dollars, they were multiplied by the ratio of the 1950 to the 1920 ENR construction index. Note too that systems are used here as individual firms.

[34] Note that there are sampling errors in the estimates of a_1 and a_2, as well as in in the estimate of π.

twenty-five years for the mikado locomotive, twenty years for the four-wheel trailing truck locomotive, twenty-five years for centralized traffic control, and thirty years for car retarders.[35]

What determines how rapidly a particular innovation spreads from one company to another? According to a simple model presented elsewhere,[36] the probability that a firm will introduce a new technique is an increasing function of the proportion of firms already using it and the profitability of doing so, but a decreasing function of the size of the investment required. Given these assumptions, and some additional ones of a technical nature,[37] it can be shown that

$$g_i^{-1} = u_0 + u_1 p_i + u_2 s_i + z_i'', \qquad (13)$$

where g_i is a measure of the rate of diffusion (the number of years that elapsed between the time when 10 per cent of the major firms had introduced the ith innovation and the time when 90 per cent had done so), p_i is a measure of the relative profitability of the ith innovation (the average payout period required to justify investments during the relevant period divided by the average payout period for investment in the ith innovation), s_i is a measure of the size of the investment required (the average initial investment in the innovation as a per cent of the average total assets of the firms), and z_i'' is a random error term.[38]

Inserting estimates of the u's based on data pertaining to a dozen innovations, the resulting equation is

$$g_i^{-1} = \begin{Bmatrix} -.066 \\ -.130 \\ -.118 \\ -.134 \end{Bmatrix} + \underset{(.034)}{.121 p_i} - \underset{(.0032)}{.0061 s_i} + z_i'', \qquad (r = .997) \qquad (14)$$

where the top figure in brackets pertains to the brewing industry, the next to bituminous coal, the following to iron and steel, and the bottom figure pertains to the railroads. Ignoring z_i'', this equation, which is plotted in Figure 5 for the railroad industry, can represent the data for

[35] E. Mansfield, "Technical Change and the Rate of Imitation," *Econometrica*, Oct. 1962, pp. 741–766; Healy, "Regularization of Capital Investment."
[36] Mansfield, "Technical Change."
[37] *Ibid.*, pp. 747–748.
[38] Actually, g_i is not used in *ibid.* as a measure of the rate of diffusion, but the measure used there is too complicated to be taken up here. The spirit and most of the substance of the original argument can be conveyed by using g_i, rather than the original measure. Equations 13 and 14 were derived from the original equations by using the theoretical relationship between g_i and the original measure.

Figure 5

Average Number of Years Between Introduction
of an Innovation by 10 Per Cent and 90 Per Cent
of Major Railroads, Given Relative Profitability
of Innovation (p) and Relative Size
of Necessary Investment (s)

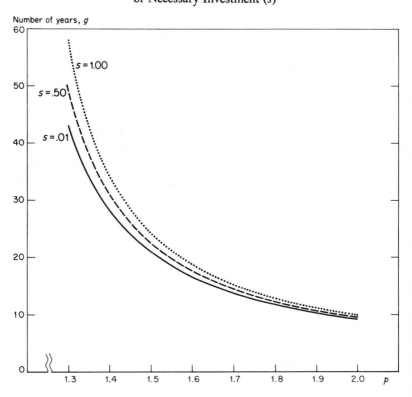

SOURCE: Equation 14.

these innovations very well. Apparently, for these innovations, differences in p_i and s_i explain almost all the variation in the rate of diffusion
within a particular industry.[39]

Comparing these various industries, p_i and s_i being held constant,
the average rate of diffusion in the railroad industry seems slower than

[39] Besides p_i and s_i, several additional variables were included—the durability of
old equipment, the rate of expansion of the industry, the phase of the business cycle
when the innovation was introduced, and a trend factor. Although the effects of all
of these factors on g_i seemed to be in the expected direction, none of them was
statistically significant.

in iron and steel, bituminous coal, and brewing. For example, if $p_i = 1.5$ and $s_i = .50$, the average time span between 10 and 90 per cent of full introduction seems to be six years shorter in steel than in the railroads, two years shorter in coal, and fourteen years shorter in brewing. However, although the difference between the railroads and brewing is highly significant, the differences among the railroads, coal, and steel could be due to chance. To the extent that they exist, these differences may be due in part to the conservatism of railroad management, the financial ill-health of the industry, and the attitude of railway labor.[40]

Finally, what sorts of railroads tend to be relatively quick to begin using new techniques, and what sorts tend to be relatively slow? To judge from data on the diffusion of fourteen innovations (five from the railroad industry), the speed with which a particular firm begins using a new technique is directly related to its size and the profitability of its investment in the technique. But a firm's rate of growth, its profit level, its liquidity, its profit trend, or the age of its management seem to have no consistent or close relationship with how soon a firm adopts an innovation. Moreover, in the railroad industry (and in most others that could be studied), only a relatively weak tendency existed for the same firms to be consistently the earliest to introduce different innovations. The leaders in the case of one innovation are quite often followers for another, especially if the innovations become available at widely different points in time.[41]

VII. Intrafirm Rates of Diffusion

The previous section is concerned with the rate at which firms in the railroad industry begin to use new techniques. This section examines

[40] For some discussion of the attitude of railway labor toward technological change, see W. Haber, "Technological Innovation and Labor in the Railway Industry," in *Technological Change and the Future of the Railways*, Evanston, 1961; and, in the same volume, G. Brown, "The Attitude of Labor Toward Technological Change in the Railway Industry." Also included in that volume are relevant papers by J. Nelson ("Technological Change and the Railway's Need for Capital") and W. Cottrell ("Sociological Barriers to Technological Change").

[41] For a detailed discussion of the factors influencing how rapidly a particular firm begins using a new technique, see E. Mansfield, "The Speed of Response of Firms to New Techniques," *Quarterly Journal of Economics*, May 1963. This study includes data on the iron and steel, bituminous coal, brewing, and railroad industries. Of course, there is no contradiction between the findings (1) that, holding the profitability of the innovation constant, the innovators tend to be large firms and (2) that there is only a fairly weak correlation between how rapidly a firm introduces one innovation and how rapidly it introduces another.

the influence of various factors on the intrafirm rate of diffusion,[42] the rate at which a firm, when it has begun to use a new technique, continues to substitute it for older methods. In particular, one of the most important recent innovations in railroading, the diesel locomotive, is singled out and a simple econometric model is described, which explains a considerable portion of the observed differences among railroads in the

TABLE 2

TIME INTERVAL BETWEEN DATES WHEN DIESEL LOCOMOTIVES
WERE 10 PER CENT AND 90 PER CENT OF ALL LOCOMOTIVES,
THIRTY CLASS I RAILROAD SYSTEMS

Time Interval (years)	Number of Class I Railroad Systems
14 or more	3
11-13	7
8-10	11
5- 7	3
3- 4	6
Total	30

Source: *Statistics of Railroads*, 1925-61.

Note: Among the 30 Class I railroad systems, entire systems are included as single units.

rate at which, after first introducing it, they substituted diesel motive power for steam.

Table 2 shows, for thirty randomly chosen Class I railroads, the number of years that elapsed between the time when each road's diesels constituted 10 per cent of its locomotive stock, and the time when they constituted 90 per cent of its locomotive stock. Although this is a crude measure of the intrafirm rate of diffusion, it is a reasonable first approximation. According to the table, there was great variation among railroads in that rate. Although nine years were required on the average to increase a firm's stock of diesels from 10 to 90 per cent of the total, six firms took only three or four years and three took fourteen years or more.[43]

[42] A more complete description of the results contained in this section is presented in E. Mansfield, "Intrafirm Rates of Diffusion of an Innovation," *Review of Economics and Statistics*, November 1963.
[43] Of course, this is a crude measure, for several reasons. First, it is based on ownership, not utilization, data. Second, it does not distinguish between various

The following model will help explain the differences. Let $D_i(t)$ be the number of diesel locomotives owned by the ith firm at time t, N_i be the number of steam locomotives owned by the firm before it began to dieselize, and r_i be the number of steam locomotives replaced by a single diesel. Assuming that the ith firm's traffic volume and r_i remain approximately constant during the relevant period,[44] the total number of locomotives owned by the ith firm at time t is

$$t_i(t) = N_i - (r_i - 1)D_i(t). \tag{15}$$

Since the firm will therefore employ N_i/r_i diesel locomotives when fully dieselized, there are $[N_i/r_i - D_i(t)]$ places left to be filled with diesels at time t.

Let ρ_i be the rate of return the ith firm could obtain by filling one of these places with a diesel locomotive (assuming for simplicity that this rate of return is the same for all places and all t); L_i be the time interval (in years) separating the year when the first firm (in this country) "began"[45] using diesel locomotives from the year when the ith firm "began" using them; S_i be a measure of its size (its freight ton-miles in 1949); and C_i be a measure of its liquidity at the time it "began" to dieselize (its current ratio). Letting

$$W_i(t) = [D_i(t + 1) - D_i(t)]/[N_i/r_i - D_i(t)], \tag{16}$$

we suppose that

$$W_i(t) = f(\rho_i, L_i, r_i D_i(t)/N_i, S_i, C_i, \ldots). \tag{17}$$

The rationale for this hypothesis is as follows: Other things equal, one would expect $W_i(t)$—the proportion of unfilled places that were filled with a diesel locomotive during the period—to be directly related to ρ_i and inversely related to the apparent riskiness of the investment. Since the latter cannot be measured directly, we assume: (1) the longer a firm waited before "beginning" to use the diesel locomotive, the more knowledge it had regarding its profitability when it "began" to dieselize; and (2) the nearer a firm was to full dieselization at time t (i.e., the

---

kinds of services, e.g., switching, freight. Third, it is based on the arbitrary choice of 10 and 90 per cent. If we use a better measure based on utilization data for freight service, however, we find there are still considerable differences among firms in the intrafirm rate of diffusion, although not so large as in Table 2. Moreover, the model described below is about as useful in explaining these data as those in Table 2.

[44] This is only a first approximation, but data indicate that it is reasonably accurate during the relevant period of time.

[45] The date when a firm "began" to dieselize is the date when 10 per cent of its locomotives were diesels.

greater was $r_i D_i(t)/N_i$, the less was its uncertainty at time t relative to its uncertainty when it "began" to dieselize. In addition, because the more liquid firms were better able to finance the necessary investment and to take the risks, one might expect them, all other things being equal, to have invested more heavily than other firms had. Finally, smaller firms might have been expected to convert to diesels more rapidly than larger ones because of the costliness of operating two kinds of motive power in a small system, because of the smaller absolute investment required to convert, and perhaps because of the quicker process of decision making in smaller units.

We assume that $W_i(t)$ can be approximated within the relevant range by a quadratic function of $\rho_i, L_i, \ldots, C_i$, but that the coefficient of $[r_i D_i(t)/N_i]^2$ is zero. Then, substituting the corresponding differential equation for the difference equation that results, and recognizing that $\lim_{t \to -\infty} D_i(t) = 0$, it can be shown that

$$4.39 Q_i^{-1} = \phi_0 + \phi_1 \rho_i + \phi_2 L_i + \phi_3 S_i + \phi_4 C_i + z_i''', \tag{18}$$

where z_i''' is a random error term and Q_i is the time interval between the date when 10 per cent of the ith firm's locomotives were diesels and the date when 90 per cent of them were diesels.[46] Using rough estimates of ρ_i,[47] it was possible to estimate the ϕ's, the result being

$$4.39 Q_i^{-1} = -.163 + .900\ \rho_i + .048\ L_i - .0028\ S_i + .115\ C_i, \tag{19}$$
$$\qquad\quad (.492) \qquad (.008) \qquad\ (.0023) \qquad (.040)$$

where z_i''' is omitted. About 70 per cent[48] of the variation among firms in the intrafirm rate of diffusion can be explained by the regression. Thus the model, simple and incomplete though it is, seems quite useful.[49]

---

[46] Actually, the analysis is carried out with another measure of the rate of diffusion, not Q_i. But using the theoretical relationship between this measure and Q_i, Equation 18 follows.

[47] These estimates were derived from correspondence with the firms. Each firm was asked to estimate the average payout period for the diesel locomotives it bought during 1946–57. The reciprocal of this payout period, which is a crude estimate of the rate of return, was used as an estimate of ρ_i.

[48] Strictly speaking, this percentage refers to the explained variation in the measure referred to in note 46, not to Q_i. See Mansfield, "Intrafirm Rates of Diffusion."

[49] Estimates were made of the effects on the intrafirm rate of diffusion (using both ownership and utilization data) of other variables besides ρ_i, L_i, S_i, and C_i. Specifically, I estimated the effect of: (1) the age distribution of the steam locomotives owned by the ith firm when it "began" to dieselize; (2) the absolute number of diesel locomotives that the ith firm had to acquire in order to go from 10 to 90 per cent of full dieselization; (3) the average length of haul of the ith firm; and (4) the profitability of the ith firm. With use of ownership data, the effect of none of these variables was significant. With use of utilization data, the age distribution of the steam locomotives had a significant effect, but the other variables did not.

VIII. Recent and Prospective Changes in Railroad Technology

In previous sections, I described measurements of the rate of technical change and presented theoretical and empirical results regarding the underlying processes of invention, innovation, and diffusion in the railroad industry, but little attention was paid to the specific improvements that have occurred recently in railroad technology. This section tries to fill the gap. It presents a brief list of the more important innovations that have come into limited or general use since World War II, and the innovations on the horizon that presidents of twenty-four Class I railroads regarded as potentially most important.[50]

First, consider the improvements in locomotives. During the postwar period almost all the nation's steam locomotives have been replaced by the vastly more economical diesel locomotive. Moreover, the diesel locomotive has been improved in a number of important ways. Tractive effort and horsepower have been increased, cooling systems have been improved, and electric circuits have been modified. In addition, experiments have been carried out by the Southern Pacific and the Denver and Rio Grande Western with diesel-hydraulic locomotives, which have proved useful in Europe.[51]

Second, consider the improvements in rolling stock, which has progressively increased in capacity and suitability for specific needs. Important developments in this area have been the three-tier, rack-type car for transporting autos, the mechanically refrigerated car, cars equipped with various shock-absorbing and lading-protection devices, cars using lubricating pads instead of oil-soaked waste packing, and hot box detectors. In addition, there has been the enormously successful use of piggybacking.

Third, consider the many applications of electronics to railroad operations. Whereas there was practically no use of radio immediately after World War II, it now is used between railroad offices, stations, moving trains, crews of different trains, and crews on the locomotive and caboose of the same train. In addition, over 8,000 miles of

---

[50] These lists were obtained by asking the presidents of thirty Class I railroads to list (1) the changes in railroad technology occurring since World War II they considered most important, and (2) the innovations likely to be introduced in the next decade and considered to be of considerable importance to the industry. Replies were received from twenty-four, or 80 per cent of the railroad presidents.

[51] On the diesel-hydraulic locomotive, see R. McBrian, "New Motive Power Technology," *Technological Change and the Future of the Railways*, Evanston, 1961.

microwave are now in service in the United States and Canada;[52] and electronic data processing equipment now is used in the area of accounting, payrolls, inventory and ordering work, car tracing and distribution, and equipment maintenance. Moreover, computers have made possible the application of various newly developed operations research techniques.[53] Centralized traffic control, first employed in the twenties, has been improved and its use has spread to over 31,000 miles of railroad. The automatic and semiautomatic classification yards, about forty of which are in operation in the United States, materially improved service and reduced operating costs.

Fourth, consider the improvements in track construction and maintenance. Probably the most important of these is the mechanization of maintenance of way, which has enabled the railroads to do with fifteen men what formerly required sixty.[54] In addition, there is the welding of rail sections to form continuous lengths of 1,000 feet or more, electronic and supersonic methods of testing rails, and improved techniques for preserving crossties.

Finally, considering innovations in railroad technology that are on the horizon (i.e., those likely to be introduced in the next decade), which, if any, are likely to be of considerable importance to the industry over the next few decades? In reply to this question, twenty-four presidents of Class I railroads gave the following answers. First, most of them listed the automated, crewless train, which is already being used in a limited way on local operations. Second, many listed new types of locomotives—the diesel hydraulic, locomotives powered by commercial electricity and eventually, perhaps, by nuclear power. Third, many listed the integral train; use of computers for simulation, train dispatching, etc.; automated freight car identification; and further containerizati on.

IX. Technical Change, Investment, and Prospective Employment

Supposing technical change in the railroad industry continues at its 1917–59 rate and that the industry's structure and work rules remain

[52] D. J. Russell, "United States Railroads: Developments, Problems and Opportunities," address before the International Railway Congress, June 22, 1962.

[53] E.g., E. Mansfield and H. Wein, "A Model for the Location of Railroad Classification Yard," *Management Science*, Apr. 1958; *idem*, "Linear Decision Rules and Freight Yard Operations," *Journal of Industrial Engineering*, Mar.–Apr. 1958; *idem*, "A Regression Control Chart for Costs," *Applied Statistics*, Mar. 1958; M. Beckmann, C. McGuire and C. Winsten, *Studies in the Economics of Transportation*, New Haven, 1956.

[54] These figures come from correspondence with the president of a major eastern road.

fixed, what will be the level of railroad employment by 1972? To help answer this question, we assume that the model in equations 1 and 2 held in the railroad industry during the past and that it continues to hold during 1960–72. Let us also assume that the estimates of λ, α, and δ derived in Section III are correct and will continue to be correct during 1960–72. If so, it follows that

$$\tilde{Q} = e^{-63.4}\tilde{L}^{.86}\left[\sum_{t=1840}^{1959} e^{.232t}I(t) + \tilde{I}\sum_{t=1960}^{1972} e^{.232t}\right]^{.14}, \tag{20}$$

where $\tilde{Q}$ is the output of the railroad industry in 1972 (1929 $=$ 100), $\tilde{L}$ is the total man-hours employed by the industry in 1972 (1929 $=$ 100), and $\tilde{I}$ is the annual gross investment (in millions of 1929 dollars).[55] Thus,

$$\ln \tilde{L} = .86^{-1}\left\{\ln \tilde{Q} + 63.4 - .14 \ln\left[\sum_{t=1840}^{1959} e^{.232t}I(t) + \tilde{I}\sum_{t=1960}^{1972} e^{.232t}\right]\right\}. \tag{21}$$

Using Equation 21 together with estimates of $\tilde{Q}$ and $\tilde{I}$, one can obtain conditional forecasts of $\tilde{L}$. Table 3 shows the values of $\tilde{L}$ associated with various levels of $\tilde{Q}$ and $\tilde{I}$.

What are reasonable estimates of $\tilde{Q}$ and $\tilde{I}$? According to forecasts made for this purpose by presidents of fourteen Class I railroads, $\tilde{Q}$ is likely to be about 144.[56] (These forecasts were expressed in terms of percentage increases over 1962, and the average forecast was a 19 per cent increase, the standard deviation being 9 percentage points.) With regard to $\tilde{I}$, use of 400 does not seem unreasonable; it is the average value of $I(t)$ during the late fifties (1954–59). Of course, these are only informed guesses, but what do they imply about $\tilde{L}$? To judge from Table 3, they imply that railroad employment in 1972 will be 35.7 per cent of its 1929 level, or 7 per cent less than its 1962 level.

How does this result compare with other sorts of forecast? According to forecasts made by the railroad presidents, employment in 1972 will be about 5 per cent below its 1962 level. (This is the average of their forecasts, and the standard deviation about this average was 12 percentage points.) Thus, their average forecast is not too different from

[55] I assume in Equation 19 that pre-1840 investment can be neglected and that gross investment can be assumed to occur at a constant rate during 1960–72. Moreover, rough estimates of $I(t)$ must be used for 1840–70, since Ulmer's figures go back only to 1870. Also, 5-year moving averages of $I(t)$ are used for 1870–1910 rather than the data for individual years used in previous sections of the paper. This should make little difference.

[56] These forecasts, like those described in the following paragraph in the text, were obtained from correspondence with the firms. The 1962 values of Q and L are estimates based on preliminary data.

TABLE 3

CONDITIONAL FORECASTS OF 1972 RAILROAD EMPLOYMENT, GIVEN 1972
RAILROAD OUTPUT AND AVERAGE ANNUAL GROSS INVESTMENT DURING 1962-72

Annual Investment (millions of 1929 dollars)	1972 Output					
	110	120	130	140	150	160
	1972 EMPLOYMENT (1929 = 100)					
400	26.1	28.8	31.7	34.5	37.4	40.3
600	24.5	27.1	29.7	32.4	35.1	37.8
800	23.4	25.9	28.4	31.0	33.6	36.2
	1972 EMPLOYMENT (1962 = 100)					
400	68	75	83	90	97	105
600	64	71	77	84	91	98
800	61	67	74	81	88	94

Source: Equation (21).

ours. However, if one uses the relatively crude, but common, procedure of extrapolating output per man-hour and dividing it into $\tilde{Q}$, the resulting forecast is that railroad employment in 1972 will be about 40.4 per cent of the 1929 level, or 5 per cent above its 1962 level.[57] This is appreciably higher than our forecast.

In conclusion, on the basis of these estimates of $\tilde{Q}$ and $\tilde{I}$, the model indicates that railroad employment will be 7 per cent below its 1962 level, if technical change continues at its 1917–59 rate. Any forecast of this sort should be taken with a generous grain of salt. First, the estimates of $\tilde{Q}$ and $\tilde{I}$ may be wrong. These variables are influenced by changes in factor prices, prices of competing means of transportation, consumer tastes, income levels, conditions in the money market, policies of regulatory agencies, and a host of other factors. To forecast $\tilde{Q}$ and $\tilde{I}$ is almost as difficult as to forecast $\tilde{L}$ itself.

Second, the production function in Equation 2 is obviously only a first approximation. For example, since economies of scale are omitted, the potential effects of the much-publicized, proposed mergers on employment are excluded. These effects are likely to be important. Third, it is assumed implicitly that the ratio of the amount of labor

---

[57] Extrapolating the regression of the logarithm of railroad output per man-hour on time, the resulting estimate of 1972 output per man-hour is 359 (1929 = 100). Dividing this estimate into the forecast of $\tilde{Q}$, we obtain 40.4 as an estimate of $\tilde{L}$.

employed to the minimum amount required to produce the forecasted level of output will be close to the ratio of actual to required employment in the past. If this ratio were to decrease, because of changes in union or public policy, the results would obviously be affected. However, the required correction might not be difficult to make.[58]

X. Summary and Conclusion

My purpose in this paper has been to estimate the rate of technical change in the railroad industry and to investigate the underlying processes of invention, innovation, and diffusion responsible for important changes in railroad practices. The principal results are as follows:

1. During 1890–1953, output per man-hour rose more rapidly in the railroad industry than in the economy as a whole but less rapidly than in all transportation. Comparing periods of relatively full employment, output per man–hour in the railroad industry rose at a relatively steady rate during that period.

2. On the assumption that technical change was capital embodied and neutral and that the production function was Cobb-Douglas, the rate of technical change in the railroad industry, defined as a shift over time in the production function, was about 3.0 per cent per year. This compares with Solow's estimate of 2.5 per cent per year for the economy as a whole.

3. To judge from Schmookler's chronology of railroad patents and important railroad inventions, there was a tendency, during 1870–1950,

---

[58] It is often asserted that there is a considerable amount of featherbedding in the railroad industry. If essentially useless "make work" accounted for a relatively stable proportion of the total time put in each year by labor, $L(t)$, which is an index number, will not be affected appreciably whether it is based on actual employment or minimum necessary employment. So long as the labor time not devoted to make "work" was allocated optimally among vintages of capital, the estimates in Table 3—as well as the estimates of λ in Section III—are unaffected by the presence of "make work." But if the latter were to be eliminated or cut substantially, the estimates in Table 3 would obviously be too high. Given any set of assumptions about changes in work rules, it should be possible to make at least an approximate correction. For some relevant discussions, see The Report of the Presidential Railroad Commission, Washington, 1962; and M. Horowitz, Manpower Utilization in the Railroad Industry, Boston, 1960.

Note too that we do not distinguish among various kinds of labor in this section. For a description of recent changes in the relative importance of various occupations, see W. Haber and others, Maintenance of Way Employment on U.S. Railroads, Detroit, 1957; and E. Jakubauskas', "Technological Change and Recent Trends in the Composition of Railroad Employment," Quarterly Review of Economics and Business, Nov. 1962.

for the rate of occurrence of these inventions to decrease with time, such a tendency being in accord with the Kuznets, Burns, and Fabricant hypothesis. There was also a tendency, in accord with Schmookler's hypothesis, for the rate of invention to be directly related to the lagged rate of capital formation in the railroad industry.

4. On the basis of a small sample of the most important innovations occurring in the twentieth century, the largest railroads seemed to do a disproportionately large share of the innovating, disproportionate in terms of their share of the industry's ton-miles. In part, this can be explained by the capital requirements needed to innovate, the minimum size of firm required to use the innovations, and the size distribution of the potential users.

5. When a new technique is introduced by one railroad, several decades usually elapse before all the others begin using it. As in other industries, the rate of imitation seems to be directly related to the profitability of the innovation and inversely related to the size of the investment required to introduce it. However, holding these factors constant, the imitation process seems to go on at a somewhat slower pace in the railroad industry than in the other industries for which we have data.

6. Judging by the diesel locomotive, the rate at which a railroad, once it begins to use a new technique, substitutes it for older methods is directly related to the profitability of the investment in the new technique, the length of time the firm waited before beginning to use it, and the liquidity of the firm; but the rate of substitution is inversely related to the size of the firm.

7. Some of the most important developments since World War II have been replacement of steam locomotives by diesels, the extension of piggybacking, use of larger and special-purpose cars, application of electronic data processing, the spread of centralized traffic control, development of automatic classification yards, and mechanization of maintenance of way.

8. According to twenty-four railroad presidents, the innovations on the horizon that are likely to be most important during the next few decades are the automated, crewless train, the integral train, the diesel-hydraulic locomotive, locomotives powered by commercial electricity, automated freight car identification, further use of computers, and further containerization.

9. If the production function continues to shift at the 1917–59 rate and if the railroads continue to invest in new plant and equipment at the 1955–59 rate, one can estimate the industry's 1972 labor requirements on the basis of forecasts of 1972 railroad output. Assuming for

the calculation a 19 per cent increase in output, which was the average forecast made by the railroad presidents, the results suggest that railroad employment in 1972 will be about 7 per cent below its 1962 level. This is fairly close to the average forecast made by the railroad presidents—that 1972 employment will be 5 per cent below its 1962 level. Note, however, that this assumes that no important mergers or changes in work rules take place.

Besides promoting a better understanding of the processes of innovation and technical change in the railroad industry, these findings may be useful in connection with the formulation of public policy. They provide information about the technical progressiveness, or backwardness, of the railroad industry relative to other industries. They provide employment forecasts which, despite their roughness, should be useful in indicating the extent of the future unemployment problem in the industry. They compare some aspects of the technological performance of large and small railroads, a relevant consideration in estimating the effect of the proposed railroad mergers on technical progress in the industry.

In conclusion, the limitations of these results should be emphasized. The model used in Sections III and IX is obviously only a crude first approximation. The data in Section IV have obvious weaknesses. The results in Sections V to VII are based on only a few innovations, which may not be entirely representative. Nonetheless, the findings should be helpful, if used with caution, to transportation economists and economists concerned with the processes of innovation and technical change.

The Determination of a Fair Return on Investment for Regulated Industries

M. J. PECK AND J. R. MEYER

YALE UNIVERSITY AND HARVARD UNIVERSITY

Introduction

Almost all common carrier transportation in the United States is
subject to profit control by regulatory commissions. The actual effect
of such profit control varies among transportation modes. For the
railroads, profits are set by competition, and the public statements of
ICC officials indicate that if they could think of an easy way to raise
rail profits they would. Motor carriers' rates, and hence profits, are set
largely by the level of rail rates. Airline earnings have on occasion, such
as the General Passenger Fare Investigation of 1956, been determined
by regulatory action. For pipelines, regulatory profit control is of more
importance. Finally, regulation is the dominant determinant of earnings in the regulated industries outside transportation, such as the
telephone and electric power industries.

Even though regulatory action plays a varying role in determining
earnings of the so-called public utility industries, it is obviously of
considerable practical importance. The purpose of this paper is to
examine various measures of profits which might guide a public agency
in determining the existence of inadequate or excess profits in a
regulated industry. Although profit standards for regulated industries
were a perennial topic for economists prior to the war, the subject has
been generally ignored since then.

The indifference of economists to regulatory standards may be
influenced in part by an increasingly widespread view that the proper
policy is the deregulation of the so-called regulated industries. We
think there is much merit in such a view; indeed, we have argued elsewhere the economic case for a substantial degree of deregulation of

the transportation industries. Nonetheless, we do not think the public utility concept completely outmoded; there are sectors of the economy where competition does not suffice to protect the public interest.[1] Furthermore, the process of removing regulation is at best a slow one; in the interim, how the regulated sector of the economy is managed is an important question.

Another source of economists' indifference may be the belief that the control of pricing rather than the control of profits should be the focus of regulation. Profit control, after all, not only has a very negative, perhaps anticapitalistic connotation, but also is a subject about which economic theory has had relatively little to say. By contrast, that theory has a great deal to say about a socially efficient set of prices as a mechanism to allocate resources, at least in the short run. But detailed regulatory control of prices in practice tends to be unworkable, especially in achieving efficiency objectives. The record of the ICC suggests that managerial freedom to set prices would produce a closer approximation to the economists' efficiency norm, at least under present circumstances, than regulation.[2]

Economists also may believe that economic analysis has nothing new to contribute to the topic of a "fair" return. We believe, on the contrary, that economic analysis has at least two important points to make. First, concepts in capital theory clearly demonstrate that measures of profits traditionally used in regulation (such as rate-of-return on original or reproduction cost of equipment) contain inherent biases which will understate or overstate true returns, basically because these usual measures do not take explicit account of the timing in the pattern of profits and the economic longevity of equipment. Second, economic analysis can provide a framework for recognizing the impact of both the changing value of the dollar and improvements in the productivity of capital equipment. Inflation deserves an explicit treatment in regulatory decisions in order to protect the adequacy of service by insuring funds for new and replacement equipment, and to recognize

---

[1] The technology and cost structure of many transportation activities do not preclude competition nor fit the economists' concept of natural monopoly. This is in sharp contrast to the electric power, gas, and water industries, where duplicating service is clearly wasteful. Indeed, a reasonably high level of competition already prevails in the transportation industry and, if not inhibited by government regulations, even more competition would almost unquestionably come into being very quickly.

[2] This leaves untouched a third aspect of regulation, control of costs. Our analysis omits this problem. For a recent and stimulating discussion on certain aspects of this problem, see Harvey Averch and Leland L. Johnson, "Behavior of the Firm under Regulatory Constraint," *American Economic Review*, LII, 2, Dec. 1962, pp. 1052–1069.

the equitable interest of investors in their real income. At the same time, explicit thought should be given to the distribution of the gains of new technology between consumer and investor. The regulatory literature now gives little recognition to the problem.

We take as our starting point for this exploratory investigation the proposition that regulation is a substitute for competition in protecting the public interest. This proposition underlies most of the judicial and legal action as well as most writing on regulation. While competition may not always produce optimum results, and regulation may aim at other goals than simulating competition, the record of regulatory efforts and of competition in numerous sectors of the U.S. economy suggests that competition produces a rough optimum, and the results of competition are, in the long run, the most workable standard for the administration of the regulated sectors of a free enterprise economy. A regulated firm operating in a competitive environment must buy its supplies at prices set by competition; it compensates its employees at wage levels commensurate with those in nonregulated industries, and, however protected its position within the industry, it competes for consumer's dollars against the nonregulated competitive industries. Most importantly, a regulated firm buys its capital at prices set in economy-wide capital markets. Any return to investors persistently below those established in the capital markets for the nonregulated firms will eventually create difficulties in attracting capital to the regulated firms and industries. The process of regulation in a free enterprise economy, therefore, must include recognition of the fact that a regulated firm and industry will follow the trends of prices, wages, and profits in the rest of the economy.

We would stress that our analysis is illustrative and tentative. The concepts used require further development and clarification prior to actual application. Moreover, our concentration upon the measurement of profits does not reflect a belief that any such measurement can substitute in the regulatory process for an examination of the risks and profit needs of an industry in terms of investment requirements and financial acceptability, or for an examination of the equitable claims of consumers against excess profits and the investors for an adequate income. Clearly it is the final impact of regulation in meeting these claims and requirements which is paramount rather than the results in terms of any one measure of profit.[3]

[3] The Supreme Court has stated "It is not the theory but the impact of the rate order which counts." See Federal Power Commission vs. *Hope Natural Gas Co.*, 320 U.S. 591 at 601–602. See also Atchison, *Fair Reward and Just Compensation*, 1954, Chapter II.

Measures of the Rate of Return

RATE OF RETURN ON A RATE BASE

The most widely used approach to a regulatory determination of reasonable profits has been through the measurement of profits as a percentage of a rate base. Two distinct definitions of the rate base are in wide use: reproduction cost—defined as the current cost of reproducing the capital equipment; and original cost—defined as the historical cost of the equipment plus working capital and minus accrued depreciation (roughly equivalent to average historical net investment).[4]

Original cost is primarily an equity concept, based upon the rationale that the investor has made a specific commitment of funds upon which he is entitled to a stipulated rate of return. Original cost also has a concreteness which facilitates administration. Such administrative convenience became a paramount consideration in the thirties when the literal interpretation of reproduction cost threatened the breakdown of effective regulation.

In a period of changing prices, however, neither the investor nor the consumer are likely to be well served by the original cost approach. The equity investor under such circumstances receives essentially a fixed monetary and a declining real return unless the permitted regulatory rate of return is promptly altered with changing price levels. Furthermore, unlike that for the bondholder, the fixed monetary return for equity holders in regulated industries is created by the regulatory process rather than by a clearly understood contract. The consumer, though, realizes at least short-run gains from the reduction in the real value of the investor's return.

However, these short-run gains of the consumer are achieved through earnings insufficient to maintain adequate service in the long run. Once it becomes clear that the equity investor in a regulated industry can receive only a fixed monetary return, equity investments normally will be forthcoming only with extremely high average returns. In the transitional period from the current return to a higher return,

---

[4] Long-term debt plus net worth represents a variation of the depreciated original cost rate base. It does have the additional advantage of being based directly on accounting records and frees the regulatory process from the necessity of a physical inventory for equipment. It also takes automatic recognition of working capital which is, however, generally included in the other two rate bases. All subsequent comments made about the depreciated, original-cost rate base apply virtually without modification to long-term debt, plus net worth.

the regulated industry is likely to be starved for capital necessary for expansion. The probable final result of such developments for the consumer will be both higher prices to pay a higher average return (to compensate the equity investor for risks which are not offset by any possibility of increased returns) and transitional periods of inadequate service. There is the further danger that the existence of inadequate service and the necessity of a higher rate of return may never be recognized, so that the consumer is perpetually deprived of sufficient capacity and the technologically best equipment.

It was this aspect of inflation that led to the introduction of the reproduction cost concept in the 1920's. Reproduction cost, by increasing profits in an inflationary period, will contribute to the maintenance of long-run adequate service. It provides an "automatic" solution to the problem of earnings dilution caused by the disparity between old and new investment costs in a period of changing price levels. Reproduction cost also treats alike companies with a different timing in their pattern of purchasing equipment. Uniformity can be important here because under conditions of secular inflation, failure to use reproduction cost or some other price correction is likely to inhibit most the earnings of those who most need to raise outside capital, i.e., firms with the oldest equipment.

Profits, however, are a smaller source of funds for purchasing new equipment in most regulated industries than the funds generated by depreciation. The underlying notion of a depreciation allowance is a flow of funds that will enable a firm to maintain its capital stock. If the prices of equipment are unchanged and the life of the equipment is estimated correctly, then depreciation practices based on original or historical cost achieve this objective. Obviously, though, price changes nullify the concept of original cost depreciation just as they eliminate the utility of an original cost rate base in regulating profits. If prices are rising, original cost depreciation may be insufficient to replace equipment, so that reinvestment either from new funds or retained earnings is required merely to maintain capital stocks at present levels.[5] This problem is not peculiar to the regulated industries, but the nonregulated companies can to some extent offset a depreciation deficiency with the higher profits which usually accompany inflation.

[5] Strictly speaking, this will hold true .only in declining or stagnant situations because, in expanding industries, price increases will be offset at least partly by depreciation expenses rising more rapidly than replacement needs. The depreciation allowance pertains under expansionary circumstances to a larger capital stock than replacement needs because of the lag between initiating depreciation charges and actual replacement.

Regulated companies do not have this option unless regulatory action is unusually prompt and perceptive.

While the determination of depreciation by reproduction cost faces up to the problems of inflation, the approach has had a dismal history in regulatory practice. During the 1920's, reproduction cost was interpreted so literally by regulatory commissions that existing equipment was assumed to be reproduced even if the equipment was obsolete, and more efficient and lower cost processes were available. This deprived the consumer of all technological gains. Furthermore, the establishment of reproduction cost relied upon the testimony of expert witnesses as to the current costs of reproduction; a cumbersome and subjective procedure that often better served the welfare of expert witnesses than consumers.

THE OPERATING RATIO AS A MEASURE OF PROFITS

The public utility industries in which many regulatory practices were first formulated were, at least historically, relatively risk free. As a result, regulation could ignore the possibility of losses and concentrate on profits. When regulation was extended to the more competitive transport sectors of motor trucking and buses, the economic character of these industries required some explicit recognition of risk. In this context the operating ratio approach was evolved, utilizing as a regulatory standard of reasonable profits the ratio of expenses to gross revenue.[6]

The rationale of the operating ratio primarily insures that short-run, unforeseen developments do not result in costs approaching or exceeding revenues so as to sharply reduce or eliminate profits. This arises in motor trucking and bus transport for two reasons: first, both expenses and revenues show relatively large year-to-year changes; second, the gap between revenues and operating expenses is extremely small. This last arises from the fact that capital is a small part of the total production process.[7]

[6] For example, if an operating ratio of 93 per cent in motor carriers serves to indicate a reasonable profit, when expenses are more than 93 per cent of revenues, a rate increase is indicated, and when expenses are less, a rate decrease is indicated.

[7] For example, the operating ratio in electric utilities (the prototype of the traditional utility involving large amounts of capital per sales dollar) in the decade 1946 to 1959 varied from a low of 83.3 to a high of 86.6—a range of 3.3 per cent—whereas buses with a small capital input per unit of sale varied from a low of 88.1 to a high of 96.1 per cent—a range of 8 per cent. In addition to a wider range in the variation of the operating ratio, the same variation in operating ratio causes a larger fluctuation in profits in an industry like buses than in electric utilities. For example, the same absolute change in operating ratio for electric utilities and buses from 1948 to 1949 (2.2 per cent) caused bus profits per unit of sales to decrease 26 per cent, whereas the electric utility profits decreased only 12 per cent.

In the operating ratio approach to regulation, profits provide a margin against financial crisis; that is, an insurance premium against unexpected losses. In the bus and trucking industry, given the breadth of the allowed safety margin, profits usually have remained sufficient to meet the extremely small capital requirements of the industry.

Though often suggested, a wider use of the operating ratio approach to regulation is undesirable for at least two reasons. First, it ignores the important problem of capital requirements which, as stated above, is a minor matter in the bus and trucking industries, but not for most other regulated industries. Second, there is no reason why a safety margin may not be provided by an adjustment in the rate of return. In fact, the historical explanation for the use of the operating ratio approach in the motor carrier industry may have been a reluctance to directly set a rate of return sufficiently large to compensate the investors for the risks involved. Aside from such considerations of administrative hesitancy, there is no reason why regulatory agencies should not recognize that some regulated industries involve very high risks and hence should be allowed to earn a rate of return greatly in excess of other regulated industries with lesser risk.

FINANCIAL RATE OF RETURN

The profit measures just outlined all share a common defect: they include no explicit recognition of the time element in investment. The time element can be explicitly recognized through the use of the discounted present value formula. Assuming that an investment is made at one point in time and is independent of all other relevant investment possibilities, and assuming that interest is compounded at regular intervals, the present value formula can be expressed in simple notational form as:

$$V = \sum_t P_t/(1 + r)^t$$

where V represents the present value of the investment; P_t indicates the annuity or profit or be realized at future time t; r stands for the interest rate; and t indicates the number of interest computation periods that separate the present (or point of investment time) from the time of the profit realization. It should be noted that P represents the *total cash return* (in a given time period) to be realized from the investment so it is *not* net of depreciation expense.

The traditional application of the discounted present value formula has been to determine the profitability of an investment in capital budgeting decisions. In this context, there are alternative procedures.

One procedure (the so-called benefit-cost ratio approach) is to compute present value just as above and then compare this with the cost of the investment; if present value exceeds cost (the benefit-cost ratio exceeds unity), the investment is considered profitable at the accepted or going rate of interest employed in the formula. The second procedure is to use the cost of the investment in place of present value in the left-hand side of the equation and to solve the equation for r which then is considered to be the earnable rate of return rather than the interest rate. If the rate of return computed in this fashion is greater than the interest rate, the investment is considered to be profitable.

Since different results can be obtained by using these alternative approaches to capital budgeting, considerable controversy exists about their relative merits.[8] In general, if maximization of V is the basic objective (which would seem to be quite plausible if consumer sovereignty is accepted), then the benefit-cost ratio will yield the best results in the widest variety of circumstances. Neither approach is infallible, even in pursing narrowly and correctly stipulated objectives, if the simplifying "point of time" and independence assumptions are eliminated; with interdependence between different investments over time, more complex techniques are required.[9]

The rate-of-return approach also suffers from a specific limitation; multiple solutions can exist for the present value formula when solved for r (the usual algorithm being Newton's approximation), specifically when P assumes negative values over some part of the time horizon. This limitation, together with the fact that the benefit-cost approach better serves the more plausible objective function, suggests that the rate-of-return calculation is the less useful of the two possibilities for capital budgeting purposes.

These limitations, however, are not serious objections to the use of the rate-of-return approach in regulatory problems. The multiple solution characteristic of rate-of-return calculations is not a real disability because the established "fair rate of return" is in practice an approximation to the correct answer, thus supplying outside information for choosing between different solutions where more than one exists. In fact, as long as the benefit-cost ratio exceeds unity at a zero rate of interest (i.e., the simple sum of benefits exceeds the simple sum of costs)

[8] Excellent discussions of these problems can be found in Jack Hirschiefer, "On the Theory of Optimal Investment Decision," *Journal of Political Economy*, August 1958, pp. 329–352; and *Management of Corporate Capital*, Ezra Solomon, ed., Glencoe, Ill., 1954.

[9] S. Marglin, *A Linear Programming Approach to Dynamic Capital Budgeting*, Rotterdam, 1962.

the "correct" rate of return will almost invariably be the lowest positive solution rate.

Once this is recognized, it is also obvious that the two capital budgeting approaches are usually identical when applied to regulatory decisions. If the rate-of-return approach is used, the calculation simply reduces to determining whether the lowest positive (or otherwise correct) solution rate is above or below the established "fair rate." Of course, if the benefit-cost approach were employed directly, the procedure would be to determine whether the benefit-cost ratio were above or below unity at the established fair rate.[10]

As long as the two approaches yield the same result, the rate-of-return approach has the advantage of being more in keeping with established regulatory traditions. Like the current practice, it involves computing a rate of return under an established rate structure and then comparing this with what is considered to be a just or equitable rate of return for investors in regulated enterprises. If the computed r is greater than the desired "just" return, the required regulatory action is to adjust tariffs downward, and thereby the P term as well, to make r equal to the established standard. Conversely, a rate of return beneath the target rate calls for regulatory action to increase P, usually by upward rate adjustments, to a point where the computed r equals the standard or accepted r.

Definitional Problems Encountered in Computing Rates of Return and Operating Ratios

Definitional problems have been a major difficulty in the regulatory use of either rate-of-return or operating ratio formulas. Indeed, a good part of the voluminous record in protracted rate hearings is devoted to disputes over definitions.

Two key definitional problems in computing gross returns on profits for regulated industries are, first, whether capital gains on inventories, fixed assets, and other investments should be counted; and second, whether returns realized on nonregulated, by-product operations should be considered in regulatory proceedings.

[10] To put the argument somewhat differently, the distinction between the rate-of-return and the benefit-cost approaches to capital budgeting are the different *rankings* of capital outlays that the two approaches yield, and these rankings are irrelevant in the regulatory context. What counts for regulation is whether the existing set of facts pertaining to only *one* investment situation are consistent with an adequate compensation to capital.

The capital gains problem as it occurs in defining gross return can be divided into two subproblems: (1) capital gains or losses realized in the course of normal operations from price level changes on the capital goods and inventories employed in the regulated production process, and (2) capital gains or losses realized on the basis of speculation in the commodities and capital goods employed by the regulated industries. Normal capital gains or losses of the first type ought to be built into the rate base and regulatory calculations, since such capital changes are as integral a part of furnishing utility services as operating costs.

For the second type of capital gains the obvious test is whether entry into the speculative activity that yields the gain or loss is restricted by grant of public franchise. If entry into speculative activities is open to both regulated and nonregulated firms, the profits and losses from these activities should be considered beyond regulatory purview. To illustrate, the grant of a unique franchise to operate an airline between two urban centers does not bestow on an airline an exclusive right to engage in speculation in plane prices. Not only can airlines operating between other points engage in such speculation but also private firms outside the airline industry can join in the speculation. Excluding speculative capital gains and losses, it might be noted, considerably simplifies the administrative problem facing regulatory agencies.

On the other hand, this simple test only applies to speculative activities sufficiently limited not to jeopardize the financial stability of the regulated firms or industries. The mass speculation that characterized substantial parts of the electric utilities industry in the 1920's must inevitably be passed on to consumers, either through higher rates to bail out the speculators or through inadequate service from bankrupt companies. The better remedy here, however, is direct control of financing or refinancing rather than through adjustments in profit measures.

The by-product or subsidiary activity problem—such as when railroads own hotels, oil wells, and timber lands—is relatively easy to solve analytically. Again, the test is whether the grant of a public utility franchise bestows upon the firm substantial market power in another sector of the economy. Such would be the case where the by-product can be economically manufactured only in conjunction with the supply of the regulated service. Of course, if the revenues of nonregulated activities are excluded from regulatory calculations, so too should be their costs and related productive assets.

While the principle is obvious, there may be substantial difficulties in practice. Often it is necessary to establish meaningful transfer prices between the regulated and nonregulated activities of the firm. Otherwise, a regulated firm might render services to a subsidiary at inordinately low prices, or conversely, purchase at inordinately high prices, thus redistributing profits from the regulated to the nonregulated sector of the firm's activities. Considerations of this kind are central to many regulatory disputes in the telephone industry.

In essence, the problem of defining costs is one of broader significance in regulatory proceedings when there is a less than competitive market for certain of the factors utilized in the production process. Without a competitive market it is, by definition, difficult to establish a going market price to use as the "cost" paid by the regulated firm. In extreme cases, the only recourse is to assume that a "fair price" represents costs of production plus a "fair return," thus placing the industries supplying regulated industries in much the same situation as the regulated industries themselves. In less extreme cases, such as the bilateral oligopoly that characterizes the equipment markets for some utilities and airlines, extending regulation is presumably not worth the effort, and it is better to rely on competition despite its imperfections.

Somewhat more tangible are the problems of defining appropriate depreciation charges for regulated industries. For example, there is considerable reluctance to count depreciation expenses as a cost when gross assets is used as the denominator of the rate-of-return ratio. (It is usually agreed that depreciation should be counted as an expense when net fixed assets is employed as the rate base.)

One approach to solving this definitional problem is to compare the results obtained by including or excluding depreciation with those obtained by using the present value formula. In general, results obtained from the established regulatory measures can be converted into present value equivalents and thus directly compared with each other and with the rate of return found from the present value formula. Such a set of comparisons is shown diagrammatically in Figure 1 for a case in which the rate of return calculated using the present value formula is 10 per cent. The upper hyperbolic-shaped function indicates the gross profit (on gross investment) return that must be earned in order that a 10 per cent financial rate of return on capital be realized. Similarly, the lower function indicates the rate of return that must be earned when using net profit (that is, when depreciation, calculated on a straight-line basis, is included as an expense, and gross investment is still used as the base) to obtain the 10 per cent financial return.

In general, if depreciation is counted as an expense, the rate-of-return ratio, with gross assets as a base, underestimates the true return.

Figure 1

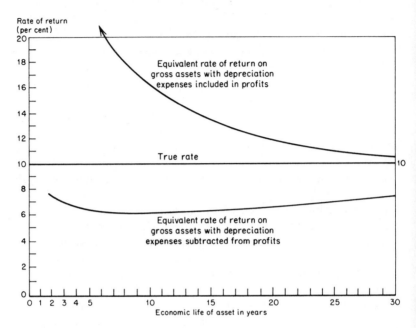

Conversely, if depreciation expense is not subtracted, the reported returns are overestimated. Which of the two functions deviates least from the "true financial rate" depends on the economic life of the equipment involved. Both give reasonably good results if the durability of the equipment is great enough, for the functions converge on the true rate as the length of equipment life increases. For equipment of very low durability, the deduction of depreciation expense yields answers closer to the true rate. At an intermediate range of durability, the retention of depreciation expense in the returns yields better estimates than its subtraction. As a rule, as the expected equipment life increases, the gross profit ratio converges to the true rate more quickly than the net profit ratio.

The preceding propositions have been based on a straight-line computation of depreciation expenses. With a declining-balance computation of depreciation, the analysis is slightly more complicated. Different effects can be achieved by the declining-balance method depending on the age distribution of the equipment stock and the relative productivity of the equipment in different periods of its life span. In the simplest case, declining-balance depreciation might accurately reflect declining productivity of the equipment. Under such circumstances, changes over time in revenue and depreciation expense would roughly cancel, yielding a good approximation of a constant annuity. This, of course, is a special case and could not be expected to hold as a general rule.

It is useful to note that the different results obtained from various regulatory rate-of-return formulas can be readily converted into one another and also into the true financial return. Accordingly, the choice of the particular measure used for regulatory purposes does not matter if it is made with a knowledge of these transformation relationships. For reference, a number of transpositions between measures of profitability on a gross asset base, with and without depreciation counted as an expense, and the financial rate of return have been brought together in Table 1.

Depreciation charges play a quite different role when operating ratios are the basis of regulation. The central consideration is the relationship of depreciation expenses to total costs, since the main economic

TABLE 1

RATES OF RETURN ON GROSS ASSETS, WITH AND WITHOUT
DEPRECIATION EXPENSE COUNTED IN PROFITS[a], COMPARED
WITH GIVEN FINANCIAL RATES OF RETURN FOR DIFFERENT LIVES
(per cent)

Financial Rate of Return[b] (years of economic life)	4 Per Cent		8 Per Cent		10 Per Cent	
	With DE	Without DE	With DE	Without DE	With DE	Without DE
2	53.0	3.0	56.1	6.1	57.6	7.6
4	27.6	2.6	30.2	5.2	31.5	6.5
6	19.1	2.4	21.7	5.0	23.0	6.3
10	12.3	2.3	14.9	4.9	16.3	6.3
15	9.0	2.3	11.7	5.0	13.2	6.5
20	7.4	2.4	10.2	5.2	11.7	6.7
30	5.8	2.5	8.9	5.6	10.6	7.3
40	5.1	2.6	8.4	5.9	10.2	7.7
50	4.7	2.7	8.2	6.2	10.1	8.1

[a]Depreciation expense estimated by straight-line methods.

[b]As estimated by using the present value formula.

rationale for the use of the operating ratio is the provision against bankruptcy and capital exhaustion from short-run fluctuations in profits. If the ratio of depreciation expense (and indeed of other book charges as well) is large relative to total cost, the firm has a cushion against sudden swings in revenue. Relatively large negative accounting profits are not accompanied by a cash drain on company funds unless revenue falls below total cost minus book charges. Thus, a high rate of book charges to total costs reduces the probability of cash drains because of random fluctuations in profit levels.

Another definitional question bedevilling rate-of-return calculations is whether unadjusted gross fixed assets or gross fixed assets minus depreciation reserves (net fixed assets) should be employed as the rate base. When net fixed assets are used as the base, it is usually accepted that depreciation expenses should first be subtracted from profits before computing the ratio and this procedure will be assumed throughout the following discussion. Defined as the ratio of net profits to net fixed assets, the rate of return becomes a good approximation of what is commonly known in capital budgeting procedures as net return on average investment. This is simply the ratio of profits after taxes and depreciation to one half the total investment. Indeed, the two measures should yield roughly identical results in the long run, that is, when averaged over the complete life of the assets involved.

When compared with the time rate of return obtained by using the present value formula, the net return on average investment uniformly overestimates the profitability of an investment (when profits are assumed to be evenly spread over the economic life of the equipment and straight-line depreciation is used). This overestimate is not too serious when economic life is short and when the correct rate of return is low, but it becomes progressively worse as economic life is extended and the true rate of return increases. These results are illustrated in Table 2.

Furthermore (again assuming straight-line depreciation and the even spread of profits over expected economic life), the use of net fixed assets as a rate base underestimates the true return during the early years after a re-equipment period and overestimates the true return toward the end of equipment life or just before a new re-equipment period occurs. When investments in equipment are made only at widely spaced periods in time, and then in very concentrated amounts, the average or long-term rate of return indicated in Table 2 will be realized as an instantaneous (i.e., a particular annual) rate of return only at the mid-point between re-equipment periods. Rates of return computed on net fixed assets under such circumstances will essentially

TABLE 2

RATE OF RETURN[a] ON AVERAGE INVESTMENT OR ON
NET FIXED ASSETS WITH A UNIFORM AGE DISTRIBUTION
FOR EQUIPMENT WITH GIVEN FINANCIAL RATE OF RETURN
AND ECONOMIC LIFE
(per cent)

Economic Life (years)	Financial Rate of Return[b] (per cent)			
	4	8	10	12
2	4.03	8.1	10.2	12.2
4	4.08	8.3	10.5	12.7
6	4.13	8.5	10.8	13.1
10	4.24	8.9	11.4	14.0
15	4.36	9.4	12.2	15.0
20	4.50	9.9	12.8	16.0
30	4.74	10.7	14.1	17.6
40	4.98	11.5	15.1	18.8
50	5.21	12.1	15.9	19.7

[a]Net of depreciation expense estimated on a straight-line basis.
[b]As estimated from the present value formula.

follow a sawtooth pattern; right after re-equipment the rate of return will drop sharply and then rise slowly in a linear fashion until it reaches a peak just before the new re-equipment period. At this point, the instantaneous rate of return will again drop and the process will be repeated. Furthermore, for growth industries, like the telephone industry and many utilities, a net fixed asset base will persistently underestimate the true financial rate.

Other biases, of course, may occur if profits are not uniformly distributed over the life of an asset or if straight-line depreciation is not used. For example, if gross profits decline more rapidly than depreciation allowances accrue, the rate of return computed on net fixed assets would in the long run underestimate the true rate of return. The instantaneous rate-of-return problem also still exists; the ratios of profits to net fixed assets under such circumstances would tend to be too great in the early years and too low in the later years.

Similarly, if net fixed assets decline more rapidly than profits, a rate of return based on net fixed assets will result, on the average, in an even more serious overestimate of true profitability than when profits are spread evenly over economic life; in the early years of the investment the average lifetime return will be very much underestimated while in the late years, just before re-equipment, the converse will hold true. This situation may occur when the introduction of new equipment is associated with learning costs that reduce profits in the early years of an investment.

Another question often raised in defining the rate base is whether working capital should be included. The usual practice has been to include it when the depreciated value of the equipment is employed as the rate base but not when gross original or replacement value is used. As a general rule, it would seem preferable to include working capital as part of the rate base and specifically recognize that it has a different economic life than physical equipment (i.e., it usually has a salvage value of 100 per cent). Working capital is as important a part of the production process as any other kind of investment and to omit it is the same as omitting part of the required investment needed to earn whatever profit is realized.

In addition, separate treatment probably should be given to returns on working capital because such investments are usually relatively liquid and consequently open to substantially less risk exposure than fixed investments in equipment. In other words, everything else equal, a regulatory body could justify a somewhat lower rate of return on total investment, including working capital, for industries with a substantially higher than average proportion of their assets in working capital.

A final class of definitional problems arises if reproduction costs rather than original costs are used as a rate base. Determination of reproduction cost necessitates a definition of the unit of productive capacity to be reproduced, which in turn raises the question of the treatment of technological change.

Regulatory agencies usually have defined reproduction costs in terms of reproducing the specific equipment now in use, thus excluding the effect of technical change. Strictly applied, reproduction cost could mean, for example, asking such irrelevant questions as what it would cost today to manufacture a DC-3, a boxcar without roller bearings, and interstate buses without diesel engines. It would be better to frame the reproduction cost question directly in terms of what it costs to create equipment capable of producing a specific unit of output. This would avoid a host of irrelevancies in rate cases, as well as a strong tendency toward reserving most of the gains of technological change for producers.

Of course, defining the appropriate unit of output is not always easy. First, a number of dimensions are usually needed to properly or fully define output in a service industry like transportation; e.g., in passenger services some distinction usually must be made between seat-miles of capacity for different trip lengths, since equipment efficient at one trip length may be very different in many important respects from that efficient at other lengths. Second, changes in technology alter the inherent properties of individual "capacity units" over time. For instance, faster plane speeds clearly make a passenger seat-mile of capacity in a jet worth more than a passenger seat-mile of capacity in a DC-3. This raises the question of how these gains should be distributed.

In general, administrative convenience and equity are usually both well served by adopting some conventional and simple measure of output and adhering to it with reasonable consistency. If reproduction costs are controlled in terms of producing equipment capable of a certain output of services, the usual consequence will be to split technological gains between producers and consumers in, admittedly, some rough and ready fashion. This occurs because most (though certainly not all) technological improvements result in producing a better product at lower cost. For example, jets produce a faster service for consumers and lower operating costs for airlines; similarly, roller bearings in boxcars result in a more dependable service for shippers and lower operating costs for railroads; and heavy diesel buses usually have superior riding and other comforts as well as lower operating costs.

At a minimum, defining reproduction cost in terms of a constantly improving service unit rather than in terms of actually reproducing a specific piece of equipment is a way of increasing the probability of transmitting to the consumer some share of the technological gains. Since reasonable profits and prices could be computed on the most efficient and newest equipment, a service-unit approach to computing reproduction cost also would provide a built-in incentive for managements to adapt to technological change. Furthermore, the administrative difficulties in the strict reproduction-cost approach are largely eliminated.

The use of a simple index of the production cost of an ever-improving unit of output is not, however, an automatic cure-all. Depending on the particular character of technological advance in an industry and the type of price index employed, the gains will be shared differently by the different participants. It remains a central problem to decide whether the results are equitable.

Despite the difficulties in computing capital reproduction costs, the effort would seem well worthwhile as long as it is accepted as a regulatory objective that the capital stock of a regulated industry should be maintained. At the very minimum, reference should be made to some sort of general price index for capital goods even if a specific index for the regulated industry appears impossible to construct. The only alternative to making a determination of capital costs is to adjust the rate of return upward when price increases occur; but these will provide only rough approximations of actual requirements unless the adjustments are based on cost and price indexes.

Some Empirical Applications

On the basis of the preceding analysis, the simplest way to construct somewhat improved estimates of rates of return from normally available balance sheets and income statements would be to: (a) use as a rate base the sum of stockholders' equity (paid-in capital and surplus, retained earnings, etc.), long-term debt, and accrued depreciation reserves; (b) define profits (for the numerator of the rate-of-return ratio) as normal accounting profits realized on activities under or closely associated with regulation, plus interest charges and depreciation expenses; (c) take explicit cognizance of the role and influence of capital longevity by making corrections in rate-of-return ratios (as defined by (a) and (b) above) so as to convert them to closer approximations of the internal rate of return that would be obtained by solving the present value formula; (d) take into account the particular differences in the durability of working capital and physical investments; and (e) correct the rate base for price, or at least take cognizance of the possibility of price inflation by attempting to measure any changes that occur in the cost of capital needed to produce specified units of output.

We will present, first, various bits and pieces of information pertinent to the price correction problem and, second, rough comparisons of rates of return realized in several transportation industries with those realized in several regulated and unregulated sectors of American industry in recent years. While these estimates will be crude in several respects, the most serious omission is the lack of appropriate price corrections for the rate bases. Accordingly, the number reported are directly comparable only to the extent that different sectors of industry have approximately the same historical age composition of their capital asset structures and have experienced similar price histories or price stability in their capital equipment acquisition markets over recent or relevant years.[11] We excuse ourselves from applying price deflation to accounting values on capital assets because it is an empirical task beyond our resources. It requires unpublished data on the historical distribution of capital asset acquisitions in order to determine the appropriate weights to assign to the index for all relevant preceding years.

These illustrations are, therefore, necessarily incomplete and are intended primarily to indicate what is possible rather than as sources for drawing substantive conclusions. The usefulness of these figures, however, might be easily underestimated. With all their imperfections and inadequacies, they are probably superior to most existing profit measures used by regulatory agencies. Furthermore, in many instances the differences between series compared are so large that no possible bias could alter significantly the more obvious conclusions or inferences. Still, care is required in their interpretation and it is hoped that their imperfections will be a challenge to others to undertake needed improvements.

PRICE INFORMATION AND INDEXES FOR TRANSPORTATION

The preceding discussion of reproduction cost developed two conclusions. First, that an adjustment in the rate base to recognize the possible impact of inflation was essential, and second, that such an adjustment could be best achieved by a price index (preferably based on a unit of service whose quality is continually improving) rather than the administratively cumbersome application of the concept of reproduction cost.

There are three types of price index which might be used in the adjustment of the rate base and hence profits: (1) a consumer or cost of living index, (2) a general producers' durable equipment index, and (3) specific indexes of equipment prices. The personal consumption index adjusts the rate base to stabilize the real income or purchasing power returns realized by investors. The other two indexes, in contrast, adjust the rate base to maintain the purchasing power of reinvested earnings. Since retained earnings as a source of reinvestment funds have become increasingly important, the maintenance of the purchasing power of profits in terms of reinvestment deserves at least equal priority with the maintenance of investors' real income.

If the particular prices paid for capital by a given industry follow the general pattern, the price index of producers' durable equipment

---

[11] Of course, there might be other fortuitous combinations of circumstances in which relative price movements and historical capital acquisition patterns would make the numbers directly comparable even without price correction.

used in national income accounts will, of course, more or less maintain the purchasing power of profits in terms of reinvestment. This index represents the price changes in a wide cross section of capital equipment (machinery, tools, vehicles), and investments in regulated industries generally fall within the categories included. Furthermore, since the typical division of profits is roughly equal between reinvestment (retained earnings) and dividends, and depreciation expense is usually about equal to retained earnings, the consumer price index and the producers' durable equipment index might be given, as a first rough approximation, weights of one and two, respectively, in the construction of a general composite index of price changes for the adjustment of rate bases. Such an index is shown in Table 3, with 1946 selected as the base year. The figures suggest a steady erosion in the value of profit dollars, though at a slow pace since 1957.

The index of prices of all producers' durable equipment, however, may often be an inadequate representation of the price changes in the equipment bought in a particular industry, especially since the general index does not reflect technological change in a particular industry (or, for that matter, in industry in general). For example, as shown in Table 4, unit of productive capacity costs for airplanes, as measured

TABLE 3

A GENERAL PRICE INDEX FOR RATE BASE ADJUSTMENT

Year (1)	Personal Consumption Expenditures (2)	Producers' Durable Equipment (3)	Composite Index 33.3% of (2) + 66.7% of (3) (4)
1946	100.0	100.0	100.0
1947	119.3	114.1	115.5
1948	126.1	123.3	124.0
1949	125.0	129.3	127.7
1950	126.7	132.0	130.2
1951	135.4	143.4	140.6
1952	137.5	144.2	141.7
1953	139.3	145.8	143.3
1954	140.5	146.3	144.6
1955	140.8	150.5	146.3
1956	142.1	160.0	154.0
1957	147.8	169.5	162.3
1958	150.5	174.0	166.2
1959	152.5	177.8	169.4
1960	155.0	178.0	170.3

Source: U.S. Department of Commerce, *Survey of Current Business,* July 1956, p. 6, and July 1962, p. 8.

for 1947–55 by prices paid for the DC-6 and DC-6B which represent efficient equipment in medium-range service, have increased less than the producers' capital equipment price index. Indeed, as can be seen by looking at column 8 of Table 4, the costs of this type of medium-range, four-engine plane capacity were remarkably stable over those years and, if anything, actually declined. The indexes reported in Table 4, it should be noted, reflect changes in the utilization patterns of the equipment as well as price changes.

A decline in the actual price of medium-range plane capacity is even more evident in more current data. In 1960, the equipment with the lowest operating costs in medium range operations would appear to be the Lockheed Electra. This plane in a conventional First-Tourist configuration has approximately 40 to 50 per cent more seating capacity than the DC-6B and, except for the period when its operating speeds were reduced for safety reasons, operated at about a 33 per cent higher over-all cruising speed. Such figures imply that one Electra is the equal in units of seats of available capacity to two DC-6B's, as long as the Electra can achieve the same number of hours of daily utilization as the DC-6B. Except for the safety problems in 1959 and 1960, the Electra, with its simple turbo-prop propulsion, should achieve a higher rate of utilization than its reciprocating engine predecessors; it should be remembered, moreover, that the DC-6 also had substantial safety problems in its early years. The Electra when new (in 1958) cost between $2.3 and $2.4 million, so that an approximate 100 per cent increase in capacity was bought at a 50–60 per cent increase in price. In 1962, a used Electra in good condition cost about $1.3 million, partially reflecting the fact that even more efficient and lower cost medium- and short-range capacity was shortly expected in pure jets.

The advent of jets into long-range service also has kept unit costs of this type of capacity more or less constant. Both the Boeing 707 and the DC-8 represent 50 per cent more seating capacity than their predecessors, the DC-7 and the Constellation, and are at least 60 per cent faster. Again, given only equal hours of utilization, this makes each DC-8 or 707 at least equal to 2.5 DC-7's in terms of available capacity. Since DC-7's cost about $2.5 million when new and the DC-8 and 707 have averaged about $6 million in price, the price ratio is also about 2.5.

In short, it would be difficult to argue that the capital costs of airline capacity have risen markedly in recent years since, if anything, they have probably declined. Given the difficulties mentioned earlier of gaining acceptance of downward price corrections and, more importantly, the fact that airline returns have not been high by any standards

TABLE 4

CAPITAL COSTS OF MEDIUM-RANGE FOUR-ENGINE PLANE CAPACITY, 1946–55
(based on DC–6 and DC–6B prices)

Year (1)	Price[a] (thousand dollars) (2)	Available Seat Miles (3)	No. of Planes of the Relevant Types in Fleet (4)	Available Seat Miles per Plane (col. 3 ÷ col. 4) (5)	Capital Costs per ASM (col. 2 ÷ col. 5) (6)	Index Based on Col. 6 (7)	New Composite Index[b] (8)
1946	587.6						
1947	658.8	549,427	83	6,655	$98.60	262.5	206.5
1948	681.8	1,857,475	102	18,210	37.50	100.0	100.0
1949	751.4	3,127,426	104	30,007	25.05	66.8	77.6
1950	857.6	3,586,964	111	32,315	26.55	71.0	80.7
1951	874.0	4,320,953	106	40,763	21.80	58.2	74.5
1952	1,016.9	1,466,068	43	34,095	29.70	79.2	89.0
1953		2,550,428	60	42,507			
1954	1,105.5	2,706,572	64	42,290	26.20	69.8	83.8
1955	1,494.4	3,223,962	70	46,057	32.30	86.2	94.7

Source: Computed from data furnished by the ATA and compiled by them in connection with the General Passenger Fare Hearings before the CAB in 1956–57.

[a]Highest price in each case.

[b]Col. 7 plus col. 2 of Table 3, weighted at .67 and .33 respectively.

in recent years, rates of return uncorrected for capacity price changes are probably reasonably legitimate and acceptable for evaluating airline operations at the moment.

Rather similar price stability for equipment purchases is observable in railroading. In that industry, however, it is more difficult to arrive at over-all impressions of equipment price behavior since so many more types of equipment are involved in a railroad operation than in an airline operation. However, there has been remarkable price stability in the last five years in several important categories of railroad equipment. For example, using actual purchase prices for specific pieces of equipment, since 1957 there has been at most a 5 per cent upward revision in the price of diesel switch and road engines, steel rail, boxcars, and specialized freight rolling stock. Since there have been improvements, in some cases of quite great significance, in the productivity of some of these categories of equipment, this relative price stability strongly suggests that the price per unit of railroad productive capacity may have declined slightly in recent years.

Some relevant figures on equipment utilization and operating efficiency of railroads are given in Table 5 along with some highly aggregate indexes relating to railroad equipment prices for the years 1953 through 1962. The price indexes reflect both price increases and some change, usually a quality upgrading, in the mix of equipment used. The year 1953 is a good base year for efficiency and price comparisons because it essentially eliminates most Korean War effects. The figures in Table 5 suggest that there has been a minimum 10 per cent increase in the efficiency of utilizing railroad equipment and probably substantially more. These figures are to be contrasted with approximate percentage increases in prices for the major types of railroad equipment during the same period: 11 per cent for diesel engines; 15 per cent for steel rail; and 43.5 per cent for freight cars. In large measure, the greater increase in freight car prices represents a substantial upgrading in the quality of cars obtained. In particular, railroad interchange rules were modified several years ago to substitute solid bearings for waste packings in freight car journals; these rules become fully effective only on May 1, 1962 (with the dramatic result, as shown in Table 5, that freight car miles per hotbox rose sharply in 1962) but have been anticipated in equipment procurement practices and prices for several years. Modern freight cars also have several other loading and maintenance cost advantages over those available a decade ago and very often provide a much higher quality of service to the shipper. The net impression is that if there has been an increase in the cost per productive unit of

TABLE 5

INDICATORS OF RAILWAY EQUIPMENT UTILIZATION,
OPERATING EFFICIENCY AND PRICES: 1953-62

Year	Net Ton Miles Per Loaded Car Mile	Car Miles Per Freight Train Mile	Freight Car Miles Per Hotbox (Monthly Due in June of each year)	Freight Train Miles Per Train Hour	Gross Ton Miles Per Freight Train Hour	Price Index for Diesel Electric Loco- motives	Price Index for Freight Train Cars
1953	32.1	63.2	n.a.	18.2	51,750	191	443
1954	31.4	65.0	n.a.	18.7	53,897	191	450
1955	32.1	66.2	n.a.	18.6	55,770	191	468
1956	33.0	67.2	n.a.	18.6	57,071	200	516
1957	33.4	69.3	n.a.	18.8	59,218	210	562
1958	33.0	70.7	n.a.	19.2	60,807	210	594
1959	33.3	69.6	n.a.	19.5	61,924	210	612
1960	34.0	70.2	159,354	19.5	63,096	210	619
1961	34.7	71.0	293,338	19.9	65,621	211	625
1962 (9 months)	35.7	71.5	938,576	20.0	67,491	211	635
Percentage Change 1953-62	11.2	11.4		10.0	31.0	11.0	43.5

Source: Operating efficiency data are from J. Elmer Monroe, "1962 Review of
Railway Operations," *Railway Age*, January 7/14 1963, pp. 87-93. Price indices for
the years 1953 through 1960 are from the American Association of Railroads Joint
Equipment Committee Report, *Costs of Railroad Equipment and Machinery*, July 1, 1961.
The 1961 and 1962 indexes for freight train cars are estimates made by the New York,
New Haven and Hartford Railroad; the 1961-62 values for Diesel-Electric locomotives
are estimates made by the present authors and are probably the most dubious numbers
reported in the Table.

railroad equipment prices, it has been very slight during the last ten
years.

Very much the same picture seems to hold true in trucking. In fact,
the price of aluminum-van dry-storage trailers seems to have declined
slightly, if anything, during the last ten years. It is a bit difficult, though,
to assess the productive characteristics of these trailers since, to a
certain extent, it would appear that durability has been sacrificed for
heavier revenue loadings and a reduction of operation costs through
less weight. On the other hand, the relative stability over the last decade
in the price of trailer-pulling tractors, in the face of some quite obvious
improvements in quality, strongly suggests that the cost of productive
capacity in tractor units has declined. Again, the over-all impression
is one of rough price stability in terms of costs per unit of productive
capacity.

Obviously, it would be useful to know whether technological gains have offset capital goods price increases for other transportation industries. Data are not readily available to answer this question; although, if the point were raised in regulatory proceedings, the data, of course, soon would become available.

RATES OF RETURN IN SOME REGULATED INDUSTRIES

The procedures suggested in previous paragraphs for developing improved estimates of rates of return in regulated industries can be applied both to individual firm and to aggregate industry data. The results obtained by these different procedures will differ, though, and the simple average of rates of return for individual firms generally will not be the same as that obtained by analyzing the aggregate figures for an entire industry. In the aggregate figures the large firms in an industry will enter in heavily, with weights more or less proportional to their asset values. The simple average of the individual firm ratios, on the other hand, weights all firms equally. Which measure is the more appropriate for general regulatory purposes is largely a matter of opinion, being dependent upon such diverse factors as viewpoints about the desirability of competition and its strength in maintaining good managerial practices, the worth of maintaining small business in the economy, and the essentiality of services in a regulated industry.

To illustrate the procedures, a fairly detailed analysis has been made of the 1960 experiences of ten American trunk airlines (all except Northeast) and nine of the larger international air carriers, using data reported to the International Commercial Airlines Organization. The results are reported in Tables 6, 7, and 8. To facilitate the computations, the somewhat arbitrary assumption was made that the airlines conducted no activities other than those that were reasonably pertinent to or an obvious adjunct of their flight operations. All profits and costs, whether realized from flight operations or from nonoperating items, were considered relevant for the rate-of-return calculations. In the case of the U.S. carriers, this means that profits and costs from such adjunct services as supplying meals and beverages for airline passengers and from the sale of surplus property or equipment were included and considered to be an indistinguishable part of the regulated airline operation. In essence, this procedure was followed not because it was considered defensible, but rather because it greatly simplified the calculations from published data. Furthermore, with a few exceptions, like American and United Airlines, the numbers involved were so small as to be of relatively minor importance in determining the final results.

TABLE 6

AIRLINE RATE BASE CALCULATIONS

(in millions of U.S. dollars at end of 1960)

Airline	Long-Term Debt (1)	Capital Stock (2)	Capital Surplus (3)	Unappropriated Balance of Profit and Loss (4)	Flight Equipment Reserves for Depreciation (5)	Grd. Prop. and Equipment Reserves for Depreciation (6)	Total (7)
American	228.8	15.2	39.8	98.2	144.2	30.3	556.5
Braniff	40.0	7.4	18.3	10.9	34.0	5.1	115.7
Delta	55.0	3.4	15.9	19.1	53.4	6.9	153.7
Eastern	165.0	3.2	27.2	80.1	180.9	21.0	477.4
National	33.8	1.8	21.2	5.9	34.5	3.8	101.0
Northwest	68.5	25.1	6.6	20.5	34.5	10.5	165.7
Pan American	317.3	5.3	72.4	60.7	183.5	24.1	663.3
TWA	123.2	33.4	48.9	43.6	185.4	22.9	457.4
United	242.0	42.2	54.1	51.8	158.1	35.5	583.7
Western	23.0	1.4	19.4	11.8	23.1	4.4	83.1
Sabena	91.5	15.0	--	--	30.1	12.5	149.1
TCA	209.9	5.0	--	--	63.0	9.8	287.7
Avianca	2.2	2.1	3.7	.6	6.7	1.7	17.0
Air France	213.3	20.4	8.7	.5	112.1	25.6	380.6
KLM	101.6	38.6	.4	.3	93.1	16.7	250.7
SAS	108.0	30.4	--	16.2	46.7	8.4	209.7
Swissair	42.1	24.4	--	.1	24.8	7.4	98.8
BEA	122.9	44.8	--	.1	38.9	11.7	218.4
BOAC	--	422.6	6.6	48.3	66.9	15.5	559.9

TABLE 7

AIRLINE PROFIT CALCULATIONS
(millions of U.S. dollars in 1960)

Airline	Net Profit After Income Taxes (1)	Interest (2)	Total Depreciation Expense (3)	Total (4)
American	11.8	9.6	38.1	59.5
Braniff	.7	1.9	7.8	10.4
Delta	3.1	2.7	13.9	19.7
Eastern	-3.6	6.0	39.4	41.8
National	-5.1	2.2	9.8	6.9
Northwest	1.6	3.2	14.4	19.2
Pan American	7.1	12.4	50.2	69.7
TWA	6.5	4.1	37.3	47.9
United	11.2	8.8	46.3	66.3
Western	2.4	1.1	9.3	12.8
Sabena	2.5	.6	7.0	10.1
TCA	--	4.2	13.7	17.9
Avianca	.6	.5	1.3	2.4
Air France	.2	8.6	32.4	41.2
KLM	2.7	2.4	21.6	26.7
SAS	-16.2	2.8	15.1	1.7
Swissair	1.1	1.3	6.0	8.4
BEA	4.0	3.6	13.5	21.1
BOAC	-7.1	13.3	29.8	36.0

As shown in Table 7, with these simplifications, the calculation of the rate-of-return numerator reduces to adding interest and total depreciation expenses to final net profits after income taxes.

The calculation of the rate base or denominator of the ratio is only slightly more complicated, given the simplified procedures assumed here. It involves adding long-term debt, capital stock, capital surplus, unappropriated balances of profit and loss, and all reserves for depreciation. The rate base calculations for the 19 airlines under analysis are reported in Table 6.

The final step in the analysis was to divide the total profit return as shown in the last column of Table 7 by the rate base estimate shown in the final column of Table 6 and these quotients are recorded in Table 8. These estimates, of course, might be converted into more refined approximations of the "true" rate of return by using the present value formula and taking into account the fact that airline equipment is now estimated, at least by the U.S. Internal Revenue Service, to have an average life of six years. In the present case, it is quite clear that performing this correction, i.e., assuming that the new Internal Revenue Service "guideline life" is correct, would mean that none of the

TABLE 8

CRUDE AIRLINE RATES OF RETURN, 1960

Airline	Rate of Return (unadjusted)
American	10.7
Braniff	9.1
Delta	12.8
Eastern	8.7
National	6.8
Northwest	11.6
Pan American	10.4
TWA	10.5
United	11.4
Western	15.4
Sabena	6.8
TCA	6.8
Avianca	14.1
Air France	10.7
KLM	10.7
SAS	8.2
Swissair	8.5
BEA	9.7
BOAC	6.4

Source: Col. 4 of Table 7 divided by col. 7 of Table 6.

domestic or international carriers earned a positive rate of return on their investments in the year 1960. (A break-even or zero rate of return would require a 16.6 per cent crude rate of return on the assumption that airline investments have a six-year useful life.) A somewhat more reasonable procedure might be to proceed on the old Civil Aeronautics Board determination that the economic longevity of flight equipment is seven years with a scrap value of 15 per cent. A seven-year life, in addition, would not appear too out of line for airline ground equipment as well. It would be even more legitimate and necessary to take into account the fact that approximately 10 to 15 per cent of every dollar invested in commercial airline operations is net working capital.

Working on the basis of these assumptions, the profit picture for 1960 airline operations is improved, but only slightly. Specifically, the break-even rate of return is lowered to 10.7 per cent. As can be seen in Table 8, this means that Delta, Western, Avianca, United, and Northwest do a little better than break even, and American, KLM, and Air France are on the margin of doing so. What these figures confirm, of course, is something that is well known: 1960 was not a very good year for either domestic or international airlines.

TABLE 9

RATE OF RETURN AND NET INCOME ON
RAILWAY OPERATIONS: 1953-62

Year	Net Railway Operating Income Before Fixed Charges But After Depreciation (million dollars)	Rate of Return on Net Investment (per cent)	Net Income After Fixed Charges (million dollars)
1953	1,109	4.19	903
1954	874	3.28	682
1955	1,128	4.22	927
1956	1,068	3.95	876
1957	922	3.36	737
1958	762	2.76	602
1959	748	2.72	578
1960	584	2.13	445
1961	538	1.97	382
1962[a]	652	2.39	494

Source: J. Elmer Monroe, "1962 Review of Railway Operations",
Railway Age, January 7/14, 1963.

[a]Twelve months ended September 30, 1962.

Some insight into the rates of return in aggregate on U.S. railway operations over the last decade can be obtained from Table 9, which reports net railway operating income, net income after fixed charges, and the rate of return on net investment computed on the basis of the net railway operating income (that is, exclusive of fixed charges) for the years 1953 through 1962. As can be seen from Table 9, these rates of return fluctuated between approximately 2 and 4.25 per cent. Conceptually, these rates resemble the return on average investment or net fixed assets discussed previously and shown in Table 2. As can be seen from that table, when the average rate of return on net fixed assets is at such a low level, it does not depart markedly from the true financial rate of return. Thus, the financial rate of return on railway operations in recent years has apparently fluctuated between approximately 1.90 and 4.00 per cent. These figures, however, are undoubtedly high because railroad assets during the period were approximately 55 per cent written off, so that a net fixed asset base results in an overstatement of the financial return. (For further information see Table 10 where the 1960 railroad return calculated by the more accurate gross asset method is presented.) Again, the figures document a well-known fact: railroading has not been a prosperous business in the United States in recent years.

Aggregate rate-of-return calculations for 1960 for both Class I railroads and other U.S. regulated industries are reported in Table 10,

TABLE 10

AGGREGATE 1960 RATE OF RETURN ESTIMATES
FOR SOME REGULATED INDUSTRIES
(million dollars)

Industry	Rate Base				Return					Crude Rate of Return (8 ÷ 4) (10)	Estim. Useful Life (years) (11)	Est. Financial Rate of Return (per cent)[a] (12)
	Long-Term Debt (1)	Capital Stock, Surplus and Unappropriated Balances and Losses (2)	Depreciation Reserves (3)	Estimated Rate Base (1+2+3) (4)	Net Income After Taxes (5)	Long-Term Interest Payments (6)	Total Depreciation Expense (7)	Total Return (5+6+7) (8)	Net Current Assets (9)			
Transport:												
1. Class I railroads	9,919	16,338	8,214	34,471	445	244	629	1,318	1,110	3.8	25	0
2. Motor carriers of property	667	751	1,003	2,421	37	37	202	276	221	11.3	8	0
3. Motor carriers of passengers	175	71	258	514	28	4	29	61	10	11.8	8	-.5[b]
4. Pipelines	1,056	1,085	1,331	3,472	169	43	118	330	206	9.5	22	8.0
Public Utilities:												
5. Natural gas	6,114	4,384	2,946	13,444	458	265	360	1,083	113	8.1	28	7.2
6. Electric utilities	21,057	18,897	9,863	49,817	1,783	727	1,183	3,693	47	7.4	30	6.2
7. Telephone	730	13,517	5,577	19,814	1,250	279	1,076	2,605	86	13.0	25	11.5

NOTES TO TABLE 10

Coverage and Sources

Line

1. Includes all U.S. Class I line haul carriers. Class I railroads have about 99 per cent of intercity rail traffic. Data from ICC, *Transport Statistics*, 1960, pp. 114–118, Part 1.

2. Includes carriers subject to ICC regulation engaged in intercity operations and reporting financial data. These are predominantly Class I carriers, i.e., those with annual revenues in excess of $1,000,000. They receive about 70 per cent of the total revenue of ICC regulated carriers. Source as above, Part I, pp. 6–10.

3. Includes all Class I intercity carriers, i.e., with annual revenue of more than $300,000. These carriers receive 88 per cent of all revenues of ICC regulated carriers of passengers. Source, as above, Part I, p. 132.

4. Includes all pipelines reporting to the ICC, source as above, Part 6, pp. 2–3.

5. All Class A and B natural gas companies, i.e., companies with more than $750,000 annual revenue. These companies account for virtually all interstate natural gas business. Source: Federal Power Commission, *Statistics of Natural Gas Companies*, 1960, Tables 1 and 4.

6. All privately owned Class A and B electric utilities, i.e., companies with annual revenues of more than $250,000. These companies receive 98 per cent of the revenue of privately owned electric utilities. Source: Federal Power Commission, *Statistics of Electric Utilities in the United States*, 1960, Tables 17 and 18.

7. All Class A carriers, defined as companies with more than $250,000 revenue. Class A carriers account for 99 per cent of industry revenues. Source: Federal Communications Commission, *Statistics of Communications Common Carriers*, 1960, pp. 28–30.

[a] Figures on useful lives were obtained from U.S. Treasury Department Internal Revenue Service, *Depreciation Guidelines and Rules*, September 1962 (except for telephones).

[a] In computing these figures an allowance has been made for both working capital needs and longevity of assets.

[b] Estimated financial rate of return here is negative.

TABLE 11

ESTIMATED AVERAGE TRUE RETURNS IN SOME
REPRESENTATIVE MANUFACTURING INDUSTRIES,
1948-54

Industry	Average Net Profit to Gross Fixed Asset Ratios[a] (per cent)			Estim. of Needs Net Working Capital as Per Cent of GFA	Estim. of Net Profit to GFA After WC Corrections (per cent)			Approximate Average Economic Life of Equipment		Approximate Financial Rates of Return[c] (per cent)		
	1946–50	1951–54	1946–50		1946–50	1951–54	1946–54	Bulletin F	Sept. 1962 *Guidelines*[b]	1946–54, Bulletin F Lives	1951–54, Bulletin F Lives	1951–54, *Guidelines*[d] Correction
Pulp and paper	18	12	15	25	14	10	12	19	16	16	13	13
Light chemicals	34	17	25	40	24	12	18	20	11	23	16	15
Heavy chemicals	22	10	16	25	18	08	13	18	11	17	12	10
Rubber	18	12	15	20	15	10	13	17	14	17	15	13
Basic iron and steel	16	14	15	25	13	11	12	25	18	15	14	13
Fabricated metal products	25	24	25	30	19	19	19	22	12	25	24	20
Other machinery	28	28	28	40	20	20	20	24	12	25	26	22
Light electrical machinery	34	18	26	40	24	13	19	19	12	22	17	16
Automotive	34	19	26	30	26	15	20	17	12	25	19	18
Household appliances and furnishing	45	30	37	35	33	22	27	18	12	33	28	23
Machine tools	23	24	24	40	16	17	17	18	12	24	24	21
Heavy electrical machinery	33	25	29	40	24	18	21	22	12	25	23	21
Basic textiles	34	08	21	15	30	07	18	25	14	22	10	08
Other textiles	24	06	15	20	20	05	13	16	11	18	08	07

using the gross asset method previously used with the airlines. As can be seen, the domestic regulated industries had widely varying experiences in the year 1960. The public utilities on the whole did well; in fact, the telephone industry did very well. An intriguing feature of the figures presented in Table 10 is the degree to which the public utilities have relatively low depreciation reserves, usually under 30 per cent of the gross rate base; this means that any rate of return using net assets as the base for these industries probably will understate the true average return.

On the other hand, all the transport industries, with the lone exception of pipelines did miserably, more or less matching the airline experience in the same year. We have, however, several reservations about our findings with respect to intercity trucking and, to a lesser extent, intercity buses. First, our calculations are based on 1960 data which, from industry accounts, appears to have been a year of atypically low profits. Second, the accounting data for trucking, an industry with a large number of small firms, may be less accurate than for other regulated industries. Finally, the economic age in the guidelines may understate the economic life of trucking equipment. Hence, we are not sure that our findings refute the widely held notion that trucking is a generally profitable industry.

The recent profit situation of the transportation industries (again with the exception of pipelines, and possibly trucking and buses) appears at least as bad when measured against the standards of unregulated manufacturing industries as when measured against other regulated industries. This is brought out by the figures shown in Tables 11, 12, and 13. In these tables, rates of return for manufacturing

---

NOTES TO TABLE 11

[a]Based on data for approximately 750 publicly listed corporations in these industries. Moody's *Manual of Industrials* and individual company reports were the principal sources.

[b]Based on Bulletin F, *Income Tax Depreciation and Obsolescence, Estimated Useful Lives and Depreciation Rates*, U.S. Treasury Department, Bureau of Internal Revenue (Washington, 1948) and *Depreciation Guidelines and Rules*, U.S. Treasury Department, Internal Revenue Service Publication No. 456 (9-62), Washington, 1962.

[c]Estimated by dividing the ratios of reported net profits to gross fixed assets by one, plus the estimated percentage needs of net working capital, and using Table 1 above (in an extended version) to convert the resulting figures into financial rates of return.

[d]These corrections were made on the presumption that Bulletin F lives had to be used by corporation accountants when recording depreciation, but that the "1962 Guidelines" were correct estimates of actual economic lives. The undepreciated portions of gross fixed asset values left at the end of the "Guidelines lives" were regarded as capital losses and considered to be 50 per cent recouped by a reduction in corporate taxes.

have been estimated both for averages of individual firms and industry aggregates.

The individual firm averages pertain to the years 1946 through 1954 and were developed from data collected for investment studies.[12] Reported in Table 11 are simple industry averages of individual firm net profit (after tax) returns on gross fixed assets; these averages, in turn, have been corrected for interindustry differences in working capital by using estimates of the average working capital needs of firms in each individual industry.[13] The samples used in constructing these averages covered virtually every firm in the designated industries that is registered with the Securities and Exchange Commission.[14] Gross fixed assets were used as the rate base in these industries mainly because of convenience: the investment studies for which the data were originally collected used gross fixed assets as a deflator when making certain cross-section statistical analyses. However, a gross fixed-asset base has the additional advantage of being less sensitive to differences in the ages of equipment used in different industries, thus avoiding the saw-tooth bias problem discussed previously.

Several different estimates of the rates of return have been presented by using different combinations of estimated useful economic lives, and by averaging the data over different sets of years. Probably the most pertinent figures from the standpoint of the present study are those shown in the last two columns of Table 11 for the 1951–54 period. While not up-to-date, they are the most recent available from the investment studies. One notable aspect of the numbers shown in the table is the way in which progressive refinements of the analyses tend to reduce the differences in the estimated rates of return in different industries, a fact which should at least be reassuring to market economists. It should be noted, moreover, that the rates of return reported in the table are, if anything, too low, since the most important single remaining bias is the omission of interest payments as a return on capital.[15]

[12] J. R. Meyer and E. Kuh, *The Investment Decision*, Cambridge, Mass., 1957; and J. R. Meyer and R. Glauber, *Investment Decisions, Economic Forecasting and Public Policy*, Boston, 1963.
[13] The estimates of working capital needs are quite crude and were based primarily on the average industry ratios of net working capital to gross fixed assets for the individual firms in the samples for the year 1954, rounded to the next lowest quinary.
[14] More detailed information on these samples can be found in Meyer and Kuh, *Investment*, Chapter 3; and Meyer and Glauber, *Investment Decisions*, Chapter 3.
[15] Another potential source of bias working in the opposite direction, however, is the fact that the actual depreciation practices followed by the manufacturing corporations included in the sample probably were slightly more conservative than

Some 1960 financial rates of return for individual manufacturing industries, based upon aggregate data, are reported in Table 12 and were estimated from figures reported in the Securities and Exchange Commission-Federal Trade Commission *Quarterly Financial Report of Manufacturing Industries*. This document presents estimates of the aggregated balance sheets and income statements for several manufacturing industries. In constructing the rates of return reported in this table, essentially the same procedures were used as were used previously when reporting estimates of financial rates of return in the regulated industries. That is, the rate base was estimated by adding together stockholder equity, long-term debt, and depreciation reserves; and the profit returns were taken as the sum of net income after taxes, depreciation expenses, and interest payments (which, however, had to be estimated because they are not available in the FTC-SEC reports). The numbers reported in Table 12 are not always directly comparable with those reported in Table 11 because of slight differences in the industry classifications employed. However, a number of direct comparisons are possible and, in general, it is clear that the numbers are not too dissimilar.[16] One point that is evident from such comparisons, though, is that rates of return, even when depreciation expense is included as a return, apparently have declined in manufacturing in the last ten years. However, some of the differences in the figures reported in the two tables may also be attributable to differences in the samples covered; the SEC-FTC *Quarterly Financial Report* includes returns for many small manufacturing corporations that are not publicly listed and may not attain as high profit levels as larger corporations. In addition, the SEC-FTC figures covered all manufacturing industries, including many of the less profitable industries not included in the investment analyses and therefore not reported in Table 11.

Somewhat more direct evidence on the behavior of rates of return in manufacturing since the end of World War II is presented in Table 13. There, crude estimates are presented of the rates of return realized in

---

those implied by the "Bulletin F" estimates reported in Table 9. Specifically, the average ratio of depreciation expense to gross fixed assets in these industries indicated in a few instances that the useful lives actually being used for depreciation were one to two years longer than the "Bulletin F" lives shown in the table. If this factor were taken into account, it would tend to further depress the rate of return very slightly; the type of adjustment involved would be essentially like that made when moving from the "Bulletin F" to the Guideline depreciation figures as shown in the last two columns of Table 9.

[16] The relationships between the industrial groupings used in the investment studies and the standard industrial classifications are explained in Meyer and Kuh, *Investment*; and Meyer and Glauber, *Investment Decisions*.

TABLE 12

AGGREGATE 1960 RATES OF RETURN IN MANUFACTURING INDUSTRIES[a]
(billion dollars)

Industry	Rate Base				Return				Net Current Assets (9)	Crude Rate of Return (8 ÷ 4), Per Cent (10)	Estim. Useful Life[b] (11)	Estim. Financial Rate of Return[c] (per cent) (12)
	Long-Term Debt (1)	Stock Holders Equity (2)	Depreciation Reserves (3)	Estim. Base (1+2+3) (4)	Net Profit After Taxes (5)	Estim. Interest (6)	Depreciation Expense (7)	Total Returns (5+6+7) (8)				
All manufacturing	33.3	164.5	89.9	187.7	15.2	2.3	10.9	28.4	80.3	9.8	12	6
Trans. equip. (incl. motor vehicles)	2.5	16.3	8.0	26.8	1.9	.2	1.1	2.3	8.6	8.6	12	4
Motor vehicle	1.6	12.5	6.2	20.3	1.7	.1	.8	2.6	6.0	12.8	12	10
Elec. mach.	2.5	10.6	3.9	17.0	1.1	.2	.6	1.9	7.0	11.2	12	9
Other mach.	2.6	13.2	5.5	21.3	1.0	.2	.9	2.1	8.4	9.9	12	8
Fab. metal prod.	1.1	7.1	3.0	11.2	.4	.1	.4	.9	4.2	8.0	12	5
Primary metals	4.8	20.0	14.4	39.2	1.4	.3	1.2	2.9	8.4	7.4	17	5
Stone, clay, and glass	.8	5.7	3.1	9.6	.6	.05	.4	1.05	2.3	10.9	15	8
Furn. and fix.	.2	1.4	.5	2.1	.1	.02	.07	.19	1.0	9.1	10	6
Lumber and wood	.7	2.9	1.4	5.0	.1	.06	.3	.46	1.3	9.2	10	5
Instruments	.3	2.7	1.0	4.0	.3	.02	.15	.47	1.8	11.8	12	9
Misc. manufs.	.4	2.0	.7	3.1	.2	.02	.1	.32	1.2	10.3	12	8
Food and kindred	2.8	13.9	6.6	23.3	1.2	.2	.8	2.2	7.6	9.5	15	7
Tobacco	.5	2.1	.3	2.9	.25	.05	.04	.34	2.2	11.7	15	10
Textiles	.9	5.6	2.7	9.2	.3	.09	.3	.69	3.4	7.5	13	4
Apparel	.3	1.9	.5	2.7	.15	.04	.08	.27	1.5	10.0	9	6
Paper	1.6	6.9	3.9	12.4	.6	.1	.5	1.2	2.5	9.7	16	7
Printing and publishing	.7	2.9	1.2	4.8	.3	.03	.2	.53	1.7	11.0	11	8
Chemicals	3.6	16.4	9.4	29.4	2.0	.2	1.2	3.4	7.3	11.5	11	8
Petroleum	3.5	28.7	21.5	55.7	2.8	.3	2.3	5.4	7.0	9.7	15	6
Rubber	.8	3.3	1.9	6.0	.3	.05	.25	.6	2.3	10.0	14	7
Leather	.2	1.1	.3	1.6	.07	.01	.05	.13	.7	8.1	11	5

all of manufacturing, again using aggregate data obtained from the SEC-FTC *Quarterly Financial Reports*. Because of a number of changes that have been made in reporting procedures and the samples used by the SEC and the FTC, consistent series for the entire period are difficult to construct. It is necessary to make a number of assumptions and to "splice" in order to join the reported numbers into a consistent set. Furthermore, because the spliced series were created for a different purpose than the measurements of rates of return (specifically by Professor Locke Anderson of the University of Michigan for conducting some investigations of financial behavior in manufacturing), no spliced series were created for depreciation reserves or gross fixed assets, series which would have been obviously useful for present purposes. As before, moreover, no interest series was available. Accordingly, the estimates developed in the table are based upon net fixed-asset rate bases and are correspondingly somewhat cruder than those reported previously, except for the railroad rates of return reported in Table 10 which are of the same type. In places where direct comparisons are available between the spliced and the original series, however, spot checks indicate that the results obtained by using the net-profit-to-net-fixed-asset approach in estimating the rate of return are not very different from those that would have been obtained if the net worth or gross fixed-asset method had been used instead.

As previously pointed out, a major difficulty with the net-profit-to-net-fixed-asset approach is that it is based on the assumption that approximately one-half of assets are written off. Therefore, the rates of return are accurate only to the extent that this assumption is approximated. Furthermore, the degree of approximation to this assumption can and usually does vary over time. Some biases are probably

---

NOTES TO TABLE 12

[a]The flow data (net profits after taxes and depreciation expense) are totals for all four quarters of the designated years; the stock data (long-term debt, depreciation reserves, stockholders equity, and net current assets) pertain to mid-year or end-of-second-quarter levels. Net current assets were estimated by subtracting total current liabilities from the total of current assets. Because no series on interest payments was available, interest expenditures were estimated by totalling all forms of long- and short-term debt and applying to them a factor of .06, assumed to be the average rate of interest paid.

[b]Based on *Depreciation Guidelines and Rules*, U.S. Treasury Department, Internal Revenue Service Publication No. 456 (9-62), Washington, D. C., September 1962.

[c]These financial rates of return were estimated on the basis of the useful lives shown in Column 11, and by taking into account differences in net working capital needs. Specifically, it was assumed that net working capital was realized in one lump sum at the end of the number of designated years of useful life.

TABLE 13

RATE OF RETURN CALCULATIONS FOR MANUFACTURING CORPORATIONS, 1947–59[a]

Year	Net Profits After Taxes	Depreciation Expense	Net Fixed Assets	Net Working Capital[b]	Other Noncurrent Assets	Crude Net Profit to Asset Ratio (per cent)[c]	Approximate Financial Rates of Return (per cent)[d]	
							Without an Interest Allowance	With an Interest Allowance[e]
1947	10.2	2.7	30.0	35.6	6.6	14.1	12.5	13.0
1948	11.8	3.4	36.5	38.7	7.5	14.2	12.5	13.0
1949	9.3	3.7	41.4	41.5	8.6	10.2	9.3	9.8
1950	13.4	4.1	44.2	45.7	8.8	13.6	11.5	12.0
1951	11.8	4.8	49.5	50.9	9.7	10.6	9.5	10.0
1952	10.8	5.3	55.8	53.0	10.3	9.1	8.0	9.0
1953	11.5	6.2	60.2	55.4	10.6	9.1	8.0	9.0
1954	11.4	6.8	64.3	56.7	10.7	8.7	7.5	8.0
1955	15.5	7.7	67.9	60.6	11.8	11.1	10.0	11.0
1956	16.2	8.4	73.8	65.4	13.9	10.6	9.5	10.0
1957	15.4	9.3	82.8	67.8	15.0	9.4	8.5	9.5
1958	12.6	9.6	88.7	68.4	16.5	7.6	7.0	7.5
1959	16.3	10.4	90.7	73.5	17.5	9.0	8.0	9.5

[a]The basic sources of data for this table were *Quarterly Financial Reports for Manufacturing Corporations* published by the Federal Trade Commission and the Securities and Exchange Commission. Because of a number of changes in the sample and sampling procedures used by the SEC and FTC, it was necessary to perform splicing operations to create series that were uniform over the entire time period. The splicing was performed by Professor Locke Anderson of the University of Michigan and it is through his generosity that these data have been made available for use here. The flow data (net profits after taxes and depreciation expense) are totals for all four quarters of the designated years; the stock data (net fixed assets, net working capital, and other noncurrent assets) pertain to mid-year or end-of-second-quarter levels.

b____ ___ ___ _____ __ _____ _____ ___ ___ _____ __ _____ assets.

introduced here; e.g., a tendency toward a systematic underestimation of the true rate of return throughout the period and particularly during the earliest years reported. In addition, a systematic tendency toward underestimation in the early 1950's may account for some of the observed differences between the estimates presented in Table 13 and those in Table 11 (although the previously reported fact that the SEC-FTC Reports cover a much larger sector of manufacturing and many more smaller firms are probably also at least partially responsible for these observed differences).

However, no matter how returns in the manufacturing industry have declined or are measured, they are still considerably larger than those realized in transportation. Indeed, even the least prosperous of all the manufacturing industries, the textile industries, do better than break even—the recent fate of most transportation industries. The

---

NOTES TO TABLE 13 (concluded)

^{c}The crude net-profit-to-asset ratio was estimated by dividing net profits after taxes by the sum of net fixed assets plus net working capital plus other noncurrent assets.

^{d}The approximate financial rates of return were estimated from the crude net-profit-to-asset ratios by using a table of conversions like those shown in Table 2 above. The simple conversions shown in Table 2 were modified, however, to take account of the fact that approximately one-third of the total investment in manufacturing is accounted for by net working capital which is not subject to depreciation and has a 100 per cent salvage value. Furthermore, because the depreciation-to-net-fixed-asset ratios range between approximately .09 in the late 1940's to .11 in the late 1950's, it was assumed that the net fixed assets invested in all manufacturing had an approximate life of twenty years; such an estimate of useful life follows almost automatically from the fact that the conversion from the crude net profit rate to the financial rate of return estimate is based on the assumption that gross fixed assets are approximately one-half depreciated at all times. While this assumption of a one-to-two ratio between net fixed assets and gross fixed assets (or, alternatively, of depreciation reserves to gross fixed assets) is not strictly true throughout the period, spot checks would indicate that it is not too gross a violation of the facts. A direct calculation of the rate of return using gross fixed assets or depreciation reserves was impossible because these two series have not been spliced to create a consistent set of numbers for the entire twelve-year period.

^{e}Because no consistent spliced series on interest payments was available, interest expenditures were estimated by totalling all forms of long-term and short-term debt, for which spliced series were available, and applying to them a factor of .06, assumed to be the average rate of interest paid. Clearly, some distortion is introduced by assuming that the average level of interest payments were the same throughout the twelve-year period, since they were almost surely higher during the tight monetary periods of 1954 and 1957 than during the other years, and were probably higher at the end of the twelve years than at the beginning. However, because such a very high percentage of total corporate debt is in the form of long-term debt, the effective movement in the actual rate of interest paid by the corporations was probably not too great over time.

substantial differences existing between returns in the unregulated manufacturing industries and transportation cannot be explained, moreover,
simply on the basis of "greater risk" being faced by manufacturers.
Indeed, in industries of such marked concentration and reputed prevalence of "oligopolistic price leadership" as basic steel, heavy chem-
icals, and pulp and paper, there is perhaps less competition and
investment risk than in transportation.

Some Final Comments and Observations

The disparity of returns between transportation and other regulated
and unregulated industries poses some interesting questions for
economic theory and policy. Above all is the question, why investments
and services in transportation continue to be forthcoming when
resources allocated to these activities realize so much lower rates of
return than in other activities.

There are, of course, indications that returns on rail operations are
really *not* adequate to keep many of the assets presently employed in
these activities in the industry. (This, though, may not be an economically undesirable objective.) The fact that the dependability of rail
returns has been further jeopardized in recent years by the rise of new
competition from trucks, buses, and airplanes only increases this
probability. Some investments in railroading, of course, may be
justified at the margin even if average returns are quite low.

In the airline industry, the continued presence of productive facilities
apparently is due to the simple fact that very large commitments were
made to this industry in recent years on the basis of highly optimistic
expectations. While these expectations have not been borne out to any
great extent (1961 was about as bad a year as 1960 for domestic and
international airlines and 1962 was only slightly improved), there are
indications that this industry may be on its way to solving most of its
problems. Four domestic carriers, Delta, Northwest, National, and
Western, reported quite handsome profits for 1962, particularly for
the second half of the year. Circumstances were even improved for
the U.S. international air carriers in the second half of 1962.

Disparities in the fortunes of different firms also may help explain
why investments continue to be forthcoming in many transportation
activities. There is always a hope, sometimes even a well-based belief,
that if one is lucky, prudent, or an intelligent manager, one can make
a reasonable return on investments in regulated industries. Optimistic
hopes of beliefs are only strengthened, of course, if there is a tendency

for regulation to gear itself to perpetuating in business the least efficient members of an industry.

Finally, it must be recognized that elimination of fixed investments in any industry requires time. In industries like railroading, involving assets of very long economic life, this transition period may be quite lengthy. Even in the airlines, recent experience suggests that the transition may be long and difficult enough to be both quite painful and not readily obvious. A regulatory agency, or even private managements, may not recognize capital consumption and the full adversity of a industry situation until the processes of deterioration are well, perhaps irreversibly, in progress. Needless to say, oversimplified, crude measures of rates of return do not increase the likelihood of early perception.

COMMENT

VERNON L. SMITH, Purdue University

Almost everyone must agree, by now, that the proper objective of regulation is to simulate the competitive process, with the appropriate incentives for service, efficiency, and technological improvement being provided at the cost of no more than transitional, abnormal profits. My difficulty with the Peck-Meyer paper (and perhaps its authors might even agree) is that I really think regulatory simulation of the competitive process is quite impossible. If profit is regulated in an attempt to keep it within competitive norms, there are not only insurmountable measurement problems, but the danger that the incentives for efficiency and technological progress will be lost. If incentive retention of profits arising out of cost improvements is permitted, how much retention should be permitted? A little more incentive for cost reduction can always be provided by increasing the share of such profits that can be retained. The competitive process requires neither measurement nor the objective formal statement of criteria, but regulatory simulation does, and that is why Peck and Meyer have set themselves a difficult task.

Despite these problems, I think their recommendations would improve matters materially; they have gone about as far as one can go with technical refinements, such as the use of present value calculations and the careful analytical definition of capital, in specifying the appropriate rate base. I say "I think," because I really do not know. When the authors come to grips with applying these principles, we find, inevitably, statements like (p. 218), "... the consumer price index and the producers' durable equipment index might be given, as a first rough approximation, weights of one and two, respectively, in the construction of a general composite index of price changes for the adjustment of rate bases." We also find wise qualifications like (p. 215), "The use of a simple index of the production cost of an ever-improving unit of output is not, however, an automatic cure-all. Depending on the particular character of technological advance ... the gains will be shared differently by the different participants."

What I am trying to say is that the attempt to simulate the competitive process requires somebody to make judgements about what is a fair return, how capital should be measured, how this or that number should be weighted, and so on. Such judgements, however rationally and objectively made, tend to become institutionalized and inflexible.

But if regulatory simulation of the competitive process is impossible, except in the roughest way, what then is the solution to the problem of regulation? I think the key to the answer is made plain in the Peck-Meyer paper, as well as in the papers by James C. Nelson and Robert A. Nelson. Peck and Meyer find that no matter how one proposes to measure the rates of return in manufacturing industries, such rates are considerably higher than those realized in the regulated transportation industries, with the lone exception of pipelines. The gas and electric utilities do about as well as manufacturing generally, with only the telephone utilities doing better. These results provide little support for the image of the American transportation system as a vast profit hungry monopoly, that would quickly bleed the country to ruin were it not for the protections provided by regulation.

With regard to transportation, the answer to the problem of regulation is not, in my opinion, the development of more refined measures of capital, rates of return, and so on. The answer is to be found in a very substantial amount of deregulation. In time, preferably soon, I would visualize the entire transportation industry subject only to regulation under the anti-trust laws, and regulations pertaining to safety. I would permit mergers between East-West and North-South air carriers; I would favor railroad and truck mergers designed to produce fully integrated, alternative-route, competitive transportation systems, provided such mergers were not in violation of ordinary anti-trust considerations. I would free most if not all classes of commodities, including passengers, from rate regulation. If there are not now enough alternative, closely competing transport facilities to permit reliance upon free competition in American transportation, then it is abundantly clear that we should be regulating most of American industry.

But I would go further than transportation, and suggest that we seriously consider deregulating the gas utilities and perhaps, in time, the electric utilities. Close substitutes for natural gas in the form of propane, heating oil, and electricity, are now sufficiently numerous, as to suggest that the regulation of the gas industry may be superfluous. I can't imagine the gas companies getting away with rates much in excess of the going equivalent prices of propane and heating oil. If this conjecture should be wrong, I could only conclude that consumers are indifferent at the higher price, and if they really are indifferent then why waste all those administrative resources trying to regulate the industry?

As for the electric utilities, it is evident that close competitive alternatives are not now commercially available. But there is a reasonably good possibility that self-contained home generating plants, employing solar conversion devices, fuel cell, or gas turbine units will in the future become economically competitive with centralized generating systems. Such a development could introduce competitive pressures on the electric utilities that would eliminate, or drastically alter, the necessity for regulation. We should be alert to the possibility of such trends, and guard against the long institutional lag that continues to characterize transport regulation.

Only the telephone utilities seem to be substantially insulated from any impending prospect of competitive substitute service. So perhaps in this industry, and for the time being in the electric utilities, we should struggle along with the Peck-Meyer improvements and a frankly imperfect attempt to simulate the competitive process.

PART III

Urban Transportation

The Commuting and
Residential Decisions of
Central Business District Workers

JOHN F. KAIN

U.S. AIR FORCE ACADEMY AND THE RAND CORPORATION

I. Introduction

During recent years, people interested in the well-being of urban communities have given increasing attention to urban transportation problems. In particular, they have been concerned with the plight of central business district commuters and the difficulties and costs confronting large central cities that wish to provide highway access facilities for the increasing numbers of automobile commuters. Many people regard automobile commuting to central areas as prohibitively expensive for both the individual and the community. Noting the apparent ability of rapid-transit systems in Chicago, Cleveland, New York, and elsewhere to maintain peak-hour ridership (even though suffering declines in over-all ridership), planners and community leaders in San Francisco-Oakland, Washington, D.C., Los Angeles, and a number of other urban areas have proposed the construction of new rail rapid-transit systems for their cities.[1]

NOTE: Views expressed in this paper are those of the author. They should not be interpreted as reflecting the views of the U.S. Air Force Academy or the U.S. Air Force, The RAND Corporation, or as the official opinion or policy of any of its government or private research sponsors.

The author thanks the sponsors and participants of the Detroit Area Traffic Study and the Chicago Area Transportation Study for making available IBM decks and other data, and for the assistance given by staff members. In particular, the author acknowledges the assistance of Douglas Carroll, Jr., director of the Chicago study; of Albert Mayer, director of the Institute for Regional and Urban Studies, Wayne State University, who made the data available; and of Sue Smock for help in interpreting the Detroit study data.

[1] Voters of three San Francisco-Oakland Bay area counties have approved a bond issue to finance a 75-mile trans-bay rail rapid-transit system with an estimated

Despite the hopes entertained for these plans, very little is known about the characteristics of central business district commuters or of their travel and residential behavior that would be crucial in determining the success of the plans. It is the purpose of this paper to examine and interpret these behavioral patterns, and in particular the interrelationships between them, for workers employed in the central business districts of Detroit and Chicago—the nation's second and fifth largest metropolitan areas—and to illustrate the usefulness of economic theory in explaining and predicting that behavior.

In Section II, below, a simple consumer-choice model is developed for analysis of the trade-off between housing cost and travel cost to explain residential choices, residential density, and commuting behavior of workers employed at high-density workplaces in major urban centers. Section II also includes a few simple and fairly obvious empirical tests of such models, using data obtained on these kinds of workers from the 1952 Detroit and 1956 Chicago transportation studies.[2] The primary

---

capital cost of nearly $1 billion. The Los Angeles Metropolitan Transit Authority, emboldened by the success of the Bay Area rapid-transit district in obtaining tax support, has expanded its proposed $300 million, 22.7-mile "Backbone Plan" to a $649 million, 58-mile system. The National Capitol Transportation Agency submitted to the President its report on Nov. 1, 1962, which proposed construction of an 83-mile, $800 million rail-transit system for the Washington, D.C. region and a substantial curtailment of the region's highway program. New rail-transit systems are being seriously proposed for Atlanta and Pittsburgh and, less seriously, for a number of other large metropolitan areas. Moreover, Philadelphia, Boston, Chicago, and New York are seeking Federal subsidies for expansion of existing rail facilities.

[2] The data describe the attributes and work-trip behavior of nearly 4,000 interviewed households representing approximately 110,000 of Detroit's central business district workers (about 100,000 whites and 10,000 nonwhites); nearly 17,000 interviewed households representing approximately 247,000 of Chicago's central business district workers; and approximately 296,000 workers employed in the area just adjacent to the Chicago central business district.

Original card records were obtained from the Detroit area traffic study and the Chicago area transportation study. The work presented here is part of a larger RAND research project, sponsored by the Ford Foundation, analyzing samples of travel data for approximately 40,000 Detroit and 50,000 Chicago households. The study considers only the "first work trip" made by each sampled household member belonging to the labor force on the day interviewed, and analyzes the journey from home to work, rather than the trip from work to home or the round trip. The morning trip was chosen over the evening trip because it is less often "distorted" by side trips for shopping and other purposes, and thus is more "normal." In addition, the study included only "internal trips," defined as trips having both ends within the study area. Since the study area is very large, workers residing outside it make only a small percentage of the total person trips: 5.3 per cent in Chicago and perhaps 7 per cent in Detroit. The percentage of such trips analyzed in this paper is of course very much smaller, with the exception of the relatively large number of rail trips entering the Chicago central business district from outside the cordon.

purposes of these simple empirical tests are to illustrate more clearly the logic of the theoretical framework used in this paper and to illustrate its consistency with widely-accepted empirical facts.

In Section III, the simple model is elaborated in order to incorporate the substantial effects of racial segregation on the residential and commuting behavior of both white and nonwhite workers employed at high-density work places. In particular, it tries to examine how discrimination affects the operation of the housing market and the spatial distribution of urban housing costs. Section III also presents empirical data illustrating some of the substantial effects of racial discrimination on the commuting behavior and residential choices of both whites and Negroes.

Section IV presents more substantial tests of hypotheses obtained from the more elaborate model, incorporating market imperfections and racial constraints. These tests deal primarily with relationships between residential space consumption and the length of the journey to work, and with relationships between housing costs and the space consumption of whites and nonwhites. The worker populations of both the Detroit and Chicago central business districts are stratified by structure type (used as a measure of residential space consumption), by city and workplace location, and by race, to examine the effects of these variables on journey-to-work length and the consumption of residential space. Journey-to-work length is measured in both elapsed time and distance in order to permit evaluation of households' trade–offs between travel and money expenditures.

Finally, in Section V the choice of transportation mode is examined in the context of the substitution of time and money costs in commuting, and in terms of the interrelationship between the choice of residential density and the costs in time and money of the alternative travel modes and combinations of modes.

II. A Model of Household Residential and Travel Behavior

The behavioral hypotheses used here to explain the residential and travel behavior of workers employed in central locations are relatively few and simple. It is assumed that households try to maximize their total real income in what is undoubtedly an imperfect way; that is, they try to obtain their preferred set of consumer services at lowest possible cost. It is also argued that the length of a worker's journey to work, and thus the distance he resides from his workplace, largely depends on a cost trade-off between transportation costs and housing costs.[3]

The essence of this trade-off is that, while workers employed at central locations can lower their housing costs by living farther from their workplaces, they increase their travel costs by doing so. The second relevant aspect of this trade-off is the fact that the magnitude of such savings in housing cost increases with the amount of residential space the worker uses, greater space consumption being associated with residence in lower-density structures. The utility-maximizing worker lives at that distance from his workplace where the money he saves in housing costs by undertaking a longer journey to work is just offset by increased travel costs.

The assumption that the portion of housing costs variously referred to by other authors as "location," "site," or "position" rents declines with distance from major workplace agglomerations is crucial to the explanation of household travel behavior developed in this paper.[4] These location or site rents are economic rents which landlords may obtain from households for sites more accessible to major workplaces agglomerations. The rents exist because of households' collective efforts to economize on transportation expenditures. Location rent surfaces having these properties have been obtained in a number of theoretical writings.[5]

It seems probable that a surface of location or site rents would be very complex and that location rent surfaces might differ for various types of accommodations (those of varying quality, density, age, etc.). The quasi-rents obtainable in one submarket defined by, say, quality differences, might differ substantially from those obtainable in another. Market disequilibrium may well be the rule rather than the exception,

---

[3] A more complete and rigorous presentation of this model may be found in John F. Kain, *Commuting and Housing Choices: An Empirical Study*, The RAND Corporation, Memorandum RM-3738-FF (in press); and *idem*, "The Journey-to-Work as a Determinant of Residential Location," *Proceedings of the Regional Science Association*, 1961.

[4] See, for example, Edgar M. Hoover and Raymond Vernon, *Anatomy of a Metropolis*, Harvard University Press, 1959; William Alonzo, "A Theory of the Urban Land Market," *Papers and Proceedings*, Regional Science Association, University of Pennsylvania, 1960; John D. Herbert and Benjamin H. Stevens, "A Model for the Distribution of Residential Activity in Urban Areas," *Journal Regional Science*, Fall 1960; Lowdon Wingo, Jr., *Transportation and Urban Land* Resources for the Future, Washington, 1961; and Ira South Lowry, "Residential Location in Urban Areas," unpublished Ph.D. dissertation, University of California, 1960.

[5] See, for example, Alonzo, "Urban Land Markets," and Wingo, *Transportation and Urban Land*.

since there are major imperfections in the market for real property, and since housing is both durable and nonhomogeneous.

Although there is apparently no empirical information that permits direct evaluation of the hypothesis that location rents in the various submarkets differ, there is some inferential evidence. For one thing, some kinds of residential services may be difficult or impossible to secure by renovating single units of the existing stock of housing. For example, if large lots, high levels of community services, and other than gridiron street patterns are highly preferred residential attributes, wholesale demolition and redevelopment would probably be necessary to achieve them in the older built-up portions of cities. Since large lots are rare in old residential areas near central business districts, the price of large-lot residential services might vary by a greater amount with distance from the central business district and other workplace agglomerations than the price of small-lot residential services would. Thus, if there are two submarkets, one characterized by modern, high-quality, large-lot residential structures and another, by obsolete, low-quality, small-lot structures, the incremental savings obtainable with distance from major workplaces might well be much greater in the former than the latter. In either case, however, we would expect the price for units in either submarket to decline with distance from the central business district. Furthermore, even given the above reservation, there is no obvious reason systematic price differentials between the various submarkets, in the absence of serious market imperfections, should persist for long periods. Housing services can be either upgraded or downgraded. Downgrading can occur through density-increasing conversions, permissive deterioration, and failure to maintain and renovate structures. Upgrading can occur by renovation, demolition, and reconstruction, and by other forms of private market renewal.[6]

Since the workers dealt with in this paper are employed in the central areas of Chicago and Detriot, where urban employment densities are highest, we would expect their housing costs per unit of residential space to decline with distance from the center. Because Chicago and Detroit differ in size and in the numbers employed in their central business districts (about two and one-half times as many in Chicago as in Detroit), it would seem reasonable to expect—assuming

---

[6] Society Hill and Rittenhouse Square, in Philadelphia, and Capitol Hill and Georgetown, in Washington, are frequently cited examples of private market renewal. In all instances, however, housing located in these areas is extremely expensive.

the above provisional hypotheses about the determinants of location rents are valid—that location or site rents would be higher in Chicago than in Detroit at each distance from the central business district. Specifically, for the purpose of the empirical testing in this study, it is postulated that the price per unit of residential space of a stated quality and amenity decreases monotonically with distance from the center, but that the price is consistently higher for Chicago. Thus it is postulated that centrally employed workers in both cities may reduce their housing costs per density unit by commuting longer distances, but that the savings per mile will be larger for Chicago workers.

It is also crucial that, in making longer journeys to work, households incur larger costs in both time and money. Since time is a scarce commodity, workers should demand some compensation for the time they spend in commuting.[7] Both the commuting distance and time a central business district worker will spend thus depend on his valuation of commuting time, the money cost of his commuting, and the savings in housing cost he is able to obtain from a longer journey to work. He will extend his distance only so long as his savings in location rent offset or just equal his increased expenditures of time and money.

His reductions in housing cost, however, depend not only on his commuting distance, but also upon the quantity or the amount of residential space he consumes. If he lives in very low–density residential quarters, his cost savings per unit of residential space are multiplied by a large number of units; if he chooses very high–density quarters, his savings may be small. For many people housing-cost savings obtained from longer journeys to work may be quickly offset by increasing travel costs.

Unless the labor forces of Detroit's and Chicago's central business districts differ greatly in their socioeconomic composition, the simple economic model used in this paper would predict that Chicago workers'

[7] The problem of valuing travel time is extremely complex. Nearly all benefit-cost analyses of urban transportation systems include a value of travel time as part of an analysis of alternative systems. Savings in travel time invariably swamp all other benefits in such analyses. Nonetheless, no one has devised an adequate empirical measurement of the value of time. Transportation studies invariably use some wage rate to value travel time, on the assumption that the value of commuting time is equal to the wage rate. Moses and Williamson have pointed out the theoretical difficulties inherent in such a procedure in two papers, which represent the best theoretical statement of the problem (see Leon Moses, "Economics of Consumer Choice in Urban Transportation," presented at Dynamics of Urban Transportation a symposium sponsored by Automobile Manufacturers Association, 1962; and Moses and Harold F. Williamson, Jr., "Value of Time, Choice of Mode, and the Subsidy Issue in Urban Transportation," unpublished; see also Fred Hoffman, "Route Choice and Valuation of Travel Time," unpublished.).

Figure 1
Cumulative Percentage Travel Times and Distances for
Chicago and Detroit Central Business District Workers

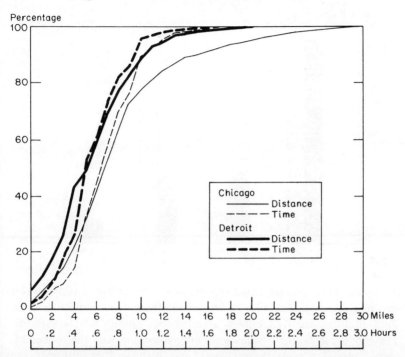

trips, measured by either elapsed time or distance, should exceed those of Detroit workers. As noted previously, we would expect larger savings in housing costs to be obtainable by commuting a given distance in Chicago than in Detroit, at every level of residential space consumption. Thus, if transportation costs in Chicago and Detroit are at all comparable, Chicago workers would be expected both to commute farther and to spend more time commuting. Precisely this relationship is shown in Figure 1: 50 per cent of Detroit's central business district workers can get home by traveling five miles or less, and thirty minutes or less; only 32 per cent of their Chicago counterparts live that nearby, and only 34 per cent can get home within that length of time.

Just as certainly, the simple consumer-choice model predicts that Detroit workers will consume more residential space since it costs less than in Chicago. Figure 2 illustrates the comparison, measuring residential space consumption according to the structure type of

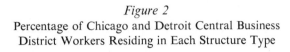

Figure 2
Percentage of Chicago and Detroit Central Business
District Workers Residing in Each Structure Type

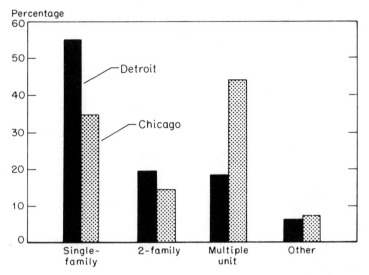

residence. It is assumed that the greatest amount of space is consumed by single-family units, followed by two-family units and multiple units. Both findings are well known and obvious empirical relationships. They are presented here because they are consistent with the consumer-choice model previously discussed, and because they illustrate the trade-off between housing cost and travel cost.

III. Housing-Market Discrimination and the Commuting of Negroes and Whites

In the absence of serious housing-market imperfections, it is possible that the simple model presented in Section II could explain household behavior adequately, especially if elaborated in terms of the heterogeneity of residential services according to attributes other than location, and in terms of the effect on travel and housing costs of other trips made by household members.[8]

[8] As an example of the latter, the housing-cost/travel-cost trade-offs of households with two or more wage earners must include all of their combined journey to work costs. Similarly, other kinds of frequently made trips may significantly affect the level of combined travel and housing costs for some households.

A far more serious omission in the model as presented thus far is the failure to consider explicitly the effects of racial discrimination on commuting and residential location. Any theory or model of the work trip and the residential-location behavior of urban households, if it pretends to be realistic and reasonably complete, should explicitly consider these effects, since racial discrimination in the housing market is a potentially enormous market imperfection with great influence on the commuting and residence patterns of both whites and nonwhites.

Racial discrimination may be thought of as a constraint on the housing-cost/transportation-cost trade-off model discussed previously. Discrimination limits the range of choice in which nonwhites are able to exercise the market calculus described above. In addition, the division of the market into two submarkets (a "free market" for whites, with unrestricted location choices, and a "segregated market" for nonwhites) affects the prices of housing services at various locations. Where such imperfections prevail, the schedule of location- or site-rents would be expected to differ from that postulated previously or obtained in the theoretical writings previously mentioned.[9]   .

Price levels in both submarkets are determined largely by supply and demand forces, but the determinants of these forces differ considerably between the two. The salient feature of both submarkets is the fact that existing housing stock makes up most of the supply. Each year's new construction is but a fraction of the total. A second important feature of the supply schedule is that the housing services represented by the stock are fixed by location and all but impossible to move to other locations. Urban development has usually occurred incrementally with distance from a single dominant center; as a result, the age distribution of the housing stock varies systematically with location.

Chicago and Detroit contain a single dominant nucleus and several much smaller subcenters around which some peripheral growth has occurred and around which, as a result, some older structures are located; but the overwhelming majority of older structures are found in and around the central business districts. The segregated market in Detroit and Chicago, as in most United States metropolitan areas, is mostly located around the dominant center, frequently referred to as "the grey area." Thus nearly all the structures in the nonwhite market are of prewar construction. Recent additions to the housing stock have been predominantly of two kinds: new lower-density structures on the periphery, and high-rise and other high-density structures at more central locations.

[9] Wingo, *Transportation and Urban Land*; and Alonzo, "Urban Land Market."

A ceiling on free-market rents and housing prices is established by the cost of providing new housing services, i.e., the cost of new construction. Of course, the costs of producing new housing vary considerably from one location to another. The greatest differences are due to variations in land costs, and the greatest of these are between the costs of vacant and nonvacant land. Site costs of developed sites are equal to the discounted value of the income streams of existing properties plus demolition costs. Thus it is hardly surprising that demolition is seldom carried out by the private market except to provide sites for very high-density and high-quality apartment developments in areas where there is substantial excess demand for them, or to provide sites for industrial or commercial use.

In any case, a price ceiling exists for any type of free-market housing, dependent on the costs of providing the desired services in a new structure or location and the differential travel costs between each site and peripheral sites. The earlier discussion makes clear that price differences equal to travel-cost differences may exist between two locations without providing an incentive for a household to locate in the lower-cost area. The critical importance of the available stock also causes a certain asymmetry in this market; price ceilings exist for each type of housing service, but no floor, except the chain of substitutes and the ability to modify the supply characteristics of the existing stock. Conversions, renovations, redecorating, and permissive deterioration are methods used by landlords and home-owners to change the configuration of the supply of housing services to correspond to changes in the configuration of demand in order to maximize their rental income.

Since nonwhites are almost entirely banned from outlying residential locations, price determination in the segregated market differs in a number of important ways from that in the free market. The price ceiling established by the cost of new fringe construction is almost entirely absent from the segregated market. The ceiling established by the cost of new construction in built-up areas still exists but, as in the free market, it is likely to be operative only at price levels considerably above those established by new construction on vacant land.

Demand for residential services in the segregated market is determined by forces similar to those in the free market. The major demand determinants for housing services in metropolitan areas during the postwar period have been increases in metropolitan populations, increases and redistribution of employment, rising incomes, and cheaper and more available housing credit. Increases in the nonwhite demand for residential services in urban areas were especially substantial during and after the war as large numbers of rural southern Negroes and of Puerto Ricans migrated to cities. Unlike whites, who can locate anywhere, nonwhites are mostly confined to areas allocated to them by convention, collusion, and the like.

While many of the same possibilities for adjusting the supply exist in the segregated as in the free market—such as the widely used device of density-increasing conversions—supply determinants in the segregated market are still considerably different. Since new construction is insignificant in the segregated market, nearly all additions to its housing supply must come from spatial expansion of the segregated market. Such expansion primarily results from very substantial increases in the nonwhite demand for housing services; it usually consists of peripheral growth—almost never of the creation of "islands" in all-white areas. Thus, the prices and changes in their level in the segregated market depend almost entirely on the relative growth of the nonwhite demand within an urban area, and the rate at which the segregated market is permitted to expand.

If demand far exceeds supply in the segregated market, as it did during and immediately after World War II, rents and housing prices are sure to rise. Wartime controls on building materials and construction kept the supply of urban housing services relatively constant. At the same time, migration to cities and higher incomes caused demand to soar, especially in the segregated market, generating enormous increases in densities and sharp increases in price levels.

The postwar housebuilding boom slowly eased the supply situation, and larger peripheral expansions of the segregated market were allowed. Large price differentials between the two markets gave whites an incentive to put housing on the segregated market. They used the profits to purchase more or better housing services elsewhere. The result was a fairly rapid expansion and consolidation of the segregated market which may have erased the former price differentials. That a positive differential still remains, however, and undoubtedly will remain so long as effective segregation persists seems likely, the reason being that the nonwhite market expands only as the result of demand pressures. Unless a Negro is willing to pay somewhat more for a particular location than a white is, white owners and landlords are unlikely to sell or rent to him. Therefore, barring a sharp decrease in nonwhite demand, price levels in the segregated market will probably continue to be higher than in the free market.

This conclusion runs counter to views widely held and accepted by real estate brokers and white home-owners. For example, it is still commonly believed that property values plummet when Negroes move into a white neighborhood. Such beliefs are consistently refuted by all the systematic empirical investigations the author has encountered,[10] but they are still held by lenders and until recently have even been approved by the Federal Housing Authority in its appraisal policies. Their full acceptance—especially by mortgage lenders, whose attitudes so crucially influence the operation of the market—makes their becoming self-fulfilling prophecies an omnipresent danger.

The author proposes that discrimination raises the cost of Negro housing above that of similar free-market housing, but that housing prices in the segregated market vary inversely with distance from major workplace agglomerations, just as they do in the free market. For the empirical testing that follows, it is postulated that: (1) housing costs in the segregated market are higher at every distance from the central business district than they are in the free market; (2) that Detroit housing costs in the segregated market are lower than those in Chicago at each distance; and (3) that housing costs per unit of residential space of a given quality decrease with distance from the central business district in each of the four markets.

The nearly absolute restriction on nonwhite residential location is illustrated in Figures 3 and 4, depicting the residential areas of Detroit and Chicago. The data shown in the two figures represent the nonwhite percentages of the total number of workers residing in each area during the study years. Given these spatial patterns of housing segregation, the reader can easily perceive that whites and nonwhites in both cities differ significantly in the distances and elapsed times of their journey to work. The effects of these constraints on Negro residential choice are partly shown in Figure 5, which graphs the percentages of Chicago and Detroit whites and Negroes residing in each two-mile interval from the central business district in which they work. The similarity in the patterns for the two cities is almost uncanny. The only significant difference is that the peaks of the distributions are about two miles closer to the central business district in Detroit than in Chicago. In Detroit, 36 per cent of the Negro labor force in the central business district reside between two and four miles from the district; in Chicago, almost an identical percentage reside between four and six miles from

[10] For example, see William M. Ladd, "The Effect of Integration on Property Values," *American Economic Review*, Sept. 1962; and Luigi Laurenti, *Property Values and Race: Studies in Seven Cities*, University of California Press, 1960.

Figure 3
Negro Workers Residing in Each Detroit Analysis Area
as a Percentage of All Workers Residing in
the Analysis Area, 1953

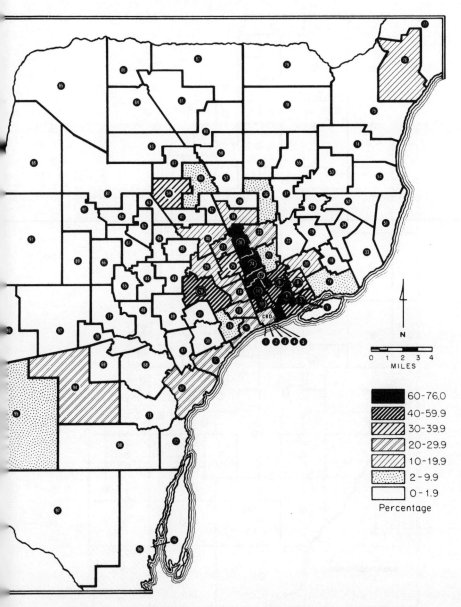

Figure 4
Negro Workers Residing in Each Chicago Analysis Area
as a Percentage of All Workers Residing in
the Analysis Area, 1956

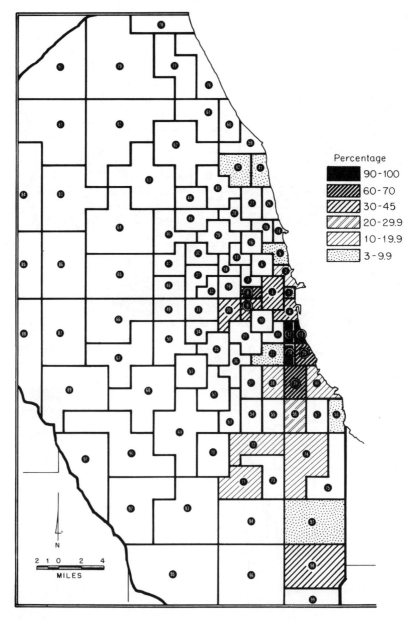

Figure 5
Percentage of White and Negro Central Business
District Workers Residing in Each Two-Mile
Distance Ring from the Chicago and Detroit Centers

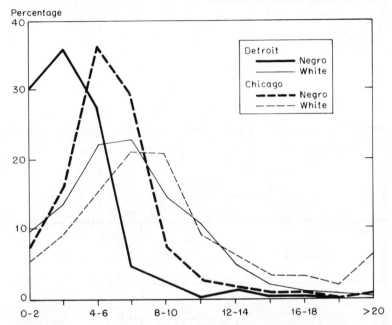

the Loop. About 22 per cent of Detroit's white workers reside in each of the distance intervals, four to six miles and six to eight miles; only about 1 per cent less of their Chicago counterparts reside in each of the six to eight and eight to ten mile intervals. These striking similarities prevail despite the fact that the two cities differ substantially in metropolitan population, central business district employment, industrial composition, area, period of most rapid development, residential density, and most other attributes that affect travel and residential patterns.

The discrepancy in the distances at which the profiles peak is due largely to differences in central business district employment levels and in metropolitan scale. For the same percentages of central business district workers to live within a given distance in both cities, the residential density of Chicago's workers would have to be several times as great. This is accentuated by the fact that in Chicago the quantity and percentage of the total area devoted to nonresidential use near the central business district are several times as great as in Detroit.

Figure 6

Percentages of Chicago White and Nonwhite Central Business District Workers Residing in Each Sector, 1956

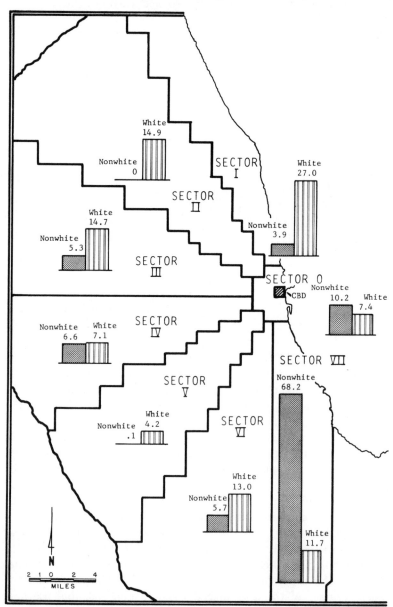

Figure 7
Percentages of Chicago White and Nonwhite
Sector O Workers Residing in Each Sector, 1956

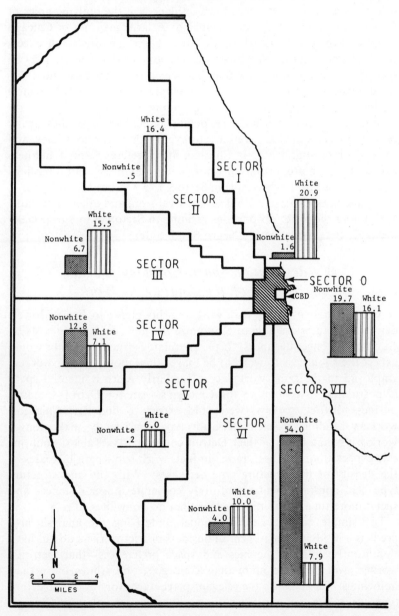

Despite the great differences in the nonwhite and white residence profiles shown in Figure 5, the full effect of segregation on nonwhite commuting patterns is still greater than suggested there. From Figure 4 it is apparent that the few Negro residences in the outlying areas of Chicago are distributed very unequally. A large majority of Chicago Negroes live in the dismal South Side. Discrimination's full effects on the commuting of Negro central business district workers may be seen more clearly in Figures 6 and 7, which show the residential distributions of workers of both races employed in Chicago's central business district and in Sector 0 surrounding it.

Segregation also affects the residential preferences of whites, many of whom have a dual motivation: to avoid living near nonwhites, and to reside in prestige areas. In Chicago, these preferences no doubt help explain the high proportions of whites employed in the central business district and Sector 0 who reside in Sectors 1 to 3 (especially in Sector 1, which includes Chicago's Gold Coast, Evanston, and other high-status areas), and the lower proportions residing in Sectors 4 to 7 (especially Sector 7, the predominantly Negro South Side).

IV. Residential Space Consumption and the Length of the Journey to Work

It was postulated above that workers who prefer to live in lower-density structures are able to economize the most on housing costs by commuting longer distances. If the postulate is true, the author would expect their journeys to work to be longer than those of other workers employed in the same workplaces. Similarly, since residential space is postulated to cost more for Chicago's than for Detroit's central business district workers, we would expect to find that Chicago's workers residing in each structure type consistently make longer work trips than those of their Detroit counterparts. Table 1 confirms this expectation; for both races, in fact, work trip length increases as the density of the structure type decreases. With city and structure type held constant, whites uniformly commute longer distances and spend more time commuting farther than do nonwhites.

The simple consumer-choice model underlying the analysis also predicts—if the two cities' central business district workers do not have significantly different incomes and space preferences—that Detroit's workers will consume more than Chicago's, and whites more than nonwhites. Table 2 lists the relevant percentages for various structure types, revealing—among other things—that the percentage of Chicago

TABLE 1

QUARTILE DISTANCE AND TIME OF TRAVEL FOR CENTRAL BUSINESS
DISTRICT COMMUTERS, BY RACE AND RESIDENCE STRUCTURE TYPE

Quartile and Residence Structure Type	AIRLINE DISTANCE (miles)				ELAPSED TIME (hours)			
	White		Negro		White		Negro	
	Chi.	Det.	Chi.	Det.	Chi.	Det.	Chi.	Det.
1st quartile								
One-family	7.7	5.0	4.0	1.8	6.4	4.5	5.1	3.3
Two-family	4.3	3.1	3.3	1.2	4.8	4.0	4.2	3.0
Multiple	3.5	1.7	3.2	0.3	4.2	2.9	3.9	2.3
2nd quartile								
One-family	10.5	7.1	7.1	3.2	8.3	6.2	7.3	4.5
Two-family	6.0	4.5	5.4	2.4	6.6	4.9	5.8	4.4
Multiple	5.7	3.1	4.5	1.6	5.5	4.4	4.8	3.8
3rd quartile								
One-family	15.3	9.4	9.4	4.1	9.9	7.9	8.9	6.1
Two-family	7.8	6.0	7.4	3.5	8.2	7.1	7.5	5.9
Multiple	7.6	4.5	6.0	2.9	7.2	5.6	6.4	4.9

TABLE 2

PERCENTAGES OF CHICAGO AND DETROIT WHITE AND NEGRO CENTRAL BUSINESS DISTRICT
WORKERS RESIDING IN VARIOUS STRUCTURE TYPES

Structure Type	White		Negro	
	Chicago	Detroit	Chicago	Detroit
One-family	36.5	58.4	9.2	30.2
Two-family	15.0	18.2	9.5	30.0
Multiple	41.4	17.4	73.0	28.7
Other	7.1	6.0	8.3	11.1
Total	100.0	100.0	100.0	100.0

whites residing in multiple units is more than twice that of Detroit whites. From this fact the author concludes that the higher price (minimum-cost combination of commuting costs and location rents) Chicago workers must pay for residential space discourages them from consuming more of it.

Part of the racial difference in residential space consumption in both Chicago and Detroit is possibly due to differences in incomes and preferences; however, the author concludes that much of it is due to the higher costs of residential space and restricted choices in the market for real property.

V. Substitution of Time and Money Expenditures in Commuting

Trade-offs between housing and travel costs are not the only alternatives available to urban households attempting to maximize their real incomes. Journey-to-work travel costs have two components: dollar costs and time costs. Commuters to the central business district may choose among fairly numerous transportation means in Detroit, and even more in Chicago, with widely varying time and money costs. The relative costs among the means partly depend on distance traveled and on the household's choice of residential density. The choice, as discussed previously, strongly affects the amount a worker can save in housing costs by commuting longer distances. The numerous transportation means can also be used in combination to provide still more alternative time and money costs.

If we consider only out-of-pocket costs, and if parking is free, the dollar costs of a railroad commuter and of a lone automobile commuter to the Chicago central business district are very similar; parking charges and car pooling, however, greatly affect the out-of-pocket costs of automobile commuting. These costs, for a single car commuter paying $1.00 a day for parking, exceed rail-commuting costs by about $0.80 a day, assuming no collection or distribution charges for the railroad commuter. If these costs are shared by two persons, auto commuting costs 20 per cent less for a trip to and from a residence area twenty miles from the Loop.

The level of transportation service, the amount of inconvenience and delay, and the portal-to-portal time of commuting by alternative travel means largely depend on the density of the worker's residence and workplace. Chicago's central business district has a combination of an unusually high level of transit service and high parking charges,

TABLE 3

PERCENTAGES OF DETROIT WHITE WORKERS USING PUBLIC TRANSIT,
BY WORKPLACE RING AND RESIDENCE TYPE

Workplace Ring (higher to lower workplace density)	Residence Type (higher to lower residential density)		
	Multiple	Two-Family	One-Family
1	60.7	58.7	50.6
2	28.5	28.6	19.5
3	29.4	23.1	18.9
4	27.3	23.1	14.1
5	17.8	11.1	8.4
6	5.8	4.1	3.5

both stemming from its very high workplace density. The result is a high rate of public transit use: 80 per cent of the central business district's workers arrive there by some form of transit. The lower rate in Detroit—53 per cent—is attributable to lower parking charges, lower levels of public transit services, and lower average residential density. Both high workplace and high residential densities usually mean more frequent transit service with wider coverage. Thus, there is a high probability that a worker employed at a very high-density workplace, such as the CBD, and residing in a very high-density residential area, will find it cheaper to use public transit than to travel by car. The probability is much lower for a worker employed at the same workplace but residing in a lower-density area, and it is nearly zero for a worker having both a very low-density workplace and a low-density residence. Table 3, which lists the percentage of Detroit workers using public transit, by workplace ring and structure type of residence, illustrates just this relationship. Reading the table from top to bottom, we find a decrease in the average workplace density and thus in the level of transit service at workplaces; and reading from left to right, we find a decrease also in the average residential density and thus the average level of transit service. The transit-use figures shown in Table 3 are just those that would be predicted if the probability of public transit use were expressed as the joint probability of use at the workplace and at the residence, where the independent probabilities are positively related to workplace and residence densities. The scatter diagram, Figure 8, illustrates the relationship between automobile use at the origin of the work trip (either by driver or rider) and the percentage of workers residing in single-family dwelling units, for all white Chicago workers. From the figure, it is clear that those

Figure 8
Percentage of Automobile Commuters in
Each of Chicago's Residence Areas,
by Percentage of Area's Single-Family Dwelling Units

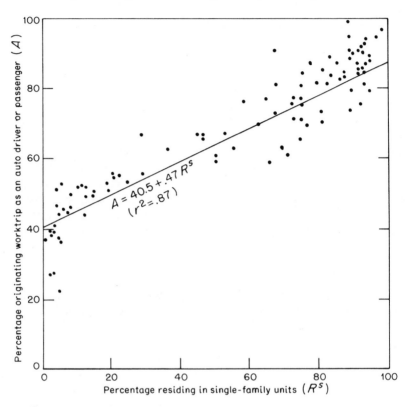

residence areas having fewer single-family units and thus lower residential densities tend to have lower rapid-transit use at the origin of work trips.

Even among those CBD workers in Chicago who reside in low-density structures, the vast majority are discouraged from commuting by automobile all the way to work, because of the high employment density and high parking charges in the CBD, and the high levels of service and abundant capacity provided by rapid transit and commuter railroads. Typically, those residing in single-family units combine the use of private automobiles, either as drivers or passengers, with commuter railroad or—slightly less often—rapid transit. Table 4

TABLE 4

PERCENTAGE OF CHICAGO CENTRAL BUSINESS DISTRICT WORKERS RESIDING IN
VARIOUS STRUCTURE TYPES, BY TRAVEL MODE COMBINATIONS

Travel Mode at Origin	Travel Mode at Destination	Type of Residence				
		One-Family	Two-Family	Multiple	Other	Total
Automobile						
Driver	Car driver	40.0	13.9	40.2	5.9	100.0
Driver	Railroad	81.9	8.1	8.8	1.2	100.0
Driver	Rapid transit	56.3	22.0	21.7	0	100.0
Driver	Bus	63.6	7.4	27.1	1.9	100.0
Passenger	Car pass.	28.3	13.4	50.9	7.4	100.0
Passenger	Railroad	85.4	6.9	5.5	2.2	100.0
Passenger	Rapid transit	60.6	13.5	25.2	0.7	100.0
Passenger	Bus	77.7	9.5	12.8	0	100.0
Railroad	Railroad	47.4	9.7	38.4	4.5	100.0
Railroad	Rapid transit	76.0	6.0	18.0	0	100.0
Railroad	Bus	57.5	1.9	29.0	11.6	100.0
Rapid transit	Rapid transit	11.4	13.3	67.6	7.7	100.0
Rapid transit	Bus	12.4	30.9	43.7	13.0	100.0
Bus	Railroad	54.7	20.5	20.2	4.6	100.0
Bus	Rapid transit	31.9	25.3	40.8	2.0	100.0
Bus	Bus	17.4	16.2	51.1	15.3	100.0
All modes		36.5	14.8	41.1	7.6	100.0

illustrates the relationship for Chicago between choice of mode combinations and the decision to reside at various densities, as measured by structure type. For example, 85 per cent of those who are combined car passengers and railroad commuters, and 82 per cent of those who are combined car drivers and rail commuters reside in single-family units; only 6 and 9 per cent of those groups, respectively, reside in multiple units. As pointed out previously, the dollar-cost and time-cost properties of these combination modes result in the highest-cost and highest average speed of all of the combination modes shown in Table 4.

The lowest money-cost, lowest speed-mode combination included in Table 4 is undoubtedly the combination of the local bus at residence and the local bus at workplace; only 17 per cent of those using that combination reside in single-family structures, while 51 per cent reside in multiple units, and 15 per cent in other dwelling units (which usually have the highest densities of all).

The interpretation offered here for the differences in the rates of use of the combinations listed in Table 4 is that they are the result of the cost-minimization, utility-maximization calculus described previously.

The large housing-cost savings per mile traveled for those residing at the lowest densities encourages them to travel long distances. As the distance traveled increases, the time savings obtainable from using modal combinations with higher speed encourages long-distance commuters to spend more money to reduce travel time. In addition, as residential density decreases, the time costs of using various travel modes from residence—railroad and rapid transit in particular and, to a lesser extent, bus—increase rapidly, usually making the private car the most economical way of originating the trip.

The situation is somewhat different for a great many people who choose to commute entirely by local bus. Their decision to reside at high density causes their potential housing-cost savings by commuting longer distances to be small and to dictate minimal transportation expenditures in both time and money. Since terminal time makes up a very large proportion of total time spent on short trips by all modes, the travel-time savings obtainable from the faster, more costly travel combinations are often too small to justify the larger dollar expenditures. Moreover, many small-space consumers employed in the Chicago central business district can use the relatively high-speed rapid-transit mode for the entire trip and walk to residences and workplaces located near the rapid transit stations; of those using rapid transit for the entire trip, the percentage residing in multiple units is higher than that for any other travel model combination—68 per cent.

The relatively small percentage of whole-trip automobile commuters, both drivers and riders, residing in single-family units (40 and 28 per cent, respectively) suggests the interpretation that a majority of automobile commuters to the Chicago central business district use their cars for work-associated purposes.[11]

The importance of cars and buses in trips from residence to the higher-volume grade-separated facilities is to be seen in Table 5, which gives the percentages of Chicago central business district workers residing within the cordon area and using each mode at their residences, and the percentages arriving in the central business district by each travel mode. (Detroit data do not permit comparable tabulations, since only the primary mode used was coded.) Table 5 shows that 20 per cent of the work trips to the Chicago central business district originate as car-driver trips, 12 per cent as car-rider trips, and 39 per cent as bus trips, while only 12.4 per cent of the arrivals represent

[11] This interpretation is supported by the finding that a disproportionate number of both car drivers and car passengers to Chicago's central business district and Sector 0 gave "sales" as their occupation.

TABLE 5

PERCENTAGE OF CHICAGO CENTRAL BUSINESS DISTRICT WORKERS USING EACH MODE
AT THEIR RESIDENCES AND WORKPLACES

Travel Mode	At Origin	At Destination
Car driver	19.9	12.3
Car rider	11.6	9.3
Railroad	13.1	22.1
Rapid transit	13.7	33.5
Bus	39.2	25.0
Taxi	--	0.3
Walk	1.3	1.3

car-driver trips, 4 per cent car-rider trips, and 25 per cent bus trips. Commuter railroad, by way of contrast, accounts for 22 per cent of destinations but only 13 per cent of origins; and rapid transit accounts for only 14 per cent of trip origins but over 33 per cent of trip destinations. Table 6 shows that the majority of commuter railroad trips combined with another mode are serviced at the origin by auto; of the 22 per cent of work trips arriving in the Loop by commuter railroad, 9 per cent originate by car, about equally divided between driver and passenger trips. Car trips are only about half as important as feeders for the rapid-transit lines: of the 34 per cent of destinations accounted for by rapid transit, only about 4.1 per cent begin by car. Buses are the important collector for the rapid transit system: almost one-half the 75,000 rapid-transit trips terminating in the central business district originate by bus, while only slightly more than one-third of the 75,000 arrivals originate on the rapid-transit line.

A comparison of Tables 5 and 6 illustrates the combined effect of lower parking fees and slightly poorer transit service on modes of

TABLE 6

PERCENTAGE OF CHICAGO WORKERS EMPLOYED IN SECTOR O
USING EACH MODE AT THEIR RESIDENCES AND WORKPLACES

Travel Mode	At Origin	At Destination
Car driver	36.8	34.3
Car rider	10.9	8.5
Railroad	4.2	6.4
Rapid transit	6.9	8.6
Bus	33.9	34.0
Walk	6.6	6.6
Work at home	1.0	1.0

TABLE 7

PERCENTAGE OF CHICAGO WORKERS USING EACH COMBINATION OF ORIGIN AND
DESTINATION MODES, BY WORKPLACE LOCATION AND RESIDENCE TYPE

Origin Mode	Destination Mode	One-Family	Two-Family	Multiple	All Residence Types
	A.	CENTRAL BUSINESS DISTRICT			
Automobile					
Driver	Car driver	13.5	11.6	12.1	12.3
Driver	Railroad	10.5	2.5	0.9	4.4
Driver	Rapid transit	3.7	3.4	1.2	2.3
Driver	Bus	1.2	0.3	0.5	0.7
Passenger	Car passenger	3.4	3.4	5.1	4.2
Passenger	Railroad	11.6	2.2	0.6	4.6
Passenger	Rapid transit	3.2	1.7	1.0	1.8
Passenger	Bus	1.8	0.5	0.3	0.8
Railroad	Railroad	16.3	8.2	10.7	12.0
Railroad	Rapid transit	0.9	0.2	0.2	0.4
Railroad	Bus	1.2	0.1	0.5	0.7
Rapid transit	Rapid transit	4.2	12.0	20.7	13.2
Rapid transit	Bus	0.1	0.6	0.7	0.5
Bus	Railroad	1.8	1.7	0.5	1.1
Bus	Rapid transit	14.1	26.7	15.4	15.8
Bus	Bus	11.0	24.1	27.7	22.3
Other	Other	1.5	.8	1.9	2.9
All modes		100.0	100.0	100.0	100.0
	B.	SECTOR O			
Automobile					
Driver	Car driver	42.8	36.9	33.0	34.2
Driver	Railroad	4.4	0.6	0.2	1.4
Driver	Rapid transit	1.1	0.5	0.2	0.5
Driver	Bus	1.8	0.1	0.1	0.5
Passenger	Car passenger	7.4	9.2	3.4	8.2
Passenger	Railroad	3.9	0.6	0.2	1.2
Passenger	Rapid transit	0.8	0.2	0.2	0.4
Passenger	Bus	2.3	0.5	0.6	1.0
Railroad	Railroad	6.5	3.0	2.5	3.4
Railroad	Rapid transit	0.4	--	0.1	0.1
Railroad	Bus	1.2	0.4	0.4	0.6
Rapid transit	Rapid transit	1.8	3.6	5.1	3.9
Rapid transit	Bus	1.0	1.5	4.1	2.6
Bus	Railroad	0.9	0.2	0.2	0
Bus	Rapid transit	5.0	5.9	4.2	3.6
Bus	Bus	16.2	32.3	35.8	29.3
Other	Other	2.5	4.5	9.7	9.1
All modes		100.0	100.0	100.0	100.0

travel used by workers employed in Chicago's Sector 0. While only about 17 per cent of the central business district workers reach their workplaces by car, either as drivers or riders, more than twice that percentage (43 per cent) of Sector 0's workers do so. Similarly, while 22 per cent of the CBD's commuters arrive by commuter railroad, only a little more than 6 per cent of Sector 0's commuters do, of whom nearly one-half start the trip as car drivers or riders; and only 8.6 per cent arrive by rapid transit as opposed to nearly 34 per cent of Loop employees. The bus is by far the most important transit vehicle for Sector 0 workers: 34 per cent of the worktrip arrivals in Sector 0 are by bus, and 33 per cent of originations; 29 per cent of those workers ride the bus all the way between home and work.

The percentage distribution for the structure types given in Table 7 suggest how the use rate of each travel-mode combination is affected by workers' choices of residential density, differences in the level of service provided by various modes, and differences in the level of parking charges between the CBD and Sector 0. Perhaps the features most sharply exhibited in Table 7 are: (1) the much greater use of private automobiles by Sector 0 than by CBD workers; (2) the much greater use of commuter railroads in combination with other travel means by CBD workers residing in single-family units than by any other group employed in either CBD or Sector 0; and (3) the minimal use of either rapid transit or commuter railroad by Sector 0 workers. The greater distance of a majority of the workplaces in Sector 0 from railroad and rapid transit stations than in the CBD, and the lower parking costs in Sector 0 apparently lead workers who do not live conveniently near a railroad or rapid transit station or who place a

TABLE 8

PERCENTAGE OF CHICAGO WHITES AND NEGROES USING
VARIOUS MODES OF TRAVEL TO TWO DESTINATIONS

| | DESTINATION | | | |
| | Sector 0 | | CBD | |
Travel Mode	Whites	Negroes	Whites	Negroes
Car driver	36.5	24.8	12.4	10.8
Car rider	8.3	9.0	4.1	6.9
Railroad	7.7	.6	23.9	4.6
Rapid transit	9.4	5.4	33.2	36.5
Bus	29.6	52.2	23.9	39.3
Walk	6.5	7.1	1.2	
Other	1.7	0.8	1.2	2.0

high value on their travel time to commute by car rather than by railroad or rapid transit. Nearly 43 per cent of Sector 0 workers who reside in single-family units drive private cars between home and work, and over 7 per cent commute the entire distance as car passengers.

Table 8 illustrates the greater use of public transit vehicles, especially buses, by Negroes employed in the CBD and Sector 0. Nearly 45 per cent of Sector 0 whites commute by car, compared with about 34 per cent of Negroes. Whites also use the longer-distance, higher-speed transit modes much more than Negroes do: nearly 8 per cent of Sector 0 and 24 per cent of CBD whites arrive by commuter railroad, as opposed to less than 1 per cent of Sector 0 and less than 5 per cent of CBD Negroes.

VI. Summary and Conclusions

The findings of this study have considerable bearing on a problem currently being debated: how to provide access to central urban workplaces for high- and middle-income commuters. The work reported here does not pretend to solve the problem, but some systematic information is presented that should help clarify it.

For example, the paper illustrates the great impact of racial discrimination on the travel behavior and residential location decisions of both whites and nonwhites. Discrimination is a central difficulty. It must be dealt with if we are to solve this aspect of the urban transportation problem, whether it be through renewal of central residential areas or by provision of high-speed rapid transit facilities.

The insights recorded which bear upon the determinants of residential location decisions and the choices among transportation means should also be useful in the evaluation of alternative urban transportation policies. Of particular significance are the data contributing to understanding of the extreme specialization of the high-speed rail facilities serving the Chicago central business district. Advocates of the rail-transit proposals noted in Section I tend to advance them as a cure-all for the transportation ills of urban communities. The findings presented here suggest that they are, instead, specific remedies for a small part of the over-all problem, and that their benefits are restricted to a narrow segment of the urban population.

The paper has a more important objective, however: the development and testing of a fairly simple but nonetheless powerful economic model that will be useful in explaining and predicting the travel and residential behavior of the urban population. The questions considered in this paper have received little economic analysis heretofore; people who have been most closely identified with these problems have tended to discount the usefulness of economic theory and analysis in solving them.

The consumer-choice model described here emphasizes several kinds of economic calculations assumed to be made by urban workers in deciding on the mode or combination of transportation modes used for the journey to work, the distance commuted, the time spent commuting, and the amount of residential space consumed (or the residential density at which they reside). The model presents these choices as being determined by the minimization of household's urban locational costs, which are the sum of housing costs incurred to reside near work and of work-associated travel costs. The model explicitly considers several kinds of cost trade-offs available to urban households in maximizing their real income. The first is a trade-off between higher housing costs and higher transportation costs. Workers employed at high-density workplaces can save on housing costs by commuting longer distances—but thus increasing transportation costs. The amount they can save on housing costs depends on both the level and rate at which housing costs per residential-space unit decrease with distance from their workplaces and on the number of space units they consume.

The second important set of trade-offs embraces the substitution possibilities between travel-time and money-cost expenditures for the journey to work. The various modes or combinations of modes have different money-cost and speed characteristics, and the differences provide another opportunity to urban households for utility maximization. Moreover, these characteristics both affect and are affected by workers' decisions about residential density.

The model also deals explicitly with the effect of racial discrimination on the operation of the housing market and on the decisions of white and nonwhite households about their travel and residential behavior. Housing-market discrimination is treated as a constraint on nonwhite behavior, which also systematically affects the preferences of whites among alternative residential locations.

Finally, hypotheses suggested by this model are tested empirically using data on work travel obtained from the Chicago and Detroit transportation studies. Over all, the empirical tests are consistent with the simple economic model used in the analysis. Although incomplete, the model and its empirical testing suggest the likelihood that economic analysis of this type can greatly increase our understanding of the problems and thus promote the sounder urban transportation planning we so urgently need.

COMMENT
BRITTON HARRIS, University of Pennsylvania

Kain has made a useful start in exploring the structure of private preference for residential space and transportation cost, and the trade-offs between them. Such an exploration is certainly necessary to the investigation of various optima under different combinations of public policies of investment, operation, control, and incentives. The reaction of private decision-makers will surely influence the magnitudes of the payoffs of these public decisions. Housing market analysis by and large appears to neglect transportation factors, and transportation analysis has certainly neglected the influence of transportation on the housing market. Kain clearly demonstrates that this neglect is un-pardonable, inasmuch as residential locators trade off freely between space and transportation costs. It is, however, not captious to suggest that serious analysis of these problems requires more accurate quan-tification than Kain has given us at this stage. Such a quantification should also take into account the interaction (or cross-elasticities) between a larger number of variables which may be subject to change over time as the metropolitan area changes. This consideration of the interaction of variables implies a more scrupulous separation of in-fluences, which I feel Kain neglected in his treatment of race and loca-tion. There is no question that the urban Negro population of Chicago is seriously disadvantaged, but Kain does not tackle the question of the extent to which this disadvantage is occasioned by income and oc-cupational factors alone, independent of segregation in housing. It is my own guess that housing segregation *per se* plays a minor role, while cultural deprivation and job discrimination are far more important in the phenomena which Kain displays. Important policy decisions depend on an elucidation of this point.

Pricing as a Tool in Coordination of Local Transportation

WILLIAM VICKREY

COLUMBIA UNIVERSITY

Use of pricing as a means of obtaining improved utilization of transportation facilities within metropolitan areas has hardly been an outstanding success in the past and, with the increasing share of this function now taken by the private automobile, pricing in recent years has been pushed even further into the background. Yet, now more than ever before, with increasingly vast sums at stake and even the whole pattern of our metropolitan areas likely to be radically affected by the manner in which transportation facilities are to be provided and used, it is becoming essential that the full potentialities of the pricing instrument be developed. That instrument is needed as a means not only of improving utilization of existing facilities in the short run, but also of developing the data essential to intelligent planning for new facilities.

A number of factors conspire to distract attention from the possibilities of using pricing for these ends. One factor is the frequent practice of discussing the subject in terms of aggregates and averages that mask sharp differences in costs and benefits. The differences are particularly sharp in the context of urban transportation, in that important time peaks compound their effects with locational peaks and with wide differences among individuals in the marginal significance of different uses. Another factor has been the relatively high cost and irksomeness of the methods hitherto employed for the direct pricing of specific transportation services. In the absence of reliable data or estimates of elasticities and cross-elasticities of demand, there has been a tendency in transportation planning to ignore price elasticities and to assume that past trends will continue, regardless of what might be done with suitable pricing policies. Particularly with respect to the pricing of roadway use, a long history of relative absence of direct charges, plus a genuine lack of functional need of such charges for use of facilities with a low level of utilization and hence low marginal cost, have tended to cause the potentialities for improvement in this direction to be overlooked. Given only a modest amount of ingenuity, however, it is not too much to say that few significant refinements in the pricing of transportation are now actually beyond reach on purely mechanical grounds.

Estimates of the costs involved in the use of urban streets and highways by private automobiles vary widely. In most cases, not enough firm data are available to pin costs down with great accuracy, but enough is known to indicate that they can reach very high levels, and that fairly drastic pricing procedures could be justified. G. J. Roth (Department of Applied Economics, Cambridge, England) estimates that an optimum tax rate to apply on the basis of traffic data for Cambridge would range from 10 to 21 shillings per hour, or 7 to 22 pence per mile. M. Bruce Johnson (University of Washington) has presented figures suggesting that tax rates of about 5 cents per mile would be appropriate for what are vaguely described as urban arterials at levels of traffic 75 per cent of "mean practical capacity," with sharply higher rates applicable to conditions of heavier traffic. Price tags attached to alternative plans for the Washington, D.C., area for 1980 indicated that, for each additional car brought into the central business district during the rush hour, capital investment in highway facilities, not including parking, would tend to increase by $23,000. In Los Angeles where, among the larger cities, conditions might be thought most favorable for freeway construction, costs of providing for peak traffic range from 3 to 12 cents per vehicle mile. While estimates of this kind vary widely and are all subject to wide ranges of error, they indicate costs sufficiently higher than vehicular charges cover to warrant serious exploration of ways and means of bringing this cost home to the individuals whose choices of transportation patterns give rise to the costs.

Suggestions that drivers on city streets should pay for them on the basis of specific trips have usually been rejected out of hand on the ground that the collection of such charges would be too costly and would cause too much interference with the flow of traffic. Even where tolls are collected for use of bridges, tunnels, and the like, suggestions of adjustment of tolls according to the degree of congestion and the time of day have been rejected, partly because of familiar and established patterns, and partly on the ground that such variation would tend to produce confusion causing further delays at toll-collection points. Recently, however, a number of alternative schemes have been proposed for the collection of such charges, any one of which would perform the job at modest cost and with practically no interference with traffic flow.

One type of system would involve equipping each vehicle with an identification unit which can be scanned by roadside equipment located at zone boundaries so that, whenever a vehicle passed from one zone into another, a record would be made of the identity of the vehicle and the time. The records taken to a central data processing unit for assembling data on particular vehicles would be the basis of billing the owners of vehicles periodically. Bills could be readily itemized to whatever extent the owner requested, so that, if he is a regular user of the highways of an area, he could modify his pattern of highway use according to the charges. In addition, current charges could be indicated by roadside notices or publicized in other ways. A number of different techniques of identification are available, some of which are actually in use for railway, bus, and other kinds of carrier. They include electronic response blocks energized from a scanning beam, small code-signal transmitters connected with the car's ignition switch, reflectorized panels scanned by photoelectric equipment, sequences of slots in an iron bar to be scanned by radar, or photographs of modified license plates with subsequent conversion to digital records by scanning equipment at the central processing bureau. There should be no difficulty in developing one or more of these methods to a satisfactory level of reliability and at reasonable cost.

Another major type of system requires a meter on the car, in most cases, arranged to display a signal visible from the outside to indicate the manner in which it is functioning. In some versions, the meter runs down at a time rate that can be varied according to traffic conditions. In one form, the driver is responsible for setting the meter to a rate indicated by wayside signals, according to time of day or traffic conditions. A slightly more elaborate form of meter would change the rate automatically in response to signals emitted at zone boundaries. Another version could be a meter running down in response to pulses or signals emitted from wayside apparatus, either in the form of pulsed signals blanketing an area or propagated from cables laid lengthwise in the road, or sequences of signals from crosswise antennae or cables. Various ways of resetting the meters can be devised, but perhaps the simplest would be resetting them by the insertion of destructible tokens purchased at service stations. Meters at an attractively low cost have been devised in England, where pricing of highway use has aroused considerable interest.

Such meters have the further advantage of adjustment to function as parking meters; as such, they are more flexible than fixed meters installed at the curb, in that payment is determined ex post and can be more directly apportioned to the time the parking space is occupied. Moreover, it is possible to vary the charge by time of day and even permit vehicle owners, presumably at their own expense, to attach devices which adjust the meter charging rate when a car is left parked over periods covering more than one rate of parking charge.

The cost of even the more expensive of such charging systems should be only a minor sum relative to the cost of the facilities to be controlled. Even for the systems using identification and central processing, the capital cost of the scanning and processing equipment should not come to more than about $20 per car for a moderately large metropolitan area. The identification unit carried by the car may involve a roughly comparable cost. The cost of processing and billing would be roughly comparable to that of accounting and billing for telephone or electric power service. Probably the greatest difficulty would be initial and simultaneous equipment of all cars that use the streets of a particular area more or less regularly.

If granted that some such scheme is a feasible possibility, what would it mean for the coordination of local transportation? The possibilities are indeed far-reaching. The most obvious immediate impact to be expected is a more economical distribution of traffic between the various modes. The imbalance between public transit and private automobile is much greater than would appear from a superficial comparison of over-all costs, and introduction of a flexible pricing system capable of differentiating between peak and off-peak usage can accomplish more than might at first appear. The reason is that public transit usage is much more sharply concentrated in the peak hours than vehicular traffic is, so that if no differentiation between peak and off-peak charges is made for either facility, public transit makes an unduly poor showing. It could be regarded as a form of "cream skimming" on the part of the private automobile.

In extreme cases, failure to distinguish rush-hour and non-rush-hour traffic can completely invert the cost comparison. As a somewhat oversimplified example, suppose a facility of type M attracts rush-hour and non-rush-hour passengers at the ratio of 1 to 4, and costs $1.00 for each rush-hour passenger provided for and 20 cents for each nonrush-hour passenger. Suppose also the costs of facility T are uniformly 25 per cent less, or 80 and 15 cents, respectively. If costs are figured on an over-all average basis, M has a cost of $1.00 + 4($0.20)/5 = $1.80/5 = $0.36; for facility T, the average cost is $.075 + $0.15/2 = $0.90/2 = $0.45, on the assumption that for T one-half the total traffic is rush-hour traffic. The planner pointing to that calculation might ask why inferior transit service should be provided at a higher cost than the preferred private automobile costs. Transit service is cheaper, however, by 25 cents in the rush hour and 5 cents in the non-rush hour, as appropriately differentiated charges show. If differentiation by time of day is impossible, it would be desirable to have the relative charges on the two facilities at least reflect the direction of the specific cost differentials at the specific times. That could be done by raising the charges on M to, say, 45 cents as compared with costs of 36 cents on the average basis, while using the excess revenues to subsidize T and make it self-liquidating by lowering the charge to 35 from 45 cents. Ruling out special charges for peak use thus creates an impressive argument for subsidizing public transit at the expense of private vehicular traffic.

One effect of such charges for street use would be to change the relative attractiveness of different forms of mass transportation. Under present conditions, buses are often entangled in the same congestion as private cars are and are further handicapped by their inferior maneuverability. Bus service, then, is not sufficiently convenient relative to use of private cars to attract the volume of traffic required for satisfactory frequency of service and a desirable variety of routes. In the absence of pricing, some form of reserved right-of-way or priority arrangement becomes necessary. In some cases, it is possible to provide a lane reserved exclusively for buses, but usually such a practice encounters difficulties in dealing with intersections and pickup points, and often leads to underutilization of the reserved lanes, since it is seldom possible to schedule just enough bus service for a whole lane of capacity. At best this is only a partial solution. Difficulties with bus service sometimes provide strong arguments for the greater expense of a rail rapid-transit system to provide higher-speed service, even where the volume of traffic might not justify such a facility.

With street use controlled by pricing, however, it is possible to insure that the level of congestion be kept down to the point at which buses will provide a satisfactory level of service. Exclusive rights-of-way, whether reserved lanes or rapid-transit tunnels, need then be provided only where they are genuinely warranted by the high volume of traffic.

Specific charging for street use can also provide conditions more conducive to better adjustment of utilization within modes as well as between modes. For example, much sporadic effort has been spent on promotion of staggered working hours to relieve peak-hour congestion on transportation facilities. However, except in particularly favorable circumstances where governments or a few dominant employers agree to maintain staggered hours, exhortation seems doomed to only partial success unless backed up by some kind of fare differentiation. In the absence of some such mild incentive, so soon as the peak-hour congestion is reduced to moderate levels by staggering, individual employers and employees tend to drift back to the more popular hours, until at least some degree of congestion is re-created. Off-peak fare differentials, even if not sufficient of themselves to initiate any marked degree of staggering, may prove essential to make whatever staggering is achieved by other means stick. In the absence of discriminating pricing applied to private automobiles, however, it may be difficult to raise public transit fares significantly during peak hours without undue increase in use of private automobiles—a situation, worse rather than better. There are thus severe limits to what can be done with peak–off-peak differentials in transit fares in the absence of a corresponding degree of differentiation in highway-user charges.

Much of the coordination provided by differentiated highway charges would be within the private-automobile mode, of course. Rapid vehicular transportation within congested areas—often not now available at any price—would be available for meeting emergency and high-priority needs, when the cost is justified. Even in a community where competition between mass transit and private automobiles is not a factor, pricing of highway usage would have an important function in coordinating the flow of highway traffic. For example, traffic between opposite sides of town often has the choice of going right through the center or of taking a more circuitous by-pass route—frequently competitive routes, even when one or both is not of limited-access type. Left to themselves, cross-town drivers are likely to choose the shorter route through the center, unless it becomes so congested that the longer way around is quicker. Pricing under such circumstances can be of considerable help in decongesting the center and increasing the share of traffic diverted to the relatively less congested and less costly by-pass routes, particularly during rush hours. If pricing cannot be used, the alternatives may be: (1) providing relatively costly and often unsightly facilities through the business center to take care of not only the traffic to and from the center but the through traffic as well; (2) tolerating the persistence of sufficient congestion to discourage the through traffic; (3) or possibly downgrading the design to make through trips artificially awkward, even in off-peak periods and for traffic going only part way through the center.

In the longer run, the availability of such pricing methods might have a fairly profound effect on city planning in general. Patterns of development could be projected on the basis of rational use of the facilities provided, rather than later distortion of plans to adjust to the tendency toward wasteful use of the facilities. While proper pricing of transportation services alone cannot eliminate the externalities involved in urban land use, it can reduce them somewhat. Without eliminating the need for zoning and other direct controls over land use, proper pricing would diminish pressures on determination and administration of zoning rules. Improvements in externalities, otherwise dependent on modification of zoning rules, would be absorbed through the transportation charges.

While many economists may agree that a fairly strong prima facie case for a sophisticated pricing scheme can be built in terms of broad over-all patterns, as outlined above, adoption of such a scheme will not come easily. The novelty of many of its features and the opposition to be expected from individuals and organizations strongly committed to the continuation of present trends are against it. Advocates of pricing must, therefore, spell out in considerable detail what the costs and benefits to be expected are. Such a study could be a means of securing adoption of adequate pricing methods in places like Washington and San Francisco, where pricing seems likely to be critical in determining the pattern of future growth. To determine more accurately how far it would be useful to extend such a scheme to less critical areas, such as Denver or Indianapolis, is also needed. The fact that Cambridge is being seriously considered for an experimental installation in England seems to indicate that there are at least some who feel that the scope for pricing extends to fairly small urban communities.

A more solidly based justification for sophisticated transportation pricing can be obtained only by a fairly elaborate analysis. The data for that are not yet available in the quantity or the form needed, though some information on orders of magnitude is available. In principle, the analysis would be a multistage one. The first stage would be a short-run cost-benefit analysis at the margin in terms of existing conditions; the second, a further short-run cost-benefit analysis in terms of conditions that might be generated by a system of charges at appropriate short-run levels; the third, a long-run cost-benefit analysis in terms of the roadways and other transportation facilities that would be needed without sophisticated pricing, compared with the needs indicated in the presence of sophisticated pricing. Finally, there would have to be a cost-benefit analysis in terms of comparing the cost of sophisticated pricing machinery with the benefits to be derived through more efficient utilization of facilities.

The basic question at the start is, given a system of transportation facilities, what price structure is appropriate? On general welfare-economics grounds, prima facie, the price should be made to vary as closely as possible with the marginal cost and to be at a level at least equal to marginal cost. The margin above marginal cost would be influenced by a number of factors. Among those justifying a margin of price above marginal cost are: (1) the presence of such margins in the prices of commodities and services that compete either on the demand side or on the consumption side of resources; (2) the fact that excess revenues can be used to lower the rates of taxes having a harmful effect in other sectors of the economy; and (3) the likelihood that users of urban-highway facilities during the periods of potential congestion are probably drawn from economic strata somewhat above average, so that excess charges considered as taxes would be moderately progressive in incidence. On the grounds of (3), justification of some slight discrimination in favor of public transit and commercial vehicles against private automobiles might be possible.

Measuring marginal cost of highway use under current conditions is a fairly straightforward problem, although it does involve a certain amount of evaluation of intangibles. While such items as contribution to smog, or added irritation or expenditure of nervous energy resulting from driving in congested traffic are extremely hard to evaluate in monetary equivalents, they are not likely to loom large in the total. Increases per vehicle mile in gasoline consumption, wear and tear on the vehicle, and increases, if any, in losses due to accidents may prove somewhat more amenable to pecuniary evaluation. The largest element of cost in most cases is, however, the delay suffered by vehicles and their occupants.

Measurement of the average amount of delay suffered by vehicles in a traffic stream as a result of congestion is a fairly straightforward procedure, given a well-defined objective and the resources for the necessary observations. Converting it into a pecuniary measure of cost, however, is subject to a considerable range of error. At one extreme, time may mean very little to a rider out for "an hour's spin" and caring little whether the hour covers fifteen miles or thirty, or to the unemployed bus rider with too much leisure. Vehicle time may also be relatively costless if the vehicle is used only for a fixed number of trips per day—by a commuter. On the other hand, the time of the busy executive may be worth a great deal, at least in terms of what he would pay to accelerate his trip. A reduction in time spent in the journey to work may be considered tantamount to a reduction in the gross working day and can thus appropriately be valued at a rate corresponding to the rate of take-home pay. Evaluation at the rate of pay is even more clearly appropriate for those whose travel falls within their working day, as truck-drivers, salesmen, taxi-drivers, or doctors.

Such an evaluation at the rate of pay might be subject to upward or downward adjustment according to whether the time spent in traffic delays is considered more or less irksome than time spent on the job. In any case, it is the average value attributable to a given traffic mix that furnishes the basis for a charge: the joy-rider is not entitled to escape the charge merely because he places no value on his time at the moment. Another element to be taken into account is the dispersion of delays. Under some circumstances, slow-moving traffic is subject to relatively little additional delay up to a certain point, as traffic density increases; faster-moving traffic is held up most severely. On the whole, faster-moving traffic probably has a higher time value than slow-moving traffic has—a reason for using a value-per-minute of delay slightly higher than a strictly statistical average. Another factor is the variability of trip time on different occasions. If trip time is more unpredictable because of interruptions of flow due to heavy traffic, or if interruptions when they do occur are more severe, significant additional cost may be entailed in the adjustment of plans, over and above the increase in average time lost in the traffic flow itself. Individuals may have to leave their origins much earlier in order to be reasonably sure of catching a train, meeting an engagement, or the like. That time would not be indicated by a comparison of average trip times between congested and uncongested conditions. Transit operators may have to schedule longer layovers in their schedules, and passengers may have to wait longer at bus stops and transfer points. These factors only add to the difficulty of evaluation, and data permitting their specific evaluation are almost totally lacking.

All of this would pertain to traffic as currently observed. Also needed is some idea of the circumstances after an equilibrium is reached, with rates justifiable in terms of the traffic conditions generated in response to the imposition of those rates. Here we know relatively little about the elasticity to be expected, either in terms of substitution between modes, between times of day, or in terms of absolute generation or suppression of traffic. Leon Moses has made some estimates of the amount of fare differential that would be necessary to divert passengers from automobile commuting to public transit. He estimated that free transit riding would convert only one-third or less of the present car commuters to public transit riding, while an increase in the cost of car commuting by 60 cents per trip might convert about half the automobile commuters. These figures indicate that the prospects of doing very much by the manipulation of transit fares are very limited. Although the assessment of charges appropriate to the costs would not eliminate the problem, it would put a very considerable dent in the problem of rush hour congestion.

In the longer run, there is the further problem of evaluating the contribution of a sophisticated pricing system in the context of optimal adjustment of the highway and transportation system to the demand, with and without pricing. It is of course conceivable that, even though the cost of a pricing system could be shown to be amply warranted in terms of the short-run situation, it might be cheaper in the long run to construct a slightly too-large highway system than to install a somewhat less costly but essentially nonproductive pricing mechanism. But while such a situation is conceivable, it seems to be rather unlikely. It would require that the elasticity of demand for highway usage be very low at levels of traffic above the optimal but fairly substantial at levels of traffic below optimal.

A complete appraisal of the desirability of pricing requires, nevertheless, that we not only estimate the appropriate levels of charges and the consequences of levying them, in the short run with existing highway facilities, but also the appropriate levels after highway facilities have been adjusted to an optimal level. Here, we are concerned not merely with the short-run cost of additional traffic as measured by costs of congestion borne by fellow motorists, but rather with equilibrating short- and long-run costs. Long-run costs in this case are costs of construction of additional facilities, including in appropriate places, the opportunity cost of devoting land to this rather than to other uses. In an optimal equilibrium, of course, the long-run marginal cost and the short-run cost should be equal. But, since short-run marginal cost is calculated in terms of the traffic conditions at a given time of day, whereas long run marginal cost pertains to the effects of expanding a facility for use throughout the year, equality can be met only in terms of aggregating the short-run marginal cost over a year. This in turn implies use of data pertaining not only to peak-hour traffic levels but also to at least some of the off-peak levels where the marginal cost, though lower than during the peak, is still not negligible. Put in another way, if an estimate is to be made of the long-run marginal cost of peak traffic, it is necessary to credit against the cost of expansion of the facilities' capacity some allowance for benefits from such expansion accruing to off-peak traffic.

To reduce the procedure for analyzing long-run marginal cost to manageable proportions, we can use the constant-elasticity formula for congestion cost, according to which the time taken to travel a given distance is $t = t_o + aq^k$, where t_o is the time required to travel a given distance under conditions of very light traffic, q is the volume of traffic in vehicles per hour and a and k are constants. The average congestion cost experienced per vehicle is then $z = t - t_o = aq^k$, and the marginal cost per vehicle trip is $a(k + 1)q^k = (k + 1)z$ in vehicle hours. Long-run optimum adjustment is then reached when the marginal cost of an addition to capacity is equal to the short-run marginal cost aggregated over all traffic, i.e., $M = \sum_i(k + 1)z_iq_i = \sum_i a(k + 1)q_i^{k+1}$. It may help to think of a "marginal cost per average vehicle,"

$$\bar{x} = (k + 1)\bar{z} = \frac{M}{\sum_i q_i},$$

which is the figure that would be obtained by dividing the cost of an increment of capacity by the total increment of traffic provided for by the increment of capacity at constant degree of congestion. A "peaking factor" can then be constructed which would be the ratio of the marginal cost of peak traffic to the marginal cost per average vehicle. Put in another way, the peaking factor would be the ratio of the proportion of total marginal cost chargeable to a given volume of peak traffic to the proportion this traffic is of the total traffic, i.e., the ratio of the marginal cost for the peak traffic to the marginal cost averaged over all traffic. The peaking factor can then be written,

$$R = \frac{a(k + 1)q_p^{k+1}}{\sum_i a(k + 1)q_i^{k+1}} \frac{\sum_i q_i}{q_p} = \frac{q_p^{k+1}}{\sum_i q_i^{k+1}} \frac{\sum_i q_i}{q_p}.$$

The peaking factor can then be calculated from data on the distribution of traffic flow by time of day, for any given value of k. The value of k will of course vary, being in general lower at lower volumes of traffic and approaching infinity as the capacity of the facility is approached. Data available seem to show, however, that over a range of from about 60 per cent of capacity to about 95 per cent, a fixed value of k can give a remarkably close fit, and it is presumably in this range that the major interest lies. Use of a value of k appropriate to the higher levels of traffic, for the purpose of imputing a share of the marginal cost to the lower levels of traffic, considerably overstates the share absorbed by the lower levels of traffic. Since the amounts involved are in any case very small, this is of little importance to the over-all results. Peaking factors obtained in this way can be applied to over-all incremental cost figures to obtain the appropriate level of charges in the long run.

Applying this method to hourly data for freeways in Los Angeles, New York, and Philadelphia gives values for R ranging from 2.08 to 5.57, for values of k ranging from 3.0 to 4.0, considering various durations of the peak ranging from 5 hours to 15 hours per week, in each direction. Long-range planning, however, would have to allow for the fact that pricing would of itself tend to flatten out the peak and thus substantially reduce the peaking factor. On the other hand, evaluating the desirability of applying the pricing mechanism in a given situation is in effect integrating over the interval running from the optimal situation, without sophisticated pricing, to the optimal situation with such pricing. The relevant peaking factor, therefore, may be some intermediate value between that obtaining under current conditions and that obtaining under ideal conditions, with pricing.

Evaluation of the scope for sophisticated pricing depends not only on demand patterns—both as to degree of peakedness and price elasticity—but also on the relative costs of the installation of the pricing mechanism and of additions to traffic facilities. The costs of the pricing mechanism are necessarily subject to a wide range of un-certainty—owing to almost no relevant experience. In *The Economist* for March 16, 1963, however, there is a report that a British firm has estimated the cost of a meter for a car at from £5 to £10, which certainly suggests the cost of sophisticated pricing is not the prime deterrent. The meter described appears to be operated by roadside signals, and the cost of the roadside equipment is likely to be far less in the aggregate than the cost of the meters themselves—indicating a fairly low-cost system. The question seems to be not so much whether a system exists that would be worthwhile where the need is greatest, but rather whether more highly refined and automatic systems would be worth the extra cost. Since it would be desirable to have a single type of system in operation in different metropolitan areas throughout the country, it may be desirable to have a system slightly less elaborate than would be ideal for the most severely congested metropolitan areas.

In estimating the cost of providing facilities for additional traffic, ranges are wider both relatively and absolutely. More data are available for freeway and expressway construction—where much recent expenditure has been concentrated—than for measures designed to increase the capacity of local street networks. It is somewhat easier, though still difficult, to reduce over-all costs of freeway construction to meaningful common units of measurement. Moreover, to the extent that expressways provide relief for local streets congested with a large share of through traffic, that is the relevant margin.

Costs of freeway construction vary tremendously. Additions proposed in January 1959 for the Maryland suburbs of Washington were to have cost an average of $0.54 million per lane mile; lanes projected at the same time within the District of Columbia were priced at $2.35 million per lane mile; 6.7 miles of projects in Manhatten were priced in 1958 at $38.4 million per route mile, equivalent to at least $5 million per lane mile (for an average of nearly eight lanes). If we assume a charge of 4.5 per cent on the value of the right of way and 6 per cent on construction costs for interest and amortization, and if construction costs are two-thirds of the total, then the charges become 5.5 per cent per year, or about $160 per million per day. Adding $17 per lane mile per day to cover maintenance and control expenditures, we have a daily cost per lane mile ranging from $92 (for a capital cost of $0.5 million per lane mile) to $767 for expressways costing $5 million per lane mile. If we suppose the average daily traffic to run from 5,000 cars per lane on the cheaper facilities (average conditions on four-lane freeways in California) to 20,000 cars per lane on the more expensive facilities (approaching the maximum observed on six- and eight-lane freeways), we get an average cost per vehicle mile of from 1.8 cents for the low-cost facilities to about 3.8 cents on the more expensive facilities. Applying relatively low peaking factors ranging from 2.0 to 3.0, we would get a cost of peak traffic of 3.6 cents per vehicle mile on the lowest-cost facilities, ranging up to 10.8 cents per vehicle mile on high-cost facilities.

Of course, these are average rather than marginal costs, in that we have not allowed for economies of scale in the construction of expressways. A six-lane expressway will not always cost 50 per cent more than a four-lane facility. Alternate routes often produce economies of scale, shortening travel distance and time for some users, plus relief of congestion. Such economies are rapidly becoming exhausted, however, in the New York metropolitan area. We find an extra tube being added to the Lincoln Tunnel, the Throg's Neck bridge is really not much more than a relief for the Whitestone bridge, and expansion is often in the form of additional lanes to existing facilities. Moreover, it appears that more than three lanes bring decreasing returns to scale through increased interference with traffic getting to and from access ramps. Costs increase, too, as the relatively less costly locations are used up.

Enlargement of existing routes provides a concrete illustration of the premature expansion that may be required in the absence of suitable pricing. The scheme of commutation rates for the Lincoln Tunnel actually encouraged a type of traffic concentrated in the peak hours. If the Port of New York Authority had been willing to experiment with a more rational toll structure, postponement of construction of the third tube might have proved desirable. If, for example, the entire annual toll charges incurred as a result of the construction of the third tube were apportioned among users that could not be accommodated on the existing two tubes, selecting for this purpose the users having the least intensive demand at each time of day, the charges might have been too high for those users. If so, it would have been better to dispense with construction of the third tube, adjusting tolls to restrict traffic to the capacity of the existing tubes. Of course, given the political constitution of the Authority, charges of exploitation and failure to cater to the demands of the public would have arisen. Use of the excess revenues to provide better alternative transit service, however, would certainly have been worth considering. On the other hand, given an inability to adjust tolls as described, construction of the tunnel may have been preferable to toleration of the existing facilities.

For local streets of downtown areas, the evaluation of long-run marginal cost is much more difficult; indeed it may be impossible to arrive at meaningful figures. The long run, in the strict sense, is longer than the life of the planners, and determining the optimal street layout (starting from scratch) is only an interesting intellectual exercise with but remote implications for even longest-range policy. Costs of occasional street-widening or -straightening projects should be a stern reminder that, in certain directions, the opportunity cost of street space is very high. At the other extreme, urban redevelopment often involves closing streets and creation of superblocks. Almost every case appears to be *sui generis*, giving little guidance for long-run expectations. Perhaps costs of local street use in downtown areas may be alleviated in the long run by the competition of expressways penetrating close to the center and siphoning off some traffic from local streets.

Arguments against meaningful charges for city-street use are often based on the notion that, in the long-run, marginal and average cost should be roughly equal, and that average cost can be computed on the basis of actual cash outlays for city street construction and maintenance. Charges for a rental value of the space occupied by the streets is dismissed as either already funded through allocation of the street space to public use, or on the ground that the value of the street area is reflected in the market and tax value of the adjacent property. Let us explore in an academic vein the opportunity cost of devoting an additional quantum of land to transportation use rather than to the support of a business activity.

In a Von Thünen-Lösch type of model of spatial economics, every commodity or service has a well-defined shadow price at every point in the space, prices which never differ from one point to another by more than their cost of transport. Firms locate at points where the relation between factor and product prices is most favorable, where there is no cross-haul, and site rents reflect transportation-cost differentials for a firm located at any given point as compared to the next best location for the firm. In such a model, generally, abstracting a piece of land from existing use will cause an increase in transportation cost in conjunction with the displaced activity. The cost can be measured by the amount of rent necessary to bid the land away from the particular use. In such a model, the opportunity cost of land in a given location for use in providing transportation facilities could be determined on the basis of the market rent of the land.

Actual cities are very far from this rational pattern, however. In many economic relationships, prices tend to be blanketed over an area, costs of transportation being borne now by the seller, now by the buyer, or sometimes shared in a rather uncertain manner. A great deal of cross-hauling goes on, most importantly perhaps in moving labor; great numbers of people with comparable skills pass each other going in opposite directions, in many cases those living near the center of the city work in the suburbs. A firm contemplating a move from a low-rent location A to a high-rent location B (or vice versa) is likely to compare the rent differential with the saving in that portion of the transportation costs which is likely to be borne by the firm; this change is likely to be substantially less than the total change in transportation costs resulting from the movement of the firm. In the extreme case of a completely blanketed market and equal sharing of transportation costs between shipper and consignee (or between employer and employee, etc.), the firm would tend to take into account only one-half the saving in total transportation costs in moving from A to B. As a result, the rent differential is likely to be bid up only to half the level that would fully reflect these transportation costs. This fact may be considered as the essence of what is sometimes vaguely referred to as the external economies of the central business district.

If all businesses have roughly the same ratio of area to transportation requirements, the result would not be serious; the only deviation from theory is that rents would be lower than they should be theoretically. To the extent that businesses differ, there will be some maldistribution of business with reference to the minimum transport locations, but the deviations do not seem to be highly systematic. If one business attempts to bid land away from another at the center of the city, the expectation would be—barring wide differences in their transportation requirements—a rough balance between the resulting increase in transportation costs for one business and decreases for the other. (In neither case, however, would all these changes be borne by the firms changing locations.) When space at the center is taken over for transportation purposes and the firm formerly occupying that space is forced to move to the periphery, total costs of the transportation services required by that firm will go up by more than the saving on rent, some of them being shifted to customers and suppliers of the firm. To justify the change for the city, the reduction in costs of transportation resulting from use of more space for it must be substantially greater than the rent the city paid to bid the space away from the firm. Not only would it be proper, then, to charge users of transportation rent for the space utilized equivalent to the rent the space would command if put to commercial use, but actually more than this—in the limiting case of random interrelationships, twice as much.

A city cannot afford to charge nothing for use of central city streets on the ground that they perform an access function, paid for by owners of abutting property in property rents and taxes. It is inappropriate to levy specific charges for use of rural and suburban access streets; but this is because the low level of traffic makes negligible the marginal cost of increased traffic, and not because of an access function. A drawback in charging for use of congested access facilities through property and other taxes is lack of creation of incentive to economize in the use of the congested facility—changing the hours of use, or shifting to a less competitive location for access.

Other proposed methods of pricing to coordinate urban transportation—among them, parking fees, cordon tolls, special licensing arrangements, and others—fail to reach the core of the problem. Its solution depends on provision of a direct incentive to the individual driver to economize in the use of high-cost facilities during periods of peak demand and potential congestion. As competition of the private automobile with other forms of urban transportation increases, a rational solution to the pricing of other competing modes depends on adoption of more rational pricing procedures for the private automobile. Without an adequate solution in this area, no fully satisfactory solution in the other areas is possible.

REFERENCES

Transportation Plan for the National Capital Region, Hearings, Joint Committee on Washington Metropolitan Problems, November 8–14, 1959, pp. 454–490.

G. J. Roth and J. M. Thomson, "Road Pricing—a Cure for Congestion?" *Aspect*, April 1963, pp. 7–14.

Gabriel Roth: "An End to Traffic Jams," *Crossbow*, July–September, 1962.

"Electronic Pricing for the Roads," *The Economist*, Mar. 16, 1963, p. 1037.

William Vickrey, "Pricing in Urban and Suburban Transport," *Proceedings of the American Economic Association*, Dec. 28, 1962.

Urban Transportation and Public Policy, Institute of Public Administration, Dec. 1961, Chap. IV, "Economic Analysis in Urban Transportation Planning."

COMMENT

HAROLD BARGER, Columbia University

William Vickrey throws down a double challenge: to the engineers and to the politicians. He asks the engineers to devise a plan for metering the use of city streets and he wishes to persuade the politicians to accept what must at best be a complicated and unfamiliar proposal. It seems a pity to opt for these complexities until it is shown that more conventional methods will not achieve the desired result. We have made a beginning with parking meters, but surely tariffs are not nearly high enough. We can tax cars by length and width—the relevant variables—rather than by weight. Instead of subsidizing parking garages, we can tax them. We can levy substantial tolls at the entrances and exits to cities. Finally, if the insurance companies can identify cars used in cities in order to impose higher premiums, city governments equally should be able to levy special taxes on them. The proceeds could be used to subsidize commuter railroads, and even buses and taxicabs. Until measures such as these have proved ineffective, it would appear premature to embrace the complexities of an electronic plan for metering automobile use of city streets.

BRITTON HARRIS, University of Pennsylvania

It is difficult to find any basic point of disagreement with Vickrey's analysis, as far as it goes. The fundamental principles of allocation of resources which he espouses are, quite clearly, economically sound. Considerable wind could be generated discussing his proposed methods of collecting tolls for highway utilization and his illustrative examples of facility costs. I propose rather to take these details as largely illustrative, with the qualification that the analysis and planning of transportation systems within the metropolitan system is substantially more subtle and complicated than Vickrey has suggested. I will explore certain other implications of Vickrey's position which he has, I feel, not treated adequately.

It is by no means clear that Vickrey's proposed policy would have the effects which he seems to seek. The collection of increased user charges for costly and high-grade transportation facilities would, he implies, result in a reduction in the use of these facilities because of the elasticity of demand. Such elasticity is perhaps less than imagined; but more important, any reduction of the utilization of a congested highway facility results in an improvement in the service offered by the facility, and consequently tends to restore demand to previous levels. If, following Vickrey's rigorously economic line of thought, we then extend the construction of such facilities to provide a new level of service until marginal revenue equals marginal cost, the result might be a highway system substantially more extensive than is presently contemplated in most urban areas.

This situation arises because we are presently allocating funds to urban highway construction only up to the point of rather high benefit-cost ratios. Vickrey implies that benefit-cost calculations should be converted into revenue-cost calculations. If, however, revenues are made to equal benefits, if there has been any realism in our benefit-cost analyses, and if these analyses become a guide to investment, it seems likely that Vickrey might be disappointed in the results.

In the Conference discussion following the above remarks, Vickrey conditionally acquiesced to the foregoing, stating that if this came to pass, he would accept such a verdict of consumer choice. Such acquiescence displays that curious stoicism of economists, who are willing to sacrifice personal values, however derived, in defense of a logical position. As an addendum to my discussion at the Conference, let me add a brief extension of my earlier remarks which suggest a way out of this dilemma. In placing his reliance on cost-revenue relationships for transportation alone, Vickrey is exploring the local optimum which may be reached from present metropolitan arrangements. New arrangements and new combinations of factors may have the effect of substantially reducing urban travel demands. The existence, the costs, and the benefits of such arrangements are difficult to establish, and no market for them exists which is comparable to and carries the same conviction as the market for transportation services in which people trade daily. Even more difficult to evaluate are the external effects on neighborhoods and urban life in general of any large program of construction of transportation facilities. These externalities are not negligible and are not excluded from an economic evaluation of the costs of transportation. It is therefore imperative that economists make some contribution to the valuation of such important consequences of metropolitan transportation development—consequences for which, again, no market exists.

MARTIN WOHL, Harvard University

There are many aspects in this paper worthy of discussion, if for no other reason than because they are so often misunderstood. Initially, one must be critical of the fashion in which Professor Vickrey has dealt with the problem of identifying and specifying the objective function; even a perfunctory reading of his paper reveals situations where he is anything but precise and where he intermixes social and economic objectives in a purely subjective fashion. For example, in his discussion of staggered working hours as a means of relieving peak hour congestion, he notes: "Off-peak fare differentials, even if not sufficient of themselves to initiate any marked degree of staggering, may prove essential to make whatever staggering is achieved by other means stick." Obviously Vickrey at least implies that even though economic (or social) gains of reduced congestion to riders are not sufficient to compensate them for whatever losses they must endure as a result of staggered hours, this free choice should be disallowed.

In another place, Vickrey states that it is justifiable to set prices above marginal costs in some situations and that "excess revenues can be used to lower the rates of taxes having a harmful effect in other sectors of the economy." Also, he comments that "the likelihood [is] that those using urban highway facilities during the periods of potential congestion are probably on the whole drawn from economic strata somewhat above average, so that excess charges considered as taxes would be moderately progressive in incidence," and ends by stating that "on this last ground it would probably be possible to justify some slight discrimination in favor of transit and commercial vehicles against private automobiles." Purely aside from the fact that he almost certainly is incorrect in his basic assumption about relative rider-income characteristics, it should be evident that he again is terribly imprecise, judgmental, and subjective in assessing the wisdom of *quasi* value-of-service pricing and certain income transfers.

More importantly, I should like to comment on his numerical example of rush-hour and non-rush-hour costing and pricing, and on his proposed technique for assessing peak-hour marginal costs.

The first example included the following data:

	Facility M (Auto travel)	Facility T (Transit travel)
Ratio of rush-hour passenger volume to non-rush-hour passenger volume	1/4	1/1
Cost per rush-hour passenger trip ($)	1.00	0.75
Cost per non-rush-hour passenger trip ($)	0.20	0.15
Average over-all cost per passenger trip ($)	0.36	0.45

Drawing upon these numbers, Vickrey then states,

> If differentiation by time of day is impossible, it would be desirable to have the relative charges on the two facilities at least reflect the direction of the specific cost differentials at the specific times. That could be done by raising the charges on *M* to, say, 45 cents as compared with costs of 36 cents on the average basis, while using the excess revenues to subsidize *T* and make it self-liquidating by lowering the charge to 35 from 45 cents. Ruling out special charges for peak use thus creates an impressive argument for subsidizing transit at the expense of vehicular traffic.

That this example and Vickrey's conclusion are absurd should be evident. First, it is clear that differential pricing can easily and cheaply be instituted on transit services; such a scheme would probably divert some peak hour riders to auto (in the absence of differential pricing for autos), would probably permit transit system economies, gain considerable off-peak riders, and reduce unit costs on two counts. But this is the point; years ago transit use during off-peak hours was high, just as the auto today, and the average over-all price and cost for transit was not only low but considerably lower than auto. (In fact, the price of transit service is still usually lower than auto—in spite of Vickrey's assumed numbers—because of transit subsidies of one sort or another.) And despite the lower price of transit travel, many passengers shifted and still continue to shift from transit to auto;

PRICING AS A TOOL IN LOCAL TRANSPORTATION

they are shifting simply because of service differentials, and because of their ability and willingness to afford higher-quality service.

The absence of any discussion by Vickrey regarding service offerings or differentials leads one to assume either that he presumes that there are no service differentials (a ridiculous case) or that he presumes that the objective of the transportation expert is to move passenger volumes at the lowest total cost irrespective of the service level and aside from questions of demand and value of higher service.

Furthermore, the volume and cost data used for this example (as well as that applied in the peaking factor examples) can hardly be described as typical, and thus useful for drawing such general conclusions as Vickrey did. Briefly, the modal data which were compared are not equivalent with respect to quality of service, volume, origin-destination pattern, and so forth; thus, the assumed set of ratios and costs was not internally consistent.

As for the proposed technique for determining marginal costs for peak and off-peak travelers, a number of comments are in order. Vickrey states: "Here, we are concerned not merely with the short-run cost of additional traffic as measured by costs of congestion borne by fellow motorists, but rather with equilibrating short- and long-run costs. Long-run costs in this case are costs of construction of additional facilities, including in appropriate places, the opportunity cost of devoting land to this rather than to other uses. In an optimal equilibrium, of course, the long-run marginal cost and the short-run cost should be equal." Thus, he recommends that system capacity be expanded until (aggregated) marginal congestion costs are equal to marginal construction costs, a point of mutual agreement.

However, his technique for allocating the construction costs of additional capacity to peak-hour and off-peak-hour users does considerable violence to this economic precept. Briefly, he derives a "peaking factor" which is supposed to (but does not) represent the ratio of marginal construction costs for peak-hour users to the marginal construction costs for all users, and which is then to be applied to the average construction cost for all users to determine the price for peak-hour travelers. It is important, though, that the peaking factor which Vickrey developed (and which he then applied to some numerical examples in a later section) was based entirely on congestion costs rather than on construction costs.

To be more explicit, Vickrey defined the peaking factor as the marginal congestion cost for peak-hour travelers divided by the sum of the marginal congestion costs for all travelers using the optimum-sized facility. Since marginal construction costs and marginal congestion costs (for a particular facility) are not necessarily equal at all output or volume levels, this *congestion* peaking factor of Vickrey's bears no necessary relationship to the incidence of construction costs. As a consequence, Vickrey's peaking factor technique for allocating construction costs and setting peak and off-peak prices (to recover construction costs) can at best only be termed an approximate value-of-service pricing technique rather than a cost-of-service pricing technique.

The technique would be approximate, if for no other reason than that Vickrey, in developing his peaking factor, has implicitly assumed that congestion cost varies directly with travel time, and thus as travel time (on a particular facility) increases exponentially with traffic volume, so does congestion cost. This assumption is subject to considerable doubt.

In summary, one must support Vickrey in his efforts to improve the utilization of urban transportation facilities through the development of better pricing tools and mechanisms. At the same time, though, one cannot help but be apprehensive on examining the material presented, its technical inaccuracies, and the somewhat subjective and rather biased attitude about the use and application of these tools. In short, Vickrey has not presented differential pricing principles and techniques properly or without regard to the outcome, but has seemingly used them to achieve certain unsupported social objectives. Further, he uses volumes, volume ratios, unit costs, and other related numbers in his examples which are at best atypical and thus improper for arriving at the conclusions which then follow. And, finally, I am most critical of his failure to properly account for service differentials in examining the relative cost structure and implications for auto and transit travel and for continually referring to the development of pricing tools for long-term objectives while using factors, volume and cost data based on existing and not necessarily optimum facilities and services.

The Economics of Transportation Planning in Urban Areas

TILLO E. KUHN

UNIVERSITY OF CALIFORNIA AT BERKELEY

I. *Urban Peak Problems*

One would think that investigations of peak phenomena should be at the very heart of urban transportation studies: The rhythm of urban traffic movements occurs daily, is predictable within very fine limits, is extremely pronounced in many instances, and causes high costs, confusion, and congestion. It primarily affects passenger transportation to and from work and is therefore a rich source of irritations and complaints. In fact, peak-hour commuter service may be regarded as the great underdeveloped area of the entire transportation industry.[1]

Clearly, something needs to be done and yet so far little systematic attention has been given to this core problem. Zettel and Carll point out that most of the contemporary metropolitan studies mention it only in passing:

The Pittsburgh report is somewhat philosophical about the congestion problem: "When these many movements overlap in time and space, and there are too few travel facilities, crowding and traffic congestion result. This is an almost inevitable result of growth and progress. Who would want to empty streets and sidewalks?" Or, as the Chicago study says: "There is natural

NOTE: Section I, "The Relevance of Economics," of the author's original version contained discussion of sociology, urban planning and other subjects which, while of considerable interest, were not deemed particularly relevant in the present volume. This part of the paper was therefore deleted to conserve space, by editorial decision, but is available upon request from the author.

[1] "Long range planners, government officials, and members of the general public alike may reasonably ask why a technology capable of producing jet passenger aircraft, manned satellites, hydrofoil ships, nuclear-powered ocean vessels, and a great array of complex weapons can not also be called upon to do something rather handsome for the weary and long-suffering commuter." Clark Henderson, *New Concepts for Mass Transit*, Stanford Research Institute, Long Range Planning Service, Menlo Park, California, December 1961.

competition for the use of highway and mass transportation facilities," adding, "people are bound to get in one another's way." But few attempts are made in these studies to consider whether congestion is in fact worsening, or is being reduced, by the current efforts to provide and maintain transport services. . . . There is notably lacking in these studies—both in the initial statements and in final reports that have been made—any extensive analysis of the development of congestion over time.[2]

With this general background in mind, the writer wishes to discuss briefly some current research on the economics of peaks.[3] The purpose is not so much to report on definitive findings, but rather to outline promising approaches. It is hoped that this will stimulate scholarly interest in the field.

PEAK PHENOMENA

Extreme diurnal peak demand patterns can be observed throughout transportation: they are manifested by vehicles on freeways, passengers in subways or buses, people in terminal lobbies, aircraft parked at gate positions or using runways for take-off and landing. But they are also quite common elsewhere; for example, in telephone, electric power, gas and water systems, retail establishments, hotels. Daily peak patterns are widespread throughout the economy.

Peak patterns are best portrayed by means of graphs. Figure 1 shows just one day's results of traffic counts which Richard Carll and Wolfgang Homburger, of the Institute of Transportation and Traffic Engineering, University of California, have been carrying out at strategic locations in the Bay Area since April 1959. The westbound peak into San Francisco reached almost 40,000 people per hour in the morning, but the eastward, homebound peak in the afternoon is sharper still, with a flow rate of 45,000 people per hour.

Note that if shorter intervals were chosen for measurement and diagrammatical representation, for example, ten minutes or five minutes, the peak patterns would be even more extreme.[4] Within limits, peak

---

[2] Richard M. Zettel and Richard R. Carll, *Summary Review of Major Metropolitan Transportation Studies in the United States*, The Institute of Transportation and Traffic Engineering, Berkeley, 1962, p. 21.

[3] Tillo E. Kuhn, Charles A. Hedges, and David C. King, *The Economics of Peaks: Concepts, Statistical Tools and the Example of Electric Power*, Technical Report, Institute of Transportation and Traffic Engineering, Berkeley (forthcoming).

[4] "Each weekday morning between the hours of 7:00 and 10:00, 1,430,000 people go to work in Mid-Manhattan. This large volume of individual travel trips converging in the 7.9 square-mile area during peak periods establishes the capacity requirements for the physical facilities . . . . The severity of the peaking problem can best be appreciated by examining the critical ten-minute periods. Between 8:55 and 9:04, 20% of the workers in Mid-Manhattan arrive at their jobs, while 32%

extremes are a function of the time interval chosen for observation. Traffic flows look rather tame when they are expressed as annual or average daily volumes as is done in the majority of reports. Dramatic fluctuations of the type shown in Figure 1 occur on many traffic arteries, five days a week, year after year, in practically all the large cities on the globe, whenever people go to work and return home.

STATISTICAL DEFINITIONS AND CONCEPTS

Among the most useful mathematical concepts in peak research are:

1. For descriptions of fluctuations: *cycle* (a periodic movement in a time-series); *oscillation* (fluctuation about the mean value of the series); *amplitude* (the value of the ordinate at its peak or trough taken from some mean value or trend line); *peak* (the maximum value of a periodically varying quantity during a cycle; a high point in the course of development, especially as represented on a graph).

2. Measures of central tendency: the familiar *arithmetic mean*, *median*, and *mode*.

3. Measures of dispersion: *average deviation*, *variance*, and *relative dispersion*.

4. Measures of skewness and peakedness: *negative* and *positive skewness*, *kurtosis* (measure of "peakedness" of a curve).

5. Demand and capacity concepts: *load factor* (the ratio of the average load to the peak load); *capacity* (a difficult and ambiguous concept; it is generally interpreted as "maximum output," or "rated output," or "maximum output under prescribed performance conditions"); *capacity factor* (the ratio of average load to capacity); *utilization factor* (the ratio of peak load to capacity).

SOME APPLICATIONS AND FINDINGS[5]

Analyses of diurnal traffic cycles on the San Francisco-Oakland Bay Bridge, were made with the quarterly data collected and tabulated by Messrs. Carll and Homburger. Some of the findings were: On the Bay Bridge, "oscillation" is a high percentage of "amplitude"; a 3:00 to 4:00 a.m. count may yield fewer than 200 vehicles, but volumes of

---

depart during the period 4:55–5:04. . . . It is important to note that head-quarters offices and service industries, which give rise to the sharpest rush-hour peaks, are the activities which are expanding most rapidly in Mid-Manhattan . . . . As professional, administrative and clerical functions continue to expand, we must look forward to experiencing greater peaks, with all the associated problems of congestion." New York-New Jersey Transportation Agency, *Journey to Work*, New York and Trenton, 1963, p. 18.

[5] This section is based on a special progress report by David C. King (unpublished).

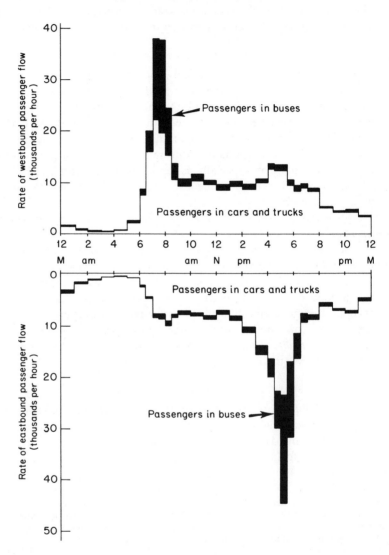

Figure 1
Rate of Passenger Flow Across
San Francisco-Oakland Bay Bridge,
Typical Weekday, January 1963

SOURCE: I.T.T.E. Traffic Survey A-16.

over 7,000 vehicles in *one direction* have been attained during an evening peak hour.

On the Bay Bridge, peaks are obviously "suppressed." Peaks have been spreading into the earlier and later hours of the rush period as congestion discourages drivers from traveling at the time most convenient to their personal schedule. Over the years, the high portions of the traffic volume curves have therefore changed from "leptocurtic" (sharp, peaked), into "platycurtic" (flat-topped) shapes.

The electric power industry has always been greatly concerned with peak problems and has developed more advanced concepts and solutions than other technologies. There is a remarkable difference, however, between the approach to peak demand of electric power and that of highway transport industries. Electric power companies are prepared, perhaps under the edict of regulatory authorities, to meet absolute peaks if necessary. Strenuous efforts are made to avoid "brownouts." They may, however, take steps to discourage peak use (through interruptable power contracts) and to encourage off-peak use (through various inducements). In the highway field, however, peak demand suppression occurs regularly. It is not even clear what degrees of suppression are regarded as tolerable or intolerable from the technical, economic and community points of view.[6] Some highway bridge authorities *encourage* peak use through cheaper commuter tickets.

There is debate on the meaning of "highway capacity." One recent technical report[7] on the Bay Bridge derives annual capacity from assumptions on hourly lane capacity and the proportion of total daily traffic represented by peak-hour traffic. For example, the Bay Bridge capacity is assumed to be 1,500 vehicles per lane per hour, or 7,500 vehicles in the peak direction. The annual capacity is then 45 million vehicles. But if a capacity of 1,800 vehicles per lane per hour is stipulated, the annual capacity of the Bridge would be as much as 54 million

[6] The American Association of State Highway Officials states: "A freeway is intended for the rapid movement of large volumes of traffic with safety and efficiency . . . but it seldom is feasible to provide facilities with a capacity to accommodate the peak-hour volumes at such speeds so that the running speeds at such times are lower. Thus, the freeway design speed should reflect the desired running speed during nonpeak hours, but not so high as to be wasteful since a large portion of vehicles are accommodated during periods of peak flow when lower speeds are acceptable." AASHO, *A Policy on Arterial Highways in Urban Areas*, Washington, D.C., 1957, p. 120. (There is no indication what the meanings of the terms "feasible," "desired," "wasteful" and "acceptable" are.)

[7] Coverdale and Colpitts, *Report on Traffic on the Existing San Francisco Bay Crossings and the Proposed Potrero Point-Alameda Crossing, Sierra Point-Roberts Landing Crossing, San Francisco-Marin Crossing*, New York, September 1962, pp. 13–14.

vehicles. A more even distribution of the traffic over the hours of the day and a flattening of the peaks would also increase the capacity estimates. Two frequently found definitions are "practical capacity" (under which drivers experience no "unreasonable" delay, hazard or freedom to maneuver) and "possible capacity" (maximum traffic volume observed).

The bridge load factor (defined as the ratio of mean hourly traffic to maximum hourly traffic) runs around 33 per cent. This indicates a very poor utilization of facilities compared with the power system which has a load factor of 75 to 80 per cent.

Average and standard deviations were found to be 1,100 and 1,500 vehicles per hour, resulting in relative dispersions of 65 to 87 per cent when compared with mean hourly traffic flows of 2,200 to 2,500 vehicles per hour. This shows the erratic character of bridge traffic as between times of day. The same measures show that electric energy demand is a great deal more stable.

Results were also obtained for bus passengers and for heavy truck traffic on the transbay routes. The number of bus passengers is particularly susceptible to high fluctuations. Load factors of less than 10 per cent, utilization factors of 90 to 96 per cent (taking capacity as the maximum number of hourly passengers recorded since April 1959), and relative dispersions of over 200 per cent were recorded for an October day in 1961. Heavy truck utilization of the Bay Bridge was not analyzed in the same manner, but work done by Carll and Homburger indicates that truckers try to avoid peak hours. The truck peak occurs immediately after the auto peak in both directions; trucks account for less than 10 per cent of the total traffic during the auto peak.

A summary comparison of findings on electric power and bridge traffic performance will be of interest:

Winter Demand, 1961

	Load Factor (per cent)	Utilization Factor (per cent)	Relative Dispersion (per cent)
Bridge westbound	33	93	74
Bridge eastbound	32	98	71
Electricity	73	86	24

Summer Demand, 1961

Bridge westbound	37	90	66
Bridge eastbound	35	93	65
Electricity	82	97	19

The poor load factors of the Bay Bridge and the erratic fluctuations of traffic on it are noteworthy. It must be mentioned, though, that the electric power figures, which were compiled for the Pacific Gas and Electric system, may look unduly favorable. Regional power demands, for example during the summer for air conditioning and water pumping in the agricultural San Joaquin Valley, or during the winter in the industrial-residential Bay Area, may show much more extreme peaks.

POSSIBLE SOLUTIONS TO URBAN PEAK PROBLEMS

The foregoing demonstrates that peak phenomena can be subjected to quantitative, statistical research. The studies can readily be extended to other technologies, for example to telephone, teletype, and data transmission networks; air transport; and gas and water supply systems. Leads and lags in peak patterns could be investigated; in the morning there are probably successive "waves" of peak uses to be observed on the airport access road, at the aircraft gate positions, the terminal building, runways, and in the air. Long-range trends can be examined and forecasts of peak behavior can be attempted: Are peaks getting "worse"? To what extent are they being suppressed? Supposing capacity had to be provided, what would unsuppressed peaks be like on urban freeways?

It is certainly possible to measure and predict the "lifebeat of the metropolis" in various ways. But the really challenging task is to devise rational, economically efficient ways of dealing with peak phenomena. Some tentative suggestions can be put forward.

1. *Peak pricing*. There has been considerable economic discussion on how to charge peak users. As is to be expected, the conclusions suggest that those who demand high-cost peak facilities, should pay more than off-peak customers. One would like to suggest that rather different questions ought also to be considered. First, urban dwellers do not become peak users for their own amusement, especially not the hapless commuters. Millions of urban workers are virtually compelled to be at a certain place at a certain time for reasons which are inherent in the general rhythm of urban life and the functioning of the urban economy. High peak-use charges may simply impose penalties on a particularly vulnerable segment of the population. At the same time, appropriate pricing regimes would discourage nonessential peak traffic and shift it into off-peak hours. Better utilization of transport facilities would be the desirable result.

2. *Planning peak service facilities*. We must ask how the capacities of the peak facilities are determined in the first place. Are some—for

example, freeways—deliberately built to less than absolute peak demands? If so, why? What is the economic rationale of the rule of thumb in highway engineering to cater to the thirtieth highest hourly traffic volume in a year, rather than to provide some other level of service? Why are other technologies geared to handle extreme peak loads? These and related questions probe into the fundamentals of long-range investment decisions under oscillating demand conditions. Pricing, by contrast, pertains more to short-range actions once the plant scale has been determined. In military terminology, we may say that investment is economic strategy and pricing represents economic tactics. The relation of both to peak problems is a most promising research area.

3. *The space and time economies of the metropolis.* We know absolutely nothing about the precise economies that are obtained by assembling people, messages, and objects in time and space (the executive, his secretary, the mail, and telephone calls are all brought together at the office at 9 o'clock in the morning). Conversely, we know nothing about the diseconomies of shifting these components of economic activity out of phase. Big cities, especially London and New York, have for years experimented with staggered working hours in the central business district. What have been the trade-offs between diminished business efficiency and enhanced urban transport performance?

4. *Encouragement of transport services with good peak performance.* In some respects private passenger cars are rather poor vehicles for carrying people in and out of central areas during peak hours. No other medium requires as much precious urban space per passenger for movement and storage; speed and safety performance is disappointing for highly peaked mass movements; nonmarket costs (air pollution) are high. Figure 1 provides a dramatic illustration of how much more efficient buses are for the purpose. It would be interesting to calculate how many millions of dollars in bridge investment would be necessary if the transbay buses were replaced by automobiles and the same peak-hour performance had to be maintained. Other transport means yet to be introduced or invented may be superior still to buses. It should be the prime function of urban transport investment analysis to ferret out and encourage these alternatives.

5. *Making peak transport demand unnecessary.* What is the possibility of rearranging urban land-use patterns in such a way as to cut down on peak movements? Are there substitutes to be found outside the transportation industry for physical movements of people? Could

message transmissions (telephone, videophone, closed television circuits) replace face-to-face meetings? Could the business executive of tomorrow operate out of his suburban home with the aid of exotic communications devices?

II. *Investment Analyses for Urban Transportation*

It is not possible within the context of this paper to develop a complete analytical framework for urban transportation planning. The excellent review of study methods by Richard M. Zettel and Richard R. Carll should be consulted.[8] Urban transportation economics proper can conveniently be seen as part of public enterprise economics; this broader field has attracted increasing attention recently and some of the works will be of interest.[9] We will discuss items of special interest only here.

TERMINOLOGY

Urban transportation, and in fact the whole field of public enterprise economics, is burdened by confusing terminology. Agreement on clear definitions of the things to be analyzed would alone be a step forward.

First, this writer wishes to express dissatisfaction with the term "benefit-cost analysis," which is quite commonly used. It can be traced back to the *Flood Control Act of 1936* which interpreted project feasibility to mean that "the benefits, to whomsoever they may accrue, are in excess of the estimated costs." Since then, four distinct aspects have become associated with benefit-cost comparisons.

1. All benefits, no matter how widely dispersed throughout the economy, must be credited to the project.

A wide analytical viewpoint is certainly desirable. In urban transportation studies, the point of reference should be set at the level of the metropolitan economy. But the analysis must not be restricted to the measurement of favorable effects only. All costs, regardless of how remote their incidence is, ought to be traced as well. Many so-called highway benefit studies credit land value increases to adjacent road development, forgetting the corresponding relative decreases in property values elsewhere. Other undesirable consequences, such as smog, accidents, noise, and scenic blight, are also often overlooked. There

---

[8] Zettel and Carll, *Summary Review.*

[9] Tillo E. Kuhn, *Public Enterprise Economics and Transport Problems*, Berkeley, 1962. (In the Appendix of this book there is a "Summary Comparison of Analytical Procedures and Criteria Proposed in Prominent Public Enterprise Documents.")

has further been a tendency to double count highway benefits which were simply transfers from one party to another.[10]

2. All benefits and costs of a project, whether they can be expressed in money terms or not, must be considered in the analyses.

Again there is agreement that all relevant evidence, whether it fits into the economist's special domain or not, ought to be studied. However, a clear distinction should be made between market and nonmarket values. The latter, while largely falling outside pure economics, must not be neglected in favor of the former. It is also misleading, arbitrarily, to convert nonmarket effects—highway accident deaths, time savings, comfort—into dollars and cents, as has been done in many highway benefit studies.

3. Benefit-cost studies provide scientific guidance for user charging and, hence, for resource allocation in transportation.

Neither of these laudable objectives has been achieved by benefit-cost studies to date. In the literature there is widespread confusion about the adherence of transport pricing to the minimum boundary condition (cost of providing the service), or to the maximum one (benefit, value, or utility derived from use), or to some intermediate position. The *Final Report of the Highway Cost Allocation Study*, for example, blindly averages conflicting results of unrelated cost and benefit formulae, some of them of questionable validity. The *Final Report* as much as admits that five years of research were in vain by inviting the policy makers to take their pick among the results:

Although it is believed that the use of these findings will assist in developing a reasonable allocation of Federal-aid highway costs among those who occasion them and reap their benefits, the fact that they were achieved by a mediation between differing results emphasizes the truth that in the field of cost allocation indisputable accuracy of findings is not possible. The report concludes that definitive answers to questions of cost allocation between users and non-users cannot be reached solely through analysis. These answers are ultimately matters of policy.[11]

[10] The Final Report of the so-called Section 210 Study states, in one of its better passages, "The benefits of highway improvement, spread out like ripples from a stone dropped in a stream, and in some respects are as elusive as quicksilver. . . . Only by an elaborate input-output analysis, on an interregional and interindustry basis, for which techniques are not now available, would it [be] possible to make any sort of approximation of the totality of nonuser benefits that will be brought about by the . . . program." U.S. Congress, *Final Report of the Highway Cost Allocation Study*, House Document No. 54, Washington, D.C., 1961, p. 31.

[11] *Ibid.*, p. 4. The *Final Report* offers to the policy makers the following "range of required payments based on study findings" for a diesel tractor-semitrailer and full trailer combination: low—$273.26 per annum; high—$3,553.20 (Table I-3, p. 17). The suggested payment ranges for other vehicle types are less extreme. But of whct possible policy use can findings of this sort be? It should be noted that their spurious accuracy extends to single cents.

On the second point, there is no guarantee at all that a meticulous transport pricing regime will automatically bring about the right investment decisions for the future. Pricing, as evidence of current consumers' acceptance of the service under the usual monopoly conditions, provides partial guidance only for planning; it becomes rather irrelevant when the investments under consideration mature five or ten years from now.

Public transport enterprises are further in the strange position that the customers (highway or rapid transit users) are also, as citizens and voters, the shareholders. Users pay for services consumed, but simultaneously they also put up capital investment funds. For example, motorists constantly invest gasoline taxes in the Interstate Highway System. It is often glibly assumed that urban transport investments which are "financially feasible" are also economically justified and socially desirable. But the availability of funds, especially under the present complex structure of intergovernmental aids and grants, is no reliable guide to planning decisions in the urban sphere. If coordinated urban transport planning is to be taken seriously, it will require coordinated physical, economic, financial, and fiscal planning. These phases cannot be separately pursued.

4. The only correct public investment planning tool is the benefit-cost ratio.

This notion must be rejected. There are other decision-making criteria which will perform much more satisfactorily. Benefit-cost ratios have a number of fundamental defects, and often rather suspect procedures have been used to arrive at them. In particular, the treatment of the time dimension has often been incorrect, interest has been neglected, time spans have been set unrealistically long, no diligent search for alternative solutions has been carried out.

In view of the checkered history and doubtful scientific reputation of some benefit-cost studies, it may be desirable to banish this expression from the urban transportation scene. Intellectually, future analyses should be firmly anchored to the economic theory of investment. The term "investment analyses for urban transportation" may therefore be appropriate. There is no reason for continuing to regard benefit-cost studies as a separate body of analytical techniques in economics.

The rest of the terminology also needs weeding out. The current literature offers a jungle of project effects which are supposed to be analyzed: pecuniary and nonpecuniary, internal and external, private and social, nontransfer and transfer, on-site and off-site, direct and indirect, market and extra-market, economic and noneconomic, measurable and nonmeasurable, monetary and nonmonetary, tangible and intangible, direct and spill-over, individual and collective, primary and secondary.

It is suggested that a simple three-tier classification of effects is all that is needed:

1. Costs (all undesirable effects of actions; inputs; sacrifices) vs. gains (desirable effects; outputs; rewards). In private enterprise investment analysis these terms would correspond to cash costs and cash revenues. In urban transportation studies a much broader interpretation is necessary.

2. Market vs. nonmarket costs and gains. This is a simple distinction between effects which are satisfactorily expressed by market prices according to the economist's rule book, and those which are not.

3. Internal vs. external costs and gains. This distinction arises entirely from the viewpoint adopted for the analysis: external effects are ignored, internal ones are considered. A public viewpoint compels study of all costs and gains within the area of jurisdiction—there are no external effects by definition.

Suppose the viewpoint is that of the San Francisco Bay Area metropolitan region, and a scenic parkway is under study. The additional tourist trade this facility generates would be an internal market gain to the metropolitan economy; its contribution to urban aesthetics, an internal nonmarket gain; the fatal accidents attributable to it, internal nonmarket costs; and the losses sustained by the hotel trade in Los Angeles, external market costs.

In this way, rather complex repercussions can be arranged systematically, precluding double counting, omissions, and confusion.

PROJECT SELECTION CRITERIA

The urban transportation analyst will be confronted by projects with diverse cost and gain patterns extending over time. It is generally agreed that discounting to present values is a convenient method for reducing these complex time profiles into flat images as it were. The standard discounting formulae are well known and need not be repeated here. Applying them, we obtain the present values of a series of gains, V, and of a series of costs, C, when both are discounted at a rate r over the functionally useful life of the project.

The most basic project selection test then is: accept projects if $V \geqq C$, reject if $V < C$. There is a mild controversy over the choice of the discount rate. Some claim that r should be determined within the project planning process itself; for example, it might be the internal rate of return of the very last (marginal) project that can still be fitted into the program. Others, this writer included, suggest than an externally derived market rate of interest or social rate of time preference is appropriate. But otherwise there is unanimity that the basic accept-reject test is sound. Even the benefit-cost ratio proponents are accommodated. Their fundamental selection rule is: Carry out all projects which have a benefit-cost ratio of at least unity, reject all those with a lesser ratio. That is to say, accept projects if $V/C \geq 1$, reject if $V/C < 1$. The two tests amount to exactly the same thing, of course.

Suppose a whole program consisting of a number of projects has to be chosen. What is the correct decision-making criterion? Some, the author among them, say that for the program as a whole maximization of $V - C$, or maximization of the present value of net gains, yields the best results. Others say that the project with the highest V/C ratio deserves first consideration, the one with the next highest ratio should come second, and so on, until the program is complete.

On reflection it becomes apparent that both procedures lead to identical results if there are no other constraints. When all projects with $V/C \geq 1$ are included in the program, the program as a whole will also show maximum $V - C$. Consequently, the involved process of arranging projects on a list by degrees of preference is really quite redundant.

Frequently, mutually exclusive alternatives have to be compared in transportation investment planning. Different designs or locations are technically possible, but one and only one solution is to be carried out. How should the best project be selected?

Here again, some advocate maximization of $V - C$, others maximization of V/C, as the correct selection criterion. We can demonstrate the virtues of both of these by working through an example contained in the AASHO report on *Road User Benefit Cost Analyses for Highway Improvements*.[12] This manual, despite numerous theoretical and practical shortcomings, still has a considerable following among members of the highway profession.

We need not examine the rationale of AASHO's gain and cost figures since we are only interested in the method of project choice. As shown in Table 1, alternate plan 1 (the existing condition) means doing nothing at all: annual highway costs would stay at $19,800 and annual road user costs (defined as the costs of operating motor vehicles) at $411,600. Alternate plans 2 to 6 represent various highway improvement projects,

[12] American Association of State Highway Officials, *Road User Benefit Analyses for Highway Improvements*, Washington, D.C., 1960. (1952 report without basic change except for use of 1959 unit costs.)

TABLE 1

AASHO METHOD OF PROJECT SELECTION

Alternate Plan	Total Annual Cost (dollars)		FIRST BENEFIT RATIO			SECOND BENEFIT RATIO		
			Differences in Costs from Alternate 1 (dollars)		Calculated Benefit Ratio (V/C)	Differences in Costs from Alternate 2 (dollars)		Calculated Benefit Ratio (V/C)
	Highway	Road User	Highway (C)	Road User (V)		Highway (C)	Road User (V)	
1 (basic)	19,800	411,600	—	—	—	—	—	—
2	22,200	356,700	2,400	54,900	22.8	—	—	—
3	23,100	354,800	3,300	56,800	17.2	900	1,900	2.10
4	25,000	336,200	5,200	75,400	14.5	2,800	20,500	7.30
5	29,200	352,100	9,400	59,500	6.3	7,000	4,600	0.66
6	29,700	352,600	9,900	59,000	6.0	7,500	4,100	0.55

Source: American Association of State Highway Officials. *Road User Benefit Analyses for Highway Improvements.* Washington, D.C., 1960, pp. 151–152.

each resulting in its particular set of highway and road user costs. Only one plan can be carried out. Which one should it be?

AASHO correctly compares the additional road improvement costs (C in our terminology) with the savings in vehicle costs (V). But use of the benefit-cost ratio as a selection criterion leads to complex calculations. In the first round, alternate plans, 2, 3, and 4 "all show justification of a high order," but plan 2, with the highest V/C ratio of 22.8, would seem to be the most preferred. However, when plan 2 is put in as the basic condition, "the extra costs of plans 3 and 4 show justification, the latter to a high extent." Hence, AASHO concludes, alternate plan 4, which emerges with a high V/C ratio of 7.3 in the second round, should be selected. Plan 3 is inferior to 4, and plans 5 and 6 can be rejected outright as they show benefit-cost ratios of <1 in the second round.

Applying our selection criterion of maximum $V - C$ to AASHO's basic data, we get exactly the same result with much less trouble:

Alternate Plan	Gains V	Costs C	Net Gains $V - C$
2	$54,900	$2,400	$52,500
3	56,800	3,300	53,500
4	75,400	5,200	70,200
5	59,500	9,400	50,100
6	59,000	9,900	49,100

As can be seen, alternate plan 4 maximizes $V - C$ and should be chosen.

It is possible to apply another variation of the $V - C$ maximization criterion to the AASHO data and still arrive at the same conclusion. According to the AASHO publication, the value to the community at large of accommodating a certain volume of highway traffic may be called V. The exact magnitude, in dollars and cents, of performing this function is not given by AASHO. However, it appears that V stays the same no matter which alternate highway improvement plan is adopted. Highways and motor vehicles can then be regarded as two factors of production which have to be combined in certain proportions to yield the desired highway transportation services. Highway costs, C_h, must be added to motor vehicle costs, C_m, to arrive at total costs of highway transportation, C. Alternate plans 1 to 6, therefore, represent different admixtures of the two factors of production, each with its particular magnitude of C.

Alternate Plan	Highway Costs C_h	Motor Vehicle Costs C_m	Total Highway Transportation Costs $C = C_h + C_m$
1	$19,800	$411,600	$434,400
2	22,200	356,700	378,900
3	23,100	354,800	377,900
4	25,000	336,200	361,200
5	29,200	352,100	381,300
6	29,700	352,600	382,300

With V fixed, the problem becomes one of straightforward cost minimization. Alternate plan 4, which results in the lowest combination of highway and vehicle costs, is obviously the best solution.

Either way, then, maximization of $V - C$ provides us with a simple, effective, and unambiguous criterion for correct project choice. The AASHO method, on the other hand, necessitates calculations of first, second, and possibly further benefit-cost ratios. There is no virtue in using this approach for choices among mutually exclusive alternatives.

Benefit-cost ratios have the further drawback that elaborate accounting rules must be followed in listing effects as gains or costs, otherwise distorted ratios are obtained. This is a serious handicap in highway analyses where the effects of positive costs (highway expenditures) may be conceived either as positive gains (user benefits) or as negative costs (savings in motor vehicle costs), as we have seen in Table 1. Following the maximization of $V - C$ rule, these bookkeeping details are of no significance and a correct answer is obtained every time.[13]

RANKING AND BUDGET CONSTRAINTS

The controversial concepts of "project ranking" or "project priorities" need to be examined carefully. Suppose, once again, that a whole program of several projects has to be submitted for approval to a top decision-making body, for example, to Congress, to a budget committee, or to a planning authority. We must assume that the proposed projects have already passed the $V \geq C$ test. Ideally, all of them should therefore be endorsed immediately. Any deletions or delays would

---

[13] Benefit-cost ratios also perform badly when there are complementary and competitive relationships among projects. These are quite common in the urban transport sphere; for example, the cross effects which freeways, feeder roads, subways, parking garages, and bus lines exercise upon each other. Such network or systems phenomena are discussed in detail in Tillo E. Kuhn, *Public Enterprise*, pp. 92–100, 116–123, 187.

mean loss of net gains. But the decision-makers, for reasons of their own, wish to trim the whole program down. It is therefore necessary, so writers on the subject claim, to arrange the projects on a priority basis in order of descending benefit-cost ratios. The decision-makers would then be able to first eliminate projects at the bottom of the list, gradually working their way to higher benefit-cost ratios until they have cut the program to the desired size.

This whole process, as described, is a little baffling. Basically, we are really concerned with a simple "accept or reject" choice: projects can only be either definitely "in" or definitely "out" of the program. Yet ranking implies that there are shades of being "in" or "out," subtle degrees of being accepted or rejected. If the ranking problem is stated in this way, it doesn't make sense. Additional circumstances have to be brought in to make it realistic.

1. Ranking over time. Most appealing is to regard ranking as an ordering in time; that is, once a priority list exists, project 1 would be done first, project 2 a little later, and so on. For example, construction companies might not have the capacity to cope with numerous projects all at once. Or if they expanded their capacity, there might be a danger of "feast and famine" cycles in construction activity. The decision-makers, with revenues coming in gradually throughout the year, may also prefer a more balanced pattern of project expenditures for financial reasons.

How can ranking over time be handled analytically? This is really a mathematical exercise in testing how much we gain and lose by shifting the starting dates of various projects backward and forward in time. Suppose there are twelve projects which all show $V \geqq C$, and each costs $1 million. The decision-makers have approved a total annual program of $12 million, with one project starting every month. Here the correct method would be to try to maximize $V - C$ for the program as a whole under these particular conditions. A trial-and-error approach is needed, if the cost and gain profiles of the individual projects are irregular.

Is it possible to use a V/C ranking if both gains and costs are expressed in present values? If the gain and cost profiles of the various projects have the same basic pattern, such ratios can be employed for determining priorities over time: the highest V/C ratio project should come first, and so on. It should be noted that in many cases net gains will grow at faster compound interest rates than the rate assumed for discounting purposes. When this occurs, the growth rate of the numerator will be larger than that of the discounting term in the denominator. Hence, such projects would show larger V/C ratios as they are postponed over time. However, maximization of $V - C$ would still be a less ambiguous project selection tool under the circumstances.

2. Budget constraint. Of importance also is the notion, frequently encountered in the water resource economics literature, that the decision-makers arrive at varying budget limits by some magical processes which are quite unrelated to the sizes and merits of the programs submitted by the analysts. Hence, lists of ranked projects must be made available, so that appropriate cut-off points satisfying the budget limits can be determined.

Once more, this procedure does not seem satisfactory. If there is an arbitrary budget limit—arbitrary in the sense that it was not arrived at with the aid of analysis—then in effect we are confronted with a constrained C. If so, then the V's for the program as a whole should be maximized in relation to the given C. If the budgeting process is fickle and there are several possible constrained C's, alternative programs must be worked out for each one of them, still following the criterion of maximizing $V - C$. The correct method under the circumstances is to compose the different programs with the aid of various discount rates: a high rate would ration out many projects and would therefore result in a conservative program; a low rate would have the opposite effect.

The most disturbing feature of arbitrary budget setting is this: it seems to treat the specified sum of C as practically costless—the money is earmarked and must be spent no matter how big or small the V's obtained; but any amount of proposed expenditure that exceeds the specified budget becomes infinitely costly no matter how large the potential additional V's may be. In other words, a completely arbitrary step function for the cost of money prevails, with the C constraint suddenly rising from zero to infinity. But in good budget planning there should really be gradually increasing penalties on larger programs. Such a smooth rationing effect can best be achieved by upward adjustment in the discount rate, for example from 4 to 5 to 6 per cent. This would be comparable to the rising interest costs faced by private enterprises in the money market, when larger and larger loans are sought.

It is suggested, in conclusion, that the ranking and budget constraint problems in urban transportation can be tackled intelligently. First, budgets ought to be based on well-prepared investment analyses; there is something wrong with the institutional arrangements if budgets are simply imposed arbitrarily. Second, if arbitrary budget limits are nevertheless a fact of life, then the program size should be fitted to the constrained C by varying the discount rate; if there is great disparity between the resulting discount rate and, say, the market interest rate in the private sector, this will at least be a signal to the decision-makers that there is something wrong with their budget constraint. Third, ranking over time can be determined by analytically postponing or advancing individual projects; maximization of $V - C$ for the program as a whole is the correct criterion.

OTHER CONSTRAINTS AND CRITERIA

Frequently distinctions are made in urban transportation planning between capital costs (K) and operating costs (O), where total cost $C = K + O$. Institutionally, different constraints are placed upon K and O and this greatly distorts the investment process. Sometimes K is subjected to budget scrutiny and rigorous analysis, but O is unconstrained because it is assumed that future project operating costs can be met from future project revenues. Consequently there is great incentive to substitute O for K. Projects with low capital intensity will be promoted, or planners will try to pass off capital costs as operating ones; because of the nebulous nature of everyday cost definitions this is not too difficult. Alternatively, funds for K may come from low-interest, low-risk, general revenue bonds, whereas O has to be found from possibly meager operating revenues. Here substitutions of K for O are advantageous. Either way, whenever costs are loaded onto an artificially low-risk, low-interest, source of finance, the economic balance is disturbed.

Other distortions occur when "foreign aid" [14] from outside the region enters into urban transport investment considerations. Usually federal or state aid is limited to capital investment items. Hence there is great pressure to favor highly capital intensive projects. In effect, massive monuments to the future in steel and concrete will be built with outside funds, even when less durable investments might be economically more appropriate.

The common practice of federal and state governments to offer liberal financial aid for urban freeways, especially those which form part of the interstate or state highway network, but not for other transportation technologies, has had particularly powerful effects. In California at the present time as much as 100 per cent of the costs of urban freeways designated for the Interstate Highway System are

---

[14] This somewhat unorthodox term is explained in *ibid.*, pp. 55–57, 200–202.

borne by the senior governments and over 90 per cent of the construction costs by the federal government; the remainder, plus all operating
expenses, by the State of California. This formula applies, for example,
to the controversial $180 million, 7.1 mile Western Freeway in San
Francisco, which has been proposed by the State but has not been
accepted locally. From the point of view of the local authorities, this
project would be a gift from the authorities in Washington, D.C. and
Sacramento, were it not for losses of tax revenues from freeway land,
destruction of community and aesthetic values, and so on.

Under these peculiar institutional circumstances[15] it is small wonder
that urban freeways have been sprouting in the big cities all over the
United States and a near miracle that local governments show any
interest at all in alternative solutions, especially rapid transit, which
are not eligible for the same massive "foreign aid" support. The
economist can only strongly urge that senior governments adopt a
policy of complete technological neutrality and offer urban *transportation* aid with no strings attached. Otherwise urban transport
investment analyses, complete with benefit-cost studies and the rest,
are a waste of time.

INVESTMENT APPROACHES TO URBAN PEAK PROBLEMS

This becomes an exercise in contrasting economic costs and gains.
Two basic lines of attack are possible. First, it may be possible to
quantify, in market terms, the gains (V) associated with different levels

[15] Richard M. Zettel describes the situation very well: ". . . in this nation we have
never met fiscal problems of the lesser units of government through *unconditional*
revenue-sharing or grant-in-aid arrangements—whereby the recipients would be
permitted to allocate funds among their several functions and activities as their
legislative bodies saw fit. Instead, the grantor seeks to establish an 'interest' in a
particular function or activity as justification for the grant; and it then sets conditions
upon use of the grant so that its 'interest' will be furthered. . . . these conditions
conspire to shift fiscal responsibility upward. And the manner in which this fiscal
responsibility is exercised tends to remove critical decisions on some governmental
activities to a seat rather far removed from the scene of the problems. The grants
take on the nature of 'foreign aid,' to be used or to be lost to the community. But
the community must abide by the conditions. It may think its school problem more
critical than its highway problem, but the highway grant will be spent for highways—
along with local resources if matching is required. And if grants are available for
highways but not for transit, then highway construction tends to become the financially feasible 'solution' to the transportation problem even though the community
might prefer to experiment with transit. And since the way is closed to shifting
funds, the dismaying alternative is to seek new grants for new purposes—grants for
education in addition to highway grants; specific grants for transit as a follow-up
to specific grants for highways." Richard M. Zettel, "Public Finance Policy and
Urban Transport," paper presented at the annual meeting of the American Society
of Civil Engineers, Detroit, 1962.

of peak performance; for example, for unsuppressed peak service (the highest V), for a slightly flattened peak (a somewhat lower V) and a severely curtailed peak demand (the lowest V). This measurement of the V's is highly problematic, but ingenious researchers may be able to accomplish it. For example, the uninhibited V would express what commuters *would be prepared to pay* if they were conveyed to their destinations with speed and comfort. Or it might be the total market gains accruing to the metropolitan economy from such a superb service. The suppressed V's would then reflect the reduced cash returns from commuters and/or the lowered efficiency of the metro economy. Given the different transport cost estimates (C) which correspond with the various V's (high C would go with high V, low with low), then the correct selection criterion would again be maximization of $V - C$.

A more promising approach, in the writer's view, would be to regard the peak V as largely nonmeasurable in market terms. The community, or its representatives, should then clearly specify the desired level of peak-hour service for everybody in the community. Exact standards should be set for door-to-door speed, safety, performance, avoidance of air pollution, external design, etc. The specifications must stress that urban transportation be seen as a *system* and be designed from beginning to end. This system must include both private and public instrumentalities, of course, as well as *all* functional components (feeders, vehicle storage, terminals, transfer facilities, etc.). In view of the backward technological performance of contemporary urban transport media, it would be a very good idea if the community transport goals were set rather high. Designers, inventors, systems analysts, and producers would rise to this challenge, just as they have risen to the challenge to get a man safely to the moon and back. There is no reason to be timid in our demands for better urban transport service.

Once the various qualities of peak-hour service have been specified by collective value judgment, the economist can help to select appropriate design configurations which will minimize C. Various other economic problems—time paths of accomplishment, trade-offs, supply and demand trends over time—can also be explored with profit by the analyst.

PREPONDERANCE OF NONMARKET VALUES

A problem that occurs over and over again in the public sector is the preponderance of nonmarket values and especially nonmarket gains. The reasons are familiar and need not be repeated here. It must be conceded that the intrusion of nonmarket values severely limits the scope of economic analysis.[16] The various gain and cost items cannot be aggregated into common money terms. Furthermore, since the relative market and nonmarket contents of costs and gains will likely differ, the two series cannot jointly be subjected to the traditional revenue-cost comparisons and calculations.

Under these circumstances, how can economists still contribute to better decisions? Fortunately, the costs of typical urban transport projects consists almost entirely of market items: the dollar outlays on men, machines, and materials necessary to build and operate these facilities. If there are distortions in the price signals generated in the market for transportation supplies, they can be corrected. Furthermore, if pure nonmarket costs are caused by specific projects, they can be entered as negative nonmarket gains if desired. For example, the smog from a freeway or the noise nuisance from an elevated rail line are just as much detractions from existing amenities as they are positive community costs. If we follow the criterion of maximizing $V - C$, it does not matter in which account they end up.

It is then necessary that the urban community or its representatives specify precisely the level of V for the transportation service. Since V will be composed of a number of desirable attributes which cannot be reduced to the common denominator of money, it is essential that they all be spelled out in detail. The specifications for a comprehensive urban passenger transportation system might for example be:

1. Under projected land-use conditions, the system must be capable of conveying peak-hour commuters in less than, say, 30 minutes from door to door (or in a larger metropolis, perhaps 60 per cent of peak-hour commuters in less than 30 minutes, 40 per cent in 30 to 60 minutes).

2. The system must adhere to certain stated standards of passenger comfort and convenience (rates of acceleration and deceleration, seat availability, air conditioning, etc.).

---

[16] Lloyd Rodwin argues that there is a gulf between traditional economics and physical (city and regional) planning: "This role [of metropolitan planning] cannot be played by the price system. The difficulties are already manifest in the widespread concern with urban maladjustments. We know the market for urban land and improvements is characterized by imperfect knowledge, sluggish or inflexible adjustments to price signals, and significant discrepancies between public and private costs. We know, too, that many of the basic decisions on urban development are not, and for some practical purposes cannot, be made by the market mechanism. They involve public policy on the character of land use control systems and decisions on public investment of capital for urban overhead." Lloyd Rodwin, "Metropolitan Policy for Developing Areas," *Regional Economic Planning: Techniques for Less Developed Areas*, Paris, 1961, pp. 221–232.

3. The fatal accident rate attributable to the system itself must not exceed 0.1 per 100 million passenger miles (or some other figure).

4. The system must not exceed stated air pollution tolerances.

5. Large portions of right-of-way must be underground, as shown on a detailed land-use map.

6. The external design of the facilities must be of high aesthetic quality and must have the approval of the civic art commission.

7. Flexibility of routing is an important quality of service aspect. The number of origin-and-destination pairs that can be served, as well as the number of nodes and interchange points, are significant and should be specified.

Given these and many additional performance standards that can be thought up, the economist can then help to choose among various means to achieve these ends. The following aspects lend themselves particularly to economic analysis:

1. Minimization of C in relation to the given V (or various dimensions of V).

2. Research on the increases or decreases of the various components of V which would result from moving the value of C up and down.

3. Study of the time paths for achieving the specified goals: over-all progress of the program; priorities for completing geographic segments of the system and for reaching different functional objectives.

4. Exploration of possible trade-offs between different goals, gains and costs. For example, more safety vs. less speed; higher aesthetic quality vs. higher cost; great portions underground vs. less passenger comfort; more air pollution vs. less cost.

5. Exploration of different technical-economic mixes on the supply sides: desirable degrees of capital intensity and combinations of factors of production.

6. Design of performance criteria, checks on operational efficiency.

7. Continued surveillance of community preferences over time; consumers' acceptance of system.

Even though the goals and performance standards of the urban transportation system will have to be determined largely by collective value judgments, the economic analyst is not likely to run out of work in this sphere.

III. *Goals, Choices and Investment Analysis*

Clear identification of goals emerges as the most important first step in any urban transportation plan. Once the ends are stated, means can be sought to achieve them. Up to the present, major metropolitan transportation studies have spent little time defining ends before rushing into the phases of data collection, field surveys, and computer programs.[17] In addition, present conditions and attitudes surely are of only limited use in determining a more desirable future.

Apparently these are general shortcomings of all urban planning. Davidoff and Reiner make the point in an important article on planning philosophy.

In each plan, the importance of placing value formulation first cannot be overstated, though there is great reluctance in urban planning to start with a search for ends. Even where goal selection is placed first, there is a tendency to underplay this and return to familiar territory—"survey and analysis." We do not understand the logic that supports ventures in research before the objectives of research have been defined. Such emphasis on research is premised on an ill-founded belief that knowledge of facts will give rise to appropriate goals or value judgments. Facts by themselves will not suggest what would be good or what should be preferred.[18]

Because value formulation is necessary in urban decision-making, planning is sometimes identified with arbitrary, undemocratic processes, manipulated by a few who impose their own preferences on the rest of the community. If this occurs, then it is, of course, not good planning. Ideally, planning should make possible more choice and particularly more intelligent choice than would otherwise be possible. It is meant to free the community from the tryanny of poor, shortsighted, selfish, and ill-informed decisions. As Davidoff and Reiner go on to say, "Values are inescapable elements of any rational decision-making process or any exercise of choice. Since choice permeates the whole planning sequence, a clear notion of ends pursued lies at the heart of the planner's task and the definition of these ends thus must be given primacy in the planning process." There is no reason why decisions on values cannot be decentralized, by putting alternatives before the voters, by informing and educating the citizens, by enlisting

[17] Regarding the need for metropolitan transportation studies, Zettel and Carll state, ". . . the review failed to turn up any extensive analysis of the urban transport problem that the studies were to investigate and help solve. The study prospectuses usually plunge directly into the technical details of fact gathering and data analysis, without attempting to define the problems on hand" (*Summary Review*, p. 20). Practically all of the studies surveyed state "preparation of a transport plan," or "formulation of a highway plan" as their basic objectives, without alluding to the higher-level community objectives that these technical efforts are supposed to serve (*ibid.*, pp. 25–26).

[18] Paul Davidoff and Thomas A. Reiner, "A Choice Theory of Planning," *Journal of the American Institute of Planners*, No. 2, May 1962, p. 111.

their advice. The purely technical decisions for implementation can then more safely be centralized.

Urban transportation planning and investment analysis must consequently be regarded primarily as a vehicle for community choices: preferences must be explored, options must be suggested, different solutions—even utopian ones—must be pursued. The difficulties are staggering, for when people decide upon one comprehensive transport system for their city rather than another one, they significantly affect the urban way of life. Furthermore, their decisions will typically not bring results this year or next, but five, ten, or twenty years from now. Quite a different generation of urban dwellers may feel the full effects.

In essence, the greater the number of alternatives considered and the more futuristic the outlook, the more powerful transport planning and analysis will be. Alas, there is as yet little evidence that this general philosophy prevails in contemporary urban transportation policy and practice.

COMMENT

BRITTON HARRIS, University of Pennsylvania

I am basically most sympathetic with Kuhn's effort as an economist to come to grips with the nature of the city and the challenges offered to economic analysis by urban problems. I perhaps disagree implicitly with his method of slicing the problem, and, as a planner speaking to economists, I shall try to suggest some of the ways in which Kuhn's discussion of applications seem to me to fail to mesh with his attempted capsulization of first principles.

The urban metropolitan scene offers half a dozen features which are somewhat intractable under conventional economic analysis.

First, it is pervaded by externalities, with individual actions having many ramifying effects upon other entities.

Second, many investments, especially in the public sector, are "lumpy." Associated with this discontinuity of investment decisions are substantial economies and diseconomies of scale.

Third, the long life of investments in land improvements introduces rigidities into the market for capital services. Under conditions of growth, an investment can be optimal for only a narrow point in time, yet once committed, it is not readily transferable.

Fourth, the great strategic importance of public investments spotlights the fact that no market exists for the services of many of these investments, and this lack of a market complicates investment decisions. Kuhn and Vickrey suggest different approaches by a cost-benefit analysis and user charges to create a pseudo-market or an actual market for certain services.

The fifth difficulty centers on the problem of identifying an optimum. Owing to the wide range of public investment channels and of public influences on private investment and behavior, many distinct combinations of factors are possible, and these may be widely separated in what might be called a "policy space." As in the economics of the farm or the industrial producer, marginal analysis can lead only to a local optimum. It cannot identify possible structurally different recombinations of factors which may result in a higher optimum.

The sixth problem arises when, as a result of a combination of difficulties four and five above, specific individual policies are pursued and judged independently of their combined effects and possible substitutes. This type of judgment, it may readily be seen, leads to suboptimization, wherein one program may tend to run away with the pattern of metropolitan development. The danger of suboptimization is particularly serious where one policy operates in a market or pseudo-market (cost-benefit) framework while its complementary or competing policies do not. Examples of suboptimization may be found in highway policy, federal mortgage insurance policy, urban renewal, and central business district planning.

REPLY BY TILLO E. KUHN

Harris offers some interesting and penetrating comments. He lists several features of urban investment decisions which are, he says, "somewhat intractable under conventional economic analysis." Although he seeks to leave the matter of degree in doubt, he conveys the impression that the pitfalls are fatal to applications of economic principles.

I am more sanguine than Harris about the potential contributions of economics. In essence my position is that if conventional economic analysis—whatever that means—is largely useless in the urban sphere, let us by all means develop unconventional economic analysis for the purpose. Otherwise "economics will fade out of this sphere by default," as I pointed out in an earlier version of my paper.

To take his easier, more technical points first, that there are externalities—lumpiness in investment and time rigidities in the capital market—is, I feel, fully recognized in my paper and elsewhere. Quite satisfactory methods to tackle these difficulties are available.

His more substantial arguments are directed against the decision standards of "suboptimization" or the "local optimum." It is difficult to define an optimum where a market mechanism does not exist, as is often the case with urban services. To act in a pseudo-market context, therefore, can be dangerous, as indeed might be an indiscriminate use of tolls such as Vickrey proposes. In a particularly perceptive passage, Harris warns against the dangers of suboptimization when one program—highways, urban renewal, mortgage insurance, and so on—runs away with metropolitan development, because it is not based to the same extent upon a market or pseudo-market framework as other programs.

I agree with Harris that proper markets for urban services do not exist. Of course, if market mechanisms conforming to the economist's rule book can be found or created, all the better. But professional economists should be on guard against the vested intellectual interests they have in the notion of the market, and all the formidable methodological apparatus it gave rise to. Simple scientific honesty compels us to state nonmarket items in other quantitative or qualitative terms. The frequently observed attempts to heroically translate all manner of effects of public action into dollars and cents are to be depreciated.

Now to the core problem of suboptimization in urban decision-making. Urban objectives have several dimensions—cultural, political, ethical, aesthetic, economic. To pursue only one dimension would indeed lead to a suboptimum from the total point of view. Likewise, once the multidimensional structure of public goals has been correctly identified, various discrete bundles of means are available. Harris uses the suggestive idea of the "policy space" within which we must move—not marginally, but by recombinations of policy sets.

In urban research, as in the social sciences generally, the need to handle multidimensional problems, the irrelevance of simple dichotomies, the absence of continuously variable relationships, create tough methodological problems. How to reconcile the different objectives? How to move up to a "higher optimum," when this is a surface rather than a point? How to select the best policy bundle? It will certainly be desirable to enlist the support of all relevant expertise, including that in economics, for the purpose. Conscientious tracing of causes and effects of various policies will be helpful. Identification of policy trade-offs—more urban mobility may detract from social, cultural, aesthetic desiderata, for example—will be highly illuminating.

In all this the scope for economic decisions, I believe, can best be delineated by the distinction between ends and means to achieve ends.

Our urban goals are predominantly noneconomic. My good friend Dick Carll would argue that they may not even be rational. We should always allow for the intuitive, the romantic, the lyric, otherwise urban life will be empty. But in the choice of human means we should endeavor to be rational.

Consequently transportation planning in urban areas ought to be pursued in this fashion: let a community pattern be set up as an end; then let us devise the optimum transport system to serve it, as a means; and then let us finally submit, for community decision-making, the question of whether the transport requirement is unreasonable for meeting the general community objectives.

This still begs the question how the multidimensional community goals should be determined. Here we get into the old hassle between "predictive" and "prescriptive" uses of economic analysis. In another article by Harris, his attitude is made clear. Speaking of "process-oriented" analysis, he describes a society of individuals, each attempting to optimize the current situation, all interacting, and all subject to resource scarcity. Given these restraints, we can analytically describe what their behavior will be. We can alter the restraints and describe a different pattern of behavior. Models based upon hypothesis about how individuals optimize their economic welfare can add to our predictive abilities.

"When we are using a model for predictive purposes," Harris continues, "normative considerations may enter in the following way: we may assume, for better or worse reasons, that we can specify a manner in which people *ought* to behave under given circumstances, which will coincide with the way they actually will behave. We impute to them an optimizing behavior which will reproduce their actual behavior." In other words, those analysts who are perceptive of values, as well as of facts, will be better prophets. But Harris hastens to add that he is not defining *standards*. The assumed behavior, he points out, need not "coincide with any normative moral code, nor need it lead to the fulfillment of any normative goals. It would thus appear unwise to equate optimizing behavior with rationality, with socially ethical behavior, or with any socially optimum results."

This may explain why Harris balks at the idea of applying economic principles for decision-making in urban public enterprises. He would probably not argue long against using economic welfare theory in private enterprise, where the behavior of persons is defined by hedonistic motives and constrained by market conditions. But in public enterprise, behavior is not compelled by impersonal forces: it is consciously directed in a particular course which reflects public choice. Applying economic principles, we are not describing a behavioral process, we are discussing *guidelines for policy*.

However, among scientifically minded people there is felt a growing need to describe public decision-making as a process of collective behavior, to outline the sequence of choices. This was the purpose of Davidoff and Reiner, and they find that the identification and formulation of values, goals, and objectives enters at every stage of the process. They feel that the planner should not only be responsible for furnishing information (including predictions about the consequences of certain decisions), but also for the evaluation of alternative choices, the suggestion of the *best* choice, the testing of values, and the identification of goals. This describes very well, in my opinion, what economists and urban transport experts in their own professional spheres also ought to do. We must, in Mumford's words, not only inform, but "educate the attitude" of decision makers.

Some Major Aspects of Urban Transport Policy Formation

KENT T. HEALY

YALE UNIVERSITY

The character of the metropolis and the directions in which it develops have in recent years become an increasing concern of public policy. The transport aspects in particular have become a center of attention at all levels of government. Economists have responded with their usual enterprise to the challenge of a new field of public concern. With the modern emphasis on analytical tools and hypothesis, they have made considerable progress.[1] But this emphasis has taken attention away from an important influence on policy formation, namely, the way policy questions are structured.

This structuring can influence the weight given or type of analysis applied to policy questions at the working level of legislative bodies or administrative branches of government where actual decisions are made. It is important, then, that what appear to be some of the more significant structural aspects in the approaches to urban transport policies be examined and their effects assessed.

The Spatial Arrangement of the Metropolitan Area

Because local leadership for urban study generally comes from top business executives and government officials whose most immediate interests and places of work are likely to be in the central business district, the urban transport problem is likely to be approached as primarily a central business district problem. It is important for transport policy formation, however, that all sections of the metropolis be considered.

The geographical pattern of the typical metropolis involves a central urban core, historically the main location of the work activities of the

[1] See John R. Meyer, "Regional Economics: A Survey," *The American Economic Review*, March 1962, pp. 48–54, for a listing of much of the pertinent literature.

city, and always a principal location. Because of this, as a metropolis increases in size there is a tendency for the average length of trips to increase. A theoretical top limit to the extent of this increase can be shown by assuming that all employment, shopping, and other activities are retained in the center. In purely geometric terms, if the metropolitan area is equally developed in all directions around the center, and residential density is uniform, the "person-trip" length increases as the square root of the increase in population. That is, if population and area quadruple, trip length doubles. Actually, decentralization of economic activity occurs and not all the trips are to the central area so that the rate of increase is always below this rate. Also, since one end of most trips is the residence, the effects of change in residential density are important. Again using the model of the single central core of work activity, the length of trips from home increases with the square root of the increase in land area per dwelling. That is, if the area for a dwelling unit quadruples, the average trip distance to the center doubles. These are not the only geometric features influencing urban transport but they are the ones of greatest significance here.

Consideration of social and economic as well as geographic factors demands a more complicated analysis than that of this simple model. The varying degrees of decentralization and intensity of land use in urban activities make significant generalizations difficult. The over-all parameters are broadly shown by recent metropolitan area transport studies.[2] Much has been learned from these studies about the spatial positioning of the demands for transport. In the first place, for large diversified metropolitan areas, some 75 to 90 per cent of all "person-trips" (which include trips by all vehicular modes of transport) involve leaving or going home. The work place provides the next largest group—some 30 to 40 per cent. The remaining trips are for such purposes as education, shopping, recreation, personal business, and social gatherings.[3]

The importance of the locations of various types of activity as they determine trip spatial patterns is further illustrated by classifying

---

[2] *Report on the Detroit Metropolitan Area Traffic Study*, Part I, *Data Summary and Interpretation* (1955), Part II, *Future Traffic and Long-Range Expressway Plan* (1956), Detroit; *Chicago Area Transportation Study, Survey Findings*, Vol. I (1959), Vol. II, *Data Projections* (1960), Chicago; *Pittsburgh Area Transportation Study*, Vol. I, *Study Findings* (1961), Vol. II, *Forecasts and Plans* (1963), Pittsburgh; *Twin Cities Area Transportation Study*, Vol. 1, *Study Findings*, St. Paul, 1962. In the footnotes which follow, these sources will be referred to respectively as *DMATS, CATS, PATS,* and *TCATS,* with the volume or part noted.

[3] Calculated from *PATS*, Vol. I, p. 92; *DMATS*, Part I, p. 81; *CATS*, Vol. I, p. 37.

destination according to basic land uses. Counting all reasons for going to residences makes their land use proportion as a destination just over 50 per cent. The sum of people going to retail and to service facilities to work, eat, shop, etc., accounts for some 25 per cent of destinations. Manufacturing and wholesale uses together account for only 6 to 7 per cent, and schools, about the same proportion. Public buildings, museums and the like, and open spaces such as parks and athletic areas, together account for another 6 to 7 per cent. Transportation facilities for external travel, stations and airports, are the destination for some 2 per cent of trips. These proportions are surprisingly stable for the three major metropolitan areas for which data have most recently been published, Chicago, Pittsburgh, and the Twin Cities.[4]

It is obvious, then, that residential location and land-use characteristics are major determinants of transport requirements. These characteristics are a result of a complex of economic and social factors which are as dynamic as technological change in transport itself. The character of residential facilities which people desire has been affected by the recent increase in the proportion of households with children under eighteen years of age. This proportion remained practically constant from 1930 to 1950, but in the following decade increased from 50 to 60 per cent. In addition, an increasing proportion of families have been receiving higher levels of income.[5] An approximate measure of this is the proportion of families and unattached individuals with incomes before taxes equivalent to over $5,000 in 1960. In 1939, about 25 per cent of

---

[4] Calculated from *PATS*, Vol. I, pp. 94–95; *CATS*, Vol. I, p. 112; *DMATS*, Part I, p. 125; and *TCATS*, pp. 92–93. Details for individual study areas are as follows:

Category of Generalized Land Use	Proportion of Person Trip Destinations for Major Categories (per cent)			
	Pittsburgh	Chicago	Detroit	Twin Cities
Residence	52	55	53	52
Retail shopping	15⎫	⎫		18
Personal services		24⎬	27	
Professional	10⎭	⎭		7
School	8⎫	⎫		6
Public bldgs. (exc. schools)		11⎬	12	
and public open spaces	6⎭	⎭		7
Transport	2	3		2

[5] Calculated from Bureau of Census, *Statistical Abstract of the United States*, 1951, p. 26, and 1962, p. 43.

the country's families and unattached individuals had incomes above this level; in 1950, 43 per cent, and in 1960, 56 per cent.[6]

Another economic factor has been the improvement in the terms of home financing. For new privately owned housing there have been reductions in down payments, extensive government guarantees of mortgage loans, some ceilings on interest rates on such loans, and income tax exemption for that part of income spent on mortgage interest. Offsetting this, the terms of financing and renting large multiunit housing for low-income and, more recently, for middle-income families have also improved. Public construction of multiunit dwellings has been undertaken and, for units of this type, relief from property taxes has been provided. More recently the incentives for private promotion of multiunit housing construction have become substantial.[7]

The preference for private homes or apartments is also affected by psychological factors about which little is known empirically. Many people have a basic desire to have their own house or land. The desire for privacy or individual expression in home ownership also plays a role. In the other direction is the desire to attain anonymity by living in a large apartment or housing development or to avoid the responsibilities of caring for a residence.

On balance, these economic, psychological, and social factors have in recent decades led to a much reduced density of living, a shift from multiunit dwellings to single ones, with an increase in the number and size of rooms. The decennial housing censuses, the first of which was taken in 1940, have indicated that the type of housing units constructed in metropolitan areas has shifted markedly since the 1920's. Of the dwelling units constructed in 1920–29 and inventoried in 1940, some 54 per cent were single-family houses and 21 per cent were structures of five and more units. For those built in 1930–39, the single-family unit proportion had risen to 70 per cent and the five and over remained at 21 per cent. Changed definitions and classifications in the later censuses make comparisons difficult, but 1940–49 building showed further increases in the single-family category—to 72 or 80 per cent depending upon whether the terms of the 1950 or 1960 census are used, and the five and over group dropped to 10 or 11 per cent. Finally, for the 1950–60 period, the proportion of construction in newly defined single-family units rose to 85 per cent and the five and over unit structures dropped from 9.7 to 9.4 per cent. The modal number of rooms per

[6] Calculated from *ibid.*
[7] *Ibid.*, 1962, p. 763.

unit has varied from five to six in the single-family house and has been three in the structures of ten units or more.[8]

These trends have been accompanied by a rapid growth in urban population, considerably more rapid than for the country as a whole. The population of the contiguous United States as a whole grew 7 per cent from 1930 to 1940, 15 per cent from 1940 to 1950, and 18 per cent from 1950 to 1960. The 1960 standard metropolitan statistical areas grew 22 per cent from 1940 to 1950 and 26 per cent from 1950 to 1960.[9]

As a result of desire for reduced residential density by more people and a general increase in population, there has been tremendously rapid growth in population outside the central cities of the metropolitan areas. For the standard metropolitan statistical areas of over 250,000 population in 1960 in the northeast, Great Lakes, southwest, and Pacific coast states (the regions defined in the last section) the growth outside of the central cities increased from 18 per cent in the 1930's to 29 per cent in the 1940's, and to 54 per cent in the 1950's. These rates may be compared with declining central city growth rates of 3, 14, and 6 per cent respectively. For the northeast and Great Lakes regions alone, these latter rates were only 1, 9, and −1 per cent respectively. This summary points up the dramatic decentralization of metropolitan residential locations and the dispersal of the major category of trip-ends which urban transport must serve.

Finally, to translate these factors into the geometry of transport, the point in space of the residence trip-end is determined by the fact that, in general, residence locations tend to spread out from the center of the city. The farther from the center, the fewer the dwelling units per acre, and the higher the proportion of land used for residences. The combined effect is made apparent by viewing the residential areas of a metropolis as a series of equal-width concentric rings around the center. The farther from the center a ring is, the greater the area it includes. The increasing size of the area and its rising proportion devoted to residences with increasing distance from the center make up for the concurrent declining density of residences. Table 1 shows these characteristics for Chicago, Pittsburgh, and Detroit. The rings, extending from three or four to ten miles from the center, each have the same general order of population proportion. Beyond this the

[8] Bureau of Census, *U.S. Census of Housing*, 1940, Vol. 2, Part 22, p. 4, and 1950, Vol. 2, Part 1, pp. 1–18; and calculations from Bureau of Census, *Metropolitan Housing*, 1960, HC (2) No. 1, pp. 1–22.

[9] Bureau of Census: *U.S. Census of Population*, 1950, Vol. 1, pp. 1–69; and calculations from *ibid., 1960 U.S. Summary*, PC (1), 1A, U.S.; and *Statistical Abstract*, 1962, p. 13.

TABLE 1

PROPORTION OF METROPOLIS STUDY POPULATION IN
EQUAL-WIDTH RINGS AROUND CENTER

Ring-Range (in miles from center)	Percentage of Population		
	Pittsburgh	Chicago	Detroit
0 - 1.9	5	3	
0 - 2.9		7	14
2 - 3.9	27	11	
3 - 5.9		25	26
4 - 5.9	19	18	
6 - 7.9	23	17	
6 - 8.9		26	21
8 - 10.9	20	21	
9 - 11.9		17	21

Source: Calculated from *PATS*, V. 2, pp. 11 and 60; *CATS*, V. II, p. 114; *DMATS*, Pt. I, p. 30.

effect of declining density seems to outweigh the added area. But residential density varies substantially, and the size of the city itself is a factor, so that the share of population living within a given distance of the center can vary considerably. About 50 per cent of the 1.5 million population of the Pittsburgh study area live within six miles of the center, while only about 30 per cent do in Detroit (with 3 million), and 32 per cent in Chicago (with 5.17 million).

At the other, nonresidential, end of the urban trip path are the activities which, in the past, were mainly oriented toward the center. A wide range of factors have tended to reorient many of these activities.[10] It is clear that changes in transport technology have been only one influencing factor though their impact is felt in several ways. Of great importance has been the growing recognition of the advantage of single-story buildings for manufacturing and distribution facilities, and the consequent requirement of larger plots of land not generally obtainable in an already built-up area. Ancillary to this are the high land values in central districts (or even some not so central) which provide an added incentive for activities requiring single-story buildings to move away from central urban areas. The flexibility in space of modern highway transport has been a facilitating factor.

[10] An analysis of these factors is presented in Raymond Vernon's *The Changing Economic Function of the Central City*. Some of the more important aspects are briefly reviewed here.

Further, the very extension of residential sites away from the center has moved the labor pool, the retail purchasing power, and the need for services out from the center. The facilities for meeting the two latter demands have themselves moved out. All these decentralizing factors have been facilitated by the ability of highway transport to provide economically for the less dense traffic flows of decentralized activities. Along with this, developments over the years in the distribution of power, water, and services required by industry have made most of them essentially ubiquitous throughout a metropolitan area.

The trend, then, is for person trip-ends away from the residence to be less predominately into urban centers. For instance, it is estimated that in 1956 only 4.6 per cent of all person-trips from the over-all Chicago area were destined to the "Loop." In 1958, the proportion was 6 per cent to the "Golden Triangle" in Pittsburgh and 8 per cent to the combined central business districts of Minneapolis and St. Paul. But the smallness of the area of these central districts does cause a very high concentration of trip-ends per square mile, twenty, or even more, times that for average residentially developed land.[11]

For the larger metropolitan areas, the dispersal also results in trip lengths shorter than might be expected from the spacing between the central business district and the distant residential areas. Half of the person-trips within the transport study area were estimated to be under 3 miles for Detroit; the average estimated actual length of person trips was 3 miles for Pittsburgh, 4.4 for Detroit and just over 5 for Chicago. Of the different categories of trips, that to the place of business was the longest, roughly half again as long as the average shopping trip. The latter, however, was made up of shorter trips to local shopping centers and trips twice as long to the central business district.[12]

Another important result of the dispersal of activity appears in the relatively small proportion of trips going to, from, and passing through the central district as compared to that for areas just outside it. For metropolitan Detroit, out of 5.2 million estimated weekday internal person-trips (by auto, taxi, and transit), 4.5 per cent were destined to the one square mile central business district; that is, roughly 9 per cent of the total trips originated or terminated there. Trips between areas outside of that district, which might pass through it if made in a straight line between origin and destination, were less than 1 per cent of all trips.

[11] Calculated from *CATS*, Vol. I, p. 115; *PATS*, Vol. I, p. 97; *TCATS*, Vol. I, p. 56.
[12] Calculated from *DMATS*, Part I, pp. 91 and 125; *PATS*, Vol. I, pp. 17 and 93; and *CATS*, Vo. I, pp. 81 and 117.

In contrast, 10 per cent of the total Detroit area trips were entirely within a ring encompassing the area three to six miles from the center. Another 10 per cent were between that ring and rings farther out; and 15 per cent were between the three- to six-mile ring and inner rings. Finally, about 10 per cent passed through the three- to six-mile ring. The total trips involving that ring were some 45 per cent of all internal trips, compared with some 10 per cent involving the central business district. However, the 45 per cent of trips were in an area of over twelve square miles, whereas the 10 per cent were in an area a little over one square mile. In the central business district, there were 2.5 times as many trips per square mile as there were in the three- to six-mile ring. Again, the high intensity of transport use of the innermost land and its small relative share of total metropolitan area transport stands out.[13]

Thus, the geometric picture portrays a demand for transport spread widely over large modern metropolitan areas. It also shows a very intense demand upon land space for transportation in the inner part of the metropolis, arising from a small share of total transport demand. Relatively small fractions of both trip ends and trip paths involve the central district. The underlying factors influencing the use of metropolitan land point in the direction of further dispersal and declining relative importance of the center. These are fundamental considerations for policy formation that should not be overlooked.

Patterns of Transport Organization

In terms of structuring the approach to policy questions, the most important institutional aspects of the urban transport picture lie in the variety of organizations for supplying transport services and the consequent variety of ways in which they are paid for. The first is public transport, where an organization, whether private corporation, quasi-public authority, or governmental department, operates vehicles and sometimes track and terminal facilities. The users pay trip by trip or, sometimes, for certain packages of trips, such as monthly commuter tickets. The sum of fare payments provides the organization's revenue. In the case of privately owned public transport—primarily bus operations—this revenue must at least meet total vehicle and general costs and may be expected to contribute for the use of streets and to general tax revenue. With government or quasi-public authorities providing public transport, revenue may be expected to meet only operating

[13] Calculated from *DMATS*, Part I, pp. 144 ff. and Table 45.

expenses, with capital cost being met by local government sources (New York Transit Authority), or revenue may be expected to meet total costs exclusive of taxes, as under some cost-of-service plans (Chicago Transit Authority).

For private transport, which involves private persons or businesses operating automobiles or trucks, on highways run by government agencies, the pattern is entirely different and is always in two parts. The costs of running the vehicles are met directly by the operators. The costs pertaining to streets and highways, provided of physical necessity by government, are, with relatively few exceptions, not met out of fares or tolls paid for trip by trip, but are provided for by user charges (such as gas taxes) or out of general government funds. Because of the established pattern for collection of user charges, almost the entire amount is collected by federal and state, rather than metropolitan governments. Thus the amount and allocation of these receipts are a matter of legislation and administrative decision removed from the metropolitan level. The dominance of rural and small town political influence at the federal and state levels has, over the years, resulted in relatively small shares of these receipts being made available for urban streets and highways, though in recent years the share has increased substantially. In general, there has been no allocation of the receipts in proportions related to the extent of metropolitan vehicular use, even though most of the imposts are related in some manner to use.

The local government departments responsible for supplying highway service thus have no direct financial incentive to increase or improve facilities. The only exception has been where a separate authority has been able to apply a toll in connection with a bridge or tunnel.

Put in another way, the user of urban transport has no direct or positive way to make his needs or his quality preferences for highway services felt. He cannot say that he would pay four mills a vehicle-mile for provision of a certain measure of highway service on a particular route, the sum of the four-mill charges to go to the city department for the costs of supplying the service.

Granting the necessity, in most cases, for highway services to rely on state and federal user taxes of various types, it follows that a most important problem for urban highway transport is how to structure the approach to user-charge allocation policies. Can user charges be channeled so as to meet the costs? It was estimated, in the course of the Chicago Area Transportation Study, that 80 per cent of the motor-vehicle miles run in Illinois were within the study area. To this must be added the fact that the gasoline consumption in much of that area was at higher rates per vehicle-mile than in the rural part of the state. The net collections in Illinois of the state and federal user charges in 1960 (the latest year for which data are available) were close to one-half a billion dollars. Eighty per cent of this would make some $400 million annually available to the Chicago metropolitan area, more than enough, with other already used sources, to meet the needs projected in the study.[14]

The varied financial characteristics and organization structures also tend to color the general approaches to policy. The public transport institutions, rail transit and bus operators, stand on one side. Strong organizational loyalties, the vested interest of employees and unions challenged by declining demand, and inevitable opposition to competitively successful private transport, create a tendency to frame policy questions principally in terms of unfairness of competition, and demands for a place in the sun. On the other hand, the urban highway system inherits pre-motor-vehicle street patterns, which are hard to change. There is a lack of market-place pricing of services provided by street and highway departments, and a lack of directly associated revenue with which to build and operate the urban system as well as an extremely rapid increase in demand for its services. All of these factors have left the responsible organizations unable or belatedly able to cope satisfactorily with their problems. The normal municipal capital programming and budgeting processes have often not risen to meet the urban highway needs. More recently new approaches have come, with federal promotion of metropolitan area transport studies since World War II. But even with forward strides in cost-benefit, demand, and other analyses, policy formation is still subject to substantial elements of political pressure based on many varieties of parochial and vested interests. Consequently, policy questions are structured in ways which overemphasize those interests.

Out of all this the tendency is for important aspects of urban transport policy to become formulated in terms of conflict between for-hire public transport and private transport on public highways. This is fraught with hazards. For one thing it can develop a restrictive influence on the growth of new forms of transport, which, in turn, restricts the growth of gross national product of which transport is a significant component. Currently, for instance, transport expenditure accounts for some 12 to 13 per cent of personal consumption expenditure.[15] It may well be that higher proportions which meet consumer preferences

[14] Calculated from *CATS*, Vol. I, p. 82; and Bureau of Public Roads, *Highway Statistics—1960*, 1962, pp. 85, 86, and 101.
[15] *Statistical Abstract*, 1962, p. 315.

will provide an even higher national product. The question is whether patterns of government finance should not be such as to allocate all or the major share of user-charge receipts to the type of transport which generates them, binding annual costs to anticipated annual receipts. Subsidiary questions involve equalization between transport types of the incidence of taxation, both in its direct burden on an organization and in relation to rates of interest on borrowed capital.

The final question then is, do the answers to the above questions provide an environment in which urban transport growth and new developments will be forthcoming at a rate and in ways consistent with the country's desire for over-all progress and increases in national product? In addition, does the environment foster effective allocation of resources and services in line with consumer preferences?

The Passenger-Mile as the Measure of Transport Service

Much of the economic analysis relating to the supply of urban transport has been oriented around the passenger-mile as the measure of service. This has led the analyses to ignore the relative merits of different urban transport services. Consideration of speed has represented the only quantitative evaluation of varying qualities of transport services. The difficulties of giving weight to qualities of service are not unique to transport but pose serious problems for economic analysis of all kinds of services; so often quality is as important (or even more important) in valuing output as the production of a unit of output itself.

Quality of transport service varies sufficiently to be vitally significant, both in considering transport as an element in the urban scene and in weighing transport alternatives. For example, a passenger-mile of service in the form of standing in a subway car has quite different qualities from driving in a comfortable seat in one's own car. At peak hours, the tight crowding of standees in the subway car must be compared with the bumper-to-bumper traffic in driving. The valuation of these qualities is always a subjective matter, not something that can be measured readily against a common scale. An analytical attack on the quality problem has been started;[16] but at the policy formation level, a passenger-mile tends still to be used as a basis for comparing alternatives in cost terms. The possibility that a higher valuation of qualities may justify a higher cost per passenger-mile does not receive adequate consideration.

[16] J. M. Meyer in *American Economic Review*, March 1962, references 95, 101, and 120.

The use of the passenger-mile tends to focus consideration of urban transport upon basic vehicle services which, from the consumer's view, are only part of the over-all trip in the urban area. With public transportation, there must be a walk from home to bus stop, a wait for arrival of a vehicle, and a walk from the destination stop to the place of work. For highway transport, the trip involves going to one's own vehicle, driving it, parking it at the other end, and walking to the place of work. The trip-maker's valuation involves the appraisal of all the elements which combine to make up his trip, not just the vehicular part. What to him may be a high-cost vehicular element may be offset by gains with respect to the other elements, such as saving in time, less discomfort, less anxiety. The difficulties of analysis in these more complicated terms are great, but failure to consider them is likely to lead to erroneous policy conclusions.

Alternative Locations of Future Population Growth[17]

The greatly increasing magnitude of urban problems, transport and others, as metropolitan area populations become larger surely raises the question of whether the population increases of future decades must inevitably converge on existing metropolises and densely populated regions. Most study effort has been devoted to the problems of existing metropolises, with the tacit assumption that their continued growth is inevitable and perhaps desirable. This is another illustration of the structuring of the approach to questions, in this case, taking attention away from the alternative of attracting population to small cities and sparsely settled areas as a solution to the problem.

Experience in the United States over the past forty years suggests rather limited possibilities of channeling population growth away from existing large cities. However, there have been significant variations in growth rates for different metropolises in the United States, with indications that under certain conditions small cities and less populated areas have absorbed large amounts of population. The variations can be most effectively analyzed by comparing growth in the four principal regions of the country, the Northeast, the Upper Mississippi-Great Lakes area, the Southwest, and the Pacific Coast. The configuration of regions as chosen is different from the usual Census groupings in order

[17] Calculated from Bureau of Census, *Abstract of the Fourteenth Census of the United States, 1920,* and *Abstract of the Fifteenth Census of the United States, 1930;* and *U.S. Census of Population,* 1950, Vol. I, and *1960 U.S. Summary,* PC (1), 1A, U.S.

to obtain a more homogeneous distribution within each region. The Northeast as defined here comprises Massachusetts and Virginia and the states lying between them, excluding the western tiers—two deep—of counties in New York and Pennsylvania. The Upper Mississippi-Great Lakes area includes the states east of the Mississippi and above its junction with the Ohio River, and those North of the Ohio to the northeast region, together with the tier of counties just South of the Ohio in Kentucky and West Virginia, and the metropolitan areas of St. Louis and Minneapolis. The Southwest includes five states: Kansas, Oklahoma, Arkansas, Louisiana, and Texas, as well as metropolitan Kansas City. The Pacific region comprises simply the three Pacific states. In 1920 these four regions accounted for 70.5 per cent of the population of the continental United States; in 1960, 73.5 per cent. In 1960, the two eastern regions each had a population of some forty-six million and the two western ones, each a population of twenty million.

The first approach in this analysis is the review of shares of growth for different ranges of metropolitan size. Size is measured in terms of 1960 populations of standard metropolitan statistical areas or consolidated areas, these areas being referred to as metropolises in this section. The earlier decennial population figures are for the areas encompassed by the 1960 metropolises. In 1960 there were twenty-one metropolises in the four regions with a population of over one million. It may be noted that these same metropolises accounted for all but one of the eighteen which were over 500,000 in 1920.

The percentage of each region's growth for forty years accounted for by the metropolises of over one million in 1960 is shown in the following table.

| | | Percentage of Region Population Growth in Metropolises of Over One Million (1960) | | |
Region	Number in Group	1920–40	1940–50	1950–60
Northeast	5	68	61	57
Upper Miss.–G. Lakes	8	67	54	54
Southwest	4	27	46	42
Pacific	4	58	53	59

In the two eastern regions, the growth proportion accounted for by these metropolises has declined significantly over the last four decades. In the Southwest it has increased, but is still below the eastern levels. The proportion in the Pacific area has not changed significantly, and is currently of the same order as that of the eastern regions. While some two-thirds of population growth from 1920 to 1940 in the two eastern regions was in metropolises of over one million, in the most recent decade, 1950–60, this has dropped to something over one-half.

In each of three regions, the Northeast, the Upper Mississippi–Great Lakes, and the Pacific, there has been one metropolis among those of over one million population substantially greater in size than any of the rest. The variations in proportions of region growth accounted for by these metropolises is significant, as the following table indicates.

Region (*Metropolis*)	*Percentage of Region Population Growth in Metropolises of Over Six Million (1960)*		
	1920–40	1940–50	1950–60
Northeast (N.Y.–Northeast N.J.)	36	28	29
Upper Miss.–G. Lakes (Chicago–N.W. Ind.)	23	15	17
Pacific (Los Angeles–Long Beach)	46	31	41

Over the decades considered, there has been some decline in the share of growth in these super metropolises. In the more mature, slower growing, eastern regions, there appear to be more active factors operating to slow down the growth of the one largest metropolis than in the Pacific region.

The share of growth among medium-size metropolises is indicated in the following table.

Region	*Number in Group*	*Percentage of Region Population Growth in Metropolises of One-Half to One Million*		
		1920–40	1940–50	1950–60
Northeast	6	6	11	9
Upper Miss.–G. Lakes	6	9	13	12
Southwest	3	12	24	17
Pacific	4	10	13	18

In contrast to the largest-size metropolises, this middle group shows a generally increased share of growth in the two more recent decades as compared with the first two decades. In all periods, the share of this middle group is greater in the West than in the East.

Finally, the share of growth in a group of relatively small-size metropolises is shown in the following table.

Region	Number in Group	Percentage of Region Population Growth in Metropolises of 250,000–499,000		
		1920–40	1940–50	1950–60
Northeast	14	8	8	9
Upper Miss.–G. Lakes	10	9	8	7
Southwest	5	11	17	17
Pacific	5	6	9	5

Only in the Southwest has the share of these metropolises increased significantly.

Another way to view the matter is to compare rates of growth for metropolises of different sizes based on the size at the beginning of each two-decade period from 1920 to 1960. The data for this second approach is shown in Table 2. The growth rate of metropolises of over one million initial population declined slightly over the forty-year period in the Northeast and increased slightly in the upper Mississippi–Great Lakes region. The over-all growth rate in the latter region was substantially higher than in the former. With one exception, growth rates of the cities in the smaller-size groups increased markedly in both regions, and for the Upper Mississippi region in the 1940–60 period they became substantially higher than for the cities of over one million.

In the Southwest in the 1920–40 period, the cities of 100,000–249,000 population showed double the rate of growth that larger cities did, but in subsequent periods the growth rates for all size groups were substantially the same. In the Pacific region, the metropolises of over one million has a markedly higher growth rate than the smaller ones for 1920–40; but, by the 1940–60 period, the smaller metropolises had attained higher growth rates.

Over-all, the average growth rates of metropolises of over one million were at their peak in the 1920–40 period, and generally exceeded those of any smaller-size class. Since then, the average growth rates for the above one million class have tended to fall below those of smaller metropolises in two of the three regions having the largest metropolises. In three of the four regions there has been relatively faster growth in smaller metropolises. Yet, as was indicated earlier, the great accumulation of the past in the largest metropolises makes their share of total growth still above half of the over-all growth, except in the Southwest.

A review of the individual states in these four regions and of individual cities for the most recent decade gives further insights into the distribution of growth. In particular, the State of Ohio provides a case where the growth of metropolises of over one million has even in absolute terms failed to equal that of the smaller metropolises in the state. From 1950 to 1960, Cleveland and Cincinnati together increased by 499,000, or 21 per cent. The group of four metropolises in Ohio with populations in 1960 of from 500,000 to one million grew in all by 552,000, or 30 per cent. The smallest-size group considered in this section—100,000 to 250,000—also grew by 30 per cent. In total, those metropolises from 100,000 to one million accounted for 47 per cent of the state's growth, while those above one million accounted for only

TABLE 2

GROWTH RATES OF METROPOLISES FOR TWENTY-YEAR PERIODS,
BY REGIONS
(per cent)

Metropolis Size (millions)[a]	1920–40	1940–60
NORTHEAST		
Over 1	31	29
.5 – 1[b]	23	20
.25 – .5	14	26
Largest over 1[c]	37	27
Total region	24	30
UPPER MISS.–GREAT LAKES		
Over 1	36	39
.5 – 1	32	43
.25 – .5	31	53
.1 – .25	11	45
Largest over 1[c]	43	39
Total region	24	34
SOUTHWEST		
.5 – 1	30	84
.25 – .5	35	85
.1 – .25	76	87
Total region	24	29
PACIFIC		
Over 1	118	117[d]
.5 – 1	--	76
.25 – .5	32[d]	232
.1 – .25	68	144
Largest over 1[c]	191	131
Total region	75	109

[a]Size as of beginning of period.

[b]Excluding Washington, D.C.

[c]For Northeast, largest is New York—N.E. New Jersey; for Upper Miss.—Great Lakes, largest is Chicago—N.W. Indiana; for Pacific, largest is L.A.—Long Beach.

[d]Too few in group to make rate significant.

28 per cent. This was in substantial contrast to the Upper Mississippi–Great Lakes region, where the respective figures were 32 and 54 per cent.

Wisconsin provides a similar contrast with a quite different pattern of population distribution. In the 1960 census there was one metropolis of over one million and all the rest were under 250,000. For the cities and metropolises of from 100,000 to 250,000—seven in all—the growth from 1950 to 1960 was 242,000, or 33 per cent, compared with Milwaukee's 165,000, or 19 per cent. Adjacent Chicago's corresponding growth rate was 21 per cent. Of the total Wisconsin growth in the period, the seven smaller places accounted for 47 per cent and the sole big one, only 32 per cent, similar to the Ohio distribution.

In that part of the Northeast region made up of the three southern New England states, growth rates from 1950 to 1960 in the medium size metropolises were just over twice that of Boston. The two with population between 500,000 and one million accounted for substantially the same absolute increase as Boston, and so did the four metropolises of 250,000–499,000.

These figures indicate that smaller metropolises under certain circumstances can provide for or attract population growth in competition with the very large ones. It would be desirable to investigate the factors accounting for this.

Some insight into these factors can be obtained by noting the common characteristics of those small cities of 1920 which have become large metropolises in recent decades. Table 3 lists the metropolises in the United States of over 250,000 in 1960 which had more than doubled in population in the twenty years from 1940 and which did not have over 200,000 population in 1920 (all data is for the population within the area encompassed by the 1960 standard metropolitan statistical areas).

These eighteen places are, with few exceptions, either centers of air- or space-craft development, or in retirement and resort areas. Many also reflect general regional growth based on development of petroleum or agriculatural resources, or both. They are all in the warmer climate belt of the United States. Two, Tucson and Albuquerque, are the seats of a principal state university. Mobile is the only one primarily dependent on general commercial and industrial development.

This indication that smaller population centers can expand substantially suggests the possibility of both private and public policy to stimulate this growth. Are there perhaps other small cities which in the future can become the larger metropolises? Can these take care of a major share of the expanding future population and relieve the existing larger cities of their already heavy burdens? This depends on

TABLE 3

U.S. METROPOLISES OF LESS THAN 200,000 IN 1920
WHICH MORE THAN DOUBLED IN POPULATION
BETWEEN 1940 AND 1960

Metropolises, by 1960 Population Categories	Population of 1960 Metropolitan Areas (in thousands)		
	1920	1940	1960
Over one million			
Houston	187	529	1,243
San Diego	112	289	1,033
500,000-one million			
Miami	43	268	935
San Bernadino	123	267	810
Tampa	116	272	772
Phoenix	90	186	664
San Jose	101	175	642
Ft. Worth	190	256	573
250,000-500,000			
Jacksonville	114	210	455
Fresno	129	179	366
Wichita	92	143	343
Ft. Lauderdale	5	40	334
Orlando	31	92	319
Mobile	121	142	314
El Paso	102	131	314
Bakersfield	55	135	292
Tucson	35	73	266
Albuquerque	30	69	262

the answers to some basic questions. First, have the desirable locations for economic activity already been pre-empted by the existing large metropolises? For instance, have all desirable coastal port locations already been occupied? Have existing large centers pre-empted water resources, which are so essential for much of industry? The answer to this sort of question may partially lie in such technological advances and engineering capabilities as have made possible port activity without nature-provided channels and basins, and cities without fresh water supply in the immediate vicinity. In general, technological advances in the fields of transportation, energy production and distribution, and climate control, along with discovery of new mineral resource locations, have tended to make many formerly localized factors more widely available. Further, there have been important changes in the character of production: de-emphasis on the basic extractive and primary stages of manufacture and an increase in the role of service industries and the secondary stages of maufacture. These changes, too, have lessened the constraint of some of the influences that have in the past led to the location of economic activity in what are now the larger metropolises.

But, is the attractiveness of the existing larger metropolises—their labor and sales markets—so great as to outweigh the other factors? Another query relates to the strength of vested interests of large metropolises in maintaining their position and even expanding it. The power of these interests is great. It has been particularly strong in the economic field, but now appears to be developing in the political sphere. Is the formulation of future public policy likely to be in terms of promoting growth in new locations where there are few voters, as opposed to supporting the metropolises to which an increasing proportion of legislators will owe their office?

COMMENT

GEORGE WILSON, Indiana University

If the denial of certainty is the beginning of wisdom, transport economists must be on the verge of major breakthroughs of knowledge. Most of the papers in the conference make reference to how little we know for sure in transportation, and all appeal for more research, which I interpret as partly symptomatic of guilt feelings for not having carried their own analyses further.

But the paper by Healy goes even further than merely pointing out how many empty economic boxes exist at present. Indeed, he is highly doubtful that, even if we had perfect knowledge and could explain correctly all the evil consequences of existing policy, nothing much of significance would or could be done about it. The answer to needed changes in public policy must therefore go beyond filling up empty economic boxes. We need somehow to chop down or at least hack away at the barriers of political bias and vested interest. And there is much truth in this contention, as anyone who has argued the impeccably logical case for user charges with representatives of the barge industry can sadly testify. If logic is a powerful force (self) love is not only a many splendored thing but equally potent.

Healy is really asking why there is so much emphasis on the central business district of the large metropolitan areas and, a related question, why there is a tendency to stress mass transit. He finds answers in two areas: political bias and lack of knowledge. The combination of these two leads to policies which, from an economic point of view, appear to border on stupidity.

For example, Healy argues that "a surprisingly small proportion of person-trips are destined for the so-called central business district" and that, from an over-all urban transportation point of view, the central business district is not very important. Furthermore, he suggests that the trend will reduce the transportation significance of the central business district even further. Aside from the dubious relevance and validity of the data cited, it is clear that Healy not only dislikes the central business district but also the present large metropolitan centers. He somewhat wistfully hopes that future population growth will not go to these areas and thus is led to examine evidence showing that medium-sized metropolises in some segments of the country have grown relatively rapidly in recent decades.

I interpret this demonstration and the rhetorical questions which suggest that all the best sites for cities have not been monopolized by existing centers as implying that it is *possible* to arrest big city growth. That it is a "good thing" to do this is an implicit value judgment. In fact, it may not be unfair to characterize Healy as a mid-twentieth century Oliver Goldsmith for whom "Sweet Auburn" has become a middle-sized city located somewhere in the South-Central United States. But, alas, nostalgia and mere possibilities are not enough. Healy knows full well that public policy is unlikely to "promote growth in new locations where there are few voters, as opposed to supporting the metropolises to which the numerous legislators owe their office." In short, Healy's value judgments suggest that most of the large metropolitan areas are beyond "optimal city size" (whatever that is!), and instead of trying to save them we should let them stagnate and funnel people into "new towns." He sees the attempt to improve movement to and from the central business district via mass transit as deliberately biased since those doing the analysis have vested interests in the central business district. Indeed, the entire approach to "The City" is apparently cleverly disguised to mask its true colors.

What I find disturbing in the Healy paper is the aura of pessimism. Here is a competent analyst and observer of the transportations scene whose contributions to the field have been numerous over the years. He now informs us that we are doomed to a policy of muddle through, that unless we are lucky enough to have a good rip-roaring crisis in transport nothing will be done. In short, "rational public policy" is virtually a contradiction in terms. Thus the economics of transportation, as far as public policy is concerned, is but the pallid hand-maiden of the politics of transportation. I suspect in the final analysis this is right.

I will not quarrel with Healy's value judgments. Let him who is without bias cast the first stone! But it is obvious that on any cost-benefit approach toward cities themselves or urban transit, one's valuations can easily determine the answer, to say nothing of influencing the "correct" rate of discount and the pricing of externalities. I doubt whether the implicit notion of optimal city size has any real meaning. I further doubt that improvements even to mass transit to and from the central business district can objectively be viewed as economic waste even if politically motivated. In short, I sympathize with Healy's viewpoint and some of his recommendations but do not think he has made a very persuasive case (except for illustrating the importance of bias), nor has he adequately demonstrated the relative insignificance of the central business district from a transportation point of view.

THOR HULTGREN, National Bureau of Economic Research

Transportation policy is a coat of many colors. In the course of time, interest has shifted from some aspects of policy toward others. Fair return on fair value has become a dormant problem in the transport area. Reinvestment of earnings and financial reorganization long ago drained the water out of railway capitalization; return on value is a smaller portion of cost for the newer kinds of transport, with their comparatively low private investment per dollar of revenue. Complaints of personal and geographical discrimination are no longer common. Two major influences have changed the emphasis. One is the growth of competition among the means of transport; the other is the growth of government and the burden to general taxation. The construction and maintenance of the newer transport facilities—highways, waterways, airports, and air navigation aids—are largely financed in the first instance by government. Should users of these facilities be required to pay for them? Should they pay enough to cover full interest at some imputed rate, actual interest on borrowed money, or only maintenance and depreciation? Should past expenditures be regarded as "sunk" costs? How should the cost of roads be divided between adjacent property owners and vehicle operators? How between small vehicles and big trucks and combinations? How should the cost of air facilities be apportioned among airlines, other private users, and the military? Taxation for nontransport governmental purposes is still largely in the form of property tax. Is it good economics to tax railroads for general purposes on their roadway while other carriers own no roadway to be taxed? Other urgent questions include pricing policy. Does it make for an efficient allocation of traffic among the various modes of transport? Low earnings of railroads and, at least recently and temporarily, of airlines have imparted new life to the merger question.

No meeting of reasonable length could deal with all aspects of policy. The paper before us deals with the important problem of metropolitan passenger transport. To what extent should this kind of transport be provided by private automobiles, and to what extent by collective riding? Should collective facilities be subsidized to reduce the cost of maintaining and policing highways? Should peak-time use be discouraged by some kind of pricing device? Where are freeways most appropriate, and where rails? Kent Healy points out that the answers to such questions depend on the social and economic background. They may differ from locality to locality. Healy draws material from the growing literature composed of detailed studies of transport conditions in specific metropolitan areas. He finds that individual home ownership and larger lots are reducing the density of population in the outer zone of the areas. Shopping centers and one-story factories are reducing the importance of travel to and from downtown. He thinks that the system of public finance results in a geographically inefficient pattern of transport expenditures. He reminds us that a rapid transit ride is often only a part of the whole origin-to-destination trip, and that quality of service as well as the number of passenger-miles is important. He wonders whether growth must occur where population is already large— a pointed question nowadays in mid-Manhattan. On the other hand, he omits two factors that have changed the pattern of metropolitan travel: the spread of the five-day week, and the growth of home entertainment in the form of television.

Perhaps for lack of time, Healy does not tie the factors that he mentions to specific transport proposals; the reader is left to find for himself the direction in which those factors point. The decline in peripheral population density tends to raise the amount of supplementary travel needed to use transit; the discussion seems to me to point toward less reliance on the latter. Healy notes that the number of trips originating or terminating in the central business district is surprisingly small—partly because of supermarkets, etc. Other studies show that a large part of other travel goes *through* the district. The argument here seems to point toward more belt and peripheral, rather than radial, facilities.

PART IV

Issues of Public Policy

The Relevance of the
Common Carrier
Under Modern Economic Conditions

ROBERT A. NELSON
AND
WILLIAM R. GREINER

UNIVERSITY OF WASHINGTON

Common carriage in the United States today is a patchwork of competition and monopoly. There is enough competition in transportation so that monopoly power, even in the absence of regulation, could not be overweening. At the same time, competition is not so complete that all monopoly power has been effectively checked. In short, the transportation business is neither more nor less competitive than many other unregulated industries. There are, however, significant features which set transportation apart from other businesses in this regard. Such competition as there is in surface transportation is generated largely by disparate sets of firms each of which has distinctly different propensities to compete. Where the railroads occupy the supply side of a market by themselves, competition is practically nonexistent. Where the truckers or water carriers can enter a market and follow their natural impulses, competition is practically perfect.

The basic policy decision regarding the economic organization of the transportation business was made by the Congress some thirty years ago. At that time Congress had several options. One was to utilize the competitive forces of the trucking industry to contain railroad monopoly. This would have emphasized the capabilities of the private sector of the economy to achieve satisfactory resource allocation. Another was to continue to concentrate decision-making power in its own hands and in the Interstate Commerce Commission. It is evident that Congress chose the latter course and in so doing created a class of common carriers (the truckers) having few of the intrinsic characteristics of common carriage as defined in the common law.[1] The question, which has been debated over and over again in the years since, is why Congress chose that alternative and seems to adhere to it so strongly.

The reason most often urged by economists and others is that the regulated transportation industries comprise a cartel whose interest lies on the side of moderating competition, and which is willing to accede to regulation for that purpose. This is undoubtedly an adequate explanation for the support given by much of the trucking industry to regulation. The railroads, too, are not disposed to open wide the gates to uncontrolled competition. But this rationale does not explain the resistance voiced by many interests to a shift toward less regulated transportation. The "preservation of the common carrier system" draws wide support and was even alluded to favorably in the President's transportation message,[2] which in general suggested that more competition would be desirable. It is evident that some benefits flow from the regulation of common carriage which would not be present in a more competitive milieu. What those benefits are and how universally they pervade the economy needs to be considered carefully before changes in public policy are made.

The primary purpose of this paper is to explore the hypothesis that public policy toward transportation has evolved largely to encourage a system in which costs of transportation have been socialized. That is to say, a public policy which has led to a system in which charges for transportation (rates) are intended to be related to ability to pay and not to long-run marginal costs. The exploration can best be done by considering the mechanism by which socialization has been accomplished as well as by inquiring into the objectives of public policy. If our hypothesis is correct, it is apparent that the value-of-service rate structure has served in a limited way as a device of income

[1] A perusal of the history of the common law regarding carriers will show that much of the legal doctrine in this field was an outgrowth of problems of what we now call imperfect competition.

[2] "For some seventy-five years, common carriage was developed by the intention of Congress and the requirements of the public as the core of our transport system. This pattern of commerce is changing—the common carrier is declining in status and stature with the consequent growth of the private and exempt carrier. To a large extent this change is attributable to the failure of federal policies and regulation to adjust the needs of the shipping and consuming public; to a large extent it is attributable to the fact that the burdens of regulation are handicapping the certified common carrier in his efforts to meet his unregulated competition. Whatever the cause, the common carrier with his obligation to serve all shippers—large or small— on certain routes at known tariffs and without any discrimination performs an essential function that should not be extinguished."

redistribution not unlike the federal income tax. We shall begin by considering briefly the economics of the problem.

For many years, value-of-service ratemaking has been regarded as a phenomenon of price discrimination. In conjunction with the economics of decreasing-cost industries, it has been given a status of economic respectability which perhaps has inhibited inquiry into its uses for public policy purposes.

The use of price discrimination as a businessman's technique to maximize profit has, of course, never turned on the resolution of any doctrinal conflict over its economic merits. Long before economists and lawmakers concerned themselves with the problem of rail monopoly, rail management had adopted value-of-service as a precept of ratemaking. No doubt the prospects of monopoly return were enhanced by the susceptibility of rail transportation to systematic price discrimination. This, in turn, may have induced the investment of greater amounts of private capital in rail plant than would have been forthcoming had discrimination not been feasible (or lawful). Perhaps demand and supply relationships in the period following the Civil War were such that discrimination was essential to induce new investment or to allow a return on existing plant, or both.

Initially, the bulk of railroad traffic was local and regional. Interregional traffic, for which demand at that time was quite elastic, did not occupy much capacity and could be handled at very little additional cost. Perhaps the revenues it produced made possible some reduction in local rates. This was the claim made in Congressional hearings and debate on the proposed long- and short-haul clause of the Interstate Commerce Act, where it was argued that uniform distance rates would kill off long-haul transport and force increases in local rates.[3]

[3] "Mr. Brown: Probably not more than 1/10th of the freight carried is through freight over some of the long competing lines. The company cannot afford to charge the other 9/10th of its freight at the rates charged for the through freight, as it cannot do so and pay necessary expenses, and if it is prohibited from carrying 1/10th or more of its freight long distances in competition with long through lines, it prevents those who are located far in the interior from reaching coast cities at all with their produce, and takes away from the company the small amount of clear money it realizes on such freight" (17 Congressional Record, p. 3830, 1886).

"Mr. Brown: Now, Mr. President, with the provision of the bill to which I have referred [long- and short-haul clause], and especially with the amendment of the Senator from West Virginia, enacted into a law and strictly carried out, it is impossible for the railroads of this country to transact the business of the country. If they attempt it they will either be driven into bankruptcy or a large part of the best territory of the United States will be driven from market and be unable to reach either Eastern cities or foreign markets with their produce. In other words, the railroads must put their local freight so low that they cannot pay fixed expenses and run, or they must put the through business at so high a figure as to prohibit the

354 THE COMMON CARRIER UNDER MODERN CONDITIONS

Perhaps Congress gave tacit approval to rate discrimination to encourage the continued flow of new capital to the railroads or to assure full utilization of sunk capital.[4] Moreover, in its first annual report the ICC acknowledged both the existence and the merit of value-of-service rates.[5] That position was perhaps wise in view of the Supreme Court's imminent holding that regulated firms had to be afforded the opportunity to earn a fair return on the fair value of invested capital.[6]

As practiced by the railroads, discrimination assumed two basic forms: discrimination based on the different commodities tendered for shipment and discrimination as between persons and places originating shipments of competitive commodities. It was clear from the very beginning of Congressional inquiry into the practices of the railroads that Congress was much more sensitive to the latter form of discrimination.[7] Debate on the act of 1887 centered largely on the

---

shipment of produce for a longer distance than five or six hundred miles" (*ibid.*, p. 3828).

"Mr. Cullom: ... the rigid enforcement of the law as now amended will result substantially in making a mileage act, so that the nearer a party lives to the seaboard the cheaper will he get his transportation. It will result, in my opinion, in destroying much of the commerce of this country" (*ibid.*, p. 4229).

[4] "Mr. Stanford: For this reason rates are oftentimes below the average cost of transportation, and freight of a low value in the market is often moved at less than average cost. Low rates, if they pay anything above the direct expenses consequent upon movement, aid to sustain the railroads and the better enable them to move the traffic at non-competing points. Railroad companies cannot ignore the various circumstances that establish competition, much of which depends on the geographical conditions of the country. The shipper for a short distance has not been charged more, but the shipper for a long distance is charged less because the carriers cannot help themselves" (*ibid.*, p. 3827).

[5] "The public interest is best served when the rates are so apportioned as to encourage the largest practicable exchange of products between different sections of our country and with foreign countries; and this can only be done by making value an important consideration, and by placing upon the higher classes of freight some share of the burden that on a relatively equal apportionment, if service alone were considered, would fall upon those of less value. With this method of arranging tariffs little fault is found, and perhaps none at all by persons who consider the subject from the standpoint of public interest. Indeed, in the complaints thus far made to the Commission little fault has been found with the principles on which tariffs for the transportation of freight are professedly arranged, while applications of those principles in particular cases have been complained of frequently and very earnestly." *First Annual Report of the Interstate Commerce Commission*, Washington, D.C., 1887, p. 36.

[6] Smythe *v.* Ames, 169 US 466 (1898).

[7] "Shippers are willing that the railroads shall receive fair and remunerative rates; they do not complain so much of the rates as they do of the unfairness of discriminations that give one section advantages over another section, one town over another town, and one set of manufacturers over other manufacturers; that makes lands in one locality worth more than in another locality less eligibly situated with

discriminatory practices which affected competitive relationships between persons and regions,[8] and the act as adopted dealt in part with the problems occasioned by that kind of discrimination.[9] It is important to note that the act of 1887 did not provide for the complete elimination of either form of discrimination. The propriety of commodity discrimination apparently was recognized[10] and, as mentioned above, some discrimination between long- and short-haul freight was tacitly approved.

---

reference to the markets. And they especially complain to see carloads of the same kind of freight passing their doors from more distant points to the same markets at less cost than they pay for transporting the same class of freight to the same market a less distance" (17 *Congressional Record*, p. 3554, 1886).

[8] One Senator summarized the complaints against the railroads in this way:

". . . I realize that there have been great wrongs, and I will enumerate some of the complaints which the people make against the railroad companies of the country as they have been summed up by the committee in its report:

The complaints against the railroad system of the United States expressed to the committee are based upon the following charges:

1. That the local rates are unreasonably high compared with through rates.
2. That both local and through rates are unreasonably high at noncompeting points, either from the absence of competition or in consequence of pooling agreements that restrict its operation.
3. That rates are established without apparent regard to actual cost of the service performed, and are based largely on 'what the traffic will bear.'
4. That unjustifiable discriminations are constantly made between individuals in the rates charged for like service under similar circumstances.
7. That the effect of the prevailing policy of railroad management is, by an elaborate system of secret special rates, rebates, drawbacks, and concessions, to foster monopoly, to enrich favored shippers, and to prevent free competition in many lines of trade in which the item of transportation is an important factor.
8. That such favoritism and secrecy introduce an element of uncertainty into legitimate business that greatly retards the development of our industries and commerce.
16. That the capitalization and bonded indebtedness of the roads largely exceed the actual cost of their construction or their present value, and that unreasonable rates are charged in an effort to pay dividends on watered stock and interest on bonds improperly issued.
18. That the management of the railroad business is extravagant and wasteful, and that a needless tax is imposed upon the shipping and traveling public by the unnecessary expenditure of large sums in the maintenance of a costly force of agents engaged in a reckless strife for competitive business" (17 *Congressional Record*, p. 3869, 1886).

[9] See 24 Stat. 379, 380 (1887), 49 USC, Secs. 2 and 3 and amendments thereto.

[10] This was made explicit by the Mann-Elkins Act of 1910. See 35 Stat. 60 (1910), 49 USC Sec. 1(6). This provision makes it the duty of regulated carriers to establish, observe, and enforce just and reasonable classifications. This recognition of the classification principle amounts to recognition of the practice of class rate discrimination. In a recent case the Commission argued that Sec. 1(6) makes classification and class (value-of-service) rates a mandatory not permissive principle of ratemaking. This argument was rejected by a three-judge District Court (see N.Y., N.H., and H.R.R. Co. *v.* U.S., 32 *U.S. Law Week* (p. 2081, U.S. District Court, Conn., Civil Action 9229, 7/23/63).

Clearly regional considerations were involved. Benefits from both forms of discrimination ran largely to the South and West, and Congressmen from those regions, though strong supporters of the act, would not have wished regulation to deprive their constituents of the benefits.

In the years between the Civil War and World War I, the economy of the West was largely undeveloped and the demand for transportation was probably quite elastic. Reduced rates on western produce were probably in the railroad's interest. It is doubtful that the Interstate Commerce Act was supposed to limit the railroads' power to continue discrimination in such cases. This is not to say, however, that the carriers and the Commission were of one mind as to how the railroads might utilize their power. Although the Commission did not act to eliminate all forms of discrimination, it did begin to develop standards covering the amount and kind of discrimination permissible. The basic rule articulated by the Commission in this early period was that no rate should be more than what the service was reasonably worth—worth being measured by some criterion other than what the traffic would bear.[11] In applying this stricture, though staying within the bounds of Smythe *v.* Ames, the Commission tended to limit rate increases on agricultural products and raw materials while being less restrictive in the treatment of proposed increases on manufactured goods.[12] That policy might have reflected a Congressional disposition to resist rail rate increases which might have slowed the rate of growth of the extractive industries in the West.

The modern history of rail ratemaking began with economic changes ushered in by World War I. By 1920 the demand for rail transportation probably had increased, relative to existing plant, so that nondiscriminating pricing might have been required without danger of crippling the railroads financially.[13] The war had greatly expanded the flow of interregional traffic and induced firms to make locational commitments in areas distant from many markets. Changes on the supply side of transportation had also taken place. Rail plant and

---

[11] See R. R. Commission of Nevada *v.* So. Pac. Co. 19 ICC 238, 249 (1910); and Advances in Rates—Western Case 20 ICC 307, 349–351, 354–357 (1911).

[12] See I. L. Sharfman (*The Interstate Commerce Commission*, Vol. III B, New York, 1936, pp. 45–83), discussing the 5 Per Cent Case of 1914 and the Rate Advance Case of 1915. In the former case, the Commission allowed eastern railroads to increase most rates by 5 per cent; in the latter case western roads were denied increases on raw materials and agricultural products. See also 31 ICC 351 (1914), and 35 ICC 497 (1915).

[13] An optimistic view of the railroads' future is expressed by W. Z. Ripley, *Main Street and Wall Street*, Boston, 1927, Chap. VIII.

capacity had diminished as a result of extensive deterioration during the war years. This allowed the railroads some flexibility of supply, in the sense that a reinvestment program could have been geared to revenues from a less discriminatory (or nondiscriminating) rate structure. Of course, a move to lessen the pattern of discrimination in rail rates might have slowed the rate of investment in rail plant in the 1920's and might have curtailed rail service to some shippers. The latter development probably would have resulted in higher rates on the movement of products of the extractive industries and less extensive service to and from areas that generated low volumes of traffic. It is doubtful that Congress would have favored such a development. Higher rates on agricultural products might have been absorbed by the farmer owing to inelasticity in the supply of such commodities. That would have worsened the already depressed state of agriculture and agricultural land values, a condition which history has demonstrated to be unpalatable to Congress.

Whatever possibilities of reducing discrimination might have resulted from expansion of demand for transportation, shifts in the location of economic activity, and diminution of rail plant can only be surmised. In the postwar period Congress clearly favored the preservation of the value-of-service rate structure.

The Transportation Act of 1920 established fair return on fair value as the rule of ratemaking to be followed by the ICC.[14] In 1924 the Supreme Court expunged any notion that full cost was the upper limit for measuring the reasonableness of any individual rate.[15] So interpreted, the act of 1920 imposed no cost ceiling on particular rates. Given the assurance that public policy condoned discrimination, the railroads tailored their investment programs accordingly. The ICC cooperated by not discouraging rail plant expansion, partly because its powers respecting such matters are limited, but also because Congress clearly favored the expansion of transportation facilities.

We do not mean to assert that there may not have been (and perhaps still are) rigidities in rail plant which called for some measure of discrimination in rail pricing. The point here is merely that the lessening of discrimination was not espoused by Congress or the Commission as an objective of public policy. Succeeding developments in the 1920's made it clear that other objectives were desired.

The railroads interpreted the act of 1920 as giving them freedom to maximize wherever possible, subject to the fair return constraint.

[14] 41 Stat. 488 (1920); as subsequently amended 49 USC 15 (a).
[15] Dayton–Goose Creek Ry. *v.* U.S., 263 US 456 (1924).

Pursuing this premise, they attempted to level up the generally depressed eastbound rates on the products of agriculture and the extractive industries. Western roads, particularly, found that the opportunities to increase revenues lay largely in the business of carrying raw materials and agricultural products, commodities which traditionally had moved at low rates. Increases in these rates were also justified by changes in rail-cost relationships. It is virtually certain that the balance of transcontinental rail traffic shifted from westbound to eastbound, so that car shortages occurred in the West and empty cars moved westward. Responding to these conditions the railroads began to level up the rates on eastbound movements.

The Commission began to balk at these efforts of the carriers to alter historic rate relationships which had existed practically from the inception of regulation. It reiterated its position that no rate should exceed what the service is reasonably worth, and in the 1920's it began to hold down or even require reductions in rates on various eastbound movements.[16] Thus, the Commission rejected the railroads' contention that the rule of ratemaking should be interpreted to allow the railroads full latitude as to the most efficient use of the discriminating rate structure, subject only to the fair-return ceiling.

That action was significant, since it revealed the Commission's view of its role in rate cases. In spite of the apparent primacy of the fair-return criterion in ratemaking, it is clear that the Commission would not allow the railroads to set rates in a way which would disturb important regional relationships. These conflicts between the carriers and the Commission appear to be inevitable consequences of demand pricing. Rates based on ability to pay, whether determined by the Commission or by the carriers, must look to both the immediate and the ultimate effect of the rate. It is clear that the two can be quite different, that the Commission and the carriers may evaluate them differently, and that such differences can reflect the economic impact of the rate. Even so, disagreements between Commission and carrier can be interpreted simply as differences in time preference (that is, the period over which revenues are maximized), and as evidence that the Commission is really only serving the long-run interest of the carriers. This interpretation ignores the fact that, while value-of-service rates may look to the maximizing of revenues and service, they are not "neutral" to the economy. Demand pricing clearly must gauge the effect of a rate on the firm or industry to which the rate applies. In

---

[16] See 68 ICC 676 (1922); 113 ICC 3 (1926); and Sharfman, *The Interstate Commerce Commission*, pp. 160–161.

that sense, the Commission must decide which sector or segment of the economy is likely to grow, or decline, as a result of change in transportation charges. It may appear, however, that the Commission has gone further in estimating the revenue consequences of a rate to the point of deciding which industries should receive the benefit of favorable rates. If such is the case, the conflicts between the carriers and the Commission are not similar to those between the manager and the members of the cartel as to the way to maximize the returns to the cartel; they are instead conflicts between an economic planner and the firms subject to its control as to how these firms are to provide service consistent with the plan. There is ample evidence to support the proposition that the Commission has been authorized to perform such a function.

Perhaps the first legislative directive to the Commission to undertake economic planning because of the impact of transportation rates came in 1925. Depressed conditions in agriculture had persisted in the years immediately following World War I. These conditions stimulated Congress to give the Commission explicit instructions regarding its role in rate cases. Western Congressmen urged the adoption of a joint resolution which would specify that agriculture, "the basic industry of the country," [17] should be afforded favorable treatment in rail ratemaking. The proposal provoked long and acrimonious debate, but finally emerged in modified form as the Hoch-Smith Resolution.[18] It gave explicit guidance to the Commission to regulate rates so that ". . . the conditions which at any time prevail in our several industries should be considered insofar as it is legally possible to do so, to the end that commodities may freely move." [19]

[17] 68th Cong., 1st sess., S. Rept. 313, "Declaring Agriculture to be the Basic Industry of the Country, and For Other Purposes," Mar. 28, 1924. Mr. Smith from the Committee on Interstate and Foreign Commerce: "This joint resolution is for the purpose of declaring the policy of the Congress as to freight rates on agricultural products and directing the Interstate Commerce Commission to carry this policy into effect.

"Congress having declared to the ICC the power to make rates, it was thought unwise to attempt to dictate any specific rate, but to direct the Commission that in the exercise of its ratemaking power the products of agriculture should carry the lowest rate in the rate structure. This is because the products of agriculture are the prime essentials in the economic structure of organized society. These products are produced under circumstances that do not permit the producer to pass the charges incident to their marketing to the consumer.

"The agriculturist pays the freight upon what he buys and sells. It seems, therefore, but just that provision should be made to make this burden as light as possible, especially upon the things he produces."
[18] 43 Stat. 801 (1925); 49 USC Sec. 55.
[19] Ibid.

Furthermore, the resolution authorized and directed the Commission to make a thorough investigation of the rate structure to determine to what extent:

> ... existing rates and charges may be unjust, unreasonable, unjustly discriminatory, or unduly preferential, thereby imposing undue burdens, or giving undue advantage as between the various localities and parts of the country, the various classes of traffic, and the various classes and kinds of commodities, and to make, in accordance with law, such changes, adjustments, and redistribution of rates and charges as may be found necessary to correct any defects so found to exist. In making any such change, adjustment, or redistribution the Commission shall give due regard, among other factors, to the general and comparative levels in market value of the various classes and kinds of commodities as indicated over a reasonable period of years to a natural and proper development of the country as a whole, and to the maintenance of an adequate system of transportation.[20]

The resolution gave particular emphasis to agriculture:

> In view of the existing depression in agriculture, the Commission is hereby directed to effect with the least practicable delay such lawful changes in the rate structure of the country as will promote the freedom of movement by common carriers of the products of agriculture affected by that depression, including livestock, at the lowest possible lawful rates compatible with the maintenance of adequate transportation service.[21]

The Hoch-Smith Resolution is the first and only explicit legislative sanction of value-of-service ratemaking. Taken literally, the resolution seems to require the Commission to adhere to the discriminatory rate structure which had been characteristic of rail pricing. At the very least, the resolution stiffened the Commission's resolve to protect the value-of-service rate structure and the historic preference in the rates afforded to agriculture. In attempting to carry out the Congressional mandate, the Commission even sought to widen the spectrum of rates in order to afford greater concessions to shippers of agricultural products.[22] When that threatened to reduce the revenues of the carriers, they appealed to the courts for relief, contending that the rule of ratemaking of 1920 made the revenue needs of the railroads the prime consideration in rate cases and that Hoch-Smith had not altered that rule. The case ultimately reached the Supreme Court where the railroads carried the day. The court held that the resolution had made

---

[20] 43 Stat. 801 (1925); 49 USC Sec. 55.
[21] *Ibid.*
[22] See, generally, Sharfman, *The Interstate Commerce Commission*, pp. 740–744.

no change in the law regarding ratemaking but had merely made explicit the legality of value of service as a ratemaking principle.[23] The Court's decision in the Ann Arbor case nullified some rate reductions which the Commission had imposed, and affirmed the contention that the rule of ratemaking of 1920 had not been altered by the resolution. The court found that the resolution expressed certain hoped-for objectives which the Commission should seek to achieve but within the limits of the law, including the rule of fair return on fair value.[24]

Certain language used in the Ann Arbor opinion gives the impression that the Court did not view the Hoch-Smith Resolution as having affected any change in the law,[25] and that view has been adopted by numerous commentators.[26] A closer reading of the case shows that it is true only in part. As interpreted by the court, the resolution had not changed the rule of ratemaking of 1920. Fair return on fair value was still the overriding requirement of that rule. Nor did the resolution make lawful anything that was not lawful prior to its adoption, value of service having been an established principle of ratemaking since the very inception of regulation. The resolution did, however, make one very significant change in the law and in the relationship between Congress and the Commission. The resolution was an assertion of the legislative power to establish standards in ratemaking and in so doing diminish the independence of the Commission in that regard.[27] The resolution also made explicit that value-of-service ratemaking was not

---

[23] Ann Arbor Ry. Co. v. U.S. 281 U.S. 658 (1930).

[24] *Ibid.*, 658, 669. This view is supported by the statements of both sponsors of the resolution in the debate on it: "Mr. Smith: It is simply a direction to the Interstate Commerce Commission that whenever there is a depression in any of the basic industries of the United States, as there has been in agriculture, the Commission should take cognizance thereof, and regulate the rates so as to facilitate the movement of the products of that industry (65 *Congressional Record*, p. 8336, 1924).

"Mr, Hoch: . . . and there is no provision here and no requirement or expectation that any rate which is not compensatory shall be levied" (*ibid.*; p. 11026).

[25] Ann Arbor Ry. Co. v. U.S., p. 668.

[26] See D. P. Locklin, *The Economics of Transportation*, 5th ed., Homewood, Ill., 1960, pp. 239–241.

[27] Sharfman has criticized the Hoch-Smith Resolution as fundamentally wrong and in breach of the principle of the independent status of the Commission (Sharfman, *The Interstate Commerce Commission*, pp. 469–472). He characterizes the resolution as "an attempt to override the judgment of the Commission . . . and to recognize the special demands of dissatisfied litigants and their supporters through the exertion of political power" (p. 470).

The authors of this paper do not hold a similar view regarding the propriety of such uses of political power. In our view, public policy is in large part an expression of political power and as such need not conform to the value system of economics or any other discipline in order to remain in the realm of propriety.

only permissible but was required, insofar as that principle is consistent with other aspects of the law. The rule of ratemaking has since been changed by Congress[28] and the federal courts have largely abandoned the rule of Smythe v. Ames.[29] The Hoch-Smith Resolution stands unaltered and its directives are still a viable part of the ratemaking law.[30]

When Congress elected to adhere to value-of-service ratemaking in the 1920's this perhaps prevented shifting to a less discriminatory rate structure. We have indicated above that the Commission might well have brought about such a change without any danger of disabling the carriers financially. By forestalling that development, the Congress effectively postponed a re-evaluation of the efficacy of value-of-service rates for another two decades.

The depression of the 1930's came close on the heels of a significant expansion of rail plant and railroad debt obligations. The high level of plant capacity and fixed charges built up in the 1920's was not appropriate to the demand conditions of the depression years. The imminent financial collapse of many carriers made necessary endeavors to secure revenues from every source possible. Presumably, the continuance of discrimination in rates could have enhanced the earnings of the railroads in that era. However, the difficulties of the railroads were not solely a product of the depression. Truck transportation had developed into a serious competitor during the twenties and had diverted much traffic from the rails. The bulk of the traffic that shifted from rail to highway was high-value, high-rated manufactured goods, the "cream of the transportation business." The existence of effective competition on a fairly wide scale made difficult the maintenance and manipulation of the value-of-service rate structure in aid of the financial plight of the railroads. The roads thus had to look to traffic in which truck competition was less effective as a possible source of new revenue.

The traffic which offered the greatest promise for increased revenue was agricultural products. The inelasticities of supply in these goods were probably of such an order that increases in freight rates would not have reduced substantially the volume of shipment, and the increased cost would have been absorbed largely by the farmer, at least in the short run. Proposed increases in these rates met with immediate

[28] 48 Stat. 220 (1933); subsequently amended 49 USC Sec. 15 (a)(2).

[29] F. P. C. v. Natural Gas Pipeline Co., 315 US 575 (1942), and F. P. C. v. Hope Natural Gas Co., 320 US 591 (1944).

[30] Apparently the Commission has held to this view. See 248 ICC 545, 611 (1942); 300 ICC 633, 686 (1957); cited by Locklin The Economics of Transportation, p. 421.

opposition. The Congress found intolerable the prospect of freight-rate increases which would worsen the economic disaster facing agriculture. As a palliative measure the Congress repealed the rule of ratemaking of 1920 by an amendment to the Interstate Commerce Act.[31] The amended rule directed the Commission to regulate rates, so that traffic would move freely at the "lowest charges consistent with the cost of providing service." [32] The revenue needs of the carriers were to be considered to the extent necessary to assure the maintenance of adequate transportation service. Fair return on fair value was abandoned as the prime objective of ratemaking. Under the new rule, the public need for cheap and adequate transportation was the prime consideration and the revenue need of the carriers was a subsidiary factor to be considered insofar as necessary to achieve the prime objective of public service. The amendment revitalized the Hoch-Smith Resolution which the Commission then used frequently to justify its attempts to maintain wide disparities in the rate structure.[33]

The act of 1933 was but a stopgap measure. The railroads were in desperate need of more revenue. Increases at the top of the rate structure were largely barred by truck competition, while increases on lower-rated goods were resisted by the Commission in accord with the new ratemaking policy. If value-of-service rates and the preferential rates at the low end of the rate spectrum were to be preserved, additional steps had to be taken. In the Commission's view the key was regulation of truck transportation,[34] since the diversion of high-rated traffic to truck movement was depriving the railroads of the traffic which supported the value-of-service structure. Such regulation was effected in 1935 with the adoption of Part II of the Interstate Commerce Act.

The support for the act of 1935 came from a coalition of interests, including large truckers who desired some modification of price competition, shippers who favored rate stabilization, and public officials who advocated a "clean-up" of the trucking business. However, for many congressmen the important thing was to do something to help the railroads.[35] Predictions made on the floor of both houses that regulation would lead to higher truck rates were not seriously denied.[36] In line with that admission, and to appease those who feared increases

[31] 41 Stat. 488 (1933); as subsequently amended 49 USC Sec. 15 (a) (2).
[32] *Ibid.*
[33] See note 24.
[34] See "The Fifteen Per Cent Case of 1931," 178 ICC 539, 582 (1931).
[35] See 79 *Congressional Record*, pp. 12197, 12210, 12214 (1935).
[36] 79 *Congressional Record*, p. 12222 (1935).

on rates for agricultural commodities, movements of such commodities were exempted from regulation under Part II.[37]

Public regulation of truck transportation has not received much support from economists—and this is not surprising. Freed of regulation, the business of truck transportation would probably come as close to the model of pure competition as is possible in the real world. The regulation of this business has been described as a cartel arrangement joining the interests of railroads and truckers under a common manager, the ICC.[38] But perhaps truck regulation may be better explained in broader terms. For example, it is clear that if, by the act of 1935, Congress sought to help the railroads, it was not solely out of concern for their employees and owners. Help for the railroads meant preservation of the rail pricing system and retention of depressed rates on some commodities. Truck competition clearly threatened the viability of that price structure and, if allowed to persist, would have necessitated the increase of some rail rates. Control of truck competition through regulation may have held out the prospect of helping the railroads, and no doubt railroad lobbying aided in the passage of the Motor Carrier Act but, nevertheless, chief among the confluence of interests which brought about passage of the act was pressure from certain shippers and representatives of certain regions to retain the benefits of value-of-service rates.

The ICC did not misunderstand the significance of the Motor Carrier Act. It gave immediate approval to truck rates and classifications which were almost exact duplicates of rail rates and classifications. Moreover, in the early days of 1935, the Commission made use of the minimum rate power to level up truck rates.[39]

Water competition, however, continued to harass the railroads. In order to have greater freedom to cope with it, the railroads suggested to Congress that the long- and short-haul clause be repealed, but the Senate was not receptive. Instead, Senator Wheeler, Chairman of the Senate Interstate and Foreign Commerce Committee, proposed that Congress bring water transportation under regulation of the Interstate Commerce Commission.[40]

Perhaps as a result of Senator Wheeler's suggestion, the Transportation Act of 1940 began as a bill to bring all domestic water

[37] 49 Stat. 544 (1935); as subsequently amended 49 USC Sec. 303 (b) (4a), (5), (6).
[38] See S. P. Huntington, "The Marasmus of the Interstate Commerce Commission," 61 *Yale Law Journal* 465 (1952).
[39] See Fifth Class Rates Between Providence and Boston 2 MCC 530, 547–549 (1936); Rates Over Carpet City Trucking 4 MCC 589 (1938); Commodity Rates of Kolahoma and Texas Transfer Co. 6 MCC 259 (1936).
[40] 84 *Congressional Record*, 1939, pp. 5874, 5882, and 6149.

transportation, except the noncontiguous trades, under regulation by the ICC, including much that up to that point had not been regulated at all. The bill, debated through three sessions of Congress, encountered much opposition from water-minded Congressmen, especially from the South. In order to prevent selective rate cutting by the railroads which might harass the water carriers, Senator Miller of Arkansas and Congressman Wadsworth of New York introduced an amendment which would have forced the carriers to comply with some kind of cost floor for rates. The amendment stated:

In order that the public at large may enjoy the benefit and economy afforded by each type of transportation the Commission shall permit each type of carrier or carriers to reduce rates so long as rates maintain a compensatory return to the carrier or carriers after taking into consideration overhead and all the elements entering into the cost to the carrier or carriers for the service rendered. It shall be unlawful to establish rates for any type of transportation which shall not be compensatory, as herein defined, whether such rates are established to meet competition of other types of transportation or for other purposes.[41]

Initially, the amendment met little opposition. In the debate on it, Senator Wheeler suggested that the language in the last sentence of the amendment might have an adverse impact on some water carriers, particularly those operating on the Great Lakes. Consequently, the last sentence of the original amendment was deleted and in that form the amendment was passed by the Senate.[42]

An amendment identical with the Miller Amendment was introduced in the House by Congressman Wadsworth of New York.[43] It met substantial opposition at the outset, but was passed.[44] Then, despite initial agreement by both houses on the Miller-Wadsworth Amendment, the conference committee refused to report a bill containing it. In debate on the conference report, Congressman Wadsworth moved that the bill be resubmitted to conference and the House conferees be instructed to insist on adoption of the Wadsworth Amendment.[45] That motion was passed and the bill resubmitted to conference.[46] A second conference report was presented to the House and once again the Wadsworth Amendment was deleted.[47] Mr. Wadsworth moved to

[41] 84 *Congressional Record*, 1939, p. 6074.
[42] *Ibid.*
[43] *Ibid.*, p. 9878.
[44] *Ibid.*, p. 9977.
[45] *Ibid.*, p. 9962.
[46] *Ibid.*
[47] *Ibid.*, p. 10146.

resubmit the bill to conference with instructions that the Wadsworth Amendment be adopted.[48] That motion was defeated.[49]

Opposition to the Miller-Wadsworth Amendment developed during the prolonged debate, as individual Congressmen recognized that the adoption of the amendment could signal a profound change in transportation policy. Their remarks and declamations provide an exceptionally revealing record of Congressional opinion about the objectives of transportation regulation.[50] The gist of the controversy as it

[48] *Ibid.*, p. 10192.
[49] *Ibid.*, p. 10193.
[50] Mr. Wheeler: "If the Miller-Wadsworth Amendment should be adopted, it would make every railroad company in this country, if a question of rates was raised, increase its rates on every branchline railroad. Not only that, but the Wadsworth Amendment provides that the Commission is to permit a floor to be placed under rates. It must be compensatory and in addition it must cover all overhead and all allowances of costs, meaning overhead, including taxes. There is considerable freight in this country that is carried at a low level of freight rates on a narrow margin because of competitive conditions or because it would not move at a higher freight rate. Many agricultural commodities are in this category, as are passenger fares" (86 *Congressional Record*, p. 11290, 1940).

Mr. Lea: ". . . We have an average cost of freight in this country. Much of it is hauled below that cost. Much freight is above that average cost.

"The Wadsworth Amendment states that the Commission shall permit the freight to be placed at a certain elevation. It must be compensatory and, in addition to that it must cover overhead and all elements of cost. That means overhead, including taxes. Without including any return on the investment we have this situation. Assume that the figure 100 involves what the Wadsworth Amendment states shall be included, compensation, including overhead, and it would carry taxes. The statistics show that in this country the average cost of transportation would be less than 80 percent of the Wadsworth standard, that is, what is rated as transportation cost. The additional costs are necessary of course for overhead and taxes.

"There is much freight at the present time that is carried as low as 80, under 100, because of competitive conditions or because it will not move at a higher freight rate. Cheap freight—low-grade freight like grain, fertilizer, sand and gravel, and building materials—must move at the lower level on a narrow margin or they do not move at all. Therefore the effect of the Wadsworth Amendment would be to require this 100 percent instead of the 80-percent floor on which the freight-rate structure is founded.

"The effect of this amendment, if put into practical effect and enforced, would be to raise the freight rates on a large portion of the heavy commerce of the United States.

"The high-cost freight, the high-priced freight, makes possible the low-cost freight in the United States. For instance, here is a passing train. One car is loaded with building materials. The railroad hauls that at a very low margin. Next to that car is a carful of merchandise, dry goods. The car that is loaded with dry goods probably pays $200 for the trip, while the car loaded with building materials pays $100. The high price that is charged for the higher grade freight makes it possible for the railroad to make something for carrying the low-grade freight. It carries the low-grade freight at a very minimum of profit, but its income is something above what it would have been had it not carried that freight" (*ibid.*, p. 18178).

unfolded was that a shift to a system of rates based on cost would result in increased rates on the movement of raw materials and agricultural products, and that this would not be in accord with past policy that such commodities should move at rates as low as possible. The clarification of that issue probably explains the ultimate defeat of the Miller-Wadsworth Amendment.

The result of the ratemaking controversy in the debate on the Transportation Act of 1940 cannot be construed as other than Congressional approval of value-of-service rates. Moreover, the *Record* is persuasive that the opponents of the amendment were more concerned with the retention of low rates on some commodities than with improvement in the level of rail revenues.[51] However, the statement of national policy in the act of 1940 does embody Congressional recognition that the carriers must be compensated if service is to be continued, *viz.*, the emphasis on fostering sound economic conditions in transportation and the proscription of unfair and destructive competition.[52] The task of carrying out these policy directives has, of course, fallen on the ICC.

About the time of the debate on the act of 1940, the Commission was developing a uniform rate scale and uniform classification. If the Miller-Wadsworth Amendment had been adopted, the class rate case probably would not have been continued. In a sense the act of 1940 and the evolution of the class rate structure were mutually confirming, and after 1940 the Commission proceeded with its refinement of an intricate value-of-service structure of class rates.

In the post–World War II period, the Commission found itself administering an internal subsidy in both rail and truck transportation. Regulation of truck transportation may have moderated the inherently competitive nature of the industry. Nevertheless, competitive pressures, though blunted, still made themselves felt in service. This competition, which the Commission has difficulty in controlling, probably squeezed out at least some of the internal subsidy which otherwise might have lodged in the truck rate structure. But even so, shippers concerned about competitive rate relationships in large degree achieved the effect of subsidy by rate equalization, and did not give up a great deal (i.e., compared to subsidized shippers by rail), inasmuch as service competition often does little more than dissipate carrier revenue. In that sense, small-lot shippers in sparse traffic areas have been benefited by

---

[51] See footnote 50.
[52] 54 Stat. 899 (1940); 49 USC preceding Sec. 1.

regulation and the extended service encouraged under it. Without it, their competitive positions would be worsened.[53]

Although it is not likely that the proponents of the acts of 1935 and 1940 envisioned this result for trucking, the Commission apparently found in the statement of policy of the act of 1940 a basis for such a result. It is true that the supporters of ICC regulation of truck and water transportation had stressed the destructively competitive effects of these modes on rail transportation and rail rates.[54] Those who opposed the extension of regulation to the other modes expressed their fear that regulation by the ICC would mean that truck and barge rates would be held up to protect the railroads.[55]

Various provisions were included in the act to allay these fears. The statement of national policy refers to the preservation of the inherent advantages of each mode as a goal of regulation[56] and, in the revised rule of ratemaking, the Commission was admonished to consider the effect of proposed rates on the movement of traffic "by the carrier or carriers for which the rates are prescribed." The statement of policy also directs the Commission to ". . . provide for fair and impartial regulation of all modes . . . ; to promote safe, adequate, economical, and efficient service and foster sound economic conditions in transportation and among the several carriers; . . . all to the end of developing, coordinating, and preserving a national transportation system by water, highway, and rail . . ." [57] Considering this language and assurances made by Senator Wheeler that the act would require the

---

[53] See the letter to Hon. John Sparkman, Chairman, Select Committee on Small Business, United States Senate, from J. H. Fles, executive vice president of Associated Truck Lines, Inc., Grand Rapids, Michigan, July 1, 1957 (Printed in Trucking Mergers and Concentration Hearings Before the Select Committee on Small Business, United States Senate, 85th Cong., 1st sess., Washington, D.C., 1957, pp. 161–162).

"Relaxation of rate policy will also mean that the shipper in the small community will not be given the service and the freight rates offered to shippers located in dense areas shipping to other dense areas. If free entry of transportation were allowed with a relaxed rate policy on the part of State and Federal regulatory bodies, Associated would give up many small service communities immediately because they are costing us money. Under our grant of authority, we are forced to serve such areas, and part of the price level granted by the Commission makes it possible to do so. Thus the lowest possible rate for a given shipper is not necessarily good for the country. We know the Interstate Commerce Commission seeks the lowest possible uniform rates so that shippers can obtain reasonably low transportation costs without discrimination" (sic).

[54] This position was summarized by Senator Wheeler at the time he introduced the bill which ultimately became the act of 1940 (84 Congressional Record, 1939, pp. 5869, 5870, 5873, 5874).

[55] See statements by Senator Bailey and Congressman South, 84 Congressional Record, 1939, pp. 6134 and 9716.

[56] 54 Stat. 899 (1940); 49 USC preceding Sec. 1.

[57] Ibid.

Commission to treat all modes impartially,[58] it is not surprising that the Commission has protected the truck rate structure as well as the rail, and has permitted or required rates which allowed the expansion of truck and barge service.[59]

The task of administering the policy impartially to preserve the inherent advantages of each mode and to foster sound and economical transportation was obviously difficult. Preserving the value-of-service rate structure requires that some freight yield revenues substantially greater than the cost of service. If both truck and rail carriers are to provide subsidized service, each must have a share of high-rated freight. But the Commission's efforts to protect the value-of-service structure, while dividing the traffic between modes, began to have adverse effects on the railroads. As volume carriers, the railroads' prime competitive weapon is price. The truckers, on the other hand, rely primarily on their service advantages to attract business. To achieve a satisfactory division of traffic between modes, the rates for each mode must reflect a balance between cost and service factors. Such a balance is not easily struck. The Commission tended to hold to the existing pattern of rate relationships and to avoid selective rate changes. This tended to give an advantage to the truckers. Moreover, the Commission was apparently reluctant to yield to the rate-cutting inclinations of the railroads because of the potentially devastating effects it could have on the truckers. At reduced rail rates, the truckers could probably continue to compete with the railroads in dense traffic areas, but at reduced revenue levels. This, in turn, would tend to eliminate trucking service to small shippers and to areas of lesser traffic volume, which would force rate increases for such shippers or areas. Similarly, if the truckers attempted to lower their rates to meet rail rate reductions, the railroads might not experience a net increase in revenue on their truck competitive movements and this, in turn, could lead to rate increases on their nontruck competitive traffic, much of which is the heavy agricultural and raw materials movements on which low rates are desired. As a result, the Commission often found such proposed rate changes, either truck or rail, to be destructively competitive and in violation of national policy.[60]

[58] See 84 *Congressional Record*, p. 6073 (1939).

[59] Petroleum Products Inc., Illinois Territory, 280 ICC 681, 691 (1951). Petroleum Carriers Division *v.* A., T. & S.F. Ry. Co., 302 ICC 243 (1957) (rail-truck competition). Wire Rods, Galveston Tex. & Sterling Ill., 277 ICC 123 (1950). Aluminum Articles, Texas to Ill. and Iowa, 293 ICC 467, 472 (1954) (rail-barge competition).

[60] See Petroleum Products Inc., Illinois Territory, 280 ICC 681, 691 (1951). Sugar from Houston, Texas, 51 MCC 775, 781 (1950). Merchandise in Mixed Truckloads, East 62 MCC 699, 723 (1954); 63 MCC 453, 483 (1955). Petroleum Carriers Division *v.* A., T., & S.F. Ry. Co. 302 ICC 243, 254–255 (1951).

The Commission's attempts to resolve these problems have been further complicated in recent years. Much of the high-rated traffic over which the railroads and the truckers have squabbled has been slipping away from the common carrier system and moving instead by exempt carriage. Legitimate private carriage has increased greatly and, of course, opportunities for profit have induced a fringe of illegitimate operations in truck transportation. The Transportation Act of 1958 has also introduced another unsettling element into an already confused situation. The 1958 amendment to the rule of ratemaking instructed the Commission that: "Rates of carriers shall not be held up to a particular level to protect the traffic of any other mode of transportation . . ." [61] How this is to be reconciled with the statement of national policy in the act of 1940 is not clear. The one test of this provision by the Supreme Court came out of a Commission attempt to hold up rates on a piggyback movement in order to protect a water carrier. The Court reversed the Commission's order and stated that, in a case where a proposed rail rate was fully compensatory, the Commission could prevent the adoption of that rate only if it could demonstrate, with satisfactory evidence, that the rate change was prohibited by national transportation policy.[62] Thus, the Commission is faced with the task of balancing competing interests of various modes of common carriage, which are subject to increasing competition from unregulated carriage, while seeking guidance from potentially irreconcilable provisions in the law.

A solution to this problem may be found in proposed revisions of the law. However, shipper interests are not neutral in the struggle among the modes, and between common and unregulated carriage. Many stand to gain if the regulated structure should be altered so as to allow greater competition in ratemaking. Others stand to lose a great deal. Generally, large-lot shippers in less densely populated areas and shippers of raw materials are in the second situation.

The Commission, preoccupied with existing law and perhaps sensitive to the very large segments of the economy which benefit by it, has found that value-of-service rates cannot be retained without new regulation to restrain competition, and thus has recommended that the agricultural and bulk-shipment exemptions be repealed.[63] Thus,

[61] 72 Stat. 572 (1958); 49 USC Sec. 15 (a) (3).

[62] U.S. v. N.Y., N.H. & H.R.R. Co., 372 US 744 (1963).

[63] See statement and testimony of Commissioner Howard Freas before the Subcommittee on Surface Transportation of the Senate Committee on Interstate and Foreign Commerce. (*Hearings on Problems of the Railroads*. Part 2, pp. 1830–1831, 1852–1857 [1958].)

it is evident that the Commission is persuaded that in order to check the drain on common carriage more restrictions must be placed on non-regulated carriage. Only in this way can a rate structure which contains massive elements of internal subsidy be sustained.

Political realities, however, make the prospects of such legislation remote. The geographic diffusion of the population and the diverse economic bases of many states and regions have diminished the political appeal of legislation to secure the low-cost movement of basic raw materials over long distances. Moreover, Americans generally have displayed a marked intolerance of efforts to interfere with their private and often free use of waterways and highways.

The Administration's proposals to admit greater competition in transportation would obviously chop down the size of the internal subsidy by reducing the degree of discrimination in rates. However, line-haul transportation by rail is still "naturally" monopolistic and will become more so with automation. Highway transportation may reach the point of such utter congestion that its provision will become a public utility function.[64] Even today, it is likely that for volume shipments there is a substantial spread between rail and highways costs, which would permit considerable discrimination to flourish.

Thus it is by no means certain that freer competition in transportation will eliminate monopolistic practices. On this score the program for less regulation has come under attack.

Continuance of regulation does not mean, however, that the full panoply of regulatory restraints should be retained. A decision to discard the discriminatory rate structure as a means of achieving public objectives might lead to more fruitful ways of blending private enterprise and public goals in transportation. The abandonment of price discrimination as a public policy should allow distinctions to be drawn between those elements of transportation service which are of a public utility nature and those which may be effectively controlled by market competition.

The provision of right of way, both rail and highway is, in the main, a public utility function as is, to a lesser extent, the provision of motive power. On the other hand, neither the public nor private costs of providing freight cars, trailers, or containers, and the provision of freight consolidation and routing service are so rigid that effective

---

[64] Our notion here is that there may be public costs associated with unlimited entry into the trucking business, which may call for at least some limitation of the number of firms allowed to operate trucks over the road. Whether this calls for continued rate regulation is doubtful—but a possibility.

competition in the supply of equipment and service is not possible.[65] These functions would be removed from the sphere of rate regulation if regulation were really to be focused on monopoly and not on the transfer of benefits from one portion of the economy to another. (Many of these services are already being performed by shippers themselves, and it would appear that this will continue in the future.) It is probable that a freeing up of large parts of the business of transportation would lead to the development of new ideas, techniques, and transport institutions.

This is not to say, however, that all discrimination can or will be eliminated from the structure of freight rates. In the past, public acceptance of discrimination among classes of goods and for certain movements favored some shippers and penalized others. For the future, we may expect public insistence on some measure of discrimination which will equalize the price of transport for similar movements, even though the costs of these movements may differ. Public support of a far-flung rail network, of mileage scales in rate structures, of a ubiquitous highway system, and of local-service airlines has provided evidence that there is general unwillingness to impose the full economic penalty on those who are unfavorably located. It is probably realistic to anticipate that this will continue. Transportation history indicates that the public's conception of what is fair and equitable transportation pricing is not based on the specifics of cost and demand. (The long-standing quarrel over the long- and short-haul problem is evidence of this.) Until technology overcomes differences in cost which are related to traffic density, climate, terrain, distance, etc., some measure of discrimination will likely be demanded by the public. If history is any guide, this discrimination will be accommodated, at least in part, through the price structure of regulated common carriers.

Conclusions

Clearly, the transportation system of the United States has been the means by which public policy has sought to promote the welfare of certain sectors of the economy. A dominant theme in regulation has

---

[65] For example, we can see how stripping away the nonpublic-utility elements from the rate structure would affect rates by examining rates under Plans III and IV piggyback. There, the rates are essentially mileage charges for locomotive power on rail rights of way. The lease costs of both trailers and flatcars are presently outside the scope of regulation. Whether they remain so will depend on the Commission's decision in ex parte 230.

been the maintenance of low rates on basic raw materials produced in areas more or less remote from the major consuming markets. The effect of this policy on the distribution of income in the United States has undoubtedly been enormous though largely immeasurable. It may be surmised that in the extractive industries, many of which have tended to be competitive, one of the effects of value-of-service rates has been to increase land rent. Insofar as this has occurred in the less-densely populated areas of the country, the result has probably been a narrowing of the differences between the values of rural and urban land. At the other end of the rate spectrum, value-of-service rates have probably imposed a larger share of the transportation burden on shippers of high-rated commodities, mainly manufactured goods, and this may have tended to dilute the quasi-rents associated with the less than perfectly competitive nature of some manufacturing.

While this may describe the effect of the internal subsidy on rail rates, it has played a different role in truck transportation. Here, value-of-service rates have probably had a marked impact on the growth of towns and smaller cities off main rail routes and on the periphery of metropolitan areas. The existence of ubiquitous truck transportation may have contributed greatly to the industrial and population decentralization which has occurred in many metropolitan areas since World War II.

Whatever may have been the exact results of value-of-service pricing, they have not been the product of aimless legislation. There is a clear and relatively consistent pattern of legislative and administrative action regarding surface transportation. The preservation of discriminating rates administered by and through the regulated common carrier system has been the dominant policy underlying transportation regulation in the United States for many years. This policy has been pursued because of the legislative expectation that it could stimulate a pattern of resource allocation and economic development desired by many members of Congress. The desire to curb monopoly power in transportation has been of marginal significance to Congress throughout the past four decades. The evidence supporting these conclusions is scattered through the record of Congressional action on transportation matters. No other interpretation is so consistent with Commission policies. One must be impressed upon reading the *Congressional Record* that Congress is willing to "skin the cat" in a variety of ways.

The problem for Congress and the nation is that increasing competition in transportation has made the enforcement of value-of-service rates virtually impossible.[66] The "preservation of the common carrier system" in its present form has depended on a coalescence of interests which is gradually breaking down. The interests of the various carriers in continued regulation are obviously different. Similarly, shippers of freight are split into different camps because of the effects regulation has on them. That shippers are not neutral in the struggle between the different modes compounds the problem of resolving the split between the truckers and the rail carriers, and makes uncertain the prospect that regulation will be abandoned. Moreover, it is clear that transport markets are still pock-marked by important elements of monopoly.

The result of forces working in transportation today, such as private transportation, experimental rates which deflate the discriminatory structure, and shipper demands for specialized equipment, may denigrate the effect of regulation. Perhaps Congress would be wise to recast regulation with a recognition that, while its objectives may need change, some measure of its protections to the public must be retained.

COMMENT

D. F. PEGRUM, University of California at Los Angeles

Because I wish to draw attention to a number of problems that cover a rather wide range of subjects it will not be possible to explore any of them in depth. I shall try, however, to make the nature of the issues

---

[66] It may be that, even without legislative action, the value-of-service concept will be laid to rest. The Federal District Court in New Haven, Conn., recently rendered an opinion on this subject which may be the harbinger of such a development. (See N.Y., N.H., and H. R.R. Co. *et al.* U.S. and ICC District Court (3 judge), Conn., Civil Action 9229, 7/23/63. Noted in 32 *U.S. Law Week*, p. 2081.)

The court struck down an ICC order which had found unlawful an all-freight rate plan proposed by the New Haven and competing roads. The Commission had found the proposed rates to violate the classification principle stated in Sec. 1(6) of the Commerce Act. The court rejected this interpretation. Judge Smith made this observation on the matter: "It would appear that the Commission here invokes Sec. 1(6) as a means of preserving a basis for the 'value of service' concept in rate-making . . . in a desire to hold fast to a past which has already slipped away beyond our reach.

"This 'value of service' principle was useful in the early years of the Interstate Commerce Act in requiring the more prosperous East to assist in the development of railroads and commercial and agricultural enterprises in the undeveloped West at a time when the existing railroads were powerful monopolies.

. . . .

The continued application of this principle is, however, contrary to the letter and spirit of the National Transportation Policy amendment to the Interstate Commerce Act, . . . which, as its legislative history makes clear, was intended to permit the railroads, no longer effective monopolies, to respond to competition by asserting whatever inherent advantages of cost and service they possessed."

clear, hopefully to force a recognition of their significance, and to encourage further discussion of them.

The Common Carrier in the Transport System

The common carrier system has never been universal in carriage for hire. Other enterprises have always participated extensively in transport. The obligations of common carriage are to serve all alike, at reasonable prices and without discrimination. That is to say, within the scope of their common carrier duties the firms cannot select their customers and they cannot include or exclude through the device of discriminatory pricing.

Whatever the reasons for the emergence and development of the common carrier concept, it is clear that with the rise of the railroad to its position of dominance, the idea of protecting the shipper from monopolistic exploitation became of paramount significance. With the failure of competition to play the role that it was assumed to be capable of under laissez-faire, and with the growth of regulation, the need for limiting competition among the railroads also became recognized. It should be noted, however, that common carriage by agencies other than railroads, water for example, was performed by competitive and nonregulated enterprises.

The development of transport regulation around the railroads, together with the accompanying comprehensive and detailed rules for common carriage under federal legislation, has resulted in an identification of the common carrier with regulation. This identification has led to the assumption that all common carriers must be regulated in the public utility mold and that entry must be restricted.

Railroad regulation came to encompass a detailed regulation of prices (rates) and also made the railroads total common carriers. Finally, in 1920, limitations were imposed on freedom of entry. In the legislation which followed 1920 these controls were extended to all common carriage in this country, except that firms engaged in common carriage by water, motor, and air were not restricted solely to that type of transport activity.

None of the foregoing conditions is essential to the status of the common carrier *per se*, and the idea of common carriage should not be identified with rate regulation and freedom of entry. If this is so, then it may be asked: what would be left of the common carrier if rate regulations were abandoned? Common carrier obligations to shippers would remain as under present law, and this seems to be the most pressing need. Appropriate authority and agencies for specifying and enforcing obligations would be retained; readiness to serve all alike would remain. These duties would relate to services rather than firms or enterprises, and would not necessarily preclude any carrier from engaging in noncommon carrier transport. Relaxation or even the abandonment of current regulation, therefore, would not necessarily result in the elimination or disappearance of the common carrier.

Freedom of Entry and the Common Carrier

Freedom of entry as a privilege to be extended to common carriers would have different effects depending on the mode of transport. For the railroads, freedom of entry in the form of new railroad lines and extensions into the territory of others, hardly seems to be feasible.

For air transport, it is complicated by the problems of subsidy and airmail payments. Restriction of entry, particularly in feeder or local service, is justified because of this. Restrictions on the operations of the trunk lines may possibly be supported on similar grounds. The administration of policy to date, however, does not seem to have encouraged outstanding efficiency, particularly on those lines where one has the greatest reason to expect it.

Freedom of entry in motor and water carriage involves somewhat different considerations than those which apply to the other two modes. The reasons for restricting entry as a means of limiting competition are not apparent. Freedom of entry for carriers in these agencies need not result in the abandonment of common carrier obligations. Certification of those wishing to serve as common carriers could be retained. Contract carriage could be restricted to certain types of service if it were so desired. Guarantee of being fit, willing, and able could be retained, as well as publication of and abidance by rates, notice of changes of rates and services, and permission to abandon. If customers want common carrier service it is difficult to believe that they will be unwilling to pay for it, or that they should be compelled to do so if they do not.

In short, not only is the competitive process completely compatible with the common carrier as such, it has existed in the past, and still does exist over an appreciable range of transportation.

Freedom of Entry and Intermodal Ownership

Freedom of entry means the freedom of undertakings to enter a particular line of transport without restrictions designed to protect the business of those already offering services.

This still leaves open the question, however, of who should be free to enter. Should the railroads be given a free hand to enter any of the other modes of transport? Should shipping companies be given a free hand to engage in domestic and overseas air transport? Should aircraft manufacturers be permitted to enter the air transport business, and the automobile manufacturers to enter the motor carrier for hire service? Complete or undefined freedom of entry would require an affirmative answer to these questions. A negative answer, however, would not necessarily imply a limitation on competition, but rather a limitation on who the new entrants or competitors might be.

Freedom of entry in this context raises two broad questions of public policy: (1) the theory of industrial organization compatible with a competitive private enterprise economy; and (2) the underlying theory of organization of a national transportation system geared to an economical utilization of resources devoted to transportation.

The implications of the first question cannot be developed here. Suffice it to say that the application of the antitrust laws to market dominance, diversification of corporate activities, and corporate agglomeration constitute areas of debate where opinions differ widely and consensus of opinion is notably difficult to obtain. There is obviously pretty general agreement, however, that some rules are necessary and that some limitations do have to be imposed, although the nature of these are vague and the lines of demarcation rather dimly perceptible.

The second question needs to be evaluated in the light of two major considerations in transport organization: (1) consolidation policy, particularly with regard to railroads; and (2) the policy to be followed on diversification or integration of the various modes or agencies.

The consolidation issue comes first, it seems to me, because views on diversification will be influenced in a vital way by the policy adopted for consolidation. The limitations on competition among railroads, which are the result of economic characteristics derived from the technology of this mode of transport, have given rise to the special issue of railroad consolidation. This focuses on the plan or policy to be followed that is consonant with private enterprise, competition, and an efficient transportation system. There are three possibilities: (1) the grouping of railroads so as to maintain very extensive competition; (2) a national, four-system plan, or something of that nature; and (3) regional consolidation, with each system enjoying extensive monopoly of rail transport in the area it serves. It is most likely that any form of consolidation that develops will have pronounced regional features with definite limitations on the geographic areas served by each railroad. Resolution, therefore, of the problem of consolidation must shape judgment on the appropriate policy regarding diversification, because of the inescapable blending of technological and regional monopoly with thoroughgoing and regionally unconstrained competition.

Diversification or integration relates to policy centering on the question of whether the formation of transportation companies should be permitted. We can therefore omit discussion of entry of one mode into another to supply ancillary services.

The desirability of new transportation companies must be considered in terms of their possible impact on competition, efficiency, and regulation. It is not readily apparent to me that the formation of such companies would of itself enhance competition in the rendering of transport services. I do not see how it could improve competition in motor, water, and air transport. Nor can I see any ready or necessary improvements in coordination; on the contrary, the possibility of the opposite is very real. Furthermore, if consolidation results in a few giant rail lines and a large amount of regional monopoly, extensive diversification would result in a highly oligopolistic transport structure, with a real threat of limitations on competition, and the dangers of "internal" subsidies. Second, economies of scale in rail transport have been the subject of some rather careful study recently. The results seem to indicate definite limitations on economical size. If this is so, it is difficult to see how diversification would do anything but aggravate the situation. Third, diversification and the formation of transportation companies would probably result in more rather than less regulation. This contradicts proposals favoring a reduction in public controls.

The Problem of Discrimination
—Its New Relevance

The problem of discrimination is noteworthy in connection with this discussion because of its bearing on competition and regulation, and because of R. A. Nelson's rather extensive attention to it.

Discrimination in economic theory refers to price differentiation among homogeneous products resulting from a producer's ability to separate his markets. The applicability of the concept to multiproduct firms with nontraceable costs is anything but simple or clear. The railroads, in particular, have significant amounts of nontraceable costs. They are multiproduct firms, although we do not seem to have reached very clear agreement on what constitutes a unit of output nor how to designate the particular products.

Nevertheless, agreement on the fact that there are nontraceable costs means that the precise total cost of each of the various services cannot be derived. This in turn means that the market (or "value of service") must be used in the making of rates if efficient utilization of the resources is to be achieved.

It seems to me that there will be no discrimination in the economic sense as long as price differences represent the recovery of nontraceable costs, and there will be no "internal subsidy" as long as any rate completely covers the costs which are directly attributable and traceable to the services which are being rendered.

The Effects of Entry Control
in Surface Transport

JAMES C. NELSON

WASHINGTON STATE UNIVERSITY

Closed or controlled entry exists in fields in which the government deems it desirable to foster monopoly of an essential service, to limit the number of firms, or to stimulate the growth of large firms. This condition is found primarily in the transport and public utility industries. Franchises, certificates of public convenience and necessity, and permits are devices used to limit entry to one firm in each market or to some number less than would have been established under free-entry conditions. In the utility industries, where monopoly organization is inevitable and clearly more efficient than competitive organization, there has been little question of the wisdom of the closed-entry policy.

The entry situation has been very different in American transport. Competition among firms in each important transport market is workable and has long existed; in trucking, the number of firms can be great enough to approach atomistic competition on dense traffic routes. The transport industries compete with one another to a far greater extent than do the utilities; despite cost and service differences, inter-modal competition is widely regarded as the most effective form of transport competition. Therefore, monopoly of one firm per route has been unacceptable.

With the exception of controls designed to prohibit or limit railroad ownership or control of Panama Canal shipping lines and other water carriers, and the "commodities clause" separating the railroad business from mining and industrial enterprises, the federal government exercised no direct entry control of transport enterprises prior to 1920. The Transportation Act of 1920 established the first direct control of entry in interstate transport by giving the Interstate Commerce Commission power to limit the establishment of new railroads and to control the extension or abandonment of railway lines by the grant or denial of certificates of public convenience and necessity. The next step was taken in 1935, when the Motor Carrier Act required that a certificate of public convenience and necessity be obtained from the ICC before inaugurating a new interstate motor common carrier service or before extending an existing one. It required that a permit be obtained before starting business as a motor contract carrier or before extending an existing contract service. "Grandfather clauses" were included to assure continuance of operations conducted at the time the Act became effective and continuously thereafter. All private carriers and several classes of for-hire carriers, particularly those of agricultural products, were exempted from entry regulation. The Transportation Act of 1940 required similar certificates and permits for domestic water carriers, with far-reaching exemptions for bulk commodity carriers; and the Freight Forwarder Act of 1942 required permits for freight forwarders in interstate commerce. The state commissions have exercised varying entry controls, much of which antedated federal regulation, over rail, motor, and water carriers in intrastate commerce.[1]

Federal regulatory statutes have long controlled the relations between modes of transport, an indirect entry control. Control or ownership by railroads of competing modes has been limited to maintain intermodal competition in full force and vigor. The landmark law was the Panama Canal Act, enacted to prohibit control by railroads of the ship lines about to begin operations through the Panama Canal, and to limit rail control of other domestic shipping to cases in which competition between water and rail carriers would not be affected. The 1935 Act significantly limited rail ownership or control of motor trucking. The 1942 Act allowed common carrier control of freight forwarders but banned control of carriers by freight forwarders. Railroads and other modes have freedom to enter the oil pipeline field without ICC approval, but the Civil Aeronautics Act of 1938 has been interpreted as virtually barring control of airlines by other modes.

The long delay in adopting federal entry controls indicates that the public was not originally convinced that a need existed for limiting the number of carriers. The wide areas of exemption signify that important groups still prefer many-firm competition in transport. Notwithstanding this, entry controls were justified as being essential to maintenance of adequate and efficient transportation by common carriers. In the idealized conception, entry controls facilitate that

---

[1] John J. George, *Motor Carrier Regulation in the United States*, Spartanburg, S.C., 1929; and Donald V. Harper, *Economic Regulation of the Motor Trucking Industry by the States*, Urbana, Ill., 1959, pp. 26–43.

objective in several ways. [First, essential common carrier services can be required of carriers given certificates and can be assured by protecting regular-route common carriers from competition of contract, private, exempt, and even of irregular-route common carriers. Second, the reduced competition due to entry restrictions can encourage adequate investment and technological change by assuring profitable returns. Third, standards of service can be improved by encouraging able and responsible carriers, by discouraging "fly-by-night" firms, and by imposing high standards of safety. Fourth, duplicating fixed investments can be avoided, excess capacity can be reduced, and large firms can be encouraged. Finally, greater coordination can result from through services and joint rates.]

In spite of the beneficial role alleged for entry control, serious issues have arisen. Certificate and permit control of motor carriers has become so detailed and laborious that the ICC has been overloaded with routine and has been unable to give adequate attention to the major public policy issues in transport regulation. In view of the costly and time-consuming regulatory procedures in competitive transport industries, questions have increasingly been raised as to whether the benefits are worth the costs.

The long-continuing decline in traffic handling of the regulated common carriers, the opposite of what had been expected under regulation, has also focused attention on entry control. Traffic diversion to exempted and private carriers has stimulated demands by regulated common carriers and the ICC that statutory exemptions be narrowed and that opportunities for private carriage be lessened, measures which are stoutly resisted by shipper groups.[2]

From the beginning, there has been criticism of the Commission's standards and policies in controlling entry, especially in trucking where regulation has been both restrictive and detailed. Motor carriers have complained of long, drawn-out proceedings, the uncertainties of the results of certificate and permit applications, and of the extremely limited operating authority often granted. Shippers have also complained of inadequate and costly service.[3]

[2] See the editorial, "Competition in Transportation," *The Journal of Commerce*, March 13, 1963, p. 4.
[3] See *Traffic World*: October 24, 1953, pp. 35–36; April 16, 1955, pp. 23–24; April 29, 1961, pp. 100–101; July 21, 1962, p. 33; and March 16, 1963, pp. 32–33 (especially the comments of August Heist, Traffic Manager, R. J. Reynolds Tobacco Co.). See also the statement of ICC Commissioner Everett Hutchison before the Surface Transportation Subcommittee, Senate Committee on Commerce, on "The Decline of the Nation's Common Carrier Industry," August 30, 1961.

The crux of the problem is whether the type of direct entry control adopted for the competitive transport industries has a solid economic foundation, and whether detailed operating authority regulation has produced over-all economies or diseconomies for the general public. Because the most restrictive entry limitations have been applied in trucking, this analysis will emphasize the entry control standards and policies applicable to motor carriers, together with their economic effects. Entry control has also been influential in the market structure and performance of air transport, but this case has been adequately treated in other studies.[4] An area which also cannot be analyzed in this paper involves the rules governing access to trailer-on-flat-car transport and the impact of existing entry controls on that notable innovation.

Administrative Standards in Control of Entry

Some reference to the statutory standards governing entry control, and to the administrative interpretations of them by the ICC, is essential to a full understanding of the economic effects of barriers to entry.

The general purpose of the "grandfather clauses" was to subject to regulation all 40,000 existing common and contract motor carriers, while preserving their operations intact. New or extended operations were to be started only after proof of the "present or future public convenience and necessity" had been shown by common carriers, or consistency "with the public interest and the national transportation policy" by contract carriers.[5] The standards in new-service cases clearly contemplated limiting the entrance of additional firms and the operating rights of existing firms; thus, some lessening of intramodal competition was desired. Except for the service, routes, termini, and intermediate and off-route points specified in the certificates of regular-route carriers and some details in other certificates and permits, the drafting of explicit models of efficient organization for the motor carrier industry was left to the Commission.

[4] This subject has been competently analyzed in Lucile S. Keyes, *Federal Control of Entry into Air Transportation*, Cambridge, Mass., 1951; and in Richard E. Caves, *Air Transport and Its Regulators*, Cambridge, Mass., 1962.

[5] In addition, under Sections 207(a) and 209(b) of the Interstate Commerce Act, common and contract carriers, respectively, have to show "that the applicant is fit, willing, and able properly to perform the service" and to conform to regulation. These tests, however, only infrequently result in denials or restrictions of a burdensome sort. See *Interstate Commerce Commission Activities 1937–1962*, Washington, D.C., 1962, pp. 23–41 (especially p. 26) for a review of the standards of entry control for motor carriers.

The actual process of obtaining authority to continue the operations begun prior to regulation proved far from automatic. The Commission early decided that applicants for "grandfather" rights must bear the burden of proof and show concrete evidence that they had been in "bona fide operation" on, and continuously since, the applicable "grandfather" date. Proof had to show that every part of the operation had been actual, conducted in good faith, and conducted continuously until the date of the decision on the application, except for interruptions beyond the carrier's control. The question was determined in adversary proceedings. The grant of "grandfather" rights quickly became a process of legally compromising private interests, with far more emphasis on protection of established common carriers than on the requirements of allocative efficiency.

As most of the approximately 90,000 "grandfather" applications by motor carriers could not be decided until 1941 or after, the Commission's rule of continuous operation led to the denial of the right to carry commodities in numerous cases.[6] The longer decisions were delayed, the greater was the likelihood that some "grandfather" operation would be denied because of traffic shifts and changes in the relative profitability of traffic or routes. The Commission frequently denied "grandfather" rights for certain commodities previously handled because they were not carried in substantial amounts and with a sufficient degree of regularity. Despite the Supreme Court's directive, in the *Carolina Freight Carriers Corp. Common Carrier Application* case, that the Commission not itemize and pulverize a carrier's operation, product by product, the restrictive policies in the grant of "grandfather" rights continued without appreciable liberalization.[7]

Several factors influenced the Commission to adopt a tight entry control policy through strict construction of the "grandfather clauses." Among these were a belief that the facts of "bona fide operation" had to be established; a desire to prevent additional persons from gaining entry by claiming "grandfather" rights; and a need to ease the administrative task through imposing the burden of proof on the applicant.

The Commission early justified its grant of restrictive commodity authority (usually special rather than general commodities) to the highly numerous irregular-route common carriers. In the case of *Powell Bros.*

[6] *Gregg Cartage & Storage Co. Common Carrier Application*, 21 M.C.C. 17, 21–23 (1939). See Commissioner Lee's dissent, pp. 23–24.
[7] *U.S. v. Carolina Carriers Corp.*, 315 U.S. 475, 478, 482–486 (1942); and 24 M.C.C. 305, 308–309 (1940).

Truck Lines, Inc., Common Carrier Application, the Commission stated its position, reiterated in many subsequent cases, as follows:

> Authority to transport general commodities throughout a wide territory over irregular and unspecified routes pursuant to the "grandfather" clause of the act should be granted to a carrier only when such carrier's right thereto has been proved by substantial evidence. To do otherwise would create the very ills which regulation is designed to alleviate, namely, congestion of highways, destructive rate practices, and unbridled competition. Common carriers which are expected to maintain regular service for the movement of freight in whatever quantities offered to and from all points on specified routes cannot operate economically and efficiently if other carriers are permitted to invade such routes for the sole purpose of handling the cream of the traffic available thereon in so-called irregular-route service.[8]

Contract carriers have generally been restricted to a highly specialized service for one or a few shippers. Where it is necessary to grant a wide range of commodities, the opportunity to add or substitute contracts has been limited to shippers of a certain type, such as meat packers or chain grocers. In other cases, contract carriers have been restricted to one or a few commodity classes. In an early leading case, *Contracts of Contract Carriers,* the Commission justified a restrictive entry policy for contract carriers, even in "grandfather" cases, in terms of an inferred need to protect common carrier service from "cut-throat competition." [9]

When service extensions or entirely new services have been proposed by motor carriers, the Commission has had complete authority to determine the actual meaning of the "public convenience and necessity" test for common carriers and the "consistency with the public interest" test for contract carriers. In such cases, the authorized services have often been limited to specified commodities and restricted narrowly as to points, routes and territories, return hauls, size of shipments, and class of shippers. Many applications have been denied in whole or in part. Large truckers have been able to round out their operations with additional grants of commodity, route, or other authority, or by purchase of rights; but highly restricted carriers, typically small firms, have not. Thus, the patterns of restrictions resulting from granting "grandfather" rights have not been basically altered.

[8] 9 M.C.C. 785, 791–792 (1938).
[9] 1 M.C.C. 628, 629–630 (1937). See also *Craig Contract Carrier Application,* 31 M.C.C. 705, 711–715 (1941); and *J-T Transport Co., Extension-Columbus, Ohio,* 79 M.C.C. 695, 701–704 (1959). See Commissioner Lee's dissent to the ICC policy of protection of common carriers in the Keystone case, 19 M.C.C. 475, 502–503 (1939).

In considering new or extended service applications, the Commission, in substance, seeks to ascertain whether the new operation would serve a useful public purpose, responsive to a public demand or need. From the beginning, however, the public need test took on protective considerations, such as whether the useful public service could be served as well by existing carriers and whether a new operation or service would endanger or impair the operations of existing carriers contrary to the public interest.[10] In regard to the effect of new or extended contract services, the Commission early held that the term "consistent with the public interest" implied that the maintenance of adequate facilities for handling general traffic was to be considered, with the convenience of a particular shipper or shippers ruled out as a conclusive test. As in "grandfather" cases, the motive of protecting common carrier service was reiterated.[11] The Commission has generally denied extensions of service by existing carriers or proposals to inaugurate new services unless applicants can make a convincing showing that the facilities of existing carriers are physically inadequate. With several regulated motor carriers already in operation, this test can be extremely difficult, even when strong support is given by shippers. Consequently, the physical inadequacy test has resulted in protecting existing carriers from new competition.[12]

Acceptable evidence of satisfactory service has varied from mere allegations of adequate service by protestant motor carriers and submissions showing the existence of several motor lines, to findings that underutilized facilities existed. Specific investigations of carrier efficiency have rarely been made. Another difficulty for new entrants was an early ruling by the Commission that the offer of lower rates to shippers cannot be considered a factor in determination of adequacy and efficiency of existing service.[13]

In the *C. & D. Oil Co. Contract Carrier Application* case, the Commission enunciated the principle, often reiterated in cases involving applications of common and contract carriers, that existing

---

[10] *Pan-American Bus Lines Operation*, 1 M.C.C. 190, 203 (1936). See also 62 M.C.C. 513, 534 (1954).

[11] *Worm Extension-Ainsworth and Johnstown, Nebr.*, 32 M.C.C. 641, 644 (1942). See also *ICC* v. *J-T Transport Co.*, 368 U.S. 81, 89–90 (1961); and *Moyer Contract Carrier Application*, 88 M.C.C. 767, 769–775 (1962).

[12] Cases in which new entrants have been approved include 1 M.C.C. 725, 735 (1937); 3 M.C.C. 465, 467 (1937); 6 M.C.C. 83, 87 (1938); and *West Coast Bus Lines Common Carrier Application*, 41 M.C.C. 269, 288 (1942). In the last, regulation was found incapable of eliminating the undesirable effects of monopoly.

[13] *Wellspeak Common Carrier Application*, 1 M.C.C. 712, 715–716 (1937). See also 368 U.S. 81, 133–138 (1961).

carriers should have the right to transport all traffic that they can handle adequately and efficiently:

> It is clear that the transportation which applicants propose to perform is now being handled with efficiency by a carrier claiming the right to a permit authorizing such operation under the "grandfather" clause... Furthermore, it appears that other motor carriers which have been in the field for some time could handle the traffic if the present operator's service should later be found unsatisfactory....
>
> ... We think that, in order to foster sound economic conditions in the motor-carrier industry, existing motor carriers should normally be accorded the right to transport all traffic which they can handle adequately, efficiently, and economically in the territories served by them, as against any person now seeking to enter the field of motor-carrier transportation in circumstances such as are here disclosed.[14]

However, the Commission does not consider rail common carrier service alone to be an indication of adequate service. Its position is that shippers are entitled to adequate service by motor vehicle as well as by rail, and motor carriers must be allowed to develop according to their inherent advantages.[15]

With substantially the same statutory requirements governing water carriers as apply to motor carriers, the Commission has been far less restrictive in regulating entry. Thus, water carriers have customarily been given "grandfather" authority to serve all ports on their routes.[16] Since proof of actual movement of specific commodities was not always required, general commodities have been granted to "grandfather" water carriers far more frequently than to the motor carriers.[17] Sample studies of recent cases reveal similar liberality in commodity and port grants in new service and extension cases.[18]

This greater liberality to water carriers probably reflected the Commission's awareness that it had gone too far in suppressing motor

---

[14] 1 M.C.C. 329, 331–332 (1936). See also 79 M.C.C. 695, 701 (1959); and Mr. Justice Frankfurter's dissenting opinion in 368 U.S. 81, 98–105 (1961).

[15] *Bowles Common Carrier Application*, 1 M.C.C. 589, 591 (1937). See *Schaffer Transp. Co.* v. *U.S.*, 355 U.S. 83, 88–92 (1957).

[16] *Pope & Talbot, Inc., Com. and Contr. Car. Application*, 250 ICC 117, 122 (1941). See also 250 ICC 249, 270–272 (1942); and 250 ICC 321, 325 (1942).

[17] *McLain Carolina Line, Inc., Common Carrier Application*, 250 ICC 327, 332 (1942). See also 250 ICC 436, 439 (1942); and 250 ICC 477, 478–482 (1942).

[18] All decisions in applications for water carrier operating authority in Volume 285 of *Interstate Commerce Commission Reports*, or those decided between April 1951 and March 1957, were examined. See 285 ICC 5, 7–8 (1951); 285 ICC 9, 11–13 (1951); 285 ICC 33, 48–50 (1951); 285 ICC 411, 413–418 (1953); and 285 ICC 667, 676–677 (1955).

carrier competition. In addition, a smaller number of firms compete on water routes, entry control for water carriers was inaugurated when the economy was in an expansionist phase, and, in general, the postwar restoration of coastal water service was a national goal.

An "easy" entry policy was also established for freight forwarders in 1942. They needed only permits which were issued on findings that "the applicant is ready, able, and willing properly to perform the service proposed, and that the proposed service . . . is or will be consistent with the public interest and the national transportation policy . . ." Most importantly, until amended in 1957, Sec. 410 (d) restrained the Commission from denying permits solely because the new service would compete with other freight forwarders.

The Commission has authorized most applications for continuing freight forwarding operations conducted in 1942 simply on proof of operation over a period of years.[19] In addition, it has been liberal in granting permits to enter forwarding and for commodity and territorial authority.[20]

The "easy" entry policy for forwarders, a close approach to free entry, reflected the emphasis by Congress on competition and a competitive structure. Freight forwarding was distinguished from other transport as not involving much investment in facilities; hence, as not requiring protection against improvident investments.

Restrictions on Operating Authority of Regulated Carriers

Under free-entry conditions, the boundaries of a firm's products or markets are determined according to the stimulus of the profit motive and under the restraints of competition, the size of the market, the economies of scale, and other limiting factors such as antitrust-law restraints on market-sharing agreements. Fragmentation of products and markets occurs when it is profitable to limit a firm's operations, but most barriers to entry or expansion arise from economic factors rather than political or protective considerations. Hence, more transport firms will use routes of dense rather than scant traffic and more

[19] Republic Carloading & Distributing Co., Inc., F. F. Application, 250 ICC 670, 673–676 (1943). See also 250 ICC 747, 751–752 (1943); and 260 ICC 307, 313–314 (1944).

[20] Lifschultz Fast Freight Extension—West and Midwest, 265 ICC 431, 440–444 (1948), upheld in 338 U.S. 855 (1949). See also 265 ICC 513, 517–518 (1949); and 285 ICC 127, 130 (1952); and 285 ICC 641, 651–653 (1955). On the other hand, see 285 ICC 425, 430–432 (1953).

carriers will compete in modes not requiring a large minimum investment.

Where entry and operations have been limited severely, as in regulated trucking, the specialization in commodities and markets gradually comes to reflect the decisions of a political authority under restrictive and protective conditions. A tendency toward fewer firms may or may not reflect economies of scale; a system of fragmented operations by franchised carriers may improve the service to the public or may cause it to deteriorate or become excessively expensive because of service competition.

A 10 per cent, stratified, random sample of intercity truckers subject to ICC jurisdiction was taken by the Board of Investigation and Research in 1941. It revealed that specialization of function had attained a high degree in the trucking industry, reflecting the operations of thousands of small carriers serving local industries and often utilizing specialized equipment. But the sample also revealed that the pattern of limitations in certificates and permits was a highly restrictive one, except for carriers already large and with well-rounded operations when regulation began.[21]

Certificates and permits for motor carriers always designate: (1) the legal characteristics of the service authorized—common or contract; (2) the routes or territories over which such operations may be conducted; (3) the points to or from which a carrier may render the specified service; (4) the commodities or classes of commodities which may be transported for compensation; and (5) the extent to which the authorized physical movement of trucks is tied to specific highway routes and gateways. While some restrictions merely confirm voluntary specialization, such detailed specification almost inevitably imposes real handicaps on efficient operations.

The most significant limitations on operating authority have been the commodity restrictions. These often narrowly restrict the traffic that a carrier may solicit or obtain for return hauls. Special commodity authorizations range from a single commodity, such as sugar or hardware, to many specified commodities. Unless highly specialized equipment is required, carriers obviously prefer general commodity authorizations.

The BIR sample of certificates and permits as of 1942 disclosed that 62 per cent of the regulated truckers had been limited to special commodities; that approximately 40 per cent of such carriers (other than

[21] Board of Investigation and Research, *Federal Regulatory Restrictions upon Motor and Water Carriers*, S. Doc. 78, 79th Cong., 1st sess., 1945, pp. 304–319.

those operating specialized equipment) had been limited to one commodity or commodity class, with 88 per cent limited to six or less; and that, in 1941, the carriers limited to special commodities conducted about two-fifths of the total regulated operations. The small common carriers, those operating over irregular routes, and the contract carriers were most frequently restricted as to commodities.[22]

Route and territorial restrictions confine carriers to designated points along the specified routes or in the described territories. Regular-route carriers have been granted points on or near their specified highway routes while irregular-route carriers have been given territories in which operations between points or from points to points may be conducted. The principal geographical limitations disclosed by the BIR sample were those on intermediate points or territories and those on choice of highway routes. Seventy per cent of the regular-route common carriers possessed less than full authority to serve intermediate points; more than one-tenth had no such authority. More than 90 per cent of the irregular-route carriers were limited to radial service; that is, their traffic had to be accepted at, or delivered to, one or more specified points within their territories. Most such carriers had no choice but to operate through points which they could not lawfully serve, "leap frogging" between noncontiguous points or areas, or between noncontiguous points and an area.[23]

Regular-route common carriers are required to follow specific highway routes. This results in circuitous operation and limits competition whenever a direct highway route cannot lawfully be used.[24]

The Commission's own "gateway" restriction requires that services between an old and a newly acquired territory must be performed through points common to the operating authority of both the acquired and acquiring carriers. This prevents an increase in competition but continues circuitous routing of traffic.[25]

The BIR sample also found that about a third of the intercity truckers had return-haul limitations, and almost 10 per cent had no authority to transport traffic on the return trip.[26]

However, the BIR study found that certificates and permits do not specify that the authorized service may be rendered only infrequently, nor do they place specific maximum limitations on the number of

[22] Ibid., pp. 27–44.
[23] Ibid., pp. 76–88.
[24] Ibid., pp. 96–110.
[25] Ibid., pp. 110–117. See map illustrations.
[26] Ibid., pp. 121–133. See also pp. 47–72.

schedules.[27] This reflects the proviso in Sec. 208 (a) (and a similar one in Sec. 209 (b)) prohibiting the placement of limitations on "the right of the carrier to add to his or its equipment and facilities over the routes, between the termini, or within the territory specified in the certificate, as the development of the business and the demands of the public shall require."

The nearest approach to a direct limitation on the frequency of service has come from specification that about three-fifths of the authorized operations be conducted "over irregular routes." The Commission has long differentiated between regular-route and irregular-route service. In the leading *Brady* case, the Commission held that common carriers over irregular routes do not have authority to render a periodical or scheduled service between authorized points in their territories unless such carriers first obtain a new-service certificate on proof of public convenience and necessity, even where no new commodities, points, or territories are involved. This was justified as necessary to protect regular-route common carriers from competition that might adversely affect or destroy regular-route service, to the public detriment.[28]

Another type of restriction, similarly justified, is the "Keystone" restriction in numerous permits. A common form limits authorized contract carrier service to such merchandise as is dealt in by wholesale, retail, and chain grocery and food businesses. Often this limits contract carriers to three shippers or less.[29]

Carriers operating both private and for-hire trucking operations on the "grandfather" dates have been permitted to continue the for-hire operations if conducted continuously thereafter. However, the Commission has frequently held that dual private and for-hire operations instituted or proposed after regulation became effective were not consistent with the public interest—applications of private carriers for contract carrier permits to facilitate return loads have generally been denied. In the *Geraci* case, the Commission explained that such auxiliary for-hire operations "might seriously affect the maintenance of adequate and efficient service by the motor common carriers upon

---

[27] *Ibid.*, p. 156.

[28] *Transportation Activities, Brady Transfer & Storage Co.*, 47 M.C.C. 23 (1947). See also 23 M.C.C. 767 (1940); 34 M.C.C. 731 (1942); and 43 M.C.C. 831 (1944).

[29] *Keystone Transp. Co. Contract Carrier Application*, 19 M.C.C. 475 (1939). See S. Doc. 78, *Federal Regulatory Restrictions*, pp. 160–163. In at least 65 cases in which contract carriers were converted into common carriers under the 1957 amendment redefining contract carriage, the Commission has continued the Keystone-type restriction in certificates. *Wall Street Journal*, March 26, 1963, p. 2.

whom the general public must depend, and by the contract carriers who do not also engage in private carriage." [30]

It is probable that a roughly comparable pattern is in existence today. In its replies to a Senate Small Business Committee questionnaire in 1955, the Commission acknowledged that the same types of restrictions as disclosed by the BIR study were still to be found in operating authorities.[31] Systematic sampling of new-service cases confirms that similar restrictions have been placed in new operating authorities; that authorizations extending service often left "grandfather" restrictions intact; and that many applications to round out operating authority have been denied.

As noted above, the Commission has been comparatively liberal in grants of operating authority to water carriers, both in "grandfather" and in new-service cases. The BIR study found that more than three-fourths of the "grandfather" grants to water carriers through May 1943 authorized commodities generally without any exceptions. Not all new-service applications have been granted, but in general the operating authority restrictions do not fragment commodities and markets as in the case of motor carriers.[32]

Representative decisions indicate that forwarders in existence when regulation became effective usually were granted commodities generally. In 1957 five forwarders had rights to serve virtually the entire United States, several others to serve all points in all but a few states, and the remaining companies to serve wide territories in most instances. Most applications to enter the field or extend operations have been granted, usually with liberal specification of territorial and commodity authority. Since the 1957 amendment, however, a somewhat more restrictive tone has been evidenced.[33]

[30] *Geraci Contract Carrier Application*, 7 M.C.C. 369, 372 (1938). See also 10 M.C.C. 183, 186–187 (1938); 12 M.C.C. 13 (1938); 14 M.C.C. 631 (1939); 28 M.C.C. 205, 211 (1941); and 33 M.C.C. 226, 227–228 (1942).

[31] *ICC Administration of the Motor Carrier Act*, Hearings before the Senate Select Committee on Small Business, 84th Cong., 1st sess., November 30-December 2, 1955, pp. 200–206 and 337–358. See the ICC's *75th Annual Report*, 1961, pp. 9–10 and 59–62; and the *76th Annual Report*, 1962, pp. 63–66, for evidence that the Commission's entry control policies have not changed. See also *73rd Annual Report*, 1959, pp. 48–52; *Competition, Regulation, and the Public Interest in the Motor Carrier Industry*, S. Rep. 1693, 84th Cong., 2d sess., March 19, 1956, pp. 1–15 and 27–29; and *Transportation Act of 1958*, S. Rep. 1647, 85th Cong., 2d sess., June 3, 1958, pp. 12–13. Finally, see the decision in *Ex Parte* No. MC-55, *Motor Common Carriers of Property—Routes and Services*, decided December 4, 1961 (mimeographed).

[32] S. Doc. 78, *Federal Regulatory Restrictions*, pp. 260–261 and 264–265; and decisions in Volume 285 of *Interstate Commerce Commission Reports*.

[33] James C. Nelson, *Controls of Entry into Domestic Surface Transportation under the Interstate Commerce Act*, Washington: U.S. Department of Commerce (multi-lithed), October 1959, pp. 177–203. Summarized in *Rationale of Federal Transportation Policy*, U.S. Department of Commerce, April 1960, pp. 10–19 and 71.

The direct controls of entry enacted in 1920 have largely been used to supervise withdrawal of marginal railway lines and extensions of relatively small segments of line to new industrial and military locations. In 1958, the Commission was granted ultimate control over passenger-train discontinuances because state commissions had delayed or blocked discontinuance of numerous hopelessly unprofitable passenger trains. With good alternatives to rail service available, the Commission has generally granted abandonments and discontinuances if little promise of restoring profitable operations exists.[34]

Consequently, the key issues over entry restrictions on railroads concern their right to diversify. Railroads are free to enter pipeline transport and the exempt areas of trucking. They have fairly easy entry, considering their resources, into regulated trucking, but are almost entirely prohibited entry into water transport. Their regulated motor carrier operations are severely limited.

The typical certificate restrictions on railroads were initially adopted in the *Kansas City S. Transport Co., Inc., Com. Car. Application* case. First, service is limited to that which is auxiliary to, or supplemental of, rail service. Second, no point may be served that is not a station on a rail line. Third, no shipments may be transported wholly by motor vehicle between the so-called designated "key points," usually large traffic-generating points. Fourth, all contractual arrangements between the motor subsidiary and the parent railroad are subject to ICC modification. Fifth, the ICC has reserved the right to impose further restrictions to preserve the supplementary character of rail motor carrier service.[35]

Certain railroads have recently tested whether the Panama Canal Act policy still prevents their control or ownership of competing barge lines. However, the purchase by the Illinois Central and the Southern Pacific of the John I. Hay Company, a profitable Mississippi barge line, was found to threaten "a sharp reduction of, and possibly complete elimination of, competition on the water routes involved."[36] In contrast, the railroads have been tolerably free, except for tariff and

---

[34] *Ibid.*, pp. 208–217. See *Interstate Commerce Commission Activities 1937–1962*, Washington, 1962, pp. 50–56.

[35] 28 M.C.C. 5, 7–11, 25 (1941). See also 42 M.C.C. 74 (1943) and 66 M.C.C. 669 (1956); and *Interstate Commerce Commission Activities 1937–1962*, Washington, 1962, pp. 200–202.

[36] *Illinois Cent. R. R.—Control,—John I. Hay Co.*, decided March 2, 1962 (mimeographed), p. 26.

motor carrier entry restrictions, to engage in and expand trailer-on-flat-car services on their own terms and at reduced rates. This affords them indirect entry into the motor carrier business.[37]

Some Economic Effects of Entry Control of Surface Carriers

Entry controls affect both regulated and unregulated carriers as well as shippers and receivers; and through these groups, the economy as a whole. The effects on carrier groups are diverse, since entry limitations favor the growth and profitability of firms protected from competition and retard the growth and profitability of firms burdensomely restricted. Such effects will be economic only if they either lead to utilization of a smaller aggregate of resources in accomplishing the demanded transport, or yield faster, more flexible, and more dependable service at the same resource costs. If users are to gain, freight rates must ultimately be lower, with services the same or better; alternatively, rates may continue to be the same or higher, with services improved. With lower transport costs and rates, the public gains from improved resource utilization and greater economic development.

An evaluation of economic effects must distinguish between gains to carriers at the expense of shippers and society, and those which ultimately result in contributions to the general economy through lessening the cost of transport or of producing goods. Economic losses of the restricted carriers may be offset by gains by other carriers. However, the protection of established firms from competition does not necessarily create lower costs and improved services. Private profit enhancement by such means may be, but cannot always be assumed to be, compatible with the general public interest.

Restrictions on entry and the scope of carrier operations necessarily modify the market structures in terms of the number and size

---

[37] For examples of motor carrier operating authority restrictions limiting some piggyback operations, see *Gordons Transports, Inc.* v. *Strickland Transportation Co.*, decided October 15, 1962 (mimeographed), pp. 4–12; *Substituted Rail Service-Betw. St. Louis & Kinder, Lake Charles, New Orleans*, decided December 31, 1962 (not to be printed); and the proposed new rules for piggyback service ordered in *Ex Parte* No. 230 (*Substituted Service—Piggyback*, 322 ICC 301, 384, 386–404, 1964). See also George L. Buland and Frederick E. Fuhrman, "Integrated Ownership: The Case for Removing Existing Restrictions on Common Ownership of the Several Forms of Transportation," *The George Washington Law Review*, October 1962, pp.163–166; and Henry P. Knowles, Jr., "A Note on the Debate over Dual Ownership in the Railroad and Trucking Industries," *Proceedings*, Thirty-Sixth Annual Conference, Western Economic Association, August 24–25, 1961, pp. 11–16.

distribution of competing firms and the character of competition and monopoly. If the purpose of entry control is minimization of resource costs, economies of scale or utilization, or both, are almost necessarily implied as the key reasons for reducing the number of competing firms. Because safety and financial responsibility can be achieved by direct regulations which involve neither entry restrictions nor minimum pricing, the effects of entry control on the market structures in transport industries are the most vital considerations in evaluating allocative efficiency.

The huge minimum investments required in the oil pipeline field, and the marked economies of scale and utilization demonstrated in it, have limited the number of firms in that field to one per route, or to not more than four firms for very large markets. Although the divorcement of common carrier pipelines from the oil refining companies has long been a contentious issue, entry regulation has apparently not been needed to obtain a tolerably socially efficient organization, that is natural monopoly, for the oil pipeline industry.[38]

Direct entry control came decades too late to influence the structure of railroading in material respects. The number of roads competing for traffic between pairs of points has changed little since entry control began in 1920. The number of sellers is small, ranging up to six railroads in direct competition or to a few more in market competition. Clearly, railroads illustrate oligopolistic or duopolistic organization between major centers.[39] The huge minimum investments, initial economies of scale, economies of utilization, and limited traffic possibilities have kept the number small.

On the other hand, the rail market structures have been influenced by the antitrust laws, the antipooling provision before 1920, and the Section 5 standards governing ICC approval of acquisitions of control, mergers, and consolidations. The railroad combination movement in progress at the turn of the century was prevented by antitrust decisions from creating regional monopolies.[40] The requirement that consolidation plans under the Transportation Act of 1920 maintain

[38] Leslie Cookenboo, Jr., "Costs of Operating Crude Oil Pipe Lines," *The Rice Institute Pamphlet*, April 1954, pp. 35–113; and *Crude Oil Pipe Lines and Competition in the Oil Industry*, Cambridge, Mass., 1955, pp. 24–32. See also J. L. Burke, "Movement of Commodities by Pipeline," United Nations Conference on the Application of Science and Technology for the Benefit of the Less Developed Areas, November 8, 1962, pp. 3 and 9–10.

[39] John R. Meyer, Merton J. Peck, John Stenason, and Charles Zwick, *The Economics of Competition in the Transportation Industries*, Cambridge, Mass., 1959, pp. 205–211.

[40] Eliot Jones, *Principles of Railway Transportation*, New York, 1929, pp. 327–352.

competitive routes and link weak and strong railroads dampened carrier interest in effectuating consolidations. It remains to be seen what influence the standards of the 1940 Act will have on the present railway merger movement.[41]

Had it not been for the Panama Canal Act prohibitions and the special regulatory restrictions placed on railroad control of motor and air carriers, many railroads would have made wide use of air, motor, and water techniques, as in Canada.[42] Such entry control standards, coupled with antitrust action, have widened competitive elements in transport as a whole.

The market structures within domestic water transport have been only slightly affected by direct entry controls. An important reason for this is that dry bulk and liquid petroleum carriage are exempt from ICC control. Also, the water pattern of entry control has not been highly restrictive. Thus, the present market organization is largely the result of economic and competitive factors.

About forty large lines, including fifteen exempt carriers, are described as operating, among other carriers, on the Mississippi system and Gulf coastal waterways; up to five or six major carriers compete for exempt or regulated traffic on each principal waterway.[43] About eight regulated and thirty-two exempt carriers operate in domestic Great Lakes shipping. Only a few common carriers and a relatively few unregulated exempt bulk and private carriers operate in coastwise and intercoastal trades.[44] Whereas in 1939 there were twelve common carriers and a number of private carriers in intercoastal shipping, seven common carriers have discontinued intercoastal water services since 1953; only Sea-Land was providing regular common carrier service

[41] W. N. Leonard, *Railroad Consolidation under the Transportation Act of 1920*, New York, 1946, pp. 267–286; and *National Transportation Policy*, Senate Committee on Interstate and Foreign Commerce, S. Rep. 445, 87th Cong., 1st sess., June 26, 1961, pp. 249–262. For present-day controversies, especially as concerns the possibility of further economies of scale, see Richard B. Heflebower, "Economic Efficiencies (Rail: a Theoretical Model)," in *Transportation Mergers and Acquisitions*, Evanston, Ill., 1962, pp. 159–173; Kent T. Healy, *The Effects of Scale in the Railroad Industry*, New Haven, May 1961, pp. 2–5; and *Rail Merger Legislation*, Hearings before the Subcommittee on Antitrust and Monopoly, Senate Committee on the Judiciary, 87th Cong., 2d sess., Parts 1 and 2, June 12–July 11, 1962.

[42] Sec. 5(2)(b) of the Interstate Commerce Act and Sec. 408(b) of the Federal Aviation Act of 1958. See D. W. Carr and Associates, "Truck-Rail Competition in Canada," in *Royal Commission on Transportation*, Ottawa, July 1962, Vol. III, pp. 41–43.

[43] *Illinois Cent. R.R.—Control,—John I. Hay Co.*, Appendix I, pp. 28–29 and Appendix "B."

[44] Meyer *et al.*, *Economics of Competition*, pp. 235–238.

in both directions in 1961. Several others provided infrequent inter-coastal sailings as part of round-the-world service or proprietory service for steel products and lumber.[45]

Only in the regulated motor carrier industry have entry controls had truly significant effects on the market structures in transport. There-fore, the effects of entry restrictions will be discussed primarily in terms of the motor carrier case.

Entry control had little effect on the organization of exempt motor transportation.[46] In the exempt areas of private carriage and for-hire trucking of agricultural products, the number of firms competing for the same types of traffic between pairs of points is still determined under free-entry conditions, that is, on the basis of economic factors such as the volume of traffic and the minimum scale for profitable operations. Nevertheless, regulatory policies have some influence on the number of exempt and private carriers, for the high rates often assessed by regulated truckers have increased the incentive to engage in private, exempt, and even unlawful for-hire operations. On the other hand, restrictions preventing private truckers from engaging in aux-iliary for-hire hauling for return loads, and those on trip-leasing of trucks on return trips, limit the feasibility of some private and exempt carriage.[47]

---

[45] *Intercoastal—Any Quantity Class and Commodity Rates*, report recommended by ICC Examiner Jair S. Kaplan, October 30, 1962 (mimeographed), pp. 2–4. See supplemental statement of Morris Forgash in *Amendment to Section 15a, Interstate Commerce Act*, Hearings before the Senate Committee on Commerce on S. 1197, 87th Cong., 1st sess., Part 2, June–August 1961, pp. 807–820 and 919–924.

[46] Compare Ernest W. Williams, Jr., and David W. Bluestone, *Rationale of Federal Transportation Policy*, U.S. Department of Commerce, April 1960, pp. 10–21. Even before federal regulation began in 1935, the need for obtaining the economies of good load factors materially contributed to a reduction in the number of intercity bus lines. However, state certification, beginning about 1921, also contributed. The state commissions typically granted rights to render intrastate service to only one firm per route. Without state rights to serve intrastate passengers, interstate bus lines experience difficulties in maintaining high load factors, low unit costs, and profitable operations. Today, between large cities, there are often only two com-peting intercity bus lines. Typically, the lines of the Greyhound Corporation's nationwide system are in a position of market dominance. Under ICC entry control, Greyhound's position has been consolidated, though to a degree the Com-mission has given encouragement to the efforts of the National Trailways Bus System to establish a competing national system. See Meyer *et al.*, *Economics of Competition*, pp. 222–224; and *Interstate Commerce Commission Activities 1937–1962*, p. 202.

[47] H. Rep. 2425, 84th Cong., 2d sess., June 25, 1956, pp. 2–7; and *Lease and Interchange of Vehicles by Motor Carriers*, 68 M.C.C. 553, 558, 560–61 (1956). See also *National Transportation Policy*, pp. 49–85 and 507–546; and Dudley F. Pegrum, *Transportation: Economics and Public Policy*, Homewood, Ill., 1963, pp. 351–353.

The market structures in exempt for-hire trucking would provide the basis for an instructive comparison of the number and size distribution of firms under free-entry as compared with regulated-entry conditions. Unfortunately, such data are not available.

Even the total number of exempt trucking firms is not definitely known to the ICC. But the Commission has estimated the number of exempt for-hire truckers subject to its safety rules. In *Gray Area of Transportation Operations*, published in June 1960, the Commission estimated the number of such truckers at 30,666.[48] An ICC Commissioner testified in April 1962 that about 37,500 persons were operating about 200,000 vehicles under the exemption for agricultural commodities, although the ICC safety regulations had been served on only 22,820 such carriers.[49] The recent Doyle Report stated that exempt commodities were trucked by more than 9,000 commercial carriers which generally operated large equipment but not a large number of trucks per firm. Their principal operations were described as "subsequent to the initial farm to market movement, between commercial establishments and often for long distances in intercity movement." [50]

The exempt for-hire truckers, which may far outnumber the ICC-regulated truckers, operate in highly competitive markets. As territorial and commodity restrictions do not exist for transport of exempt agricultural commodities, the most likely assumption is that large numbers of firms compete for the traffic between points which have a heavy seasonal or recurrent traffic flow. The small-scale character of exempt trucking operations supports that assumption, as does other evidence in U.S. Department of Agriculture studies. According to this evidence, exempt for-hire truckers most frequently compete with other exempt carriers, and rates for exempt hauling are based on demand and supply conditions rather than on individual-carrier price policy or on agreements among carriers.[51] A USDA study of the role of truck brokers in the movement of exempt agricultural commodities

[48] Bureau of Transport Economics and Statistics, Statement No. 6010, p. 81.
[49] *Control of Illegal Interstate Motor Carrier Transportation*, Hearings before the Surface Transportation Subcommittee, Senate Committee on Commerce, in S. 2560 and S. 2764, 87th Cong., 2d sess., February and April 1962, pp. 99 and 108.
[50] *National Transportation Policy*, pp. 511 and 517.
[51] C. P. Schumaier, "Characteristics of Agriculturally Exempt Motor Carriers," *Conference on Private and Unregulated Transportation*, The Transportation Center, Northwestern University, October 29–30, 1962, pp. 3–4 and 8–11; and *The Role of Truck Brokers in the Movement of Exempt Agricultural Commodities*, U.S. Department of Agriculture, Marketing Research Report No. 525, February 1962, pp. 8 and 20–27.

found that, on the average, each truck broker booked loads for 118 truckers, the regional averages varying from 94 in Florida to 160 in the North Atlantic region.[52] This high average per broker suggests that a large number of carriers are in competition at each origination for volume traffic to principal destinations.

A recent USDA study, based on a sample of 1,514 exempt for-hire truckers hauling agricultural commodities (27 per cent of the 5,584 firms sent questionaires), reveals some significant indications of a many-firm market structure. Forty per cent, or 607 firms, reported operations with only a straight truck, or with one tractor-trailer rig, or with one of each of these vehicle types—the average firm had about 2.2 tractors and 2.5 semi-trailers. A number of exempt truckers reported operating several straight trucks or several tractor-trailer rigs, but only thirteen firms reported ten or more straight trucks per firm and only fifty and fifty-one firms reported 10 or more tractors and 10 or more semi-trailers per firm, respectively. The tonnage carried was concentrated in grain, livestock, milk and cream, vegetables, and fruits and berries.[53]

It can be concluded that the exempt trucking markets almost certainly conform to the large-numbers case, with an absence of dominant firms exercising price leadership but with the vigorous competition in rates characteristic of tramp shipping.

In sharp contrast to the many-firm and small-scale characteristics of exempt trucking under free-entry conditions, the market structures of regulated trucking have evidenced a marked reduction in the total number of carriers; a rapid growth of very large trucking firms; a decline in the number of competing regulated truckers to a small number in many markets (although a large number continues to exist in some); a substitution of rate bureau and group action for individual action and competitive determination of rates; and widespread substitution of service competition for rate competition. In short, in the transport of regulated commodities, the market structures have been substantially modified by entry control.

A study by the National Resources Planning Board of the first six years of federal motor carrier regulation found that entry and minimum rate controls had resulted in fewer interstate trucking firms, larger companies, and the organization of rate bureaus from the beginning.

---

[52] *Ibid.*, p. 13.
[53] Schumaier, *Characteristics*, p. 2; and *For-Hire Motor Carriers Hauling Exempt Agricultural Commodities*, U.S. Department of Agriculture, Marketing Research Report No. 585, January 1963, pp. 2–3, 6–10 and 13.

The strong influence of the NRA and ICC rate regulations was evident in the organization of more than twenty-five motor rate bureaus within a few months after regulation became effective in 1935. Such organization for concerted action, supported by ICC rate suspensions and minimum rate orders, reduced the independence of individual firms in making rates; resulted in higher, more stable, and more uniform rates; and tended to groove service into rigid molds.[54]

The total number of ICC-regulated freight motor carriers has not grown with the marked increases in total traffic and revenues. On the contrary, it has fallen from an estimated 26,167 in 1939 to 17,502 in 1959.[55] In contrast, the intercity ton-miles carried by Class I, II and III intercity motor carriers under the ICC rose from 19.6 billion in 1939 to 101.4 billion in 1959; and between 1939 and 1961, the total estimated freight revenues of Class I, II and III regulated truckers rose from $792.2 million to almost $7.5 billion.[56] Unless the economies of scale would have been sufficiently persuasive to have brought about a similar reduction in the number of firms under free-entry conditions, a wholly unlikely assumption in view of the economic characteristics of the trucking industry, the decrease in the number of truckers must largely be attributed to entry control.

A more significant measure of market structure is the change in the number of regulated truckers who divide the traffic between significant pairs of points. In many markets, the number of effectively competing certificated truckers has been drastically lowered by drop-outs, mergers, and numerous denials of new entries and extended services.[57] However,

[54] James C. Nelson, "New Concepts in Transportation Regulation," *Transportation and National Policy*, Washington, May 1942, pp. 216–32.

[55] C. S. Morgan, E. V. Breitenbach, and J. O. Riley, "The Motor Transport Industry," *Transportation and National Policy*, pp. 403–404; ICC, *73d Annual Report*, 1959, p. 57, and *76th Annual Report*, 1962, p. 75. In 1960, there were 14,879 motor carriers of property included in the ICC's statistics for such carriers—1,066 Class I carriers, 2,035 Class II carriers, and 11,778 Class III carriers. See ICC Statements No. Q-800, Year 1961; No. Q-850X, Year 1961; and No. 6203, June 1962. This may indicate an even larger drop in the number of ICC-regulated motor carriers since 1939—as do the data in *1962 American Trucking Trends*, American Trucking Associations, Inc., p. 13. But see Allan C. Flott's apparent understatement in *Transportation Mergers and Acquisitions*, p. 28.

[56] ICC, Bureau of Transport Economics and Statistics, *Intercity Ton-Miles 1939–1959*, Statement No. 6103, April 1961, p. 17; Statement No. 531, January 1953, p. 4; and *Transport Economics*, January 1963, p. 2.

[57] *Interstate Commerce Commission Activities 1937–1962*, pp. 26 and 199; and *ICC Administration of the Motor Carrier Act*, pp. 327–330 and 501. On the basis of samples of new service cases assigned in 1947 and 1953, the ICC reported in the latter source that 46.8 per cent of the applications for certificates and permits had been granted, the remainder having been denied, dismissed or withdrawn.

until the Commission's long-announced inventory of motor carrier operating authorities is effectively operating, only fragmentary data on the number of firms in each market will be available. These data come from field explorations, application and rate cases, and motor carrier directories.[58]

A considerable number of regulated truckers still operate on dense traffic routes between large, relatively close population centers. For example, David Axelrod found that between twenty-five and thirty-nine motor carriers of general commodities operated daily in 1961 between Chicago and such cities as Detroit, St. Louis, Milwaukee, Indianapolis, Cincinnati, and Minneapolis and St. Paul.[59] On the other hand, there are numerous light-density routes that are served by only two or three regulated carriers having like authorizations, or by one carrier in some instances.[60] Even on many routes generating fairly dense traffic flows, the number of general commodity motor carriers authorized to give single-line service varies from two or three up to six or ten common carriers.

Only about a dozen motor carriers of general commodities have been authorized to render single-line service on the regular long-haul transcontinental routes, and the numbers authorized between specific pairs of terminal cities are fewer. In 1963, the number of Class I motor common carriers authorized to transport general commodities in single-line service between Seattle or Portland and Chicago was two over direct routes and four over direct and circuitous routes; between San Francisco and Chicago, five over direct routes and seven over direct and circuitous routes; between Los Angeles and Chicago, six over direct routes and nine over direct and circuitous routes; between Seattle or Portland and Minneapolis-St. Paul, three over direct routes; and between Los Angeles and New York, two over direct routes and three over direct and circuitous routes (one of these, Navajo Freight Lines, Inc., through a controlled carrier beyond Chicago). Some additional general commodity motor carriers, such as Garrett Freight-lines, Inc. and the Interstate System, provide through trailer or two- or multiple-line interchange service between transcontinental centers. The single-line transcontinental carriers, for example, Consolidated Freightways, Inc. and Pacific Intermountain Express Co., are among the largest trucking firms in the nation, and have registered rapid growth through mergers as well as additional traffic. Thus, a small

[58] *67th Annual Report*, 1953, pp. 59–60; *70th Annual Report*, 1956, p. 71; *71st Annual Report*, 1957, p. 47; *76th Annual Report*, 1962, p. 76; and *Interstate Commerce Commission Activities 1937–1962*, p. 252.

[59] *Transportation Mergers and Acquisitions*, pp. 110–111.

[60] *ICC Administration of the Motor Carrier Act*, pp. 189–190.

number of large-size carriers characterizes transcontinental market structures, with even fewer carriers authorized to render specialized service in liquid or dry bulk commodities.

The available data indicate, too, that only a few carriers are authorized to haul general commodities in single-line service over Pacific Coast and Intermountain routes. The number of regulated carriers competing intramodally in particular markets in 1963 was no greater than about ten. Thus, between Portland and the major California cities, there were six such motor carriers authorized to serve over direct routes and seven, over direct and indirect routes (one, Pacific Motor Trucking Co., is a Southern Pacific subsidiary); between Seattle and Tacoma and major California cities, four carriers by direct routes and five by direct and indirect routes; between Salt Lake City and the major California cities, six carriers by direct routes and seven by indirect routes; between Portland and Southern Idaho and Utah cities, four carriers over direct routes; and between Seattle and Portland, ten carriers over direct routes.[61]

Entry control has contributed to a marked increase in the size of many regulated truckers. In 1939, the largest carrier had revenues of $6.6 million; and only fifty-nine carriers had revenues in excess of one million dollars. By 1960 and 1961, there were about 965 regulated truckers engaged in intercity service with revenues of one million dollars or more—they accounted for 67.2 and 66.2 per cent of the total revenues of Class I, II, and III regulated truckers in those years, respectively. In 1961, Consolidated Freightways Corp., the largest regulated trucker, had revenue of $86.8 million; and among the 100 largest involved as acquiring carriers in unifications with other regulated truckers were thirty-three firms having revenues in excess of $10 million, and thirteen firms with revenues in excess of $20 million each.[62] In 1961, there were 181 Class I common carriers of general commodities having revenues in excess of $5 million, compared with 154 such large carriers in 1959; of the 1961 group, twenty-three had revenues of more than $20 million and 86 had revenues of $10 million or more.[63]

[61] See my testimony in the *Western Pacific Control Case*, ICC Finance Docket Nos. 21334–21335, Exhibit No. 136, July 31, 1961, pp. 7–14.

[62] ICC, *76th Annual Report*, 1962, pp. 27, 221, and 230–231. Tables showing participation of the 100 largest motor carriers of property have been included in all ICC annual reports, beginning with the 1958 issue. For 1939, see *Transportation and National Policy*, pp. 210 and 403.

[63] John W. Jalonen, *Financial Position of the Motor Carrier Industry for 1961*, American Trucking Associations, Inc., Washington, pp. 20–21 and 31. See Kent T. Healy, "The Merger Movement in Transportation," *American Economic Review*, May 1962, pp. 436 and 441.

Whether the degree of concentration in the trucking industry under regulated-entry conditions has become serious is a matter of some dispute.[64] Nevertheless, the evidence at hand indicates that concentration has been growing steadily as the combined result of restricted entries and the many mergers approved by the Commission. A large number of the mergers involved regulated carriers from the 100 largest.[65]

In a study published by the Senate Small Business Committee in *Trucking Mergers and Concentration*, Professors Walter Adams and James B. Hendry found that under the merger policies of the ICC the extent of concentration in the regulated trucking industries had become disturbing by 1956. Their data revealed that the largest Class I common motor carrier of general freight accounted for 1.84 per cent of the 1955 revenues of carriers of that class; and that the 100 largest common carrier truckers accounted for 44.62 per cent of the 1955 revenues of Class I regulated truckers of general freight (25.49 per cent of the 1954 revenues of all Class I, II, and III regulated truckers). Greater concentration was found in three of the groups of specialized common carriers—in household goods carriage, the four largest common carriers accounted for 49.1 per cent of the 1955 revenues of Class I household goods truckers; in automobile hauling, the twenty-five largest truckers earned 70.3 per cent of the 1955 revenues of the Class I automobile carriers; and in liquid petroleum carriage, the twenty-five largest truckers had 51.2 per cent of the 1955 revenues earned by Class I petroleum carriers.[66]

The Commission has not brought the Adams-Hendry series on concentration up to date, but it has reported some additional data in

[64] This is partly because of lack of data on the number and size distribution of firms in each market. Occasionally, data relating to the dominance of particular firms in specific markets can be found in ICC decisions, such as, for example, in *Substituted Rail Service between Jackson, Miss., and New Orleans, La.*, decided December 27, 1962 (mimeographed), pp. 5–7. Here, there were five motor common carriers authorized to transport general commodities between St. Louis and Jackson and New Orleans, but the tonnage data given for shipments by each firm between those points were for varying periods, thus not designed to reveal dominance. The proposed substituted trailer-on-flat-car service, by Dixie Highway Express, Inc., between those points was found unlawful because Dixie's highway routes were circuitous compared with those of motor competitors and of the Illinois Central and "Dixie would be in a position to compete for traffic which it cannot handle over its authorized routes as economically as can its competitors."

[65] *Interstate Commerce Commission Activities 1937–1962*, pp. 117, 150–153, 197–200, and 202–203.

[66] *Trucking Mergers and Concentration*, Hearings before the Senate Select Committee on Small Business, 85th Cong., 1st sess., July 1957, pp. 240, 242, 250, 252, 255, and 320.

its recent annual reports. A summary of the data on the percentage distribution of carriers and revenues, by revenue groups, is given in Table 1.

The above data indicate clearly that the growing concentration revealed in the Adams-Hendry study continued after 1955. Taken in conjunction with the small numbers of regulated truckers competing on many routes and the tremendous scale achieved by some firms, the data warrant an expectation that in many markets a structure now exists conducive to an oligopolistic pattern of action on rates.[67]

Whether or not the surviving regulated truckers on each route would engage in intramodal price competition under unregulated conditions, it seems certain that entry control has encouraged a re-duction in the number of firms in many highly fragmented markets and in those having dense traffic flows. The dominance of very large firms obviously has facilitated concerted action on rates, now universal under regulated conditions.

TABLE 1

DEGREE OF CONCENTRATION IN REGULATED TRUCKING, 1957-59

Regulated Carriers, by Revenue Group (million dollars)	Per Cent of Carriers			Per Cent of Revenues		
	1957	1958	1959	1957	1958	1959
General commodity carriers:						
Over 10	0.97	1.11	1.40	32.84	34.71	39.48
5-10	1.35	1.31	1.76	17.09	15.72	16.77
Total	2.32	2.42	3.16	49.93	50.43	56.25
Over 1	9.64	10.32	11.44	79.52	80.23	82.50
Household goods carriers:						
Over 10	0.32	0.36	0.40	39.12	41.78	41.48
5-10	0.32	0.36	0.59	9.41	10.57	15.64
Total	0.64	0.72	0.99	48.53	52.35	57.12
Over 1	2.28	2.37	2.77	64.26	67.71	70.67
Special commodity carriers:						
Over 10	0.15	0.21	0.32	6.94	10.88	14.69
5-10	0.55	0.46	0.61	12.93	10.14	11.22
Total	0.70	0.67	0.93	19.87	21.02	25.91
Over 1	6.03	6.05	7.23	55.83	56.86	61.02

Source: *75th Annual Report of the Interstate Commerce Commission*, Fiscal Year 1961, p. 79.

[67] Robert A. Nelson, "The Economic Structure of the Highway Carrier Industry in New England," in *Public Transportation for New England*, The New England Governors' Conference, November 1957, pp. 40–41. See also W. David Maxwell, "The Regulation of Motor-Carrier Rates by the Interstate Commerce Commission," *Land Economics*, February 1960, pp. 79–91.

In addition, entry control has supported the use of government power to curtail the intramodal rate competition not curbed by rate bureau procedures and agreements. With fewer and larger firms, the rate suspension and minimum rate procedures can be utilized more effectively to thwart independent action. It seems pertinent that the number of rate adjustments filed with the ICC which were protested has risen markedly from 567 in 1946 to 5,170 in 1962. The number of the protested rate adjustments involving rate decreases, i.e., protests by carriers against rate competition, has risen even more rapidly—from 227 in 1946 to 4,712 in 1962, or from 40 per cent to more than 90 per cent of the total. In recent years, almost 50 per cent of the protested rate agreements have been suspended by the ICC.[68] A sample study of formal ICC decisions during 1955 revealed that 70.9 per cent of the suspended rate reductions had been disapproved by the ICC.[69] Entry control has been a factor in elimination of intramodal rate competition, such as is characteristic of exempt trucking.

Whether effects of entry control on the market structure, noted above, promote or obstruct the general interest depends on the effects of fewer and large-scale firms on unit costs and on the availability and quality of service. A key aspect is whether the trucking industry is subject to economies of scale. If the very large regulated firms that have emerged have yielded marked economies of scale or utilization and/or distinctly improved services, there would be little reason to object to the trends, provided regulation, or the remaining intramodal and intermodal competition, had been effective in passing on such economies to consumers. Even so, attention would have to be given to the cost-increasing effects of many certificate and permit restrictions and of the processes for administration of regulation. But in the absence of substantial economies of scale or utilization, not attainable under free-entry conditions, the entire economic case for employing entry control to stimulate oligopoly or duopoly organization would have to rest on the possibilities for improved services.

Although rational limitation of the number of firms to encourage large-scale trucking depends on specific knowledge of cost behavior, the Commission has never published a study designed to throw real light on the economies of scale in trucking. When the Senate Small

---

[68] James C. Nelson, *Railroad Transportation and Public Policy*, Washington, 1959, p. 140; and ICC, *76th Annual Report*, 1962, pp. 42–43.

[69] James C. Nelson, *Railroad Transportation*, p. 142. See *ICC Administration of the Motor Carrier Act*, pp. 360–361, for the Commission's admission that entry limitation is indispensable to regulation of minimum rates.

Business Committee requested such information in 1955, the Commission was unable to report data other than on operating ratios by size of trucking firms. The data submitted for Class I intercity motor carriers of general commodities showed somewhat more favorable operating ratios for groups of carriers with the larger revenues. Pressed to comment on whether those data indicated that only large truckers can be efficient, Commissioner Mitchell testified in the negative and agreed that the lower operating ratios and higher profitability of some large firms often reflect factors other than scale economies, such as operations over good routes, participation in hauling profitable commodities, and the amount of competition.[70]

After reviewing the ICC motor carrier cost studies, John R. Meyer and his associates concluded that the "observable economies of scale in the trucking industry are ... probably a function of the intensity to which a given geographical route pattern is utilized and not of the total volume of the firm"; and that such "economies of scale in a high traffic density are equally available to the absolutely large and small firm." [71] They found in recent studies by other economists that the differences in unit costs between trucking firms have largely been explained by variations in length of average haul, and concluded on the basis of all available evidence that "in the trucking industry the small and large firms are on a cost parity." [72]

The available data, therefore, do not necessarily suggest lower unit costs and rates for the public. Thus, except on routes of extremely light traffic, economies of scale and utilization do not provide a firm basis for monopoly or oligopoly organization. On the other hand, since there are no, or only slight, diseconomies of scale in trucking, an industry organization with some or all large firms would not necessarily bring higher unit costs but might yield service improvements.[73] These might reduce the cost of agricultural, manufacturing, or marketing processes or yield service qualities of value in themselves. But if higher unit costs

[70] *Ibid.*, p. 195. Dr. Charles S. Morgan, long the Commission's Chief Carrier Research Analyst, inferentially drew attention to the Commission's lack of information on the economies of scale and stated that an "area which calls for searching analysis is the increasing concentration of regulated motor transportation into the hands of a relatively limited number of large carriers." See "The Function of Research in a Regulatory Agency," *ICC Practitioners' Journal*, May 1957, p. 833.

[71] Meyer *et al.*, *Economics of Competition*, p. 88.

[72] *Ibid.*, pp. 95 and 97. See Merrill J. Roberts, "Some Aspects of Motor Carrier Costs: Firm Size, Efficiency, and Financial Health," *Land Economics*, August 1956, pp. 230–236; and Healy, "The Merger Movement in Transportation," p. 441.

[73] George W. Wilson, "Current Criticisms of the Interstate Commerce Commission," *Current Economic Comment*, August 1959, pp. 14–15.

are imposed through emphasis on service competition, or if the total costs of regulation are significant, policies giving encouragement to large firms might have adverse economic effects even though diseconomies of scale were absent.

Only fragmentary information is available on the additional costs imposed by entry control on the numerous, highly restricted truckers.[74] However, the aim of promoting efficient operations has always been distinctly secondary to that of protecting the existing carriers in the Commission's entry cases. Regulatory emphasis has been on fostering greater profitability, more stability in rates and services, and less "destructive" competition. The Commission has largely ignored the cost-increasing effects of commodity authorizations insufficient for a return haul and of route authorizations forbidding use of direct routes.

The BIR study found that restrictions in certificates and permits of motor carriers had created large amounts of unnecessary empty mileage, additional mileage over circuitous routes, and idle truck time.[75] A more recent study sought to ascertain the economic effects of certificate restrictions on regulated motor carriers in New England. The carriers reported on the average that 17.2 per cent of total miles operated were empty in 1954; and that their average load factor was 60.5 per cent in intercity operation. The great majority indicated that their operations would be more efficient if their certificates were broadened.[76] The Senate Committee on Small Business reported several cases of wasteful operations from certificate restrictions that might have been avoided if alternate route applications had not been denied because they would increase competition, or if return-haul restrictions had not been placed on operating authorities.[77] In its proceeding, Ex Parte No. MC-55, the Commission invited comments from carriers and other parties on five proposals to relax restrictions on routes, gateways, radial points, and regularity of service for irregular-route carriers. A number of carriers replied that such restrictions caused poor service, wasteful additional mileage, empty mileage on return hauls, and partial loads, all of which contributed to higher costs of operation. For example,

[74] For example, in *The Maryland Transportation Company Extension—Specified Commodities*, decided June 19, 1959 (mimeographed, p. 4), elimination of the Frederick, Maryland gateway would have saved the applicant carrier 53.4 miles on each one-way trip, or $29.93 per trip. The application was denied, although 732 truckloads were transported between September 1957 and February 1958.

[75] S. Doc. 78, pp. 32–33, 70–72, 108–110, 116–117, 133–145, 153–156, 162–163, and 281–283.

[76] Robert A. Nelson, "Economic Structure," pp. 31–32.

[77] *ICC Administration of the Motor Carrier Act*, pp. 458–459, 461, and 507–508; and S. Rep. 1693, pp. 3–9 and 30.

the Pacific Eastern Refrigerated Lines, Inc., of Mount Vernon, Wash., submitted a tabulation showing that from 35 to 470 excess miles were required on each trip from Midwestern cities to Seattle, San Francisco, or Los Angeles because circuitous operations through Rapid City, South Dakota, were necessary under the carrier's operating authority.[78]

The Senate Small Business Committee in 1955 sought information from the Commission on the manner in which commodity, route, gateway, return-haul, service, and other restrictions affect operating efficiency and whether they result in lower rates to the public. Except for statements that limiting the number of carriers avoids "cutthroat and destructive competition" and "spreading of traffic too thin for economic operation," the Commission reported uniformly to the Committee that it had "no figures available as a basis for answering those questions."[79] Four years later, the Commission reported to the Department of Commerce that it still had no analyses of the effects of certificate restrictions on the cost and adequacy of service by motor and other types of carriers.[80] Neither Examiner Frank R. Saltzman nor Division 1 referred in specific terms to the wasteful mileage and other cost-raising effects of certificate restrictions. Instead, their reports in *Ex Parte* No. MC-55 emphasized the legal and protective aspects of that proceeding.[81]

Empty mileage from insufficient commodity or return-haul authority, added mileage from route and gateway restrictions involving circuitous routes, and idle truck time occasioned by commodity and class-of-shipper restrictions obviously increase excess capacity and raise unit costs. This is not true, however, where no return flow of traffic takes place, or when trucks must move circuitously or partially loaded for service reasons, or when seasonal traffic peaks necessitate more equipment than can be used fully at all times. Meyer and his associates estimated that only about 50 per cent of the physical capacity of trucking equipment is utilized.[82] Much of this unused capacity, because of the factors mentioned, cannot be considered an inefficient result either of competitive conditions or of entry restrictions. But as a recent Highway

[78] Statement filed by John S. Wallace, Office Manager, April 10, 1959.
[79] *ICC Administration of the Motor Carrier Act*, pp. 170–172, 205, 336–337, 339, and 343–345.
[80] Letter of September 11, 1959, from Robert J. Test, Acting Secretary, ICC, replying to inquiries submitted by me as Consultant to the Under Secretary of Commerce for Transportation, by letter of September 3, 1959.
[81] *Motor Common Carriers of Property—Routes and Service*, proposed report by Examiner Frank R. Saltzman, December 1959 (mimeographed), pp. 3–19; decision by Division 1, December 4, 1961 (mimeographed), pp. 12–22.
[82] Meyer *et al.*, *Economics of Competition*, p. 216.

Research Board study has shown, payload ton-mile cost, when a freight vehicle is empty on its return trip, "is closely equivalent to twice the unit payload ton-mile cost when an equivalent vehicle is loaded in both directions." Certificate restrictions creating the described effects obviously do elevate the unit costs and require a higher rate level to maintain services by restricted carriers over the long run.[83]

Such additional costs are socially wasteful unless more than offset by the economies of scale achieved by the less restricted carriers that become large firms, or by the economies of utilization achieved by such firms because of restrictions on competitors. As economies of scale do not appear promising, attention must be directed to whether restricted entry provides sufficiently higher average loads and average mileage per vehicle to yield cost reductions large enough to offset the added costs imposed on the highly restricted firms.

The HRB study, *Line-Haul Trucking Costs in Relation to Vehicle Gross Weights*, suggests that common carriers more frequently have full loads in both directions, and less frequently have wholly empty loads on return, than the private, exempt for-hire, or contract carriers. Thus, on the basis of a sample of 23,610 line-haul loadings in reports from 611 highway freight carriers involving 23,384 trailer combinations, 52.4 per cent of the loadings by common carriers were in connection with trips having full loads in both directions, while 7.9, 7.3, and 5.2 per cent of those by contract, private, and exempt carriers, respectively, were in that category. Only 13.9 per cent of the common carrier loadings were in connection with trips full in one direction and empty on return, whereas 57, 53.8, and 50 per cent of those of private, contract, and exempt carriers were in that category. On the other hand, the exempt carriers achieved the highest average annual mileage by trailer combinations (73,300 miles compared with 64,000 for common carriers, 59,000 for private carriers, and 46,700 for contract carriers). Likewise, the exempt carriers far more frequently operated their vehicles seven days per week than the other classes (77.8 per cent versus 26.6, 15.4, and 14.6 per cent of the common, contract, and private carriers, respectively).[84] By comparing a sample of twenty-five exempt carriers with 134 Class I and II regulated common carriers in the Middle Atlantic region, C. P. Schumaier found that the exempt carriers had an average load of about nine tons per round trip compared

[83] *Line-Haul Trucking Costs in Relation to Vehicle Gross Weights*, Highway Research Board Bulletin 301, 1961, p. 83; and Schumaier, *Characteristics*, p. 7. See supplemental statement of Morris Forgash, *Amendment to Section 15a, Interstate Commerce Act*, pp. 803–806 and 928.

[84] Bulletin 301, pp. 114 and 119.

with 10.1 tons for the regulated carriers. Applying the nine-ton average load to the line-haul costs per vehicle-mile of the regulated group yielded average costs of 43.8 mills per ton-mile, or a cost level of 4.5 mills, or about 11 per cent higher than the average costs for that group at the actual average load of 10.1 tons.[85]

The fragmentary data cited do not show whether the total economies of utilization attained by regulated carriers having adequate authorizations fully offset the additional costs forced on the more numerous highly restricted carriers. They refer to exempt and private carriers which are largely limited to exempt agricultural commodities for back-haul opportunities.[86] The higher percentage of two-way loads and the higher average loads of regulated common carriers compared with exempt carriers suggest that the regulated common carriers probably do attain at least modest cost economies from higher load factors, owing in part to the restrictions placed on their actual or potential competitors. On very low-density routes (i.e., with minimal trucking schedules) economies of utilization may justify limiting the number of firms or the operations of existing firms.[87] However, evidence of offsetting utilization economies due to certificate restrictions is hardly strong enough to validate the existing pattern of regulatory restrictions; nor can it be assumed that this pattern achieves lower total operating costs for all regulated and unregulated trucking services.

In contrast to entry control in Great Britain, the ICC type limits the number of regulated motor carriers and the scope of their operations rather than the total supply of truck equipment units in relation to the total demand for them. Any regulated motor carrier can add or subtract from the pool of truck and truck combinations which it maintains at will. Under such a scheme of entry control, and through regulated minimum rates which are often set high relative to costs and on a parity with rail value-of-service rates, the regulated motor carriers are pressed by market forces to engage in costly service competition. This is because intramodal rate cutting by certificated carriers as a competitive means of dividing traffic efficiently is greatly restrained by rate bureau procedures, rate suspensions, and minimum rate orders.

[85] Schumaier, *Characteristics*, p. 7. See *Costs of Operating Exempt For-Hire Motor Carriers of Agricultural Commodities*, U.S. Department of Agriculture, ERS-109, February 1963.

[86] Schumaier, *Characteristics*, p. 5. USDA interviews during 1962 indicated that only about 20 per cent of the exempt truckers engaged in any trip leasing for backloads.

[87] Meyer *et al.*, *Economics of Competition*, p. 221; Robert A. Nelson, "Economic Structure," p. 40.

Adding to the schedules offered is one means of service competition, especially in local and short-haul operations. But this decreases the average load and raises the unit cost of service. Excessive solicitation, another means of service competition, also raises the cost of service. C. P. Schumaier found that the line-haul costs per vehicle-mile of exempt carriers, for a gross vehicle weight of 60,000 pounds, were "very considerably below that for all carriers computed by the Highway Research Board . . . and for Class I and II common carriers in the Middle Atlantic region computed by the cost finding section of the Interstate Commerce Commission." [88]   Also, line-haul payload ton-mile costs at similar percentages of loaded mileages were some 10 per cent lower for exempt carriers than for the predominantly common carriers in the HRB study; they were about 30 per cent lower than comparable ICC estimates for the regulated common carriers of general freight in the Middle Atlantic region, with total costs of exempt trucks well below the line-haul costs of the common carriers.[89]

Although the reasons for such cost differences could not all be documented, Schumaier noted that the additional costs of the common carriers for collection, terminal, and delivery operations not ordinarily performed by exempt carriers, had not been included in the comparison of line-haul costs. Among the factors cited for lower costs of exempt carriers were the payment of drivers on a commission, or share-of-revenues, basis rather than on a time and mileage basis; the minimum need for terminals, garages, and office buildings; and the considerably reduced need for administrative and sales overhead, because exempt carriers use brokers rather than salesmen and advertising, concentrate on full-load operations, and eliminate the need to file tariffs and to obtain operating authority.[90]

In addition to the cost-increasing effects for many carriers of certificate and permit restrictions, regulatory limitations on back hauls, and the emphasis on service competition in regulated markets, there are probably enormous direct and indirect administrative costs of special economic regulation. These must be set against the modest load factor economies which common carriers of general commodities, having adequate operating authorizations, probably attain in part as a result of entry restrictions. Comprehensive estimates of such costs, including both direct expenditures by the regulatory body and the expenditures by carriers and shippers for preparing and presenting

[88] Schumaier, *Characteristics*, p. 6.
[89] *Ibid.*, pp. 7–8.
[90] *Ibid.*, p. 8.

evidence before regulatory bodies and the courts, appear generally to have been ignored.[91]

In the 1955 hearings before the Senate Small Business Committee, representatives of the Commission acknowledged that the costs associated with regulation do increase the cost of transport, particularly in the case of motor carrier regulation which accounted for more than 40 per cent of the Commission's work.[92] This cost increase was regarded as a price to be paid for the benefits of regulation. The $22.6 million appropriated to the Commission for fiscal 1963 is only a small fraction of the total expenditure. The parties pay for participation in cases, for legal fees, for purchases of operating rights having monopoly value only because of entry restrictions, and for protective activities connected with regulation.[93]

The costs of regulation can only be illustrated. The Bee Line Express Co. of Birmingham, Alabama, a small carrier specializing in service to small towns, spent approximately $1,500 for an application in which the Commission granted limited authority to serve Albertville, Alabama (population, 5,037) but declined to approve service to Boaz, Alabama (population, 3,078). The Shipley Transfer Co., of Baltimore, spent $9,000 in attorney fees to process its applications for operating authority in liquid latex. The company did not obtain satisfactory grants despite strong shipper support. The Yeary Transfer Company's estimated litigation expense to safeguard its rights under an agricultural exemption amounted to between $15,000 and $20,000. A study of merger applications approved in Volumes 57 and 59 of *Motor Carrier Cases* found that the average price paid for operating rights by the largest group of motor carriers was $45,852—that paid by other carriers was $12,157.[94] Such costs rest heaviest on the small carriers.

Unless load-factor economies for some carriers, because of entry restrictions on other carriers, are more than offset by the costs attributable to service competition under regulated entry and by the regulatory costs of protection from competition, it would appear reasonable to expect that the rates of regulated carriers, at least of large common carriers of general freight, would be lower than those of the exempt for-hire carriers and lower than the costs of private trucking. But the available data point precisely to an opposite conclusion.

[91] James M. Landis, *Report on Regulatory Agencies to the President-Elect*, 86th Cong., 2d sess., December 1960, pp. 9–11.

[92] *ICC Administration of the Motor Carrier Act*, pp. 96, 158, 210, and 325.

[93] ICC, *76th Annual Report*, 1962, p. 6.

[94] *ICC Administration of the Motor Carrier Act*, pp. 58–62, 92–94, and 97–102.

The removal of agricultural products from entry and minimum rate control has resulted in a sharp reduction in rates because new trucking entries occurred; existing firms shifted to hauling the freed commodities; regulated carriers met the rate competition of exempt carriers; and rates again were fixed by demand and supply forces rather than by administered pricing. The USDA found that truck rates charged by carriers during 1956–57—the first years of free-entry—were approximately 33 per cent below the 1952 rates on fresh poultry, and 36 per cent below the 1955 rates on frozen poultry.[95] Truck rates on frozen fruits and vegetables during 1957 ranged from 11 to 29 per cent below the regulated rates in 1955.[96] Another USDA study reported that rates on exempt agricultural commodities had remained relatively stable during the last decade while rates on regulated commodities had gradually risen; and that despite lower exempt rates, sufficient capital investment had occurred to provide growing capacity and modern equipment for exempt trucking.[97] A follow-up study revealed that freight rates on frozen fruits and vegetables since August 1958, when those commodities were again placed under regulation, had changed notably, with increases predominating.[98]

The lower rates under free-entry conditions do not necessarily indicate that the costs of service competition and regulatory processes completely offset the utilization economies which some regulated carriers obtain. They may reflect lower labor standards and lower labor earnings under exempt carriage, or an incentive compensation system for drivers of exempt trucks that lowers operating and maintenance costs. Very likely, too, monopoly pricing under rate agreements and sympathetic minimum rate regulation accounts for part, or possibly most, of the differentials in rates above those in free-entry markets. To the extent this is true, regulation must be ineffective compared with free competition in passing on utilization economies to the public. In any case, evidence is scarce to support an assumption that entry restrictions have netted the public a better deal in terms of rates. Although the USDA findings involved limited commodities and the

[95] *Interstate Trucking of Fresh and Frozen Poultry under Agricultural Exemption*, Marketing Research Report No. 224, March 1958, pp. 1, 3–4, and 67–78.

[96] *Interstate Trucking of Frozen Fruits and Vegetables under Agricultural Exemption*, Marketing Research Report No. 316, March 1959, pp. 1, 3–4, and 50–65.

[97] *The Role of Truck Brokers in the Movement of Exempt Agricultural Commodities*, p. 23. See Thomas C. Campbell, "Agricultural Exemptions from Motor Carrier Regulation," *Land Economics*, February 1960, pp. 14–25.

[98] *Supplement to Interstate Trucking of Frozen Fruits and Vegetables under Agricultural Exemption*, Supplement to Marketing Research Report No. 316, July 1961, p. 3.

deregulation effects pertained to relatively short periods, the restrictive design for entry control and minimum pricing, the lack of any significant economies of scale in trucking, and the continuing traffic diversion from regulated common carriers to unregulated carriers all logically support the expectation that the tendencies observed in the USDA studies would be fairly general. The Commission itself has stated that deregulation would mean lower competitive rates for shippers.[99]

At this point it is pertinent to question whether the effects of regulation on the availability and quality of truck service makes paying higher rates for regulated service worth while. Is service by larger and financially stronger carriers better than service by many small carriers and fewer large ones? If it is, would the shippers still choose to pay higher charges for regulated service than for somewhat less attractive service under unregulated conditions if both types of service were offered at rates reflecting their respective costs?

Although supporters of current regulation do not emphasize that the process inevitably leads to lower unit costs and rates, they do strongly claim that it results in improved service, greater financial responsibility to shippers, and greater public safety on the highways. Before the Senate Small Business Committee, the Commission claimed that "curtailment of entries for the purpose of limiting competition often is warranted as a means of developing a financially responsible and reliable transportation industry." [100] The Commission further stated that the fitness and willingness tests for operating authority provide "considerable assurance" that the licensed carrier will maintain his equipment in proper condition; will observe proper safety practices and hours of service for drivers; will maintain public liability, property damage, and cargo insurance; will observe the special safe handling requirements for explosives; and will be trustworthy, as the licensing procedure is a deterrent to gangsters, knaves, and irresponsible persons entering the trucking field.[101] Acknowledging that even regulated carriers prefer to serve points generating substantial traffic, the Commission indicated that "in some instances" it had imposed the duty of serving small intermediate points by including them in a carrier's certificate even though an authorization was not sought. The

[99] *ICC Administration of the Motor Carrier Act*, pp. 182–186, 326–327, and 336–337.
[100] *Ibid.*, p. 326.
[101] See *Investigation of ICC's Administration of Motor Carrier Act*, Hearing before a Subcommittee of the House Committee on Interstate and Foreign Commerce 86th Cong., 2d sess., August 30, 1960, p. 3; and *Independent Regulatory Commissions*, Staff Report to the Special Subcommittee on Legislative Oversight, the same committee, pp. 51–63, especially p. 58.

Commission also noted that entry controls have aided the small-town merchant and small manufacturers by insuring the availability and prompt transportation of less-than-truckload shipments by common carriers.[102] Manifestly, the Commission has been acting on the theory that restrictive entry regulation improves service, at least by the regular-route common carriers.

Several considerations enter into any over-all economic evaluation of the effects of entry control on service. The most obvious concerns the safety and hours-of-service regulations which undoubtedly have contributed to higher standards of public safety on the highways. As those regulations apply equally to private and exempt for-hire carriers which are not subject to entry control, it would seem that economic and safety regulation do not necessarily depend on each other. The convenience of having the same agency administer both safety rules and economic regulation does not make a logical case for economic regulation. Limiting numbers and encouraging the growth of very large carriers may simplify enforcement of safety regulations, but that advantage hardly justifies the resulting market structures. The same point applies to public liability insurance standards, which could be required without restrictive entry control. Fitness-and-willingness-to-serve tests to insure trustworthy and financially responsible carriers could be applied without restricting entry on grounds of competition.

In addition, there is no adequate market test of the shippers' general willingness to pay for higher service standards under regulated conditions. The large and continuing diversion of regulated commodities to private carriers, the widespread shipper use of gray area for-hire operations, and the quotation of low competitive rates by regulated carriers when they participate in hauling exempt commodities, suggest that substantial parts of the traffic now moving by regulated truckers would not continue to demand the presently high regulated service standards if lower-quality service at lower rates were amply supplied in the market.

Aside from these pertinent considerations, it is not at all certain that all regulated services conform to the high standards claimed by advocates of restrictive entry policies. Thus, in its recent annual reports, the Commission has reported about 15,000 informal complaints each year from shippers and receivers of freight, passengers, and others, alleging unsatisfactory service or unlawful practices.[103]

---

[102] *ICC Administration of the Motor Carrier Act*, pp. 166–168, 172–174, 342, and 507.

[103] For example, see *76th Annual Report*, 1962, pp. 113–114. See *Independent Regulatory Commissions*, p. 62.

Numerous complaints of underestimating charges, slow payments for loss or damage, delayed deliveries, and other service deficiencies have long been levied against household goods carriers and have been the subject of ICC proceedings (during 1960, there were 2,338 shippers making such complaints).[104]

Before the Senate Small Business Committee, Commissioner Anthony F. Arpaia testified that there "is not a shipper in this country who would not prefer to have single-line haul." [105] But it is precisely the route and territorial restrictions in certificates and permits and the denials of applications for new or extended operating authority that prevent numerous capable and efficient motor carriers from competitively offering improved single-line service where it is now unavailable. The formation of long-haul transcontinental and regional truckers, through end-to-end mergers, has been alleviating the single-line service deficiency to an extent. However, this has resulted in dominant firms, duopoly and oligopoly markets, and no relaxation of service rigidities due to regulatory restrictions.[106] Despite the common practice of trailer interchange for truckload shipments, there is still a vast amount of interchange of traffic that might be avoided were it not for operating authority restrictions. In fact, evidence exists in extension and new-service application cases, such as in *Wilson Extension-Dairy Products*, that lack of sufficient opportunities for single-line service has been an important factor in driving shippers into operation of leased or private trucks.[107] A representative of Land O'Lakes Creamery testified before the Senate Small Business Committee that, though he had sought single-line service from common carriers, his company had been unable to obtain the requisite service on an efficient basis and had to turn to a lease-type operation and finally to private trucking when advised by the ICC that leasing was unlawful.[108]

---

[104] *Ex Parte* No. MC-19, *Practices of Motor Common Carriers of Household Goods*, recommended report by Examiner Richard S. Ries, served June 15, 1962, pp. 3–5, 7, 11, 13, 18, 30, and 36. See also *Traffic World*, March 16, 1963, pp. 5–10.

[105] *ICC Administration of the Motor Carrier Act*, p. 176. See also *Interstate Commerce Commission Activities 1937–1962*, p. 200; and *T.S.C. Motor Freight Lines Extension—New York*, 62 M.C.C. 499, 501–502 (1954).

[106] See Allan C. Flott, *Transportation Mergers and Acquisitions*, pp. 27–29; ICC, *70th Annual Report*, 1956, pp. 75–77; *71st Annual Report*, 1957, pp. 53–56; and average-haul-per-carrier data in supplemental statement of Morris Forgash, *Amendment to Section 15a*, pp. 870, 883–895, and 908–913.

[107] 61 M.C.C. 51, 52–53 (1952).

[108] *ICC Administration of the Motor Carrier Act*, pp. 30–39.

Agricultural associations, cooperatives, and the USDA have long defended service by exempt truckers. They have strongly opposed adoption by the Congress of restrictive entry control and minimum rate regulation for those carriers, or adoption by the Commission, under pressure from regulated carriers, of leasing rules making trip-leasing on back hauls unlawful.[109] Agricultural groups have claimed they not only benefit from lower rates under free-entry conditions but also from maintenance of greater service flexibility and more ample supplies of service. The ability of exempt haulers to travel on short notice to a given producing area and to transport perishable products to any destination, provides flexible services of a type that cannot be rendered under limited certificates or by the railroads. Using an exempt carrier, a shipper can start his product moving while he is finding a market, and has maximum freedom to divert shipments in transit to any market, without transferal of lading to another carrier who has the requisite operating rights and without costly delays. The tendency of exempt truckers to migrate from area to area during periods of peak harvest operations provides a more ample supply of trucks than regulated carriers could supply efficiently.[110] Unless extremely wide nonradial territorial grants were made, it would not be possible for certificated truckers to meet peak agricultural demands without maintaining many trucks that could not be utilized much of the year.

Other studies by the USDA throw further light on the effects of regulation on trucking service. These studies sampled opinions of agricultural processors on service characteristics before and after court decisions making for-hire motor transport exempt from entry

---

[109] This position was reiterated recently by twelve national farm and related shipper organizations which declared "support of the approach of removal of minimum rate regulation from the transportation of agricultural and bulk commodities recommended to the Congress by President Kennedy on March 5, 1963." Press release of United Fresh Fruit and Vegetable Association, March 20, 1963, p. 1. See *Interstate Commerce Act—Agricultural Exemptions*, Hearings before a Subcommittee of the House Committee on Interstate and Foreign Commerce, on H.R. 5823, 85th Cong., 2d sess., April 1958, pp. 66–69.

[110] Order M.V. No. 76940, Hearing No. 4313 of the Washington Utilities and Transportation Commission, June 25, 1962 (mimeographed), pp. 6 and 11. In peak harvesting seasons in eastern Washington, 1,500 trucks engaged in hauling sugar beets and 800 trucks in hauling potatoes; 80 per cent of these trucks were from other states. An easy-entry permit and freedom to negotiate rates were adopted for these seasonal agricultural carriers, but their authorized hauling was limited to hauls not exceeding 50 miles, over the objections of some shippers. The large intercity regulated carriers, including Consolidated Freightways, admitted they could not supply the needed service efficiently.

and rate control. Three-fifths of the processors of fresh and frozen poultry reported an increase in the number of for-hire trucks available after regulated entry ceased; about three-fourths of the processors of frozen fruits and vegetables had the same experience. In both cases, this effect was attributed primarily to entrance of exempt motor carriers into the field. The principal advantages of regulated motor carriers reported by processors of fresh and frozen poultry were better service, greater financial responsibility, greater reliability, and the expenditure of less managerial labor for supervision. Aside from higher rates, the principal reported disadvantages of regulated carriers were unavailability of sufficient trucks, unwillingness to serve off-line points, slowness in deliveries, and difficulties in obtaining service to distant markets. The principal advantages claimed for the exempt truckers hauling fresh and frozen poultry were a greater availability of trucks, faster service, and a greater willingness to serve out-of-the-way points and distant markets, while the principal disadvantages were less financial responsibility, unsatisfactory equipment, trucks not readily available, and the necessity of exercising more supervision.[111] Processors transporting frozen fruits and vegetables gave a similar report.[112]

In a subsequent study, the USDA sought to check on the effects of placing frozen fruits and vegetables back under entry and minimum rate control in 1958. In October 1960, 75 of the 107 processors in the earlier study were queried. While a majority reported that for-hire truck service had not changed, in the East, Middle West and the South "many processors reported that service needed by them became more difficult to find, particularly service to new markets." Some processors had entered or expanded private trucking in order to serve new origins and destinations—others had discontinued serving customers requiring less-than-truckload shipments. Charges were now uniformly made for stop-offs and the number permitted to complete loading or to make partial deliveries was being limited.[113]

Obviously, both service advantages and disadvantages accrue from regulated conditions as well as from free-entry conditions. But it must be concluded that service by exempt carriers has been adequate on the whole and that agricultural shippers, if given a choice, would often be unwilling to pay the higher rates for whatever advantages regulated

[111] Marketing Research Report No. 224, pp. 2 and 44–55.
[112] Marketing Research Report No. 316, pp. 2–3 and 30–42.
[113] Supplement to Marketing Research Report No. 316, p. 3.

service may have.[114] However, without more facts on shipper willingness to pay when both superior and inferior services for industrial products are available at appropriate prices, it cannot be definitely known whether net gains or losses to shippers have accrued from regulation in that sector. Nevertheless, the continuing diversion of industrial traffic to private or leased trucking must be attributed either to the higher rates charged by regulated carriers, or to inadequacies in the services rendered by the regulated carriers.[115]

Conclusions

Entry control came late in modern American transport development and has been applied most vigorously where it was needed least. Conceptually a tool for preventing overinvestment in fixed-cost industries and for achieving the economies of scale, it has been most used in the competitive modes of transport having small fixed costs and slight, if any, economies of scale in terms of size of firm.

In the transport industries having large fixed costs and marked economies of scale, direct entry control has not been employed. Thus, the oil pipeline industry was organized as a natural monopoly without government limitation on entry. And the railroad industry, for better or worse, was organized into its long-existing oligopolistic patterns without entry regulation other than the controls separating the modes of transport and preventing monopoly firms. On the other hand, in motor trucking, government entry control has limited the number of firms and encouraged large firms in spite of the small fixed investments and the negligible evidence that large firms were more efficient than small or medium-size firms.

With its handmaiden, minimum rate control, entry limitation was adopted by the Congress as an alternative to deregulating the railroads in the 1930's and as a measure for protecting these carriers from the forces of depression and the competitive onslaughts of new modes of transport. But whatever the design of the Congress, the ICC's interpretations of the Motor Carrier Act and the Transportation Act of

---

[114] In Docket No. 32912, *Rates on Formerly Exempt Commodities*, a traffic representative of the USDA testified in favor of maintaining the present diverse tariffs that offer the shippers a choice of rates on the same commodity between the same pair of points, for the reason that "the low-rate carriers may render a service suitable for the warehousing or marketing of numerous commodities which do not require a minimum of in-transit time to fulfill shipper needs, and leave the high-rate carrier for those shippers which demand fast in-transit time to meet their obligations." Testimony of Clarence H. Williams, March 1963, p. 4.

[115] *National Transportation Policy*, p. 509.

1940 have been highly restrictive of intramodal competition in the trucking industry and protective of the "grandfather" carriers (particularly those of large size) and the regular-route common carriers of general commodities. Thus, entry regulation has become a means of bringing about soft rather than hard competition between motor carriers, through extreme fragmentation and itemization of markets. Along with minimum rate control, it has fostered administered pricing and service competition.

To many transport people, a most surprising economic effect of protective entry control has been its adverse long-term impact on the economic position of the very carriers it was supposed to strengthen. By stimulating a rate parity policy based on value-of-service rates, and by channeling competitive forces into service competition, protective regulation has contributed importantly to the decline of the railroad common carriers in the spheres of traffic and haul in which they have substantial cost superiority. Instead of meeting price competition with motor carriers, the railroads were encouraged to play the fair-share-of-the-market and service-competition games until the resulting deterioration in their traffic and revenue positions finally forced a change in competitive policy.

Through substitution of private carrier, exempt carrier, and gray area transport for regulated common carrier service, the shipping firms have often had effective tools for avoiding the high rate and inflexible service effects of administered pricing and of operating authority limitation. But the safety valves of private and exempt or unlawful for-hire carriage have not saved the shippers and receivers, and through them the entire public, from all uneconomic effects of protective entry control of competitive transport industries.

Since economies of scale in size of firm have not been found in motor trucking, beyond very small companies, it seems likely that the cost level for regulated trucking as a whole tends to be higher than it would be under free-entry conditions. The costs—probably enormous—to carrier and shipping firms of detailed regulatory procedures must be added to other costs. The higher cost levels forced on numerous specialized motor carriers, whose back-haul, direct-route, full-load, and full-service opportunities have been limited by restrictions in certificates and permits, have to be considered. The imposition of restrictions on operations that result in inefficient use of resources can only raise the transport costs for those who must use highly restricted carriers, without necessarily reducing the cost level for those served by carriers not subject to burdensome restrictions. While a distinct possibility exists that the favored regulated carriers may be able to operate with modestly higher load factors because of restrictions placed on competitors, the higher costs occasioned by service competition, the administration of regulation, and burdensome restrictions probably offset such economy gains.

Whether because of the higher costs of trucking operations under restrictive and protective regulation or because of the monopoly power of regulated carriers through association in rate bureaus and entry restrictions, rates for regulated motor service are typically higher than rates in free-entry trucking. If service by regulated carriers is worth the differentials in rates, the higher costs and rates might be economical. But there is little clear evidence that the economies to shippers from regulated services justify the higher rates. Where alternatives exist, the shippers voluntarily resort to private, exempt, and gray area types of carriage. Agricultural shippers strongly oppose the extension of regulation to the present exempt areas. Industrial shippers as strongly oppose even the submission of private carriage to a registration requirement so that the regulatory body can know the total number and location of such carriers and their facilities. The current strong shipper support for a policy of deregulation suggests that regulated services are not generally regarded as worth the higher rates. Industrial shippers, as well as agricultural shippers, have come to believe that adequate standards of service can be expected under competitive conditions.

Brief attention should be accorded the view that the economic effects of entry control have been slight because competitive organization has not been eliminated in motor trucking. While it may be true that there are enough other firms in some markets to facilitate effective competition, the fact remains that the number of regulated truckers has been reduced in many markets; very large carriers are achieving a dominating position through mergers, entry denials, regulatory restrictions, rate suspensions, and minimum rate orders. Price competition between regulated motor carriers has been dampened almost to the point of extinction.

Finally, with essential data at many points deplorably inadequate, definitive information on some of the final economic effects of entry control will have to await the publication of data from the ICC's inventory of motor carrier operating rights. Further research is needed by the ICC and others into economies of scale and utilization and other critical areas bearing on the economic consequences of entry control as presently practiced in surface transport.

Manpower in Operating
Classifications on the Railroads

JOHN T. DUNLOP

HARVARD UNIVERSITY

The two most significant studies made by the Presidential Railroad Commission concern manpower in operating classifications and the wage structure.[1] Irrespective of how one appraises the Commission's recommendations (and there are its supporters and detractors), it is agreed that these two studies provide significant new information to economists, government agencies, and the carriers and brotherhoods. In an industry as old as railroading, regulated in detail by government agencies and with a long history of collective bargaining, it is portentous that such large gaps could have existed in our information regarding the manpower profile and the wage structure of operating employees.

The Commission was in complete accord in its direction of the studies, and the methods used were approved by experts representing the carriers, the brotherhoods, and governmental agencies. Thus, the studies possess both a high degree of technical competence and wide-spread confidence.

This paper is concerned solely with manpower problems, despite the greater richness and novelty of the wage data and my own professional interest in wage structure issues. The wage structure of operating employees is so distinctive and involves such grotesque inequities[2] that discussion of its problems has relatively little general relevance except as another instance of a "demoralized" incentive

---

[1] The Commission was established by Executive Order 10891 in accordance with the agreement of October 17, 1960, between the carriers and the five operating brotherhoods. The *Report of the Presidential Railroad Commission* was presented to the President on February 26, 1962. The reports are *Studies Relating to Railroad Operating Employees, Employment Trends and Manpower Characteristics of Railroad Operating Employees*, Report of the Commission, February 1962, Washington, Appendix III, pp. 1–105, and *Pay Structure Study, Railroad Operating Employees*, Report of the Commission, February 1962, Washington, Appendix II.

[2] See *Report of the Railroad Commission*, Chaps. 8, 9.

system. The manpower study appears to have a wider range of applicability not only in transportation but in industry more generally.

Manpower Study

Employment in the railroad industry has been declining over the past forty years, except for the period of World War II. Average annual employment of Class I railroads was 2.0 million in 1920, 1.5 million in 1930, 1.0 million in 1940, and 780,000 in 1960. The 1961 figure was 716,000, and that for 1962 may be expected to be below 700,000. This is a decline of over 60 per cent in forty years.

Operating employment on Class I railroads declined from 366,000 to 261,000 in the postwar years 1948–59. This decline of 29 per cent was at a lesser rate than the 47 per cent decline of total employment on these roads, reflecting the larger decline in nonoperating employment. In the postwar period, the number of railroad employees attached to the industry (Railroad Retirement Board data) declined at a more rapid rate than the number of railroad jobs (Interstate Commerce Commission data) as certain employees, particularly in nonoperating and lower-seniority categories, left the industry.

The Commission started its work with the conviction that a careful manpower profile of the work force was a prerequisite to any policy prescription in an industry with forty years of secularly declining employment, and faced with further market competition, additional labor-saving technological change, a merger movement among carriers, and disputes over work rules that concerned manning schedules. It was not enough to project a continued decline in average employment or attachment to the industry; it was imperative to be informed of the age distribution, length of service, and other characteristics of employees in various occupations and types and grades of service, and also to know the rationale of hiring rates and separation rates. The study of manpower was designed to tabulate and analyze data on these characteristics of the work force in the operating classifications.

The railroad retirement system uniquely provides data on the manpower of the railroad industry. (Data in such detail are not available by occupations for other industries.) The Commission arranged for universe counts of operating employment, new entrants, and retirements; it secured 4 per cent samples of data relating to age, service, death, and withdrawals, and 2 per cent samples of unemployment and sickness beneficiaries. These tabulations were generally made for the years 1948–59. The RRB data on employees attached to the operating occupations in January of each year contain a great deal more detailed information than the mid-month employment counts derived from the ICC M-300 report forms reflecting the number of jobs.[3] For the year 1959, the RRB data showed a total of 260,952 employees attached to operating classifications as compared with 210,673, the average of the mid-month count from ICC reports.

It would be impractical to summarize here the rich statistical detail this manpower study makes available, but four illustrations will show the relevance of the data to manpower planning and policy making.

1. The median age in 1959 of the major operating occupations was as follows: engineers, 59; firemen (helpers), 42; conductors, 53; brakemen, 41. The age distribution within each occupation adds important information. The percentage distribution figures for engineers (35,525) and firemen (67,000), for instance, were as follows.

Age Distribution	Engineers	Firemen
Under 20	—	1.0
20–24	.3	6.0
25–29	1.2	9.1
30–34	2.2	12.7
35–39	5.1	14.7
40–44	12.5	15.9
45–49	8.9	12.5
50–54	7.7	8.9
55–59	16.2	8.5
60–64	23.6	6.9
65–69	17.0	2.8
70–74	4.2	.8
75 and over	.9	.1

SOURCE: *Report of the Railroad Commission,*
Appendix III, Table 15.

Thus, 22.1 per cent of the engineers, or 7,850, were over 65 years of age; another 23.6 per cent, or 8,384, were between 60 and 64 years. The distribution of firemen shows that 7.0 per cent, or 4,690, were under 25 years of age and another 9.1 per cent, or 6,097, between 25 and 29 years. Such details can be elaborated into distributions by

[3] See Technical Note, "Comparability of Railroad Retirement Board and Interstate Commerce Commission Employment Statistics," *Report of the Railroad Commission,* Appendix III, pp. 10–11.

branch of service, such as road and yard, passenger and freight, and other categories. Age distributions are clearly vital to consideration of manpower policy-making in an industry with a history of sharply declining employment.

2. The length of service of employees by occupation, type, and grade of service as well as by age distribution is another dimension of the work force measured by the manpower study. The percentage distribution of years of service[4] completed at the end of the same year (1959) by the same employees (engineers and firemen) are shown as follows.

Years of Service	Engineers	Firemen
0–4	2.4	17.8
5–9	2.0	13.8
10–14	7.0	20.6
15–19	19.0	29.0
20–24	12.4	6.2
25–29	7.5	3.5
30–34	12.4	2.6
35–39	12.7	3.2
40 and over	26.7	3.2

SOURCE: *Report of the Railroad Commission,* Appendix III, Table 17.

Thus, 31.6 per cent of all firemen had less than ten years and 17.8 per cent less than five years of service, while 26.7 per cent of all engineers had forty years of service and more.

Tabulations by length of service and age distribution for 1959 show that, of the 11,950 firemen defined as attached to the industry with less than five years of service, 670 (5.6 per cent) were less than 20 years old; 8,300 (69.5 per cent) were in the 20–29 age group. Among the 9,225 with five to nine years of service, 1,800 (19.5 per cent) were in the 20–29 age bracket. However, when one considers the bracket of ten to fourteen years of service, as might be expected, virtually no one was under 30 years of age.[5] Since industrial societies often measure attachment and equities in jobs by length of service and age, the detailed

[4] A year of service is equal to twelve months of cumulated compensated service; a month of service is any calendar month in which compensated service of any amount, creditable under the Railroad Retirement Act, is completed.
[5] *Report of the Railroad Commission,* Appendix III, Table 18.

data presented in this manpower study are essential to private and public policy-making.

3. The study shows that, even though the number of employees in operating classifications had decreased steadily from 366,000 in 1948 to 261,000 in 1959, there were in that year 8,934 new entrants with no previous railroad experience. The firemen classification recruited 2,455, or 27.5 per cent, of the new recruits alone.

4. The study also analyzes closely the annual separation rates for operating employees in recent years in regard to the effects of retirements, deaths, and withdrawals. The tabulations are available by age and occupation. They are essential to any careful projections of the work force and to building various models of adjustment in manpower to projected changes in demand and manning schedules. Thus the number of vacancies available to firemen or trainmen in the next five or ten years will depend upon the projected separation rates—retirements, deaths, and withdrawals—not only in the immediate classifications but even more in the engineer and conductor classifications, which are the next step in the promotion ladder.

This section has been designed to call attention to the rich source of raw materials made available in the manpower study of the Presidential Railroad Commission. Study of them can serve as a pattern for a number of industries, such as maritime, printing, and basic steel, which face continued long-term contraction in employment.[6] The railroad manpower study was greatly facilitated by the specialized data made available through the railroad retirement system, and comparable studies in other segments will require extensive collection of new information. It is imperative that studies be begun in these other sectors at the earliest possible date by cooperative programs of labor, management, and government.

Technological Change and Collective Bargaining

The widespread newspaper publicity campaigns on technological change—or the lack of it—in the railroad industry and the emotional changes surrounding "featherbedding" have materially complicated reasoned public discussion of adjustment to change not only in railroads but in industry generally. While railroad managements were divided to some degree on the advisability of these campaigns, partly because

[6] Ewan Clague and Leon Greenberg, "Employment," in John T. Dunlop, ed., *Automation and Technological Change*, Englewood Cliffs, N.J., 1962, pp. 114–131.

morale of employees and efficiency would be adversely affected, the publicity campaigns reflected managerial judgment that their previous attempts to negotiate in collective bargaining had not been successful and that further attempts could only succeed in the spotlight of an aroused public opinion.

The labor organizations were understandably concerned that this campaign so prejudiced many segments of public opinion that it would be difficult to secure a fair hearing even before informed neutrals, that their subsequent bargaining position had been adversely affected, and that public opinion had been emotionally prejudiced. Nor did the contemporaneous flight-engineer problems help to secure a sympathetic public reaction. The railroad brotherhoods resented the fact that their resources for public countercampaigns were small. Despite some pioneering activities, they tended, by and large, in this hostile environment to stimulate their memberships to resistance rather than to the need for accommodation.

This sort of atmosphere in the newspapers is suitable neither for constructive problem solving at the bargaining table nor even for scholarly discussion. In view of the state of public feeling on these questions relating to the railroads, it is essential to devote a brief section to technological change and collective bargaining more generally, and to identify the special circumstances that have aggravated the railroad situation. This discussion is designed to place railroad problems in a more dispassionate setting. Two general propositions are asserted.

The first is that, on balance, collective bargaining has stimulated rather than retarded the rate of technological change.[7] Collective bargaining has required top managements to pay greater attention to the work place and to the managerial line of communication to and from the first level of supervision. Labor organizations have placed managements under strong pressure to seek greater efficiencies and cost reduction. Agreements in most industries provide, in the event of a dispute, for managements to make technological changes and a variety of adjustments in job asssignments, wage structure, benefits, safety, and other conditions of work, through an orderly grievance procedure without resort to work stoppages. Labor organizations have typically emphasized the need for broad training in a work force. There are notable exceptions to this proposition and some agreements have developed significant rigidities, but they should not be allowed

---

[7] Sumner H. Slichter, James J. Healy, and Robert E. Livernash, *The Impact of Collective Bargaining on Management*, Washington, 1960, pp. 342–371, 946–961.

to distort the general picture. Indeed, the exceptions call for explanation.

The second proposition is to remind ourselves that resistance to technological change is widespread in the community and not the distinctive attitude of any group. "Turnpike companies profiting from tolls, and owners of stage coaches were among the most active opponents of railroads. They were supported by tavernkeepers along the route of the roads, and by farmers who felt that the introduction of the railroads would deprive them of markets for horses and for hay." [8] The railroads may have been more sophisticated but probably no more charitable toward their latter-day competitors (the Panama Canal, the St. Lawrence Seaway, the pipelines, the trucks, and the airlines). There are certain human qualities which suggest that attitudes and responses depend, at least in part, upon whose ox is being gored. Moreover, Professor George Taylor wisely reminds us, "It is a sign of the times, perhaps, that the short-shrift treatment is so largely confined to those rules which benefit hourly paid workers while work rules prevalent in the professions, including college teaching with its tenure appointments, are more sympathetically viewed." [9] Efficiency needs to be weighed against other values.

In the light of these general propositions, the question arises of the reasons for the failure of the railroad industry to make a more orderly and rapid adjustment to technological changes, particularly with regard to various work rules relating to the use of manpower. Collective bargaining developed early in this industry, and the statesmanship of leaders on both sides was widely acclaimed. While there is a tendency among outsiders to minimize the extent of the change in technology that has in fact taken place in the past decade, and to fail to appreciate the degree of accommodation to it on particular railroads, the problem remains a significant one with many facets. These include the recruitment and development of managements, managerial methods and techniques, availability of capital, and government regulatory policies aside from the collective bargaining arrangements. The quest here is for the more proximate factors.

It has sometimes been said that the craft organization of railroad operating employees primarily accounts for their policies toward work rules and manning schedules. This is a temptingly easy solution and

[8] National Resources Committee, *Technological Trends and National Policy*, Washington, June 1937.

[9] George Taylor, "Collective Bargaining," in John T. Dunlop, ed., *Automation and Technological Change*, New York, 1962, p. 94.

congenial to economists since it relies on the inelasticity of demand for a single craft. While the form of organization and the bargaining arrangements do play a role, as will be indicated, the craft explanation is not very significant or perceptive. Thus, the same diesel engine which so drastically altered the work operations of the fireman (helper) also virtually eliminated the boilermaker from the railroad shops. This change eliminated almost 50,000 jobs in the postwar period and caused some difficult adjustments in the structure of the Boilermakers' Union, at least in railroads. But this sweeping change was accomplished without serious dispute or public notice. A number of contrasts between the situation involving the fireman and the boilermaker are most instructive.

The boilermakers had a craft which was transferable to other industries, but the skills of operating employees have little use outside their industry. The boilermakers often were able to command as high or even higher compensation in construction, shipbuilding, and boiler-manufacturing enterprises. It is hard to discover jobs in industry which would provide annual incomes to match those of operating railroad personnel with skills of little transfer value. The Boilermakers' Union is engaged in a number of industries and could directly facilitate the transfer of displaced workers through knowledge of job opportunities, hiring arrangements, and personal contacts. The railroad operating unions have few collective bargaining relationships outside the railroad industry. The disappearance of the jobs of boilermakers on the railroads did not involve the threat of disappearance of the union as an organization. The railroad operating unions, however, are tied almost exclusively to railroads. While the work operations and the jurisdiction of boilermakers were defined in scope rules, there was no collective bargaining provision or state law establishing a manning rule for boilermakers or providing for the employment of so many boilermakers in each shop. In contrast, the national diesel agreement of 1937 requires the use of firemen, and various state laws prescribe the size of the train crew. Finally, the boilermakers were not confronted by a rival union in their jurisdiction, nor did they share a promotion ladder with another craft, as in the case of the firemen and engineers.[10] It is the combination of these various factors which is responsible for the differences in adjustment of two crafts to the same technological change.

[10] George R. Horton and H. Ellsworth Steele, "Unity of the American Railroad Engineers and Firemen," *Industrial and Labor Relations Review*, October 1956, pp. 48–69.

In general terms, the degree of difficulty in adjusting manpower to technological change can be related to five factors. Their identification will assist in locating the sectors of the economy which may involve most problems in adjustment to change.

1. A sector with long-term decline in employment magnifies the problems of adjustment.

2. A high degree of turnover, as is typically the case in occupations characterized by women employees, or in industries with casual employment, tends to mitigate the severity of adjustment problems. The long-term attachment of men in railroads complicates the task of adjustment.

3. Occupations with specialized skill, as among railroad operating employees, compared to skills with wide transfer value, involve greater problems, particularly when wages are relatively high compared to other wages in the communities in which many operating railroad workers live. Employees are often required to make changes in both location and occupation to secure alternative employment.

4. The concentration of a union in a single craft in a single industry makes adjustment more difficult in the face of adverse technological change, since the question of institutional survival of the labor organization complicates adjustments. Merger among labor organizations in the railroad industry, as in others, has proven most difficult. The problems are magnified by the fact that ladders of promotion, such as fireman and engineer, are served by rival unions, and work rules and seniority arrangements defining work opportunities between the crafts on the same ladder impede merger. Further, the future of the labor organization, its officers, and its bargaining rights are at stake in addition to jobs. Labor organizations confront budgets also, and when employment and dues have fallen below a certain level the organization may cease to be financially viable.

5. The inclusion of explicit manning rules in collective bargaining agreements or in state statutes or regulations further complicates adjustments since such rules become symbolic and often provide a barrier to review of new technological possibilities. Moreover, a single national rule is likely to prove more difficult than a variety of locally bargained rules which permit local experimentation with new processes and a variety of compromises. There has been little opportunity for local or regional experimentation on firemen questions, although there has been much more variation in the case of rules on crew composition.

Policies to Facilitate Manpower Adjustments

The lesson of history is clearly that work rules cannot for long frustrate technological change. The labor movement early learned that a policy of obstruction[11] could not succeed. In the language of President Perkins of the Cigar Workers: "No power on earth can stop the at least gradual introduction and use of improved machinery and progressive methods of production." Matthew Woll stated in 1929 the position of the labor movement: "It is not the function of the labor movement to resist the machine. It is the function of the labor movement to turn the installation of machinery to the good of the workers."

The central problem of collective bargaining raised by technological change is, accordingly, accommodation to the change. These problems are most acute in the types of situations identified by the list of five factors noted in the last section. Irrespective of the wider effects of a particular change on the economy as a whole, technology does destroy or erode job opportunities and skills for particular groups; this destruction is analogous to the destruction of capital values and rents. In an advanced industrial society the task is to design procedures to secure orderly adaptation to continuous change rather than to fight through an isolated technological change.

Economists tend to think of the flow and direction of manpower solely in terms of the concept of the labor market. While concern with the labor market is appropriate, it involves only a portion of the relevant flows of manpower in the economy. A more complete analysis of labor flows requires equal attention to the flows of manpower within enterprises or other units established by collective bargaining, and also the relations between such internal flows and the exterior markets.

It is appropriate, perhaps, to emphasize the importance of this concept to economists. The flow of manpower within a unit, and to and from the exterior market, is largely regulated by a series of rules of the work place affecting ladders of promotion, seniority districts, overtime allocation, work allocation, manning rules, retirement, and the like, as well as by the internal wage rate structure. Thus, the rules governing the definition of seniority districts and the criteria for layoffs will determine whether employees are discharged from the enterprise

[11] Sumner H. Slichter, *Union Policies and Industrial Management*, Washington, 1941, pp. 201–227.

and returned to the exterior labor market or whether they remain partially employed or attached to the enterprise. Moreover, these rules determine which particular employees are affected. Still other rules will determine the rights to promotion, the division of overtime or other work opportunities, and other flows of manpower within the enterprise or other units. Further, narrow seniority districts may result in hiring new workers from the exterior market while other workers are on layoff status in other seniority districts. Any attention to the efficient allocation of the labor force must involve both the traditional exterior labor market and the rules directing the internal flows of manpower and their interchange with the exterior market.

The significant question of policy concerns the measures that can be taken to increase the effective use of manpower already attached to the industry and to provide an orderly adjustment of manpower to technological and market changes in prospect. The following measures may be suggested to apply to manpower in operating classifications in the railroads.

1. There is need to broaden seniority districts and even to create new carrier-wide or even industry-wide pools or lists so that employees, particularly of long service, are given rights to employment elsewhere on a railroad or even elsewhere in an industry on other carriers before new people are hired. In an industry with declining employment totals, it is less than a rational use of manpower to continue to attract and to train new employees to very specialized jobs while other workers, often older with these same skills, are being released permanently. One of the significant features of the Kaiser-Steelworkers plan provides for a plantwide labor pool below the separate departmental seniority districts. The Commission proposed such a national roster for firemen separated or furloughed as a result of its recommendations. But wider seniority districts are generally required, particularly with regard to permanent layoffs.

2. An industry with declining employment totals should gradually adopt a program of compulsory retirement at age 65. This policy is the more appropriate in an industry with adequate or even generous pension or retirement benefits as compared to industry generally. In an industry with 22.1 per cent of the engineers and 15.8 per cent of the conductors over 65, revised retirement policies should play a role in the necessary adjustment of manpower to further technological change. It may well be that the gradual adoption of a compulsory retirement program, starting at age 70 and working down to 65, should be associated with some increase in retirement benefits to encourage even

earlier retirement in some cases. These suggestions are opposed by senior men who have spent a long time looking forward to the opportunity of choosing certain select runs which provide considerable overtime or short hours of work. But a retirement program has nonetheless a major contribution to make in the adjustment of manpower to changes taking place in the railroad industry.

3. Changes in the hours of work of certain operating employees, particularly in local freight service, also have a contribution to make to more orderly manpower adjustments. Among local freight engineers, 75.5 per cent worked forty hours or more a week, 60 per cent fifty hours or more, 34 per cent sixty hours or more, and 15.1 per cent 70 hours or more. In contrast, 53.9 per cent of through-freight engineers worked less than thirty hours a week, another 24.7 per cent between thirty and forty hours, a further 14 per cent between forty and fifty hours, and only 7.4 per cent over fifty hours a week.[12] While these hours are related to the wage system and other rules, it is clear that one way to adjust to employment declines is to provide in local freight service for lower weekly hours of work for some employees with the longest hours, even at the expense of weekly earnings.

4. An industry which has highly specialized jobs and a long-term record of declining employment has an obligation to encourage the retraining of its labor force. Programs should be made available particularly to employees in the age brackets below 30 years, who have least seniority, are more vulnerable to unemployment, and are also most likely to move voluntarily. There may well be a case for sharing costs between the industry and the community, but it is imperative to a manpower policy to encourage such training while workers have jobs rather than to defer training until they are unemployed.

5. The proposal has been made by a number of labor organizations and adopted in some agreements that the orderly adjustment of manpower to further technological changes in the railroad industry requires the adoption of some limitation on the right of management to abolish positions. In some instances the proposal is for a "controlled attrition approach," as in the Southern Pacific agreement with the Order of Railroad Telegraphers, under which the rate of job abolition is limited to natural attrition or a fixed percentage of the working force, whichever is less. This approach, it has been said, protects something more than people; it protects the job itself. In other instances the proposal is for the limit of "natural attrition," which restricts the rate of job elimination

[12] *Report of the Railroad Commission*, pp. 112–113.

to the rate of labor turnover resulting from death, retirement, resignation, discharge for cause, and possible promotion outside the bargaining unit.[13]

In the language of Emergency Board 151, "The only appropriate objective of natural attrition consonant with public policy is the leveling of peaks and valleys of employment, not the impeding of necessary innovation. Meaningful employment security cannot be achieved at the expense of change. The goal of a natural attrition program should be to assure that technological and organizational change will be introduced on a planned, orderly basis, and its result should be an average level of employment no higher than would be the case in its absence."

In some circumstances an attrition program may be a useful contribution to a manpower program in an industry faced with continuing technological change. But it is not a universal or general-purpose tool. Some industries and companies are expanding as others are contracting; some have higher natural attrition rates than others, depending on the proportion of women employees, age composition, location, and other factors; some have a higher proportion of temporary employees typically excluded from any attrition program. It may not always be feasible or practical to distinguish between changes in employment attributable to variable output and economic conditions and changes in employment directly related to new technology or new methods. An attrition program may be effectively frustrated by seniority rules which permit little or no transfers among related jobs. An attrition program confined to a single occupation may have little purpose other than to restrict the rate of introduction of technological change. A program of attrition may be applied to a group of employees above a certain age or with longer service records, rather than to all employees. The Presidential Railroad Commission proposed such a program for firemen in other than passenger service. Thus, its appropriateness must be examined separately in each situation.

6. Manpower displaced by technological change should be provided a schedule of lump-sum payments or weekly benefits, above normal unemployment compensation, to facilitate transfer to new jobs and locations and in partial compensation for the loss of preferred positions and economic rents. This principle has now come to be recognized as the first requisite to orderly adjustment of manpower. The benefits should be higher the longer the period of service.

[13] See the excellent discussion of Emergency Board 151, December 31, 1962, pp. 24–31.

In view of a continued decline in demand, these policies are designed to facilitate a more orderly withdrawal of labor resources from operating classifications, to discourage unnecessary new recruitments, and to use more effectively the labor force remaining in these occupations in the industry.

COMMENT

GEORGE WILSON, Indiana University

Dunlop's treatment of railroad-industry problems differs from that of other contributors to this volume in that it is more narrowly based. His immediate goal is to help effect an orderly transition of internal labor flows in the railroad industry in the face of a combination of technological change and a relative decline in the demand for railway service. This is a vexing problem but at least it is specific. It lends itself to political compromise on behalf of union and management, assuming emotions can be held in check. In the long run the ultimate solution is clear. We can only question the way in which it should be effected. This question does not require any sophisticated analysis of economically optimal solutions. Rather, the problem is to devise a pattern of adjustment which both sides will find acceptable.

But Dunlop is not content merely to summarize a program for orderly readjustment. He is concerned as well with why adjustment has been so difficult in the case of firemen and engineers. I find his five factors, which have general applicability in the context of technological change, to be convincing if not very exceptional. His method of moving from the specific to the general is more informative and provides a more satisfactory outcome than, for example, the Healy paper. This is no criticism of the latter since it is always easier to discuss a specific problem whose nature is clear and in which the direction of desirable change is uncomplicated by doubt.

It is obvious that ignorance expedites vested interest and bias while knowledge at least restricts unwavering irrationality. Dunlop's discussion is reassuring in this regard although I suspect that he is not confident that strikes can be averted despite careful analysis of the manpower structure. We can hope that our findings will at least guide public policy and attitudes on to approximately correct paths despite innumerable small instances of inefficiency, waste, and inequity. We can also hope that needed changes can be induced by our work before the crisis stage is reached.

THOR HULTGREN, National Bureau of Economic Research

A currently important transportation problem is that of finding a useful place for labor displaced by technological improvement. The problem is especially acute in the case of train and engine labor. The Diesel locomotive has made the usefulness of a whole craft, the firemen, questionable. The system of wage payment in train and engine service is peculiar. And the industry is relatively stagnant in size. The Presidential Railroad Commission of which John T. Dunlop was a member developed a large body of data bearing on the problem. In his paper, Dunlop considers six lines of policy. One is reliance on attrition—no separation from service except that occasioned by death, retirement, voluntary quitting, dismissal for cause, and perhaps decline of traffic. On the whole, Dunlop rejects that solution, which would greatly delay the realization of economies. He favors broader seniority districts, compulsory retirement at age 65, reliance on additional workers rather than overtime, training for other jobs before present jobs are lost, and protracted separation allowances. Broader districts would certainly often be better than firing old employees on one part of a railroad system while hiring new ones on another part. Because a railroad is territorially far-flung, however, wider districts would sometimes involve considerable social dislocation. As to hiring additional workers rather than paying overtime, it is often not feasible to replace a train crew at the end of straight time. Some people would question whether workers should be thrown out of the labor force automatically at any specified age; this is a growing problem in the economy at large. Dunlop points out, however, that train and engine workers are unusually old and do not possess broadly transferable skills. He draws an ingenious contrast between locomotive firemen and boilermakers in railroad repair shops. Diesels threatened the jobs of both, but boilermakers had a transferable skill and put up much less resistance.

For firemen employed less than ten years, PRC recommended separation, with allowances to be paid for periods as long as four years, depending on length of service. Similar allowances have been required by the Interstate Commerce Commission for workers displaced by railway mergers. Railroad managers complain that there are no analogous arrangements in other industries. Certainly it is not fair to cast the entire social burden of transition on the displaced workers. On the other hand, law and policy urge the railroads to be efficient; the ICC is told to consider efficiency when passing judgment on the level of rates and fares. Should railroads nevertheless be deprived for a time of the benefits of efficiency? If displaced workers are not absorbed elsewhere, that would seem to indicate imperfection in the labor market, a responsibility of the economic community at large. However, when separation results from greater efficiency, there is at least new income out of which allowances may be paid. In contrast, when the Rutland went out of business, the ICC refused to burden the estate of the defunct railroad with separation allowances.

Dunlop draws an optimistic lesson from history. I can think of a work rule in newspaper printing that has seemed to "frustrate technological change" for at least two decades. How long is long?

Research and Public Policy Issues: Some Canadian Comparisons

F. W. ANDERSON

UNIVERSITY OF SASKATCHEWAN

Canadians have always observed American affairs with interest, enthusiasm, or alarm. While the sheer size of the American nation and what we regard as the complexities of its institutional systems make it difficult for us correctly to categorize all the developments in our powerful neighbor, nevertheless the orientation of our interest is predominantly southward. Our interest continues to be whetted by news of what appear to be significant advances in your economic, political, or social progress, even as it is piqued by your problems.

Anyone who undertakes a critique of a situation which has become unstable through general dissatisfaction runs the risk of seeing the problem he is examining solved between the preparation and delivery of remarks, should the inertia of the political system be overcome and action taken. It is entirely possible that this may happen in this instance. General dissatisfaction with transportation policies in Canada has grown to such an extent, beginning first with railway policy and spreading rapidly to other transportation policies, that pressure has grown on all sides upon the federal government. Policy action has been promised during the present sitting of the federal Parliament.

The rising tide of interest in transportation policies evident on both sides of our border is an indication of similar dissatisfaction with outmoded policies. Yet it does not follow that comparable types of policies have been in existence in the two countries throughout the past century. Coincidently, rising dissatisfaction in the United States and Canada with transportation policies does not mean that the policies are similar. I take it as the main purpose of this paper, not to draw a comparison between the policies of the two nations but, more simply, to set out in a broad framework the nature of the policies which have existed in Canada and the extent to which they have failed to meet the demands of the nation for a modern transportation system.

Governmental acknowledgment of policy dissatisfaction takes a course in Canada different from that in the United States. When a problem becomes acute enough, the technique of the Royal Commission is invoked. Following this technique, an attempt is made to set out the problem and a group of commissioners is appointed to gather a staff, hear evidence, and propose solutions. The parties that appear before a Royal Commission present their briefs, and eventually their argument, and the Commission then prepares a report of recommendations for the consideration of the government. The government accepts or rejects the recommendations as it sees fit, and the proposed policy changes are introduced into the legislature where debate takes place. In matters of transportation, this process has been undertaken at least three times by federal Royal Commissions since the end of World War II. In addition, there have been numerous special and provincial inquiries into particular aspects of transportation problems. Certain remedial legislation was offered following the reports of the first two federal Royal Commissions, but the basic problems continued, and general dissatisfaction grew. In order to present the nature of these basic problems faced by the most recent Royal Commission, appointed in 1959, some historical recapitulation is necessary.

Transportation in National Policy in Canada

In many aspects of the political life of a nation one could agree with Edmund Burke that we read principles into history only after the event. But the first sixty-year period of Canadian nationhood is a notable exception. Before the Confederation, during its negotiations, and for at least sixty years following the passage of the British North America Act in 1867, policy on a broad scale, policy with principles easily discernible, characterized the national growth. The measure of success was not due entirely to the policy; good fortune and world affairs contributed to economic growth. But without some such policy, the economic growth would most likely not have occurred within the framework of a Canadian nation. The contention that Canada is economically and logically bound with the continental United States would have been demonstrated before the end of the nineteenth century, if the advent of the steam railway had not enabled an otherwise inexorable economic pull to be resisted.

Canadian developmental policies have always embraced transportation policies. The transportation policies of the Dominion after 1867 merely intensified and extended the policies of the pre-Confederation colonies, with emphasis more particularly upon railways than upon other modes.

The colonial provincial governments of British North America before Confederation had built certain main highways as public works. Toll roads were little used and private turnpike companies were unknown.

The Canadian and Imperial governments built nearly all the canals of the St. Lawrence system as public works. Those, like the first Welland Canal, which were built by private companies, received help from government and were without exception taken over as public works. The magnitude of these works and the lack of adequate private capital made state action necessary and inevitable. Military needs often reinforced the need for state action.

The same considerations applied in a varying degree to railway construction, ownership, and operation. As in the United Kingdom, public opinion and government policy at the beginning of the railway age were divided as to whether railways should be built and operated as public works or as private enterprises. In Canada, because of the size of the country, the sparce population, the lack of private capital, and the imperative need of improved communications to develop the country, the decision was rarely or wholly in favor of outright private construction, ownership, and operation. Private enterprise seldom proceeded without state aid in one form or another. Thus, after the prolonged discussion between 1846 and 1862 on the construction of the Intercolonial Railway to link the St. Lawrence region with the Atlantic provinces, all assumed that the political and military considerations governing the construction of the railway would see it progress as a public work. The construction of the Grand Trunk Railway to parallel the canal system of the St. Lawrence is an outstanding example of how Canadian government, before Confederation, aided the construction and operation of railways by private companies to a degree which exceeded the help given railways in the United Kingdom and even the United States. The company was given a bonus of £3,000 a mile, about one-third the cost of construction, and government support was extended in other ways. When the Grand Trunk Railway encountered early financial difficulties, guarantee of a new bond issue was made in 1855. In 1856, a further guarantee followed and an outright grant was voted; further aid was given in 1857.[1]

---

[1] A. W. Currie, *The Grand Trunk Railway of Canada*, University of Toronto Press, 1957, Chaps. 1 and 2.

The construction of the Grand Trunk was an act of provincial policy, designed to give Montreal a share in the trade of the American Middle West and a winter port in Maine by meeting the competition of American railways and canals.

The Pacific railway was not less necessary, but it was an even more complex and enormous undertaking. The acquisition of Rupert's Land and union with British Columbia had to be first negotiated. Then the incomparably longest railway of its time had to be built over some of the most difficult terrain on the continent. Manitoba entered the Confederation on the understanding that a railway would be built to connect it with the outside world. Its public lands, purchased from the Hudson's Bay Company in 1870, were to be "administered by the government of Canada for the purposes of the Dominion." Of these "purposes of the Dominion," two transcended all others—railways and settlement. Those public lands were to provide the railways which would link the scattered regions of the Dominion and were to encourage the settlement, which would in turn support the railways and give stimulus to the older regions. In 1929, sixty-two years after Confederation, it was officially declared these "purposes of the Dominion" had been fulfilled, and the process of returning the remaining public lands to the prairie provinces began.[2] When British Columbia entered the Dominion in 1871, the terms of union required the national government to begin a railway to the Pacific within two years and to complete it in ten—that is, by 1873 and 1883, respectively. Railway construction was thus an integral part of national union and national expansion.

The decision to utilize railways to create and bind the nation carried with it the decision to utilize all-Canadian routes. The railway policy evolved before Confederation was designed to create a railway system, paralleling the water system, to penetrate the heart of the American hinterland. While there is no evidence that this pre-Confederation policy was to be abandoned, it was definitely relegated to second place. The Grand Trunk Railway finally gained access to Chicago in 1880. Since that time, the St. Lawrence canals have been continuously improved and deepened. But the construction of a transcontinental railway system implied that the means of access from eastern Canada to the prairies and the Pacific coast should be contained entirely within Canadian borders. This decision meant that the costs of construction were increased, and that a much larger participation by government would be necessary. In the budget speech of Samuel Leonard Tilley

[2] Chester Martin, "Dominion Lands Policy," *Canadian Frontiers of Settlement*, Vol. II, Toronto, 1938, pp. 223–228.

on April 1, 1873, some indication of the hopes for this new policy are revealed. In justifying the proposal of ambitious expenditures of $10 million on the Intercolonial Railway, $30 million on the Pacific railway, and $20 million on canals, he referred to the great benefits which would come to all parts of the Dominion as a result of these national investments. The construction of these great facilities was intended to have a stimulating effect upon all the established centers in central Canada and the Atlantic provinces, and the increase in trade was intended to yield tax revenues to the Dominion. The Dominion government confidently expected to recoup its investment in transportation.

Certain other national policies inevitably followed from this decision to capture and settle the western lands for Canada by the establishment of all-Canadian transportation routes. For trade to move through the channels constructed by massive public assistance, Canadian railroads required some degree of monopoly, or imports and exports would be free to move from the more settled portions of the United States across the border into the Canadian frontier. So, the third national policy of development, the promotion of industrialization by protective tariff, was established in 1879. The tariff wall, in conjunction with railway rates, was designed to assure effectively that trade would move east and west to and from the more populous centers of central Canada, and to Canadian river and sea ports. Thus it was intended that, by heavy public investment, the Canadian nation would obtain a viable economic place, and the necessarily great investment would be recovered through the expanding volume of imports and exports of the growing nation.

Public Concern with Railway Pricing

The task of railway construction was far more imperative in the first generation of railway building than were the rates the railways might charge when in operation. Furthermore, the economic philosophy of the day led to the assumption that competition would protect the interests both of the general public and of private persons. Obviously, until additional railways could be built by other companies, such competition was not present. Even after additional railway schemes were promoted with varying degrees of public support, it became obvious that competition between railways was not pervasive enough to protect the shipper. Other modes of transport to insure equitable treatment through intermodal competition were unavailable in many sections of the country.

When public complaints began in the 1870's, the Canadian government, under the British North American Act of 1867, had full jurisdiction over interprovincial railways. The right of Parliament to limit or regulate rates charged by railways was never in doubt; as the creator and benefactor, certain presumptions of control were expected. In addition, the current doctrine of public responsibility attaching to common carriers gave residual and remedial powers to government. Federal statute in 1879 gave power to the government to limit rates when railway dividends exceeded 15 per cent of capital expended on construction. In 1881, when the Parliament of Canada chartered the Canadian Pacific Railway, that principle was extended to permit rate control if dividends of 10 per cent on capital expended were exceeded.

The principle of public regulation, important as it was, could not alone create a national policy of rate regulation. Because of the lack of water competition in western Canada, rates were generally higher there than in central Canada, and the imposition of the tariff policy after 1879 prevented the most settled portion of the prairies, the Province of Manitoba, from enjoying the benefits of competition it might have had from U.S. railroads. The tariff operated to diminish the flow of goods northward from the United States and thus diminished the competitive capacity of American railroads to haul exports from Manitoba. The general effect was to make the prairie provinces an area in which Canadian railways were sheltered from the competition of American railroads.

Until 1888, the Canadian Pacific Railway had an effective monopoly of railway transportation in western Canada due to a guarantee in its charter that no other railway would be permitted between its main line and the American boundary. The withdrawal of this monopoly clause in 1888 allowed the entry of the Northern Pacific Railway to Manitoba, but its competition was restrained and forced only slight reductions of rates.[3]

It was not until 1897 that national policy sought a means of modifying the monopoly position of the railways in western Canada and of reducing the disparity between rates charged in central and western Canada. In that year, the first statutory limitation was placed upon certain railway rates in an *ad hoc* attempt to control the prices of railway services in an area where other modes of transportation were lacking.

The circumstances surrounding the introduction of that measure need not concern us here in detail. It is sufficient to recall that the federal government, in return for a cash subsidy and a land grant to

[3] G. P. Glazebrook, *A History of Transportation in Canada*, New Haven, 1928, p. 309.

enable the Canadian Pacific Railway to build a line through the Crows' Nest Pass in southern British Columbia to the rich mining area in the Kootenay Mountains, required the railway to reduce its rates on specified commodities moving to Western Canada and on grain and flour moving east for export. Those statutory rates were the first and fundamental attempt to achieve a national policy of minimizing differentials in freight rates in the interregional and export trade of Canada. The rates on commodities moving to the west have long since been released from statutory limitations, but the rates on grain and grain products moving to export positions from western Canada have remained the same since 1897, with the exception of a few years following World War I. That exception was brought to an end with the re-establishment of the statutory rates, about the same time that the second national attempt was made to devise a transportation policy to mitigate the disadvantages of great distances from the more outlying sections of Canada to its center.

In 1927, as a result of agitation from the Maritime Provinces of Canada and after examination by a Royal Commission, the Parliament passed the Maritime Freight Rates Act. Since the economic welfare of the Maritime regions did not depend upon any single staple product, as the western prairies did, no attempt was made to fix statutory rates on specific commodities. Rather, a new device was introduced. The federal government undertook to pay 20 per cent of the railway freight charges on commodities moving within the "select" territory, either point to point. or from points to the western boundary of the territory. The Act did not extend its benefits to goods imported from overseas through Maritime ports or to goods moving into the select territory from central Canada. In spite of the fact that the Maritime area has accessible water transportation, the Act reduced only railway freight charges. Since 1957, the rate reduction has been 30 per cent on the select-territory portion of outbound rail shipments to other parts of Canada. This further rate reduction has not been incorporated into the Maritime Freight Rates Act, but has been authorized by annual vote of Parliament.

The third major component of national policy in transportation is relatively new. It is highly significant, and indicative of the failure of the older policies to adjust to a new situation, that the third policy was not introduced until 1951, long after the emergence of highway transportation as a complicating factor in the provision of rail transportation.

Following World War II, increasing complaints of regional in-equities in railway freight rates caused the establishment of a Royal

Commission in 1949. Faced with mounting costs of railway operation and loss of much lucrative traffic to intercity highway operators, the railways had sought and received permission to apply a number of "horizontal" percentage increases to traffic considered able to bear them. Basing its analysis and recommendation upon the well-established principle of national responsibility for assuming part of the costs ascribable to overcoming long distances in transportation, the 1951 Royal Commission made the following comment:

Various submissions were made to the commission as to steps which ought to be taken to lessen the burden of freight rates for the western provinces whose geographic location necessitates a haul of traffic inwards and outwards over a long stretch of unproductive or only partly productive territory.[4]

The territory referred to was the long stretch of railway through northern Ontario. The recommendation was that "the cost of maintaining that portion of our transcontinental railway system which serves as a link or bridge between east and west be charged upon the general revenues of the country." [5] Such a step was expected to "be particularly effective as a measure of relief in the case of charges on westbound traffic passing over this bridge." [6] The recommendation was approved by the government and a bill to amend the Railway Act was introduced in Parliament in 1951. This act, known as the Freight Rates Reduction Act, but popularly as the "bridge" subsidy, provided among other things for an annual payment of $7 million to the transcontinental railways to cover the cost of maintaining the "bridge." The act clearly set out the method by which the $7 million was to be apportioned between the two transcontinental railways, but it did not establish the method by which it should be applied toward reduction of freight rates. It was left to the Board of Transport Commissioners for Canada to work out the formula.

From time to time, there have been other special provisions from the public treasury for assistance to the movement of certain classes of commodities within Canada. But the principles implicit in the three main pillars of transportation policy are the bases from which policy issues today arise. Each of the three, Statutory Grain Rates, Maritimes Freight Rates Act, and the Freight Rates Reduction Act, although separated by over half a century, are logical only if a railway enjoys a monopoly in overland transport and if, as a monopoly, needs restraint, is able to recoup possible losses from other traffic, and can be used as a

---

[4] *Report of the Royal Commission on Transportation*, Ottawa, 1951, p. 253.
[5] *Ibid.*
[6] *Ibid.* p. 254.

vehicle to pass on public assistance to shippers. If any or all of these conditions do not hold, then in one measure or another, the policies misallocate resources, distort market demands for transport, or fail to ensure benefit where it is intended.

The Search for Transport Policy

In the Canadian past, great national aspirations were reflected in national policy, of which transportation policy was a part. At no time was it discernible that careful economic criteria were the parameters of transportation policy. Transportation, which meant primarily railway transportation, was intended to serve the national interest and, in so doing, was expected to be extensively endowed by the public purse in capital construction and protected sufficiently to see the private investor adequately rewarded. Imperfectly as it might appear in terms of an economic analysis, the transportation function was well defined in relation to national policy.

The forms of public investment in a multimode transportation environment are so diverse, and the intermodal effects of it so implicating, that transportation policy has shifted its focus and, in shifting, has become blurred. Rather than designating the function of transport, policy has been turned inward until it has become a series of expedients for permitting each mode to live regardless of the effects upon the adequate total provision of transport service. Each mode has its voice, and each voice seeks to achieve a better competitive posture in the face of other modes. Public policy recommendations in Canada, since 1949 at least, have been based on studies initiated by the breakdown of the older identification of transportation with railways, and have been aggravated by special interests. The definition of special interest in this context ranges from proximate administrative necessity to resolve special problems created by the failure of policy to keep abreast of technology, through vested public and private interest in the regulatory *status quo*. Between these limits are set the terms of reference for specific research, which means that research begins with its broad directions predetermined. These factors have been determining because study at a more fundamental level to define a simple standard of national interest in transportation is lacking. The continuing collection of pertinent data is inadequate, and there is insufficient basic research on the economically strategic aspects of industry, on regional structure, economic behavior, organization, and interrelationships. These failures leave transport-policy studies disoriented to the present and continuing needs for transport services in the economy and, therefore, defenseless against special interests. Unless and until a long-range and far-ranging program of study receives legislative and public support, any attempts to rationalize the transport functions must inevitably be limited in scope, and be in the nature of palliatives to meet emergent shorter-run crises.

The economic and political shape of Canada, the constitutional forms, and the distinct development of national policy may superficially obscure the relevance of American problems to the Canadian situation. But the similarity is real. The smaller size of the economy and the parliamentary system of government do help us to focus attention on economic problems with which transportation is closely associated. But, at least until recently, the legacy of past policy has successfully kept Canadians from isolating the symptoms from the real causes. The transportation requirements of technological progress in industry, growing regional diversification, and changing consumption patterns have been met by adding to the total private and public investment in transportation, without sufficient consideration of the total transport needs, and without sufficient concern for the changed environment in which regulation operates. As each new mode appeared, *ad hoc* regulatory arrangements have been set up without regard for the inevitable impacts upon other modes. In response to regional and national demands, new investments of significant magnitudes have been undertaken without regard to the need for a policy which defines the roles of each mode, and without policy adjustments suited to changing roles.

Constitutionally, in Canada, regulation of all modes of transport are, or can be, concentrated at the federal level, either totally or for interprovincial segments. In practice, all modes except highway transport are federally controlled in varying degrees. This has not brought the uniformity which might logically have been expected in a relatively simple economy. So far as experience shows, there is no coordination of regulation or of policy between numerous federal authorities separately charged with transport responsibilities. Theoretically, such coordination and responsibility for policy coalesce in the federal Cabinet which, under the parliamentary system, is responsible to the Legislature. The evidence is that the Canadian system has been no more successful than the American has been in achieving unity of outlook. Even after a generation of intermodal competition, the most recent Royal Commission set up by the federal legislature was directed to investigate railway transport problems and to seek solutions to the many regional complaints, solely within the framework of railway operations. Fortunately the Commissioners interpreted their terms of reference more broadly.

Canadian Royal Commission reports on transportation, like similar investigations in the United States, have been accused of being pro-railway. This is true of the most recent report. That it appears so is purely an accident of history: the only form of overland transport available at the time the Canadian nation set its course was the railway. Consequently, transportation policy was almost entirely railway policy. The close association of railways and politics throughout our history still leads many Canadians to believe in the continuing political and economic influence of railways. The sheer size of our two railway systems gives some validity to this conviction, but it distorts public objectivity. Canadians have not yet realized that the wealth, size, and number of interests vested in other modes make them politically more powerful, considerably more vocal and, in some cases, create interests more vested in the *status quo* than those of the railways.

To the casual reader, or to one whose assumptions respecting the relative and relevant role of each mode of transport in Canada are biased by special interest or failure to allow for the rapid pace of change, the report of the most recent Royal Commission on Transportation is very little different from any other. Set up at a time when transportation was the most vexatious of all domestic problems in Canada, its purpose was interpreted by many as solely to find a solution to rising freight rates without public subsidy, without substantial restriction on the freedom of competition, and without withdrawing every Canadian's inherent right to regular and frequent rail service. Now, two years after the substantive report, the national anguish over transportation problems seems to have subsided. And, as yet, no part of the recommendations has been implemented.

I am convinced that, in spite of the prejudicial circumstances which surround research into policy, the Report of the Royal Commission on Transportation succeeded in reaching down toward some understanding of basic transportation functions in a multimode environment. Short-term solutions had to be found, and I believe they were found, consistent with the longer-term assessments. The Commission recognized the changed role of rail transport, and the redefinition inevitably implied definition of some other roles. It recognized the fact of competition and that public investment is the single largest determinant of the degree of competition. The Commission recognized and attempted to illustrate structural differences in various segments of the transport industry and suggested the nature and extent of regulation in keeping with those differences. It divested itself of any suggestion that the purpose of policy is to keep any segment of the industry alive, save for clear and evident nontransport purposes, and further suggested that the costs of those purposes are a national burden. Furthermore, it had the humility to say that no single investigation could hope to solve permanently the problems associated with a dynamic and unpredictable industry serving a growing nation, and it proposed continued research. It had the foresight to see the limitations to continued study without adequate universal data, and without the relevant cost data collected and collated in a manner useful for increasingly sophisticated costing processes. Finally, the Commission embarked timidly into the federal constitutional problems associated with coordination in public policy, but could only recognize the necessity of federal leadership.

In any nation, the allocation of resources in transportation cannot be determined at less than the national level, although not necessarily exclusively there. Coordination of public investment or, at the very least, full knowledge of public investment plans in transport is absolutely essential. The resolution of issues of public policy today must begin with some attempt at their definition, some understanding of the quantitative significance of the issues, some study of the effects of past and projected policy enactments, some assessment of the impacts of public investment. In the modern idiom these are all embraced in the word "research."

Research regards its tasks as essentially nonnormative preparation for policy decisions. Canadian experience in transportation policy decisions does nothing to encourage such an attitude. The reverse is often apparent: some special regional or interest groups are convinced that policy decisions are justified on the grounds of special need, and that the sum of "good" enactments must be the larger good. This fallacy of composition and reliance on the doctrine of the invisible hand applied to public policy is far from dead in Canadian transportation.

No one dealing with policy questions is naive enough to believe it will ever really be otherwise. The great lack in Canada has been the refusal of policy makers to see the need for larger examination of transportation problems on a continuing basis. This failure is the more regrettable, because there is no serious constitutional limitation to the creation of an impartial and continuing research group removed from the daily administrative decisions requiring study. Instead, there has been a multiplication of administrative branches and boards, each charged with regulation of one mode or one aspect of one mode, in an excessive growth of departmental rigidity, to the detriment of the cabinet system of government. With the growth of heavy federal financial responsibility in the past twenty-five years, a perfect rationale exists for creation of a research group to examine the needs, size, and impact of public investment in transportation in the light of national policies of growth and development. It would place in the hands of policy makers an improved defense against importunate regional or special demands, and provide at least one rational basis for positive national policy decisions.

From a study of transportation investment—past, present, future— almost every other aspect of the whole transportation problem would open up. An explicit recognition that public investment is the single largest determinant of the degree of competition within the whole industry is invaluable in assessing the validity of competitive pleas from various segments of the industry for public help or pleas to equate somehow the flow of public bounty between modes.

Early in December, 1963, the first statement of legislative intention was given to the present federal Parliament. The statement indicated that this government, which is not the one which set up the most recent federal investigation into transportation problems, is going to attempt to find solutions without the establishment of a research group for continuing investigation over all modes. The closest intention is to exert considerable effort toward dismantling some of the railway plant that is excessive by means which will cause the least economic disturbance. This, like some other recommendations of the Royal Commission, is useful, but it does not get down to the basic issue of the role of each of the modes of transportation in the national policy of development. Until that is at least begun, disputatious public policy issues in transportation will continue to be met by intuitive response to special pressures, inaccurate assessment of competitive realities, inept and contradictory *ad hoc* measures which will surely be fuel for future burning issues.

Index

Adams, Walter, 404–405
Air France, 226
Airline Finance and Accounting Conference, 96
Airlines:
  advertising costs, 95–120
    budget relationship, 115
    CAB policies, 96–99
    competitive, 96
    cost of traveling by air or auto, 97
    effect of rates and advertising on profit, 105
    effect on market share, 98, 106
    institutional, 96
    intraindustry use of, 96–97
    in peak seasons, 99
    ratio of advertising expense to revenue, 114–115
    regulatory policy concerning, 99–106, 116
    revenues, 106–116
    selling costs, 95–96
    size-value relationships, 113–114
    types of advertising, 98
  airport operations, measuring, 82
  costs and managerial efficiency, 61–94
    aircraft and traffic servicing, 64, 81–86
    Boeing 707, 65, 66, 219
    Boeing 720, 65, 66, 67, 70, 79
    Constellation, 73, 219
    Convair 880, 67, 70, 79
    Convair Piston, 74
    DC-6 and DC-7, 71, 74, 219
    Douglas DC-8, 77, 219
    flying operations, 64–75
    Lockheed Electra, 69, 219
    maintenance, 64, 75–80
    overstaffing problem, 83–84, 88–90
    standard cost factors, 93
    Vickers Viscount, 67, 70
  decline in profits, 61
  earnings, 199
  economies of scale, 106, 118
  equipment price behavior, 218–220
  fare increases, 90
  financial and operating reports, 111
  fleet structure, 66, 70, 79

  freedom of entry, 377
  jet operations, 62, 219
  mail subsidies, 95, 104, 107
  mergers, 61n, 90, 240
  personnel utilization, 72–75, 83, 88–90, 93–94
  pilot salaries, 64, 70, 72
  pilot staffing, 72–73, 79
  producers' durable equipment index, 218–220
  rate of return, 87, 90, 223, 238–239
  route structure, 82–83, 91
  sales promotion, 64, 92–93
  scheduling, 58
  seats departing, 83, 92
  staffing index, 73, 74–75, 79
  technological improvements, 215
All American Certificate Renewal Case, 102
Alonzo, William, 248n, 253n
American Airlines, 79, 81, 82, 83, 91, 112, 221, 223
American Association of State Highway Officials, 301n, 309–312
American Overseas Airlines, 100
American Transportation Research Forum, 20n
Anderson, F. W., 439
Anderson, Locke, 235
Anti-trust laws, 240
Arpaia, Anthony F., 417
Automobiles:
  competition with urban transportation, 291
  relative cost of traveling by, 97
  use of, 279
Averch, Harvey, 200n
Avianca Airlines, 226
Axelrod, David, 402

Bandeen, R. A., 121–138
Bankruptcy, railroads, 55
Barge lines, 30, 368, 394
  costs, 5
  rate policy, 20
Barger, Harold, 172n, 175, 291
Baumol, William J., 4n, 11n
Baylis, A. E., 44